GOVERNMENT OFFICE
FOR THE SOUTH EAST

The South East Plan

Regional Spatial Strategy for the South East of England

May 2009

Communities and Local Government

London: TSO

TSO
information & publishing solutions

Published by TSO (The Stationery Office) and available from:

Online
www.tsoshop.co.uk

Mail, Telephone, Fax & E-mail
TSO
PO Box 29, Norwich, NR3 1GN
Telephone orders/General enquiries: 0870 600 5522
Fax orders: 0870 600 5533
E-mail: customer.services@tso.co.uk
Textphone 0870 240 3701

TSO@Blackwell and other Accredited Agents

Customers can also order publications from:
TSO Ireland
16 Arthur Street, Belfast BT1 4GD
Tel 028 9023 8451 Fax 028 9023 5401

Communities and Local Government, Eland House, Bressenden Place, London SW1E 5DU
Telephone 020 7944 4400
Web site www.communities.gov.uk

© Crown copyright 2009

Copyright in the typographical arrangements rests with the Crown.

This publication, excluding logos, may be reproduced free of charge in any format or medium for research, private study or for internal circulation within an organisation. This is subject to it being reproduced accurately and not used in a misleading context. The material must be acknowledged as Crown copyright and the title of the publication specified.

For any other use of this material, please write to Office of Public Sector Information, Information Policy Team, Kew, Richmond, Surrey TW9 4DU.

Any queries relating to the content of this document should be referred to the Government Office for the South East at the following address:
Government Office for the South East, Bridge House, 1 Walnut Tree Close, Guildford GU1 4GA

ISBN 978 0 11 753998 3

Printed in Great Britain on material containing 75% post-consumer waste and 25% ECF pulp
N6122215 C16 05/09

Contents

Section A

1 Introduction and Overview 7
2 Challenges and Context 11
3 Vision and Objectives 15

Section B - Core Regional Policies

4 Spatial Strategy 17
5 Cross Cutting Policies 31
6 Sustainable Economic Development 43
7 Housing 53
8 Transport 65
9 Natural Resource Management 83
10 Waste and Minerals 117
11 Countryside and Landscape Management 145
12 Management of the Built Environment 153
13 Town Centres 161
14 Tourism and Related Sports and Recreation 169
15 Social and Community Infrastructure 181

Section C - Sub-Regional Policies

16 South Hampshire 189
17 Sussex Coast 201
18 East Kent and Ashford 209
19 Kent Thames Gateway 219
20 London Fringe 229
21 Western Corridor and Blackwater Valley 239
22 Central Oxfordshire 249
23 Milton Keynes and Aylesbury Vale 259
24 Gatwick 267
25 Isle of Wight and Areas Outside Sub-Regions 273

Contents

Section D

26 Implementation, Monitoring and Review 283

27 Appendix 1 - Saved Policies 287

28 Glossary 289

POLICY SP1: SUB-REGIONS IN THE SOUTH EAST 17
POLICY SP2: REGIONAL HUBS 18
POLICY SP3: URBAN FOCUS AND URBAN RENAISSANCE 25
POLICY SP4: REGENERATION AND SOCIAL INCLUSION 26
POLICY SP5: GREEN BELTS 27
POLICY CC1: SUSTAINABLE DEVELOPMENT 31
POLICY CC2: CLIMATE CHANGE 31
POLICY CC3: RESOURCE USE 32
POLICY CC4: SUSTAINABLE DESIGN AND CONSTRUCTION 33
POLICY CC5: SUPPORTING AN AGEING POPULATION 35
POLICY CC6: SUSTAINABLE COMMUNITIES AND CHARACTER OF THE ENVIRONMENT
 36
POLICY CC7: INFRASTRUCTURE AND IMPLEMENTATION 37
POLICY CC8: GREEN INFRASTRUCTURE 39
POLICY CC9: USE OF PUBLIC LAND 41
POLICY RE1: CONTRIBUTING TO THE UK'S LONG TERM COMPETITIVENESS 43
POLICY RE2: SUPPORTING NATIONALLY AND REGIONALLY IMPORTANT SECTORS AND CLUSTERS 44
POLICY RE3: EMPLOYMENT AND LAND PROVISION 46
POLICY RE4: HUMAN RESOURCE DEVELOPMENT 47
POLICY RE5: SMART GROWTH 49
POLICY RE6: COMPETITIVENESS AND ADDRESSING STRUCTURAL ECONOMIC WEAKNESS 50
POLICY H1: REGIONAL HOUSING PROVISION 2006 - 2026 54
POLICY H2: MANAGING THE DELIVERY OF THE REGIONAL HOUSING PROVISION ... 57
POLICY H3: AFFORDABLE HOUSING 58
POLICY H4: TYPE AND SIZE OF NEW HOUSING 59
POLICY H5: HOUSING DESIGN AND DENSITY 62
POLICY H6: MAKING BETTER USE OF THE EXISTING STOCK 63
POLICY T1: MANAGE AND INVEST 66
POLICY T2: MOBILITY MANAGEMENT 67
POLICY T3: CHARGING 68
POLICY T4: PARKING 69
POLICY T5: TRAVEL PLANS AND ADVICE 69
POLICY T6: COMMUNICATIONS TECHNOLOGY 70
POLICY T7: RURAL TRANSPORT 70
POLICY T8: REGIONAL SPOKES 71
POLICY T9: AIRPORTS 71
POLICY T10: PORTS AND SHORT SEA SHIPPING 72
POLICY T11: RAIL FREIGHT 73
POLICY T12: FREIGHT AND SITE SAFEGUARDING 73
POLICY T13: INTERMODAL INTERCHANGES 74
POLICY T14: TRANSPORT INVESTMENT AND MANAGEMENT PRIORITIES 74

Contents

POLICY NRM1: SUSTAINABLE WATER RESOURCES AND GROUNDWATER QUALITY ... 85
POLICY NRM2: WATER QUALITY ... 86
POLICY NRM3: STRATEGIC WATER RESOURCES DEVELOPMENT ... 87
POLICY NRM4: SUSTAINABLE FLOOD RISK MANAGEMENT ... 88
POLICY NRM5: CONSERVATION AND IMPROVEMENT OF BIODIVERSITY ... 91
POLICY NRM6: THAMES BASIN HEATHS SPECIAL PROTECTION AREA ... 99
POLICY NRM7: WOODLANDS ... 102
POLICY NRM8: COASTAL MANAGEMENT ... 103
POLICY NRM9: AIR QUALITY ... 105
POLICY NRM10: NOISE ... 106
POLICY NRM11: DEVELOPMENT DESIGN FOR ENERGY EFFICIENCY AND RENEWABLE ENERGY ... 108
POLICY NRM12: COMBINED HEAT AND POWER ... 109
POLICY NRM13: REGIONAL RENEWABLE ENERGY TARGETS ... 110
POLICY NRM14: SUB-REGIONAL TARGETS FOR LAND-BASED RENEWABLE ENERGY ... 111
POLICY NRM15: LOCATION OF RENEWABLE ENERGY DEVELOPMENT ... 113
POLICY NRM16: RENEWABLE ENERGY DEVELOPMENT CRITERIA ... 115
POLICY W1: WASTE REDUCTION ... 118
POLICY W2: SUSTAINABLE DESIGN, CONSTRUCTION AND DEMOLITION ... 119
POLICY W3: REGIONAL SELF-SUFFICIENCY ... 119
POLICY W4: SUB-REGIONAL SELF-SUFFICIENCY ... 122
POLICY W5: TARGETS FOR DIVERSION FROM LANDFILL ... 122
POLICY W6: RECYCLING AND COMPOSTING ... 123
POLICY W7: WASTE MANAGEMENT CAPACITY REQUIREMENTS ... 125
POLICY W8: WASTE SEPARATION ... 127
POLICY W9: NEW MARKETS ... 128
POLICY W10: REGIONALLY SIGNIFICANT FACILITIES ... 128
POLICY W11: BIOMASS ... 129
POLICY W12: OTHER RECOVERY AND DIVERSION TECHNOLOGIES ... 129
POLICY W13: LANDFILL REQUIREMENTS ... 130
POLICY W14: RESTORATION ... 131
POLICY W15: HAZARDOUS AND OTHER SPECIALIST WASTE FACILITIES ... 131
POLICY W16: WASTE TRANSPORT INFRASTRUCTURE ... 132
POLICY W17: LOCATION OF WASTE MANAGEMENT FACILITIES ... 133
POLICY M1: SUSTAINABLE CONSTRUCTION ... 136
POLICY M2: RECYCLED AND SECONDARY AGGREGATES ... 137
POLICY M3: PRIMARY AGGREGATES ... 139
POLICY M4: OTHER MINERALS ... 140
POLICY M5: SAFEGUARDING OF MINERAL RESERVES, WHARVES AND RAIL DEPOTS ... 142
POLICY C1: THE NEW FOREST NATIONAL PARK ... 145
POLICY C2: THE SOUTH DOWNS ... 146
POLICY C3: AREAS OF OUTSTANDING NATURAL BEAUTY ... 146
POLICY C4: LANDSCAPE AND COUNTRYSIDE MANAGEMENT ... 147
POLICY C5: MANAGING THE RURAL-URBAN FRINGE ... 148
POLICY C6: COUNTRYSIDE ACCESS AND RIGHTS OF WAY MANAGEMENT ... 150
POLICY C7: THE RIVER THAMES CORRIDOR ... 151
POLICY BE1: MANAGEMENT FOR AN URBAN RENAISSANCE ... 153
POLICY BE2: SUBURBAN INTENSIFICATION ... 155
POLICY BE3: SUBURBAN RENEWAL ... 156
POLICY BE4: THE ROLE OF SMALL RURAL TOWNS ('MARKET' TOWNS) ... 157

Contents

POLICY BE5: VILLAGE MANAGEMENT 158
POLICY BE6: MANAGEMENT OF THE HISTORIC ENVIRONMENT 158
POLICY TC1: STRATEGIC NETWORK OF TOWN CENTRES 163
POLICY TC2: NEW DEVELOPMENT AND REDEVELOPMENT IN TOWN CENTRES 166
POLICY TC3: OUT-OF-CENTRE REGIONAL/SUB-REGIONAL SHOPPING CENTRES 166
POLICY TSR1: COASTAL RESORTS 170
POLICY TSR2: RURAL TOURISM 172
POLICY TSR3: REGIONALLY SIGNIFICANT SPORTS FACILITIES 173
POLICY TSR4: TOURISM ATTRACTIONS 174
POLICY TSR5: TOURIST ACCOMMODATION 175
POLICY TSR6: VISITOR MANAGEMENT 177
POLICY TSR7: PRIORITY AREAS FOR TOURISM 177
POLICY S1 : SUPPORTING HEALTHY COMMUNITIES 181
POLICY S2 : PROMOTING SUSTAINABLE HEALTH SERVICES 182
POLICY S3: EDUCATION AND SKILLS 183
POLICY S4: HIGHER AND FURTHER EDUCATION 184
POLICY S5: CULTURAL AND SPORTING ACTIVITY 184
POLICY S6: COMMUNITY INFRASTRUCTURE 186
POLICY SH1: CORE POLICY 190
POLICY SH2: STRATEGIC DEVELOPMENT AREAS 191
POLICY SH3 – SCALE, LOCATION AND TYPE OF EMPLOYMENT DEVELOPMENT 192
POLICY SH4 – STRATEGY FOR MAIN TOWN CENTRES 194
POLICY SH5: SCALE AND LOCATION OF HOUSING DEVELOPMENT 2006-2026 196
POLICY SH6: AFFORDABLE HOUSING 197
POLICY SH7: SUB-REGIONAL TRANSPORT STRATEGY 197
POLICY SH8: ENVIRONMENTAL SUSTAINABILITY 199
POLICY SH9: IMPLEMENTATION AGENCY 200
POLICY SCT1: CORE STRATEGY 201
POLICY SCT2: ENABLING ECONOMIC REGENERATION 202
POLICY SCT3: MANAGEMENT OF EXISTING EMPLOYMENT SITES AND PREMISES
.... 203
POLICY SCT4: EMPLOYMENT PRIORITY IN NEW LAND ALLOCATIONS 204
POLICY SCT5: HOUSING DISTRIBUTION 204
POLICY SCT6: AFFORDABLE HOUSING 206
POLICY SCT7: IMPLEMENTATION AND DELIVERY 206
POLICY EKA1: CORE STRATEGY 210
POLICY EKA2: SPATIAL FRAMEWORK FOR ASHFORD GROWTH AREA 212
POLICY EKA3: AMOUNT AND DISTRIBUTION OF HOUSING 213
POLICY EKA4: URBAN RENAISSANCE OF THE COASTAL TOWNS 214
EKA5: THE GATEWAY ROLE 214
POLICY EKA6: EMPLOYMENT LOCATIONS 215
POLICY EKA7: INTEGRATED COASTAL MANAGEMENT AND NATURAL PARK 217
EKA8: EFFECTIVE DELIVERY 217
POLICY KTG1: CORE STRATEGY 220
POLICY KTG2: ECONOMIC GROWTH AND EMPLOYMENT 221
POLICY KTG3: EMPLOYMENT LOCATIONS 222
POLICY KTG4: AMOUNT AND DISTRIBUTION OF HOUSING DEVELOPMENT 223
POLICY KTG5: THE ROLE OF THE RETAIL CENTRES 224
POLICY KTG6: FLOOD RISK 225
POLICY KTG7: GREEN INITIATIVES 226
POLICY LF1: CORE STRATEGY 230
POLICY LF2: ECONOMIC DEVELOPMENT 231

Contents

POLICY LF3: BROAD AMOUNT AND DISTRIBUTION OF FUTURE HOUSING DEVELOPMENT 232
POLICY LF4: AFFORDABLE HOUSING 233
POLICY LF5: URBAN AREAS AND REGIONAL HUBS 234
POLICY LF6: DEVELOPMENT AT FORMER DERA SITE, CHERTSEY 235
POLICY LF7: TOWN CENTRES 235
POLICY LF8: SUB-REGIONAL TRANSPORT HUBS AND SPOKES 236
POLICY LF9: GREEN BELT MANAGEMENT 236
POLICY LF10: SMALL SCALE SITE TARIFF 237
POLICY WCBV1: CORE STRATEGY 240
POLICY WCBV2: EMPLOYMENT LAND 243
POLICY WCBV3: SCALE AND DISTRIBUTION OF HOUSING DEVELOPMENT 244
POLICY WCBV4: THE BLACKWATER VALLEY 246
POLICY WCBV5: THE COLNE VALLEY PARK 246
POLICY CO1: CORE STRATEGY 250
POLICY CO2: ECONOMY 251
POLICY CO3: SCALE AND DISTRIBUTION OF HOUSING 252
POLICY CO4: GREEN BELT 254
POLICY CO5: TRANSPORT 255
POLICY MKAV1: HOUSING DISTRIBUTION BY DISTRICT 2006-2026 261
POLICY MKAV2: SPATIAL FRAMEWORK FOR MILTON KEYNES GROWTH AREA 262
POLICY MKAV3: SPATIAL FRAMEWORK FOR AYLESBURY GROWTH AREA 263
POLICY MKAV4: EFFECTIVE DELIVERY 265
POLICY GAT1: CORE STRATEGY 268
POLICY GAT2: ECONOMIC DEVELOPMENT 268
POLICY GAT3: HOUSING DISTRIBUTION 269
POLICY IW1: ENABLING ECONOMIC REGENERATION 275
POLICY IW2: HOUSING DEVELOPMENT 276
POLICY IW3: RURAL AREAS 276
POLICY IW4: STRATEGIC TRANSPORT LINKS 277
POLICY IW5: INFRASTRUCTURE 277
POLICY AOSR1: SCALE AND LOCATION OF HOUSING DEVELOPMENT 2006-2026 277
POLICY AOSR2: SCALE AND LOCATION OF HOUSING DEVELOPMENT 2006-2026 278
POLICY AOSR3: THE WHITEHILL/BORDON OPPORTUNITY 278
POLICY AOSR4: SCALE AND LOCATION OF HOUSING DEVELOPMENT 2006-2026 279
POLICY AOSR5: SCALE AND LOCATION OF HOUSING DEVELOPMENT 2006-2026 280
POLICY AOSR6: SCALE AND LOCATION OF HOUSING DEVELOPMENT 2006-2026 280
POLICY AOSR7: MAIDSTONE HUB 281
POLICY AOSR8: TONBRIDGE/TUNBRIDGE WELLS HUB 281
POLICY IMR1: MONITORING THE RSS 284

Contents

The South East Plan - Regional Spatial Strategy for the South East

1 Introduction and Overview

Why Produce a South East Plan?

1.1 The Regional Spatial Strategy (RSS) for the South East of England (known as the South East Plan) sets out the long term spatial planning framework for the region over the years 2006-2026. The Plan is a key tool to help achieve more sustainable development, protect the environment and combat climate change. It provides a spatial context within which Local Development Frameworks and Local Transport Plans need to be prepared, as well as other regional and sub-regional strategies and programmes that have a bearing on land use activities. These include the regional economic and housing strategies as well as strategies and programmes that address air quality, biodiversity, climate change, education, energy, community safety, environment, health and sustainable development. In addition, policies in this Plan carry weight in decisions made on planning applications and appeals for development.

1.2 The Plan includes spatial policies for:

- the scale and distribution of new housing
- priorities for new infrastructure and economic development
- the strategy for protecting countryside, biodiversity and the built and historic environment
- tackling climate change and safeguarding natural resources, for example water and minerals

1.3 The Plan also incorporates the Regional Transport Strategy (RTS) and will be supported by an implementation plan.

What is a Spatial Strategy?

1.4 Spatial planning, which has its legislative underpinnings in the Planning and Compulsory Purchase Act 2004, recognises that there are policies, processes and decisions capable of shaping the future geography of an area other than those associated with the traditional remit of land use planning. Examples include investment decisions on infrastructure, the working of the property market, personal preferences on where people want to live and work, and what people value about their area. A spatial plan needs to understand these processes and set out a range of policy levers to influence them.

1.5 A successful spatial strategy must:

- understand the South East Region - how it functions, what its strengths and weaknesses are, and what differentiates it from other regions. This needs to be evidence based.
- understand the forces of change that will affect the region in the long term. A summary of *key drivers of change* in the region is set out in Chapter 2.
- set out its *vision* for what the region should be like in 2026, and its *objectives* for managing this change. Chapter 3 sets out this vision and the accompanying objectives.
- include a clear spatial strategy for managing anticipated change. This is set out in Chapter 4, and is accompanied by a key diagram showing the core strategy.
- identify the policy levers that it can use to manage these changes. In this Plan these are grouped into cross-cutting policies (Chapter 5), topic-based policies (Chapters 6 to 15) and policies specifically relating to the eight sub-regions identified in the spatial strategy (Chapters 16 – 24). A further chapter (25) covers areas outside defined sub-regions, including the Isle of Wight.
- set out a clear implementation and monitoring framework to explain how policies are to be delivered, by whom, and whether changes are being managed in the way the Plan anticipates (Chapter 26, and the separate implementation plan which will be updated over time by the regional planning body).

Introduction and Overview

The Regional Spatial Strategy (RSS) - Principles

1.6 A key factor in the preparation of the Plan is the level of detail that it should go into. On the one hand, it should reflect the considerable degree of technical work and expert input which underpinned its preparation. On the other, it should be as short and succinct as possible, to make it easy to understand and use. The Plan should only contain policy and proposals that are appropriate to its scope and scale, where it is not possible or desirable to make that policy at a more local level. It should also add value to the planning process by not replicating national policy, and should be specific to a region. Further background on policy and procedure for regional planning is set out in Planning Policy Statement 11: *Regional Spatial Strategies* (PPS11). This can be downloaded from the Department for Communities and Local Government website at www.communities.gov.uk.

Relationship to the Previous Regional Spatial Strategy

1.7 This Plan replaces existing Regional Planning Guidance for the South East (RPG9, March 2001). RPG9 became the statutory RSS for the region in September 2004 when the Planning and Compulsory Purchase Act came into force. It covers a smaller administrative area than RPG9, and no longer includes Bedfordshire, Hertfordshire and Essex (now part of the RSS for the Eastern region), and Greater London (now covered by the Mayor's London Plan). The Plan also replaces RPG9a (*Thames Gateway Planning Framework*) and RPG9b (*Strategic Guidance for the River Thames*), where they apply to the South East region.

1.8 This Plan also incorporates policy stemming from partial reviews to RPG9 carried out since 2001. These are:

- Regional Transport Strategy, July 2004
- Ashford Growth Area, July 2004
- Renewable Energy and Tourism, November 2004
- Milton Keynes and South Midlands Sub-Regional Strategy, March 2005
- Waste and Minerals, June 2006

1.9 These documents are now replaced with the exception of the Part A Statement of the Milton Keynes and South Midlands Sub-Regional Strategy, which continues to apply. In the event of any conflict, the South East Plan will take precedence.

Relationship with County Structure Plans

1.10 The publication of this final version of the South East Plan means that all the saved policies which had been extended by the Secretary of State in the following structure plans are no longer in force:

- Berkshire Structure Plan 2001-2016
- Buckinghamshire County Structure Plan 1991-2011
- East Sussex and Brighton & Hove Structure Plan 1991-2011
- Surrey Structure Plan 2004
- Hampshire County Structure Plan 1996-2011 (Review)
- West Sussex Structure Plan 2001-2016

1.11 The saved policies in the Oxfordshire Structure Plan 2016 were extended by the Secretary of State in September 2008 after the publication of her Proposed Changes to the draft South East Plan. It was not possible, therefore, to set out at that stage which of those policies would be expressly replaced by policies in the South East Plan. These are now set out in Appendix 1. In relation to the Kent and Medway Structure Plan 2006, the Secretary of State has decided that none of its policies should be extended so these will cease to have development plan status when their three-year saved period expires on 6 July 2009.

Introduction and Overview

The Process

1.12   There were three main stages in reviewing the South East Regional Spatial Strategy:

- The South East England Regional Assembly prepared a draft South East Plan between 2003 and 2006. It submitted this draft to the Government on 31 March 2006; a copy can be found on the Assembly's website at www.southeast-ra.gov.uk. A period of public consultation then drew some 17,000 responses from over 7,000 separate individuals and organisations.
- An independent Panel of inspectors examined the draft South East Plan at a public examination between November 2006 and March 2007 testing it for soundness. Their report, published in August 2007, can be viewed on the GOSE website at www.gos.gov.uk/gose.
- The Government considered the Panel report and in July 2008 issued a Schedule of Proposed Changes to the Plan for public consultation. The responses to that consultation have been considered, and as a result the Government has produced this final version of the South East Plan.

Sustainability Appraisal and Habitats Regulations Assessment

1.13   The Planning and Compulsory Purchase Act 2004 and European Directive 2001/42/EC require strategic environmental assessment (SEA) of plans, including this Plan. This is contained within a wider sustainability appraisal (SA), which looks at the implications of the plan against environmental, economic and social considerations. Under the Conservation (Natural Habitats &c) Regulations 1994, a Habitats Regulations Assessment (HRA) is also required, to assess the potential impacts of development proposals in the plan on nature conservation sites of European importance. Both the SA and HRA are iterative - they are plan-making tools that help guide the preparation of the plan, making sure that it has taken both sustainability considerations and the need to protect the integrity of important wildlife sites into consideration. The draft South East Plan, as prepared by the Regional Assembly, underwent separate assessments for SA and as required by the Habitats Regulations. The draft SA report was published for consultation with the draft Plan submitted to the Government in March 2006, and a separate draft HRA was published in October 2006 – termed 'Appropriate Assessment' at the time.

1.14   Both were available to the independent Panel which examined the draft Plan. The Government then commissioned an updated sustainability appraisal and Habitats Regulations Assessment. The results of these were taken into account in the preparation of the Proposed Changes document, and there has been a further iteration of the combined appraisal following the further changes that were put into this final version of the Plan. A summary report of the findings and recommendations of both the SA and HRA are set out in the Supporting Document that is being published at the same time as this Plan, and the full appraisals are also being published.

Introduction and Overview

1

Challenges and Context

2 Challenges and Context

The South East - Present and Future

2.1 The South East and London are strongly inter-linked: the wealth and influence of the city spreads by varying degrees throughout the region. There are large commuter flows, with 370,000 South East residents travelling to London each day while 128,000 Londoners travel outwards to jobs in the South East. However, the South East also has a number of nationally significant centres such as Reading and Oxford that generate their own wealth and jobs and in turn their own commuting flows. The result is a multi-centred or 'polycentric' region gathered around London, a city that operates on a global scale. The challenge for this Plan is to manage development whilst dealing with the inequalities and accessibility issues between the eastern and western halves of the region, the threat of dangerous climate change and the ongoing need to protect the extensive and precious natural resources which contribute to the region's character.

A South East Pen Picture – A Region of Contrasts?

"Many people think that most of South East England is sprawling suburb and continuous seaside resort. Like many popular ideas of different regions of Britain this is far from the truth. There are large tracts of glorious countryside and a fascinating series of towns." [1]

There is much to cherish.

The South East is a rich region - in wealth, natural resources, culturally and in terms of quality of life.

It is an affluent region…

At £126.6 million, gross disposable household income in the South East in 2006 was higher than that of any other region - 55% more than the total of the neighbouring East of England region, for example. London and the South East are the only UK regions to have a GVA (Gross Value Added) per head higher than the UK average. The region has a strong research presence, and a strong service sector based economy with better paid and higher skilled jobs. The South East has historically had the highest employment rate of any UK region at 79.5% and the lowest unemployment rate at 3.8%.

…and also one of the most beautiful.

80% of the South East is classified as 'rural' [2] and the region is home to almost a third of all England's Areas of Outstanding Natural Beauty, in turn covering a third of the South East. It contains the New Forest National Park, with a further national park now declared in the South Downs. 16% of the region is designated as Green Belt, [3] and the South East contains 40% of the nation's ancient woodland. [4]

It benefits from exceptional cultural and natural assets…

The South East draws visitors from around the world – to the towns of Windsor, Oxford and Canterbury, to the landscapes of the Chilterns, Wessex Downs and the New Forest and to the coasts and beaches of Sussex and Kent. The region has a rich heritage of historic buildings and contains over 300 museums and galleries, attracting over 10 million visitors a year.

…and healthy credentials…

---

1. David Lloyd, *Historic Towns of South East England*, quoted in Living Places – Urban Renaissance for the South East, URBED for Department of Transport and the Regions and GOSE, December 2000
2. Around 80% of the land area is classified as rural under the ONS classification derived from census data
3. Department for Environment, Food and Rural Affairs, 2007
4. Environment Agency, South East State of the Environment Report 2007

The South East is considered to be the least deprived and the most healthy of all the English regions. The region has a comparatively low percentage of people with limiting long term illness: 14.8% compared to 22.1% in the least healthy region.

... and is seen as a good place to live...

Nine out of ten residents in the South East rate their quality of life as good or very good - nearly half (49%) of the residents are very satisfied with the South East. Generally they are more satisfied with where they live than residents elsewhere in the country and the trend has been upwards since the first MORI survey in 2002. [5]

...which means that more people want to live here.

In 2006, 225,000 people moved into the South East from the rest of the UK while 221,000 moved out. The biggest net migration is from London - in 2006, 96,000 people arrived from London, while 56,000 moved to the capital.

Not all South East districts are facing migration pressures...

While 10 out of the 67 South East districts had a net in-migration of 1,000 or more between 2005 and 2006, five districts had a net out-migration of 1,000 or more. Altogether, 17 districts - including many of the region's larger towns and cities - had more people moving out than moving in.

...and not all areas are benefiting the same way from the region's economic growth.

Apart from London, the South East is the region with the widest range of social deprivation and economic disparities. There are over 400,000 people classed as deprived (the worst 20% of the overall Index of Multiple Deprivation) in the South East. [6]

Economic success brings its own set of problems...

The development pressures, both national and international, call for more land. Some people contend that the region is already 'full up'; others point out that around 90% of its land mass remains undeveloped.

...with housing affordability worsening...

In 2006, the average first time buyer deposit needed to get on to the housing ladder in the South East was £37,319. The ratio between lower quartile house prices and lower quartile incomes in 2007 was 8.9, compared to 5.8 in 2001.

...and our ecological footprint is growing.

South East residents remain relatively wasteful in their use of natural resources, leading to the region having an ecological footprint 17% above the national average, [7] the highest of any region. Per capita production of pollutants, greenhouse gases and CO_2 is higher than any other region as is per capita water consumption.

Yet the region has learnt to use its land resources more wisely.

In 2006/7, 82% of new homes were built on previously developed land and 80% of new homes in the South East were built at densities of 30 dwellings per hectare or more.

---

5   MORI, for The South East England Regional Assembly - *Perceptions of the South East and its Regional Assembly*, June 2008
6   *The Profile of South East England*, SEEDA, February 2005
7   South East England Regional Assembly and Partners - *The South East Regional Sustainability Framework - Towards a Better Quality of Life,* June 2008

Challenges and Context

Key Drivers Of Change - Challenges And Opportunities

2.2 Much progress has been made in making the South East one of the best regions in which to live and work. However, the regional context is being transformed by significant socio-demographic, economic, technological and environmental trends. The rapidly changing future context demands that the region needs to seize the opportunities and meet the challenges ahead so that all those who live and work in the South East in 2026 will enjoy an even better quality of life than that enjoyed by most residents at present.

2.3 **The region is facing unprecedented levels of population growth.** In mid-2006, the South East was home to about 8.2 million people living in 3.5 million homes.[8] The population is projected to grow by an unprecedented 64,300 per year over the next 20 years, exceeding a total of 9.5 million by 2026.[9] This means potential for significant economic growth, significant pressures on social and physical infrastructure and challenges to the aim of stabilising the region's ecological footprint.

2.4 **The South East population is ageing.** Over 64% of the population growth in the 20 years to 2026 is projected to come from those who are, or will be, aged 60 or above. In 2006, there were about three economically active people to support every one person of 60 or over. This will reduce to about two by 2026.[10] There is therefore a need to 'age proof' all key plans and strategies that aim to shape the region's future.

2.5 **Globalisation has changed the economic landscape.** Notwithstanding the current recession, it is widely predicted that the global economy will double in size over the next 20 years. The economic impact of globalisation is, however, proving to be both uneven and unpredictable with international competition increasingly moving from low-skilled to highly-skilled sectors. This trend means that businesses and individuals in the region will have work to remain competitive in terms of the interplay between type and level of skills, adaptability and productivity. Globalisation helps to promote productivity and economic growth allowing market leaders to expand further, creating new markets for existing products and services as well as to create new products and services altogether. A particular challenge for the Regional Spatial Strategy is to create a spatial context that helps businesses and individuals to adapt swiftly, to minimise adjustment costs and to make the most of new opportunities as they arise. This will be especially important in enabling the South East to emerge as strongly and as quickly as possible from the current recession. Flexible and open regional economies are best placed to serve the interests of the regional business and resident communities as well as the needs of the UK economy.

2.6 **The pace of technological change** is having an increasing effect on the way we live, work and do business. The premium on skills and rewards for innovation are increasing and strength in activities higher up the value chain is increasingly essential if the region is to remain competitive in the global market. The region needs to continue to enhance and update its skills and knowledge base. This also means re-training to avoid some people being 'left behind' and area specific efforts to ensure that all parts of the region are set to share the benefits of the knowledge economy.

2.7 **The size of households (i.e. the number of people) in the UK and in the region has been declining,** leading to a rate of household growth in the South East that is more than twice as fast as that of population growth. For the region, this means a need to focus on sustainable strategic solutions for addressing the need and demand for more housing while taking an innovative approach towards preventing, minimising and mitigating the impacts of housing and economic growth.

2.8 **Housing supply in the South East has been lagging behind population growth and housing affordability is worsening.** About 208,400 households remain on local authority Housing Registers, with 7,680 homeless households listed as being in temporary

---

8   Office for National Statistics, 2006 Revised Mid Year Subnational population estimates, published 2007
9   Office for National Statistics, 2006-based Subnational population projections, June 2008
10   Based on a proxy economically active age group of 15-59

Challenges and Context

accommodation.[11] In the South East between 2001-2006, there has been a 70% increase in average house prices, an 88% increase in lower quartile house prices, and a nearly 30% increase in the average deposit required by first time buyers. Although current market conditions have led to a fall in house prices in the region, long-term pressures on housing supply and affordability remain. Constraints on supply in the current market will only increase the unmet need for housing. When access to credit returns, a lack of supply will exacerbate housing pressures - the long term housing supply and affordability challenge therefore remains.

2.9 **The South East is already being affected by signs of climate change.** The 1990s was the warmest decade in 100 years, and the twelve-month period to April 2007 was the warmest since records began.[12] Given its large ecological footprint, the region needs to do much more to contribute to the national target of reducing greenhouse gas emissions and to prepare itself better for the impacts of climate change. Balancing affluence with the need to live within environmental limits will mean changes in the behaviour of residents, businesses and all others who live, work, visit or invest in the region, and will be one of the biggest challenges for the next few decades.

---

11 South East England Regional Assembly Annual Monitoring Report 2007, Department for Communities and Local Government Statutory Homelessness Statistics 2007.
12 Environment Agency, South East England State of the Environment Report 2007

3 Vision and Objectives

A Healthier South East

3.1 This Plan has been developed to help deliver the following vision for the South East, as set out in the Regional Sustainability Framework: [1]

> **A socially and economically strong, healthy and just South East that respects the limits of the global environment. Achieving this will require the active involvement of all individuals to deliver a society where everyone, including the most deprived, benefits from and contributes to a better quality of life. At the same time the impact of current high levels of resource use will be reduced and the quality of the environment will be maintained and enhanced.**

3.2 A healthier region means working to improve:

- the physical and mental health of its citizens, their wellbeing and productivity
- the health of the environment around us, including water and air quality, vegetation, habitats, wildlife and landscape
- the health of our neighbourhoods, underpinned by a sharing of the benefits of growth, good quality housing and the provision of community facilities with sustainable transport links between them, green space and a feeling of security
- the health of the region's built environment and historic buildings.

3.3 This will involve pursuing policies that strive to manage growth in a way that maintains a high quality of life and increases prosperity and opportunities for all, whilst nurturing and enhancing the region's environmental assets and increasing the efficiency with which we use resources. In practice this will require a combination of good forward planning – the right development in the right place at the right time and connected in a way that encourages healthy travel choices to be made - and recognition of the need for behavioural change.

3.4 This vision is supported by a core set of objectives that have underpinned and guided its development. These objectives will be pursued through implementation of policies in this Plan and should be used as a basis for the development of local development frameworks.

Core Objectives

i. a sustainable balance between planning for economic, environmental and social benefits will be sought, to help improve quality of life for everyone in the South East
ii. economic growth and competitiveness in the region will be sustained, with Gross Value Added (GVA) in the region increased by 3% per annum over the period 2006-2016
iii. new initiatives to tackle skills deficits will be promoted
iv. a closer alignment between jobs and homes growth will be pursued
v. economic and social disparities within the region will be reduced
vi. a sufficient level of housing development will be delivered
vii. a substantial increase in the supply of affordable housing will be pursued, through a package of measures to deliver this goal
viii. adequate infrastructure will be provided in a way that keeps pace with development
ix. key transport links will be improved, providing access for all, especially disadvantaged groups
x. health provision and access will be improved

---

1 South East England Regional Assembly and Partners - *The South East Regional Sustainability Framework -Towards a Better Quality of Life,* June 2008

Vision and Objectives

xi. spatial planning in the region will take into account the needs of an ageing population and its implications

xii. crime and the fear of crime will be reduced

xiii. better natural resource management and efficiency will be pursued, leading to reductions in the consumption of water and energy and the production of waste

xiv. new development will be delivered in a manner which mitigates the effects of, and adapts to, climate change

xv. the best of the region's historic, built and natural environment will be protected and where possible enhanced, both for its own sake and to underpin the social and economic development of the region

xvi. new development will be of high quality sustainable design and construction, and be an asset to the region

4 Spatial Strategy

A Spatial Strategy for the South East

> The South East Plan is based on the following six spatial planning principles:
>
> 1. A co-ordinated approach to managing change within the region's key settlements and their hinterlands. This will be achieved through the coordination of policy in nine identified *sub-regions* (Policy SP1).
> 2. Focusing new development on the South East's network of *regional hubs*, according to their role and function, whilst promoting their accessibility and inter-linkages between them. This will include new development in five strategic development areas (Policy SP2). (A further two SDAs where specific development opportunities exist not linked to hubs will also be pursued).
> 3. Pursuing a continuing strategy of *urban focus* and *urban renaissance*, by encouraging accessible mixed use development in the region's network of town centres and by seeking a high quality built environment in all areas (Policy SP3).
> 4. Spreading opportunities more evenly around the region through co-ordination of *regeneration and social inclusion activity* in the region's lagging areas (Policy SP4).
> 5. Respecting and maintaining the general pattern of the South East's settlements and undeveloped areas, through the protection of the region's identified *Green Belts* (Policy SP5).
> 6. Supporting the vitality and character of the region's *rural areas*, whilst protecting the valuable natural and historic assets of the region (policies set out in box at the end of this chapter).

Spatial Planning at a Sub-Regional Level

> **POLICY SP1: SUB-REGIONS IN THE SOUTH EAST**
>
> Sub-regions identified in this Plan will be the focus for growth and regeneration. This will require co-ordinated effort and cross-boundary working to better align economic and housing growth, deliver adequate infrastructure in a timely manner and to plan for more sustainable forms of development.
>
> The sub-regions are defined as:
>
> 1. **South Hampshire**
> 2. **Sussex Coast**
> 3. **East Kent and Ashford**
> 4. **Kent Thames Gateway**
> 5. **London Fringe**
> 6. **Western Corridor and Blackwater Valley**
> 7. **Central Oxfordshire**
> 8. **Milton Keynes and Aylesbury Vale**
> 9. **Gatwick**

4.1 The South East is a particularly large and diverse region. This means that perhaps more than any other region it does not have towns, cities and rural areas that share similar characteristics. Different parts of the region often have a distinctive set of issues that need to be addressed through joint working across local authority boundaries. This Plan responds to that challenge by identifying nine sub-regions, defined according to the functional relationships between key settlements and their surrounding areas, and driven by the need to apply a consistent set of policies across their areas. Policies for these areas have been developed to overcome any 'strategic policy deficit' that demands co-ordination of planning activity at a regional and sub-regional scale.

4.2 Sub-regions have been identified where they show strong economic potential or particular regeneration needs. This supports the principle of *'sharper focus'* which helped inform the development of this strategy, and aims to help support the economic competitiveness of the region whilst spreading the benefits of prosperous areas more evenly round the South East.

4.3 The Key Diagram shows areas covered by sub-regional designations - this is set out inside the rear cover of this document. Chapters 16-24 of this Plan set out the particular challenges and specific policy guidance for these areas. A further chapter (25) sets out strategic policy on areas outside the identified sub regions, including the Isle of Wight, Whitehill/Bordon and the two hubs at Maidstone and Tonbridge/Tunbridge Wells.

Regional Hubs

> **POLICY SP2: REGIONAL HUBS**
>
> **Relevant regional strategies, local development documents and local transport plans will include policies and proposals that support and develop the role of regional hubs by:**
>
> i. **giving priority to measures that increase the level of accessibility by public transport, walking and cycling**
> ii. **encouraging higher density land uses and/or mixed land uses that require a high level of accessibility so as to create "living centres"**
> iii. **giving priority to the development of high quality interchange facilities between all modes of transport**
> iv. **focusing new housing development and economic activity in locations close to or accessible by public transport**
> v. **delivering long term development in strategic development areas where identified around hubs.**

4.4 Chapter 2 explained the changing geography of the region and how the South East exhibits a very 'polycentric' structure, with a patchwork of cities and towns scattered throughout the region, each demonstrating varying degrees of self-containment and influence on each other. Whilst transport and economic activity in the region remains dominated by London, commuting patterns and business relationships in the region are becoming increasingly more complex, with major settlements often becoming more economically self-contained but also more dependent on one another for labour and knowledge capital. On average 70% of the wider South East population lived and worked in the same Functional Urban Region in 2001, although this figure varies widely depending on proximity to London. [1]

4.5 This represents a challenge for the forward planning of the region. On the one hand there is a need to support the development of these centres and acknowledge that there will be a great deal of interaction between settlements in the region and beyond, on the other there is a need to make settlements as self-contained as possible, to reduce the need to travel and make the best use of targeted investment - particularly infrastructure.

4.6 The South East Plan's approach to this challenge is to recognise that there is a network of cities and towns where most employment, leisure, retail and cultural activity in the region will gravitate, by virtue of their more developed transport networks and their wide mix of services combined with demand from accessible populations. As dynamic 'hubs of activity', they are the logical areas within the South East within which the various components of growth will need to be focused and co-ordinated to help deliver more sustainable forms of development. A major part of this approach will be reducing the need to travel through closer alignment of local labour supply and demand.

---

1 Trends & Messages from Polynet, ICS/Young Foundation, 2005

Spatial Strategy

4.7 The South East Plan therefore identifies a network of 22 regional hubs. The 22 hubs are listed in Table SP1 and identified on the key diagram. The designation of the term 'hub' is not intended to imply that all hubs share similar characteristics, and they vary in function and scale.

4.8 Regional hubs will be:

- a focus for investment in multi-modal transport infrastructure both within and between hubs, supported by initiatives to re-balance travel patterns through behavioural change
- a focus for other new infrastructure, including health, education, social and green infrastructure, and public services
- a focus for new investment in economic activity and regeneration, including skills and training investment
- a focus for new market and affordable housing, to support the creation of higher density 'living centres'
- a focus for new major retail and employment development

4.9 The following table provides further information on the designation of each hub. It is anticipated that given demand in the area hubs in the sub-regions in the Inner South East (Gatwick, London Fringe, Western Corridor/Blackwater Valley and Central Oxfordshire) will accommodate a large component of additional growth in the region, and may need to expand beyond their current development boundaries. Two regional hubs – Maidstone and Tonbridge/Tunbridge Wells – are not located within one of the nine sub-regional areas. Both are identified as accessible settlements of regional significance with Maidstone identified as having the potential to accommodate significantly higher levels of development during the Plan period than other urban settlements located outside the sub-regional strategy areas. Policy is provided for the 22 hubs in Chapters 16-24 of the Plan, along with guidance for the areas of the region that fall outside the sub-regions (Chapter 25).

4.10 Before and during the preparation of the South East Plan initiatives were brought forward which will influence the role of each hub. In particular:

- the Government's Sustainable Communities Plan of 2003 set out a plan of action to accelerate new development in designated growth areas at Milton Keynes/South Midlands, Ashford and the Thames Gateway. Subsequent partial reviews of Regional Planning Guidance for the South East (2001) took this initiative forward, and policies in these partial reviews have been incorporated (and in some cases updated) within this RSS. Five of the hubs lie in these growth areas (Aylesbury Vale, Ashford, Ebbsfleet, Medway and Milton Keynes)
- the Government announced its Growth Points initiative in October 2006, which aims to support high rates of housing delivery over the first ten years of the South East Plan. Nine growth points were announced at the end of the bidding processes (Basingstoke, Didcot, Maidstone, Oxford, Reading, South Hampshire, Reigate & Banstead, Dover and Shoreham), all of which are designated as hubs by this Plan, with the exception of Didcot (Shoreham is included within the Brighton hub). Areas with Growth Point status are shown on the Key Diagram. Growth at Whitehill/Bordon in Hampshire is also proposed in this Plan. In April 2008 this site was announced by the Government as one of three potential 'eco-towns' in the South East. A further two eco-towns have been short listed in the South East (Ford in West Sussex and Weston Otmoor in Oxfordshire). At the time of publication, the Government had not yet announced decisions on eco-towns. Local development documents and any future reviews of this Plan will need to take account of the outcome of any eco-town announcement. It is expected that any future RSS review will test the longer term issues that arise from the eco-town proposals - such as the ultimate size of settlements
- eleven hubs were covered by the eight areas designated as 'Diamonds for Investment and Growth' by the South East England Regional Development Agency. These diamonds are identified as being capable of stimulating prosperity, with

Spatial Strategy

further growth being unlocked through targeted investment in infrastructure. Diamonds for Investment and Growth are shown on the Key Diagram

- in addition, hubs are intended as a focus for new major retail development. Following the advice of the independent Panel which examined the draft plan, this Plan (see Chapter 13 – Town Centres) names certain hubs as 'Centres for Significant Change', 'Primary Regional Centres' and 'Secondary Regional Centres'.

4.11 Although all these designations were driven by various initiatives and different consideration of their functions there is a great deal of synergy between each designation. The following table clarifies and summarises the role of each hub according to these initiatives.

Hub Reason for Designation	Growth Point	Growth Area	Centres for Significant Change	Primary Regional Centre	Secondary Regional Centres	Diamond For Growth
1. Ashford High level of access to strategic rail and road networks. Existing international rail station served by Channel Tunnel Rail Link. Interchange opportunities between international and local rail services.		●	●			
2. Aylesbury Administrative centre and county town for Buckinghamshire, identified for major growth in the Milton Keynes and South Midlands Sub-Regional Strategy and in this RSS. This opportunity to realise the longer term potential of the town to provide higher order functions and fulfil role of a regional hub will be dependent upon improved strategic transport connections.		●	●			●
3. Basingstoke Major focus for commercial activity, in particular administrative and headquarter related functions. Well related to strategic rail and road networks. Interchange point for inter and intra-regional rail services.	●			●		●
4. Brighton Largest settlement on the South Coast. A historic centre, tourist destination and a focus for media and cultural activity. An important commercial centre providing higher order and administrative functions, and a transport hub. Growth expected at Shoreham. A key interchange for Coastway intra-regional services and inter-regional rail services. High level of access to the strategic road network.	●			●		●
5. Canterbury				●		

One of the largest town centres in the South East with an existing role as a population and service centre. Canterbury is also an important centre for culture, history and tourism, and is classified as a 'tourism' hotspot.						
6. Crawley-Gatwick Commercial and administrative centre providing a wide range of higher order functions. Proximity of London Gatwick Airport serves to attract organisations requiring good access to international and European markets. Rail station acts a key interchange between inter and intra-regional rail services. High level of access to the strategic road network, with the coach station at Gatwick acting as a national hub for coach services.		•			•	
7. Dover Important transport interchange and gateway to the region, Dover port is also the largest roll-on/roll-off gateway in Britain and forecast to grow significantly. Dover is also an area for economic growth and regeneration, and housing development. It is an identified growth point.	•			•		
8. Ebbsfleet Key development node in the Thames Gateway sub-region that provides the opportunity to create a new transport hub of regional significance. Identified location for major business district in a mixed settlement. Development will be focused on the new international rail station located on the Channel Tunnel Rail Link.		•			•	
9. Guildford Historic town that is an increasingly important regional administrative and commercial centre serving a wider area. Some interaction with activities and facilities available at Woking. Key interchange on rail network between inter-regional, intra-regional and local rail services. High level of access to the strategic road network.			•			
10. Hastings A number of strategic, multi-modal services converge on the town. The town is a major employment centre, supporting higher order activities and both current initiatives and future plans for Hastings and Bexhill will strengthen this role. It is a focus for future major development for employment, housing, retail and leisure uses. Increasing accessibility is a central plan of the integrated regeneration package for the town. Regeneration initiatives				•		

are intended to meet the social and economic needs of both the urban area and the wider local economic area.						
11. High Wycombe High Wycombe is a relatively large service centre and acts as a focus for economic activity for surrounding areas. The inclusion of High Wycombe as a hub reflects its location on the M40 and the Chiltern rail line between London and Birmingham, providing high frequency connections with both major cities. Strategically situated in between the Western Corridor/Blackwater Valley and Milton Keynes/Aylesbury Vale sub-regions.				•		
12. Maidstone The county town of Kent serving as the focus for administrative, commercial and retail activities. Well related to strategic rail and road networks. Interchange point between intra and local rail services.	•			•		
13. Medway Towns An identified regeneration opportunity within the Thames Gateway sub-region, but the longer-term potential of the towns to provide higher order functions and fulfil role of a regional transport hub dependent upon improved strategic transport connections.		•	•			•
14. Milton Keynes Major administrative and commercial centre. High level of access to strategic rail and road networks. Key interchange point between inter-regional, intra-regional and local rail services, with the scope to improve opportunities for public transport through development of East-West rail corridor. Identified as a Growth Area in the Sustainable Communities Plan.		•	•			•
15. Oxford Historic and cultural city of international status, drawing tourists from around the world. County town for Oxfordshire serving as the focus for administrative, educational and higher order commercial and retail activities. Well related to strategic rail and road networks. Interchange point between intra and inter-regional rail services, including services connecting with London. Located on strategic north-south road corridor.	•		•			•
16. Portsmouth		•	•			•

Spatial Strategy

#	Settlement / Description	1	2	3	4	5	6	7
	Historic port and long-standing administrative centre. A major employment centre that provides a focus for retail activities. Well related to strategic rail and road networks. Major ferry terminal for services linking to Isle of Wight with direct interchange with passenger rail services. Second largest roll-on/roll-off ferry port in the region providing cross channel services.				•			
17.	**Reading** — Largest settlement in the Thames Valley and long-standing administrative centre. Focus for higher order commercial and retail activities. The location for European and international corporate headquarters. Second largest interchange on national rail network outside of London, with connections provided between inter-regional, intra-regional and local rail services. Well related to strategic road corridors. Direct coach link with Heathrow Airport. Main rail station identified as the focus for major redevelopment opportunity that would maximise interchange opportunities between all modes.	•		•				•
18.	**Reigate/Redhill** — Settlements that have a high level of access to the strategic rail network and road network. Redhill provides a key interchange between intra-regional services and to Gatwick Airport, with the potential to develop orbital movements as an alternative to established radial links to London afforded a high priority.	•		•				
19.	**Slough** — Administrative and commercial centre. Strong interaction with activities at Heathrow Airport. Interchange point on rail network between local and intra-regional rail services. Regeneration opportunities within the town centre could provide the catalyst for delivery of a long-term vision for the town that is consistent with its regional role.				•			
20.	**Southampton** — Largest settlement in the South Hampshire sub-region and long-standing administrative centre. A major employment centre that provides the focus for higher order commercial and retail activities and port related industries. Well related to strategic rail and road networks. Interchange point on rail network between inter and intra-regional rail services. Second largest deep-sea container port in the UK, which is forecast to grow significantly. Southampton International Airport is a regional airport of significance serving a large business community.			•			•	
21.	**Tonbridge/Tunbridge Wells**				•			

The joint hub reflects not only the proximity of the two centres, but also their complementary roles: Tunbridge Wells as significant economic and service centre and Tonbridge as a major transport interchange.						
22. Woking Important centre of economic activity. Some interaction with activities and facilities available at Guildford. Key interchange on rail network between intra-regional and local rail services. Direct coach link with Heathrow Airport. Well related to the strategic road network.			•			

Strategic Development Areas (SDAs)

4.12　Seven strategic development areas for major mixed-use development schemes are identified in this Plan. The seven locations are:

- South East Milton Keynes
- South West Milton Keynes
- Fareham, Hampshire
- North of Hedge End, Hampshire
- South of Oxford
- Shoreham, West Sussex
- Whitehill/Bordon, Hampshire

4.13　The rationale for the designation is twofold. Firstly, the South East performs strongly on the economic level with much of its wealth generation coming from the highly networked information-rich knowledge economy centred in the 'Golden Arc'[2] – from Bournemouth and Poole and South Hampshire and extending into a Western Crescent taking in Reading and Oxford and onto Milton Keynes to Cambridge. This success brings with it challenges for managing expected growth including predicted labour shortages, high housing demand and transport congestion. Research indicates that it would be inappropriate to limit the natural growth to the west of the region[3] as it would inhibit wealth creation and lead to more pressure on existing housing stock and longer journeys to work.

4.14　This Plan therefore promotes development surrounding towns in this arc to support current spatial patterns of service economy clustering, economic growth potential and to better align employment and housing growth. As part of this strategy, five strategic development areas are identified around hubs in this arc comprising mixed-use developments of more than 4,000 dwellings and where the direction of growth is known. Secondly, further opportunities for significant new growth and regeneration also exist on land formerly in public use in mid Hampshire (Whitehill/Bordon) and through the redevelopment and regeneration of land on the south coast at Shoreham. The two areas are designated as SDAs accordingly.

4.15　Further information and policies for SDAs are included in the relevant sub regional sections of this document. Any further review of this Plan should identify further opportunities for growth in the Golden Arc to support wealth generation in the South East.

2　*Connecting England: A Framework for Regional Development*, Town and County Planning Association,' The Hetherington Commission', May 2006

3　South East England in Northern Europe: Trends & Messages from Polynet, ICS/Young Foundation 2005

An Urban Focus/Renaissance

> **POLICY SP3: URBAN FOCUS AND URBAN RENAISSANCE**
>
> The prime focus for development in the South East should be urban areas, in order to foster accessibility to employment, housing, retail and other services, and avoid unnecessary travel.
>
> Local planning authorities will formulate policies to:
>
> i. concentrate development within or adjacent to the region's urban areas
> ii. seek to achieve at least 60% of all new development across the South East on previously developed land and through conversions of existing buildings
> iii. ensure that developments in and around urban areas, including urban infill/intensification and new urban extensions are well designed and consistent with the principles of urban renaissance and sustainable development
> iv. use strategic land availability assessments to identify the scope for redevelopment and intensification of urban areas, seeking opportunities for intensification around transport hubs and interchanges.

4.16 The spatial strategy is based on an urban focus, which aims to concentrate development and support services, thereby making the best use of already developed land and setting out opportunities for sustainable urban expansions. Policy SP3 sets out a regional level policy designed to achieve this aim, and includes a target for the proportion of new development on previously-developed land.

Town Centres

4.17 The development of dynamic and successful town centres is central to the achievement of sustainable development in the South East. A strategic network of town centres is identified in Policy TC1 (Chapter 13). Out of the twenty-two centres identified as primary regional centres, twelve are expected to evolve significantly in terms of their range of town centre uses through the life of this strategy, and have been identified as 'Centres for Significant Change'. Local authorities, in partnership with other organisations should work to develop proactive, integrated strategies for their future. They are:

1. Ashford
2. Aylesbury
3. Crawley
4. Chatham
5. Guildford
6. Milton Keynes
7. Oxford
8. Portsmouth
9. Reading
10. Reigate-Redhill
11. Southampton
12. Woking

Tackling Regeneration and Social Inclusion

POLICY SP4: REGENERATION AND SOCIAL INCLUSION

Local authorities and other national, regional and local partners in the public, private and voluntary sector will align policies and programmes to reduce the overall extent of, and as a result the significant spatial disparities in, socio-economic deprivation, including health inequalities across the region. Specifically they should focus funding and initiatives to:

i. address the extensive regeneration needs within the sub-regions of East Kent and Ashford; Kent Thames Gateway; South Hampshire; Sussex Coast; and the Isle of Wight

ii. implement appropriate actions to address the pockets of deprivation and broader exclusion issues facing other parts of the region both inside and outside sub-regional strategy areas.

Local communities should be involved in the design and implementation of such regeneration initiatives. Particular efforts should be made to involve "hard-to-reach" groups and understand their needs.

4.18 Indicators, including the Indices of Multiple Deprivation, show that despite its general prosperity there are significant areas of deprivation in the South East. The deepest and most extensive levels of deprivation are in the economically under performing coastal parts of the region, across an area broadly corresponding with the sub-regions of Kent Thames Gateway, East Kent and Ashford, Sussex Coast, South Hampshire, and the Isle of Wight. This contrasts with the scattered pockets of intense deprivation that can be found within the economically strong sub-regions. Examples are found within the urban areas of Oxford, Milton Keynes, Reading and Slough. Other, predominantly rural, parts of the South East outside the sub-regions are characterised by relatively strong socio-economic performance but with small scattered pockets of localised deprivation.

4.19 Policy SP4 identifies spatial disparities in economic performance and deprivation, and advocates co-ordinated and consistent intervention by a range of partners to address them. Securing the objectives of Policy SP4 will be dependant on the successful delivery of a wide range of policies in the Plan that address these objectives, as well as other regional and local strategies including the Regional Economic Strategy.

Numerous regional policies in this strategy also seek to tackle intra-regional disparities, in particular:

- CC7, to bring forward necessary infrastructure
- RE3, to bring forward appropriate sites and premises
- RE4, S3 and S4 addressing educational and skills issues
- RE6, tackling underlying weaknesses in the economic structure
- H1, H3 and H4, regarding the location of housing, seeking renewal where necessary, and addressing affordability
- T1, enabling improvements to strategic accessibility
- BE1 and BE3, enabling urban renaissance and suburban renewal
- TC2 and TC3, encouraging management and regeneration of town centres
- S6, promoting increased provision of community infrastructure
- S1 and S2, tackling public health issues and health service provision
- TSR1, TSR4 and TSR7, facilitating and managing tourism-based regeneration, and diversifying the coastal economies.

Spatial Strategy

Maintaining Separation of Settlements

> **POLICY SP5: GREEN BELTS**
>
> The existing broad extent of Green Belts in the region is appropriate and will be retained and supported and the opportunity should be taken to improve their land-use management and access as part of initiatives to improve the rural urban fringe. However, in order to meet regional development needs in the most sustainable locations, selective reviews of Green Belt boundaries are required
>
> i. in the Metropolitan Green Belt to the north east of Guildford, and possibly to the south of Woking, and
> ii. in the Oxford Green Belt to the south of the City
>
> In addition, a boundary review will be required in the area of the former DERA site at Chertsey.
>
> Smaller scale local reviews are likely to be required in other locations, including around Redhill-Reigate, and these should be pursued through the local development framework process.
>
> These reviews should satisfy national criteria for Green Belt releases, accord with the spatial strategy, and ensure that sufficient land is safeguarded to avoid the need for further review to meet development needs to at least 2031. Where reviews cover more than one local authority area they should be undertaken through a joint or co-ordinated approach. Where selective reviews are undertaken local authorities should satisfy themselves that there will not be a need for further review before 2031. In undertaking this exercise the same annual rate of development as set out in Table H1b of this strategy should be assumed for the years 2026-2031.

4.20 Any strategy aiming to focus new development into sub-regions and existing settlements needs to be reinforced by a strong policy to maintain a separation of settlements. The region contains tracts of designated Green Belt (the Metropolitan Green Belt, the Oxford Green Belt and a small part of the south east Dorset Green Belt). Government has confirmed its continuing commitment to the Green Belt as an instrument of planning policy, and consultation on this Plan has confirmed very strong public support for the concept. Green Belts fulfil five main functions (as set out in Planning Policy Guidance Note 2: *Green Belts*):

- to check the unrestricted sprawl of large built-up areas
- to prevent neighbouring towns from merging into one another
- to assist in safeguarding the countryside from encroachment
- to preserve the special character and setting of historic towns
- and to assist in urban regeneration by encouraging the recycling of derelict and other urban land

4.21 Policy SP5 seeks to protect these functions notwithstanding the need for selective reviews of Green Belt boundaries at Oxford and Guildford, and possibly south of Woking. Small scale local reviews may also be required at Redhill/Reigate. These reviews are considered necessary to support these town's roles as regional hubs. Reviews are termed 'selective' rather than 'strategic' as the direction of growth is known through work carried out on previous structure plan reviews. If there are any cases for small scale local review these should be pursued through the local development framework process. If, as a result of these reviews, Green Belt land is lost, as part of the long term assessment of the land use implications of the development proposed, consideration should be given to whether a broader review of Green Belt is needed with a particular view to determining whether additional land should be designated as Green Belt.

4.22   In addition to Green Belts there are a number of policies in this Plan which will influence settlement size and shape. These are:

- SP2 (Regional Hubs)
- RE3 (Employment and Land Provision)
- NRM4 (Sustainable Flood Risk Management)
- NRM8 (Coastal Management)
- BE4 (Role of Small Market Towns)
- BE5 (Village Management)
- TC1 (Strategic Network of Town Centres)

Supporting and Protecting our Rural Communities

4.23   Extensive parts of the region are largely undeveloped and offer a high landscape value and agricultural resource. These areas are often punctuated by small towns and villages that contribute to the particular character of the region, and which provide essential homes, jobs and services for the local population. These settlements are highly accessible to those living and working in the region's urban areas, which increases pressures in terms of demand for homes, for recreation and for work. Planning policy must therefore balance the need to protect the countryside and retain the charm and heritage of the region's enviable patchwork of smaller settlements whilst making sure that thriving and socially inclusive communities are maintained and developed, to serve the needs of both their locality and the wider region. Whilst the policies of this Plan seek to focus new development into and around existing larger settlements, there remains a need to recognise that local authorities should consider the need to plan for some new development outside these areas to support rural communities and services.

4.24   This strategy does not contain a single generic spatial policy or set of policies relating to rural areas. Instead, policies influencing the spatial development of rural areas are threaded throughout this strategy. The box below sets out four key principles for rural policy development and signposts which policies in this Plan are expected to help achieve more sustainable forms of development. Chapter 25 also contains some guidance on spatial planning for areas which fall outside the nine sub regions covered by area-specific policy.

Four key principles for rural policy development in the South Est Plan, and location of relevant policies

	Core Policies
i. **Sustainable rural communities** which are inclusive, tackle disadvantage and provide a range of affordable housing, access to essential services, and support for local community-based activities and decisions.	RE3 – Employment and Land Provision H1 – Regional Housing Provision H3 – Affordable Housing H4 – Type and Size of Housing T7 – Rural Transport BE4 – The Role of Small Rural Towns BE5 – Village Management TSR2 – Rural Tourism S3 – Education and Skills CC5 – Supporting an Ageing Population

	CC7 – Infrastructure and Implementation
ii. **Sustainable rural economies** which support and develop both a profitable land-based economy, as well as the rural-based manufacturing and service economy, and high quality tourism.	RE3 – Employment and Land Provision BE4 – The Role of Small Rural Towns BE5 – Village Management TSR2 – Rural Tourism
iii. **Sustainable rural environments** which celebrate and enhance character and distinctiveness; accept change and development which respect that character; provide for a wide range of recreation and retreat.	CC6 – Sustainable Communities and Character of the Environment CC8 – Green Infrastructure C1 – The New Forest National Park C3 – Areas of Outstanding Natural Beauty C4 – Landscape and Countryside Management C5 – Managing the Rural-Urban Fringe C6 – Countryside Access and Rights of Way Management C7 – The River Thames Corridor BE4 – The Role of Small Rural Towns BE6 – Management of the Historic Environment
iv. **Sustainable natural resources** where they are used more prudently with more thought given to alternative energy sources, and the most valuable are protected and conserved.	CC1 – Sustainable Development CC3 – Resource Use CC4 – Sustainable Design and Construction NRM1 – Sustainable Water Resources and Groundwater Quality NRM2 – Water Quality NRM5 – Conservation and Improvement of Biodiversity NRM7 – Woodlands NRM11–16 – Renewable Energy.

5 Cross Cutting Policies

Sustainable Development

> **POLICY CC1: SUSTAINABLE DEVELOPMENT**
>
> The principal objective of the Plan is to achieve and to maintain sustainable development in the region. Sustainable development priorities for the South East are identified as:
>
> i. achieving sustainable levels of resource use
> ii. ensuring the physical and natural environment of the South East is conserved and enhanced
> iii. reducing greenhouse gas emissions associated with the region
> iv. ensuring that the South East is prepared for the inevitable impacts of climate change
> v. achieving safe, secure and socially inclusive communities across the region, and ensuring that the most deprived people also have an equal opportunity to benefit from and contribute to a better quality of life.
>
> All authorities, agencies and individuals responsible for delivering the policies in this Plan shall ensure that their actions contribute to meeting the objectives set out in this policy and in the Regional Sustainability Framework. [1]

5.1 The principles of sustainable development, as reflected in the Regional Sustainability Framework (RSF) and the UK Sustainable Development Strategy underpin this Plan. A cross-cutting policy (CC1) has therefore been incorporated in the Plan to emphasise the importance of working towards more sustainable development. A clear obligation is therefore placed on all delivery authorities to demonstrate their commitment through specific and identifiable actions.

Climate Change

> **POLICY CC2: CLIMATE CHANGE**
>
> Measures to mitigate and adapt to current and forecast effects of climate change will be implemented through application of local planning policy and other mechanisms. Behavioural change will be essential in implementing this policy and the measures identified.
>
> In addition, and in respect of carbon dioxide emissions, regional and local authorities, agencies and others will include policies and proposals in their plans, strategies and investment programmes to help reduce the region's carbon dioxide emissions by at least 20% below 1990 levels by 2010, by at least 25% below 1990 levels by 2015 and by 80% by 2050. A target for 2026 will be developed and incorporated in the first review of the Plan.
>
> Adaptation to risks and opportunities will be achieved through:
>
> i. guiding strategic development to locations offering greater protection from impacts such as flooding, erosion, storms, water shortages and subsidence
> ii. ensuring new and existing building stock is more resilient to climate change impacts
> iii. incorporating sustainable drainage measures and high standards of water efficiency in new and existing building stock
> iv. increasing flood storage capacity and developing sustainable new water resources
> v. ensuring that opportunities and options for sustainable flood management and migration of habitats and species are actively promoted.

---

1 *The South East Regional Sustainability Framework -'Towards a Better Quality of Life',* South East of England Regional Assembly and Partners, June 2008
http://www.southeast-ra.gov.uk/documents/sustainability/rsf_2008/rsf_main.pdf

> Mitigation, through reducing greenhouse gas emissions, will primarily be addressed through greater resource efficiency including:
>
> i. improving the energy efficiency and carbon performance of new and existing buildings and influencing the behaviour of occupants
> ii. reducing the need to travel and ensuring good accessibility to public and other sustainable modes of transport
> iii. promoting land use that acts as carbon sinks
> iv. encouraging development and use of renewable energy
> v. reducing the amount of biodegradable waste landfilled.

5.2 In recent years, the evidence that significant climate change is occurring on a global scale has become increasingly compelling. These changes will particularly affect England, and research suggests that the South East could be more affected by these changes than other regions.[2] The precise impacts of climate change are not clear, although there will be some opportunities as well as problems. It is, however, already evident that climate change will particularly affect many facets of development and land use. This Plan recognises that challenging measures for mitigation and adaptation relating to climate change will be needed over the Plan period. And Policy CC2 includes a commitment for the spatial development of the region to play its part in pursuing the Government's stated targets for reduction of carbon dioxide emissions.[3] These will not be delivered by this Plan in isolation and require positive planning to implement energy efficiency and renewable measures through waste management, transport and housing initiatives. One key goal will be the achievement of the Government's aim that all new homes should be 'zero carbon' by 2016[4] and all new non-domestic buildings should follow by 2019.[5]

5.3 Organisations in the South East, including the South East of England Regional Assembly and Climate South East are already at the forefront of tackling climate change issues through the application of spatial planning. ESPACE (European Spatial Planning: Adapting to Climate Events)[6] is a four year European project aimed to promote awareness of climate change and investigate how action to tackle climate change can be supported through spatial planning. In June 2007 the partnership published its final Strategy *'Planning in a Changing Climate'*, which offers practical advice on how spatial planning practitioners can embed climate change considerations into their work. The draft Sustainability Appraisal of this RSS, along with work on water resource issues formed case studies for the initiative. The South East of England Regional Assembly subsequently published a practical guide for planners for local councils, developers, regulators and service providers to inform their plans, and a Climate Change Mitigation and Adaptation Implementation Plan in March 2007.[7]

5.4 The *"New Performance Framework for Local Authorities and Local Authority Partnerships"* contains national indicators for the reduction in CO_2 emissions. Targets against these national indicators have been negotiated through Local Area Agreements (LAAs), and action to meet these targets will be expected to contribute to Policy CC2.

Resource Use

> **POLICY CC3: RESOURCE USE**
>
> A sustained programme of action to help stabilise the South East's ecological footprint by 2016 and reduce it by 2026 should be incorporated into plans and programmes. Such actions will include:

---

2 *Counting Consumption,* World Wildlife Fund and Partners, 2006
3 Section 1 of the Climate Change Act 2008
4 *Building a Greener Future,* Department for Communities and Local Government, 2007
5 *Budget Report 2008,* HM-Treasury, para 6.59
6 www.espace-project.org
7 http://www.southeast-ra.gov.uk/southeastplan/key/climate_change/START.pdf

Cross Cutting Policies

i. **increased efficiency of resource use in new development**
ii. **adaptation of existing development to reduce its use of energy, water and other resources**
iii. **changes in behaviour by organisations and by individuals.**

5.5 The South East remains wasteful in its use of natural resources. Research has shown that at 2001 its 'ecological footprint' per head was 17% higher than the UK average.[8] Ecological Footprint analysis measures the impact of human activity on nature, and expresses the productive land and water area that a human population requires to produce the resources it consumes and to absorb its waste. The Region's consumption of water, energy and minerals must stabilise and begin to reduce in the future, with new development adopting increasingly rigorous standards to reflect a movement towards sustainable construction, using more recycled materials, producing less waste and consuming less water and energy per unit. But the focus must not be simply on new development. Existing development must also heed and follow the same themes, taking particular advantage of opportunities afforded by renewal or upgrading of property and equipment. Adaptations of lifestyle and business practices will also need to accompany these development changes. Attitudes towards consumption of energy and the production of waste, are probably more important drivers of change than physical development.

5.6 Policy CC3 aims to help stabilise and reduce the South East's ecological footprint. We need to make sure that where the policies set out in this Plan run the risk of increasing the region's footprint (for example through increased housebuilding levels and further economic growth) measures are put in place to offset and ideally reduce this impact. An example of such measures would be the move towards more sustainable production and consumption promoted through the Regional Economic Strategy.

Sustainable Design and Construction

POLICY CC4: SUSTAINABLE DESIGN AND CONSTRUCTION

The design and construction of all new development, and the redevelopment and refurbishment of existing building stock will be expected to adopt and incorporate sustainable construction standards and techniques. This will include:

i. consideration of how all aspects of development form can contribute to securing high standards of sustainable development including aspects such as energy, water efficiency and biodiversity gain
ii. designing to increase the use of natural lighting, heat and ventilation, and for a proportion of the energy supply of new development to be secured from decentralised and renewable or low-carbon sources
iii. securing reduction and increased recycling of construction and demolition waste and procurement of low-impact materials
iv. designing for flexible use and adaptation to reflect changing lifestyles and needs and the principle of 'whole life costing'.

Local planning authorities will promote best practice in sustainable construction and help to achieve the national timetable for reducing carbon emissions from residential and non-residential buildings. There will be situations where it could be appropriate for local planning authorities to anticipate levels of building sustainability in advance of those set out nationally, for identified development area or site-specific opportunities. When proposing any local requirements for sustainable buildings, local planning authorities must be able to demonstrate clearly the local circumstances that warrant and allow this and set them out in development plan documents.

8 *Counting Consumption*, World Wildlife Fund and Partners, 2006

5.7 Sustainable construction can be defined as creating or renewing buildings so that they reduce or avoid adverse impacts on the built and natural environment, in terms of the buildings themselves, their immediate surroundings and the broader regional and global setting. It is a vital tool in combating climate change and reducing the region's ecological footprint. Sustainable construction encompasses the following principles:

- constructing development to reduce non-renewable resource consumption including building materials
- ensuring development, through its construction and use, reduces the use of energy and water and protects valuable soil resources
- eliminating or minimising the use of toxins and the production of waste associated with the construction and use of development.

5.8 At the national scale, Government is committed to amending national Building Regulations to increase energy efficiency in new buildings.[9] It has outlined a timetable to achieve a 20% reduction in carbon emissions from new homes by 2010, and nearly 50% by 2013, before reaching zero carbon in 2016. It announced in the 2008 Budget an ambition for all new non-domestic buildings to be zero carbon from 2019. The Government has also indicated its intention to bring forward an amendment to the Building Regulations to include a requirement for a minimum standard of water efficiency in new homes from 1 October 2009 and will review the Water Supply (Water Fittings) Regulations 1999 later in 2009.[10] The Code for Sustainable Homes - a new national standard for sustainable design and construction of new homes also now operates. Since April 2007 the developer of any new home in England could choose to be assessed against the Code, and rating against the Code has been mandatory since May 2008. It replaces the EcoHomes scheme, developed by the Building Research Establishment. For non-residential buildings, a number of sustainability assessment tools are well established and should be used throughout the region. For waste, Site Waste Management Plans became a legal requirement from April 2008, and require better management of waste on construction and development sites to improve materials resource efficiency.

5.9 The use of sustainability checklists, such as those promoted by Climate Change South East and SEEDA can help deliver new homes that outperform the existing stock in terms of efficiencies in resource use.

5.10 Progress is being made – for example, work to support the setting of zero-carbon targets in Milton Keynes, including the development of low carbon emitting housing on sites such as Oxley Wood, and the deployment of decentralised energy systems by Woking Borough Council. Local authorities are ideally placed to identify where place-specific opportunities may arise to improve energy and water efficiency and promote lower emissions. Planning Policy Statement: *Planning and Climate Change* (PPS1 Supplement) confirms that it could be appropriate for local planning authorities to expect higher levels of building sustainability than the standards in national Building Regulations. Local requirements should be brought forward through development plan documents and focus on known opportunities, with local authorities demonstrating clearly the local circumstances that warrant and allow local requirements. An example is where higher standards of water efficiency would make development in areas of water stress more sustainable. Any local requirements should be specified in terms of the achievement of nationally described sustainable buildings standards. Local authorities also have duties under the Home Energy Conservation Act to improve the energy efficiency of housing stock and there is also considerable scope to improve the efficiency of current public buildings through retrofitting.

5.11 The Government's water strategy for England, *Future Water*, was published in February 2008. It sets out the long-term vision for water and the framework for water management in England. This includes an ambition to reduce per capita consumption of water, through cost-effective measures, to an average of 130 litres per person per day (l/p/d) by 2030.

---

9   *Building a Greener Future*, Department for Communities and Local Government, July 2007, and *Water Efficiency in New Buildings – A Consultation Document*, Department for Communities and Local Government, Department for Environment, Food and Rural Affairs, December 2006.
10 http://www.communities.gov.uk/publications/planningandbuilding/water-efficiency

Cross Cutting Policies

5.12 The Government has set out its programme for introducing water efficiency standards through the Building Regulations and the Code for Sustainable Homes. In particularly water-stressed areas, local planning authorities may seek higher standards for water efficiency than those set nationally, through their local development frameworks. This will need to be proportionate and evidence based, and will be tested through the planning process.

5.13 Other ways of reducing water efficiency in line with *Future Water* include:

- water metering - Water company customers who are metered typically use 10% less water than other customers. All new build is fitted with water meters and water companies in the South East are looking at strategies for existing property. Some companies, such as Folkestone and Dover Water Services Ltd, are already undertaking programmes of metering for all properties, whilst Thames Water is undertaking metering pilots. Southern Water has proposed, in its draft Water Resources Management Plan, to introduce compulsory metering for all properties by 2015; and Portsmouth Water has announced its intention to meter all customers starting in 2010. The Southern Water and Portsmouth Water proposals for metering are dependent on the Secretary of State for the Environment, Food and Rural Affairs being satisfied that the options appraisals in the plans support metering as a cost effective solution to ensuring a sustainable supply of water.
- water efficiency targets – Ofwat have introduced water efficiency targets for water companies for the period 2010 – 2015. The new targets will require water companies to undertake activities to meet annual minimum water saving targets of 23 million litres per day across all water companies.
- review of the Water Fittings Regulations – A review of Water Fittings Regulations is taking place in 2009. The Water Supply (Water Fittings) Regulations will be revised with a view to setting new performance standards for key water using fittings such as WCs, urinals, dishwashers and washing machines. These measures will apply to individual appliances installed in both new and existing houses and non-domestic buildings and are intended to complement the overall performance standard set within the Building Regulations.

5.14 Policies NRM 11-16 contain a more detailed approach to the deployment of renewable energy technologies in the region.

Supporting an Ageing Population

POLICY CC5: SUPPORTING AN AGEING POPULATION

In order to reflect a significant increase in the proportion of older people in the region over the Plan period, local authorities and public agencies should pay particular regard in local development frameworks and other programmes to assessing and planning for the social needs that will arise. Policies and programmes should particularly address the following issues:

i. **the need to adapt the existing housing stock, make provision in new housing developments and sheltered and extra care housing to support older people living independent lives in their own homes (*National Strategy for Housing in an Ageing Society*)** [11]

ii. **the provision of reasonable access to services, through the provision of public transport and the extension of communications and information technology**

iii. **the provision of leisure, recreational and community facilities (including greenspace) that help older people maintain active and healthy lifestyles**

iv. **facilitating access to training and development opportunities that support available employment for the workforce beyond the existing retirement age.**

---

11 *Lifetime Homes, Lifetime Neighbourhoods - A National Strategy for Housing in an Ageing Society*, Department for Communities and Local Government, February 2008

Cross Cutting Policies

5.15 Projections for the UK suggest that the South East will have the third largest number of people over 65 of all the English regions. The South East already has some of the greatest concentrations of those aged over 75 in the country, particularly along the South Coast. By 2027 a large swathe of authorities in the coastal belt plus West Oxfordshire are projected to be home to populations within which between 25-37% are aged 65 or more.[12]

5.16 Although to date the elderly are tending to live longer and be healthier, this major rise in the very elderly will present challenges for housing provision, health and social support. At present 25% of pensioners live alone and this may increase as more people chose to remain single. Coupled with the complexity associated with changing lifestyle and housing aspirations, and the Government's desire to provide greater housing choice for older people, this means there will be a need for a variety of housing options to be made available, including support for older people living independent lives in their own homes, sheltered housing and extra care housing. While it is recognised that staying put is the preferred option for many older people, for a significant number the benefits of sheltered or extra care housing will be essential if they are to maintain an independent lifestyle. The provision of such housing offers choice, frees up under-occupied family sized homes and offers an improved quality of life including improved mental and physical well-being of older people.

5.17 The elderly population are a major contributor to community life, particularly the voluntary sector, and more people are now working beyond age 65. Older workers can represent a significant resource in the employment market, and can make an important contribution to smarter growth. Policy CC5 also addresses this need to help older workers enter and maintain employment. Transport plans should reflect the need to ensure continued mobility of the elderly.

Sustainable Communities and Character of the Environment

POLICY CC6: SUSTAINABLE COMMUNITIES AND CHARACTER OF THE ENVIRONMENT

Actions and decisions associated with the development and use of land will actively promote the creation of sustainable and distinctive communities. This will be achieved by developing and implementing a local shared vision which:

i. **respects, and where appropriate enhances, the character and distinctiveness of settlements and landscapes throughout the region**
ii. **uses innovative design processes to create a high quality built environment which promotes a sense of place. This will include consideration of accessibility, social inclusion, the need for environmentally sensitive development and crime reduction**

5.18 The South East has a high quality environment with a rich heritage of historic buildings, landscapes and habitats. This is reflected in the coverage of protective designations and contributes to the region's identity and the quality of life residents and visitors enjoy. It is also subject to a high degree of development pressure. Forward planning must therefore actively seek to promote sustainable communities whilst protecting and, wherever possible, enhancing these valuable assets and their contribution to the sustainable development of the region in the long term.

The Government's vision for Sustainable Communities is set out in its 'Homes For All' Five Year Plan.[13] Sustainable communities are defined as:

- active, inclusive and safe
- well run

---

12 *Ageing Assets Implications of Population Ageing for the South East Region*, Population Ageing Associates for the Social Inclusion Partnership for the South East, October 2005
13 Five Year Plan, Sustainable Communities for All, Department for Communities and Local Government, January 2005

Cross Cutting Policies

- environmentally sensitive
- well designed and built
- well connected
- thriving
- well served
- fair for everyone.

Infrastructure and Implementation

POLICY CC7: INFRASTRUCTURE AND IMPLEMENTATION

The scale and pace of development will depend on sufficient capacity being available in existing infrastructure to meet the needs of new development. Where this cannot be demonstrated the scale and pace of development will be dependent on additional capacity being released through demand management measures or better management of existing infrastructure, or through the provision of new infrastructure. Where new development creates a need for additional infrastructure a programme of delivery should be agreed before development begins.

Funding will be provided by a combination of local government and private sector partners, and substantial contributions from central government.

To help achieve this:

i. infrastructure agencies and providers will aim to align their investment programmes to help deliver the proposals in this Plan
ii. local development documents (LDDs) will identify the necessary additional infrastructure and services required to serve the area and the development they propose together with the means, broad cost and timing of their provision related to the timing of development
iii. contributions from development will also be required to help deliver necessary infrastructure. To provide clarity for landowners and prospective developers, local authorities should include policies and prepare clear guidance in their LDDs, in conjunction with other key agencies, on the role and scope of development contributions towards infrastructure.

The phasing of development will be closely related to the provision of infrastructure. In order to create confidence and assurance in the timely delivery of infrastructure in relation to new housing a more proactive approach to funding will be adopted. This will involve a joint approach by regional bodies, local authorities, infrastructure providers and developers. Consideration will be given to the pooling of contributions towards the cost of facilities, development tariffs and local delivery vehicles. Mechanisms to enable forward funding of strategic infrastructure will be agreed between regional bodies and Government. One of these, a Regional Infrastructure Fund is currently being developed for the South East Region.

In order to further secure effective delivery of the Plan, and particularly the timely delivery of the necessary supporting infrastructure, an Implementation Plan will be prepared, monitored and reviewed by the regional planning body, which will set out the requirements and obligations for public and private sector bodies at the national, regional and local levels. The Implementation Plan will include a regional and sub-regional investment framework identifying the strategic infrastructure schemes needed to deliver the Plan.

5.19   The provision of adequate infrastructure to support new development was a source of much debate in the preparation of this Plan. Government agrees that the timely provision of infrastructure is a fundamental tenet of this Plan, and key aspect to improving the quality of life of all those in the region.

Cross Cutting Policies

5.20 The South East Plan therefore promotes a 'Manage and Invest' strategy, with delivery arrangements focusing on the three elements of implementation that impact on infrastructure delivery. These are:

- delivering efficiency through better use of existing infrastructure
- reducing demand by promoting behavioural change
- providing additional capacity by extending or providing new infrastructure

5.21 To deliver best value this will firstly require a full understanding of how the use of existing infrastructure can best be optimised. Secondly, an understanding of the scope to reduce demand for infrastructure is needed, for example through increased energy efficiency or reduced water usage. Thirdly, we need to understand where additional demand will arise, and whether it is driven by increasing populations or by changes in household size. For example, demand for energy and water usage increases as the size of households falls, but this on its own may have less effect on the overall demand for other types of infrastructure (such as transport infrastructure), as there is no population increase.

5.22 Implementation of a strategy that ties together additional population growth and movement with supporting infrastructure will require improved delivery arrangements compared with the past, the creative assembly of public and private resources and a sustained effort. This is particularly the case in Growth Areas (Milton Keynes and South Midlands, Ashford and Thames Gateway), in the Strategic Development Areas set out in this Plan and the nine Growth Points announced by Government (Basingstoke, Reading, Oxford, Didcot, Maidstone, South Hampshire, Reigate & Bansted, Dover and Shoreham), where large scale development offers additional opportunities for capturing uplift in land values and higher rates of development are anticipated to come forward before the year 2016. Where new development comes forward in the form of a large number of small sites local authorities should consider the possibility of tariffs on new properties to pool contributions, or funding through the Community Infrastructure Levy.

For the purposes of this Plan infrastructure is defined as:

Transport	airports, ports, road network, cycling and walking infrastructure, rail network
Housing	affordable housing
Education	further and higher education
	secondary and primary education
	nursery schools
Health	acute care and general hospitals, mental hospitals
	health centres/primary care trusts
	ambulance services
Social Infrastructure	supported accommodation
	social and community facilities
	sports centres
	open spaces, parks and play space
Green Infrastructure	see box following Policy CC8
Public Services	waste management and disposal
	libraries
	cemeteries

	emergency services (police, fire, ambulance)
	places of worship
	prisons, drug treatment centres
Utility Services	gas supply
	electricity supply
	heat supply
	water supply
	waste water treatment
	telecommunications infrastructure
Flood Defences	

Green Infrastructure

> **POLICY CC8: GREEN INFRASTRUCTURE**
>
> **Local authorities and partners will work together to plan, provide and manage connected and substantial networks of accessible multi-functional green space. Networks should be planned to include both existing and new green infrastructure. They need to be planned and managed to deliver the widest range of linked environmental and social benefits including conserving and enhancing biodiversity as well as landscape, recreation, water management, social and cultural benefits to underpin individual and community health and 'well being'. They will be created and managed as a framework of green spaces and other natural features that will boost the sustainable development of settlements and increase the environmental capacity of the locality and region as a whole, helping communities to be more resilient to the effects of climate change.**
>
> **The provisions of this policy apply region-wide. However, the successful designation and management of green infrastructure will be particularly important in areas designated as regional hubs, where growth may impact on sites of international nature conservation importance[14] or where there is a need to enhance the existing environmental capacity of an area.**

5.23   For the purposes of spatial planning the term green infrastructure (GI) relates to the active planning and management of sub-regional networks of multi-functional open space. These networks should be managed and designed to support biodiversity and wider quality of life, particularly in areas undergoing large scale change.

5.24   Whilst provision and maintenance of GI will be particularly important on the urban fringe and within new development, the value of green infrastructure networks is evident across all spatial scales, from the neighbourhood to the wider region, with the creation and maintenance of linkages between spaces being a prime concern. A list of green infrastructure assets is included in the box below.

5.25   Planning and management of green infrastructure must be undertaken in consultation with relevant partners with the following multi-functional objectives in mind:

- protection and enhancement of biodiversity, including the need to mitigate the potential impacts of new development

---

14   This is the term used to encompass sites that have the highest level of protection in the UK either through legislation or policy. These include Special Areas of Conservation (SAC), candidate SAC (cSAC), Special Protection Areas (SPA), proposed SPA (pSPA) and Ramsar sites.

Cross Cutting Policies

- creating a sense of place and opportunities for greater appreciation of valuable landscapes and cultural heritage
- increasing recreational opportunities, including access to and enjoyment of the countryside and supporting healthy living
- improved water resources, flood mitigation and reduced flood risk through sustainable surface water run-off management
- making a positive contribution to combating climate change through adaptation and mitigation of impacts
- sustainable transport
- minimising the potential for crime and disorder, and the fear of crime
- improved educational opportunities.

5.26 Policy CC8 is included in this Plan to ensure that connected networks of green spaces around new built environment are treated as integral to a planning and design process which is conscious of its place within wider GI networks. GI should not just be considered as an adjunct to new development, and policies and strategies relating to GI assets in local development frameworks should have a spatial expression and not just be restricted to its definition.

5.27 Future revisions to this Plan should identify and map existing regionally and sub-regionally significant networks of GI in the South East. The 'Framework for Green Infrastructure in the South East', which is currently being prepared by Natural England, the Environment Agency and other regional partners, will help this approach. The Framework seeks to establish GI as an integral and essential component of sustainable communities, develop a common understanding of the role and importance of GI, help implement the South East Plan's GI policy and provides detailed guidance on how GI can be delivered through the planning system and local partnerships.[15]

GREEN INFRASTRUCTURE ASSETS

The following areas can form part of networks of Green Infrastructure:

- parks and gardens - including urban parks, country parks and formal gardens
- natural and semi-natural urban greenspaces - including woodlands, urban forestry, scrub, grasslands (e.g. downlands, commons and meadows) wetlands, open and running water, wastelands and derelict open land and rock areas (eg cliffs, quarries and pits)
- green corridors - including river and canal banks, cycleways, and rights of way
- outdoor sports facilities (with natural or artificial surfaces,either publicly or privately owned) - including tennis courts, bowling greens, sports pitches, golf courses, athletics tracks, school and other institutional playing fields, and other outdoor sports areas
- amenity greenspace (most commonly, but not exclusively, in housing areas) - including informal recreation spaces, greenspaces in and around housing, domestic gardens and village greens
- provision for children and teenagers - including play areas, skateboard parks, outdoor basketball hoops, and other more informal areas (e.g. 'hanging out' areas, teenage shelters)
- allotments, community gardens, and city (urban) farms
- cemeteries and churchyards
- accessible countryside in urban fringe areas
- river and canal corridors
- green roofs and walls

---

15 Following the publication of the Framework, the Regional Group will continue to provide a consistent regional voice for GI, add value to existing regional GI activity and broker strong partnership working arrangements, resulting in the proactive planning and delivery of high quality GI. The Framework is published by regional environmental partners, who will continue to provide strategic support for implementing this work. A copy of the Framework can be downloaded from:http://www.gose.gov.uk/gose/planning/regionalPlanning/?a=42496

Cross Cutting Policies

Use of Public Land

> **POLICY CC9: USE OF PUBLIC LAND**
>
> In order to identify potential development and land management opportunities, Government departments and public landowners should undertake strategic reviews of their land holdings, taking into account the objectives and policies of the Plan as a primary consideration in the use and disposal of their land. They should consult the regional planning body and other partners on the disposal and development of major sites, paying particular attention to the need to bring forward land for housing, especially affordable housing.

5.28 The South East region has a substantial portfolio of public land, particularly land held by the defence and, to a lesser extent, health sectors. Development of this land offers opportunities for additional affordable housing, employment land and GI provision. Reviews of health sector land have been undertaken and strategic land releases are under way, with land transfers to the Homes and Communities Agency. The Ministry of Defence has also embarked on a fundamental, long-term review of its operational requirements and landholdings, which will lead to the release of significant land and property holdings across the region. Some sites offer considerable potential, and the scale of likely release over the Plan period makes the issue of strategic importance. Where such sites have potential, their public land ownership could assist both implementation and the forward-funding of necessary infrastructure, in order to achieve high standards of development.

5.29 Policy CC9 sets out this Plan's policy on the use of major sites in public ownership. In the context of this policy 'major sites' are defined as those sites that would be referred to the regional planning body as major planning applications.

5 Cross Cutting Policies

Sustainable Economic Development

6 Sustainable Economic Development

Context

6.1 The Government's regional policy is focused on enabling every region to perform to its full potential in both economic and employment terms. The contribution of the South East's economy to the performance of the UK as a whole is of critical importance. The key challenge for the Regional Spatial Strategy is to maintain the region's national and international significance as one of the most successful regions in the world. And to enable it to make its full contribution to the UK's overall competitiveness, in a way that best respects the principles of sustainable development and improves the quality of life of all those who live and work in the region, for now and in the future.

6.2 The economic vision of the Regional Economic Strategy 2006-2016 (RES) is to be a world class region achieving sustainable prosperity. The RSS will assist the implementation of the current RES. Under the new single Regional Strategy, the RSS and RES will form one integrated strategy.

6.3 It is also important for the region to have regard to the inter-regional context and in particular to strong inter-connection between the economies of the South East and London.

6.4 Planning policies in this RSS should be read in conjunction with policy in draft Planning Policy Statement 4: *Planning for Sustainable Economic Development* once it is published in its final form.

Contributing to the UK's Long Term Competitiveness

POLICY RE1: CONTRIBUTING TO THE UK'S LONG TERM COMPETITIVENESS

Local development frameworks will provide an enabling context to ensure that the regional economy contributes fully to the UK's long term competitiveness. Local planning authorities will ensure that local development documents will be sufficiently flexible to respond positively to changes in the global economy and the changing economic needs of the region.

The regional planning body and the regional development agency (SEEDA) will work with local authorities, business support organisations and the business community to seek to ensure that the spatial requirements for market flexibility are fully met in all parts of the region, respecting the principles of sustainable development.

6.5 Globalisation is changing the economic landscape dramatically. It is likely to have an even more profound effect on both the UK and the South East economies over the 20-year horizon of this RSS. Notwithstanding the current recession, it is widely predicted that the global economy will double in size over the next 20 years. The economic impact of globalisation is proving to be both uneven and unpredictable with international competition increasingly moving from low-skilled to highly-skilled sectors. Globalisation helps to promote productivity and economic growth allowing market leaders to expand further, creating new markets for existing products and services as well as to create new products and services altogether. A particular challenge for the regional spatial policy is to create a spatial context that helps businesses and individuals to adapt swiftly, to minimise adjustment costs and to make the most of new opportunities as they arise. This will be especially important in enabling the South East to emerge as strongly and as quickly as possible from the current recession. Flexible and open regional economies are best placed to serve the interests of the regional business and resident communities as well as the needs of the UK economy.

6.6 Global competition is not limited to enterprises. Cities and regions also compete with each other and, increasingly, the competitors are territories in other countries. The South East England Development Agency (SEEDA) should work together with the regional planning body (RPB) to assess the dynamics of globalisation and to keep under review the attractiveness of the region as a global business location. They will also promote action to better understand the spatial dimension to the region's competitiveness and to help the public understanding of the impact of globalisation on economic prosperity and employment prospects of the region's communities.

6.7 In their strategic approach to increase the region's competitiveness, the RPB and SEEDA should engage actively and constructively with regional partners in neighbouring regions. In particular, they should work with regional partners in London and the East of England to exploit the greater South East's collective strengths and its competitive advantage. Local planning authorities within sub-regions adjoining London should work with the neighbouring authorities within London to take appropriate account of cross-boundary implications in their local development documents (LDDs).

Supporting Nationally and Regionally Important Sectors and Clusters

> **POLICY RE2: SUPPORTING NATIONALLY AND REGIONALLY IMPORTANT SECTORS AND CLUSTERS**
>
> The development of nationally and regionally important sectors and clusters will be supported through collaborative working between local authorities, local strategic and economic partnerships, SEEDA and the business community.
>
> SEEDA, business support organisations and higher and further education establishments should maximise the potential of the sectors and clusters. They should promote a culture of innovation, foster inter-university connection to create synergies and links with other research establishments in the local area, other regions and internationally and establish centres of excellence in key industries as they evolve.
>
> Local authorities, through regular employment land reviews, combined with local knowledge and working with other partners, will identify the key sectors and clusters within their local area, and any opportunities that exist for the development or expansion of sectors and clusters.
>
> Where appropriate, local development documents will include policies that:
>
> i. ensure that land and premises are available to meet the specific requirements of nationally and regionally important sectors and clusters
> ii. enhance, develop and promote local assets that can facilitate the development of sectors and clusters
> iii. promote and support non-land use initiatives that benefit and foster the growth and development of new and existing nationally and regionally important sectors and clusters.

6.8 Supporting both innovation and the role of the knowledge-driven industry is important to realise the Plan's objective of sustainable economic development in the South East. The focus of this policy is on supporting and encouraging types of businesses that will help the regional economy to continue to develop successfully. The region has a number of sectors that will be significant to realising this objective. Assisting their development and supporting and promoting opportunities for enhanced networks and cluster development will help enhance the region's competitive advantage, broaden the region's economic base, and encourage economic growth.

6.9 The RES itself identifies six key sectors of the economy which have the greatest capacity to deliver growth through a sectoral focus on innovation and development of new products and services. These are:

- digital media
- marine technologies

- health technologies
- environmental technologies and services
- built environment
- aerospace and defence

6.10 These sectors have been selected because of their high potential to innovate and grow; because they are clustered within the South East; because of their importance in delivering a sustainable future for the region; and because there is evidence that a sectoral focus (on supply chains or other business-to-business links) has particular potential to deliver benefits.

6.11 Responding to climate change and promoting a low carbon, low waste economy is a key challenge for the region. Legislation and policy incentives to respond to such needs have created a global market for environmental technologies and services. The RES sets out transformational action aiming to achieve a global leadership in environmental technologies by exploiting business opportunities created in this sector. The market for new environmental products and technologies will be given a boost by the region's growth programme for homes and work places where new development is required to be supported by technical infrastructure that meets the highest standards of environmental sustainability. The RPB and local authorities will work in collaboration with SEEDA in facilitating the growth of this business sector. SEEDA should also work with the business sectors to develop an evidence base on opportunities for economic and technological interventions that may promote behavioural change that facilitates a low carbon future.

6.12 The RES identifies key sectors that need to be supported through the provision of appropriate land and premises. However, as the region's economy is constantly evolving, the RPB and SEEDA should work with the business sectors to keep the key sectors/clusters and their needs under review.

6.13 To identify whether, in their local economy, key regional sectors are represented and/or there is the potential for the development of new or existing clusters within their area, local planning authorities should draw on:

i. their own employment land reviews
ii. the local knowledge of partners such as SEEDA's Sector Groups, Local Economic and Strategic Partnerships, adjoining authorities and the business community
iii. research undertaken for the RPB and other regional partners, and the expertise of SEEDA.

6.14 Where regionally important sectors or clusters, or the potential for their development are identified, LDDs should include policies that address the specific requirements of these sectors. These should include land-use and non land-use interventions, with the aim of exploiting, enhancing and fostering favourable conditions to assist sector, cluster or network development (see the following box).

Interventions at a sub-regional and local level may include:

i. the provision and safeguarding of land in appropriate locations (which may include: proximity to existing sector concentrations, research and development facilities, good transport links, particular environmental assets)
ii. the provision of premises of an appropriate type, size, price and quality (which may include: small and incubator units, managed workspace, move-on workspace, business parks, science parks)
iii. the provision of advanced ICT infrastructure
iv. the improvement and exploitation of other assets in the local area (which may include location, environmental quality, strong transport or research and development links)
v. non land use interventions such as sector skills programmes, business support and business development programmes, marketing initiatives to attract new investment, the establishment

of centres of excellence, and strategies to establish and enhance networks between businesses and sectors.

Supply of Employment Land

POLICY RE3: EMPLOYMENT AND LAND PROVISION

In preparing local development documents (LDDs), local authorities will have regard to strategic and local business needs and the relevant sub-regional strategy. In planning for the location, quantity and nature of employment land and premises, they will facilitate a flexible supply of land to meet the varying needs of the economic sectors.

As an input to LDDs, local authorities will undertake employment land reviews working with adjoining authorities as appropriate, and in consultation with business interests. This will include reviewing all extant allocations of employment land for their suitability to meet future needs. Where land cannot be economically developed, or which for other reasons is not suitable for employment purposes (including mixed use schemes), alternative allocations may need to be made and the original land reallocated to alternative use(s). Where possible, both housing and employment land reviews should be undertaken at the same time.

Joint employment land reviews should identify strategic employment land to provide for the future needs of businesses, including qualitative needs, in those sectors showing potential for growth in that part of the region, whilst recognising the need to safeguard the environment and meet targets for reducing CO_2. Strategic employment land should be focused at locations identified in the sub-regional strategy, or more generally at the regional hubs or gateways, and allocated or safeguarded in the relevant LDD.

Based on the evidence from employment land reviews and other market intelligence, provision should be made in each relevant LDD for a range of sites and premises to meet more general needs in locations that:

i. are or will be accessible to the existing and proposed labour supply
ii. make efficient use of existing and underused sites and premises, through increasing the intensity of use on accessible sites
iii. focus on urban areas
iv. promote the use of public transport.

Accessible and well-located industrial and commercial sites should be retained where there is a good prospect of employment use. In particular, key sites of importance to the marine industry identified through SEEDA's Waterfront Strategies should be safeguarded in relevant LDDs.

LDDs should address the particular economic needs of rural communities and be supportive of agricultural, horticultural and forestry industries, and rural economic diversification and non-land based business proposals in towns and villages or on farm sites where applications show positive benefits, based on clearly defined criteria and evidence-based assessments.

6.15   The sectoral composition of the South East's economy has been changing. As more goods are manufactured outside the UK there is an increasing need to protect the best industrial land as well as to make the most efficient use of existing and surplus industrial land. At the same time, the region needs to offer a high quality portfolio of sites to meet the needs of growing sectors and to attract inward investment. Working together with SEEDA, the regional planning body will seek to develop a strategic and co-ordinated approach to the management of employment land. This will include co-ordinating the employment land reviews across the region to help develop a better understanding of the future demand and characteristics of change, including those resulting from industrial restructuring and the supply of land and premises at the regional and sub-regional levels.

6.16 LDDs will need to ensure that there is an adequate quantity and high quality of employment land and a range of sites that can be adapted for a broad range of employment uses to meet the current and future requirements of local economies. It is important to enable flexibility in the range of premises while at the same time ensuring better use is made of existing developed land. Land identified as surplus by employment land reviews may be released for other uses, including housing, provided it meets locational criteria and can contribute towards meeting identified local or strategic needs.

6.17 Economic diversity should also be supported through the promotion of small and medium enterprises and businesses in rural areas.

6.18 The currently available evidence on jobs is not robust enough to provide any more than interim job numbers and these are given in the table below. These include trend based projections for some areas and policy based forecasts for others. Their respective status in relation to the preparation of local development frameworks (LDFs) needs to be considered in line with the relevant sub-regional strategy.

Interim Job Numbers

Sub-Region	Jobs
South Hampshire	59,000 (2006-26)
Sussex Coast	30,000 (2006-16)
East Kent & Ashford	50,000 (2006-26)
Kent Thames Gateway	58,000 (2006-26)
London Fringe	39,500 (2006-16)
Western Corridor and Blackwater Valley	79,300 (2006-16)
Milton Keynes	49,950 (2006-26)
Aylesbury Vale	21,500 (2006-26)
Central Oxfordshire	18,000 (2006-16)
Gatwick	17,400 (2006-16)
Isle of Wight	7,000 (2006-16)
Rest of Kent	15,000 (2006-16)
Rest of Hampshire	14,500 (2006-16)
Rest of the region	20,500 (2006-16)

Footnote: These figures should be seen as indicative and for monitoring purposes only.

6.19 An early review of the RSS on employment land will provide robust guidance on the scale and location of employment land and floorspace required. As part of the development of the single Regional Strategy this should also include indicative job estimates/targets for sub-regions or for groups of districts within the sub-regions or rest of region areas as appropriate. This will provide a stronger steer for LDFs and ongoing monitoring. Joint employment land review work may well provide a bottom up input to these estimates, but a major contribution will still be needed from top-down employment projections in order to give regional consistency and to incorporate strategic needs. The RPB and SEEDA should work with principal authorities to provide up to date evidence to meet the need for more robust strategic evidence in the interim period.

Human Resource Development

POLICY RE4: HUMAN RESOURCE DEVELOPMENT

Local authorities should work jointly with business sectors and education and training providers to deliver co-ordinated programmes to ensure that the skills provision meets business requirements and the workforce is equipped to access and benefit from existing and new job opportunities in the labour market.

Sustainable Economic Development

> Regional and local agencies will work together to maximise the number of people ready for employment at all skill levels and help raise economic activity and growth. The Regional Skills for Productivity Alliance (RSPA) should work with local employers, local authorities and local learning partnerships to ensure a healthy labour market in which employers and individuals get effective help in meeting their skills needs. Partners should focus on:
>
> i. addressing intermediate and technician-level skills shortages
> ii. improving skills and qualifications, including provisions to facilitate up-skilling especially in sub-regions where the level of productivity is below the regional average
> iii. addressing the need for quality information, advice and guidance on skills improving basic numeracy and literacy levels and addressing access to appropriate learning infrastructure throughout the region and particularly meeting the significant increase in demand in Growth Areas, Growth Points, areas surrounding strategic development areas and specific skills problems in deprived areas
> iv. further and higher educational establishments need to plan for an increase in demand for places on courses and continuous development in the workplace and particularly to expand provision in the Growth Areas, Growth Points, and in areas surrounding strategic development areas
> v. local authorities will ensure that sufficient and accessible premises are available for training and education purposes to meet the requirements identified through the relevant strategies, including the Regional Economic Strategy, the RSPA Prospectus and Delivery Plan and those drawn up by Learning and Skills Councils and Lifelong Learning Partnerships.

6.20 A highly skilled, flexible and adaptable labour force is the foundation for the future competitiveness, productivity and prosperity of the UK and the South East. The Government therefore aims to achieve a world class skills base in the UK by 2020. The Government's Enterprise Strategy (Enterprise: Unlocking the UK's Talent, BERR, March 2008) emphasises the need to develop a broad range of skills and knowledge including management skills and entrepreneurial capacity. The RES recognises skills at all levels as a key driver for the region's prosperity and a core component of the RES, particularly given the challenge of an ageing population.

6.21 The qualification profile of the region's workforce is higher than in many other English regions. However, there are considerable skills shortages and gaps in the region. For instance, working age people in Kent Thames Gateway, East Kent and the Isle of Wight are less likely to have high-level skills than their counterparts in the north and west of the region. The RPB and local authorities need to work through the Regional Skills for Productivity Alliance (RSPA) and Local Skills for Productivity Alliances (LSPAs) to ensure that spatial issues are addressed. Learning and Skills Councils (LSCs) also have a role in addressing spatial issues.

6.22 The key actions required to ensure a thriving labour market include:

i. maintaining a sustainable supply of skilled labour at all levels
ii. addressing intermediate and technical level skills shortages which occur across all sub-regions in the South East
iii. providing information, advice and guidance on skills
iv. meeting the skills needs of the knowledge economy
v. removing persistent pockets of low skills attainment.

6.23 Approaches to Integrated Employment and Skills in the region should be further developed. For example, an Accord has been signed between the LSC, Jobcentre Plus and SEEDA and work is taking place within the Partnership for Urban South Hampshire (PUSH) to deliver a new inter-agency service to lead residents out of long-term unemployment and into sustained and increasingly skilled sustainable employment.

Sustainable Economic Development

6.24 All areas are expected to experience growth in training requirements and the LSCs, working with Lifelong Learning Partnerships[1] and other partners, need to continue to carry out Strategic Area Reviews to assess the requirements and ensure that provision develops in every local area. In the Growth Areas, Growth Points and in settlements surrounding Strategic Development Areas there will be a particularly significant increase in demand for education and training. Planning agreements should be used to secure funding for training measures where appropriate. Appropriate learning infrastructure should be located in deprived areas and local people should be encouraged and supported to access these opportunities.

Smart Growth

> **POLICY RE5: SMART GROWTH**
>
> Working with environmental partners, the achievement of smart economic growth will be encouraged throughout the region, namely to increase the region's prosperity while reducing its ecological footprint. Local authorities will seek to enable businesses to work as efficiently as possible, through considering their needs for land and premises, movement, housing and ICT as reflected in other policies of this Plan.
>
> Local authorities will work with local strategic and economic partnerships, SEEDA and the business community to promote smart growth in line with the principles set out in the Regional Economic Strategy.
>
> i. In the more economically buoyant parts of the region, the focus will be on raising the level of innovation, creativity and global competitiveness and on ensuring adequate and timely investment in relevant sector skills, ICT and other infrastructure.
>
> ii. In all parts of the region, but particularly in the coastal areas, local authorities, SEEDA and Learning and Skills Councils will seek to assist more people to join the labour force by removing barriers to work and enhancing skills levels.
>
> Through local development documents and local transport plans, local authorities will support and promote advances in information and communications technologies (ICT) and new ways of working by positively promoting the development of ICT-enabled sites, premises and facilities suitable to support changing and flexible working practices and home based businesses.
>
> SEEDA will work with local authorities and other public and private sector partners to:
>
> i. enable and promote the take up of ICT by businesses, the public and voluntary sectors, and local communities, and encourage the innovative use of ICT to improve productivity and competitiveness and to encourage flexible working practices
>
> ii. promote and support the introduction of accessible, effective and socially inclusive e-services and e-education.

6.25 The RES identifies Smart Growth as one of the three key challenges for the region and aims to achieve it by lifting under performance with a focus on the six drivers of productivity:

- employment
- enterprise
- innovation and creativity
- skills

---

1   Lifelong Learning Partnerships bring together educational providers, learners and employers to improve the provision of learning and address skills shortages. There are 18 partnerships in the South East. It is proposed to dissolve LSCs in 2010 with their proposed successor bodies being the Young People's Learning Agency and the Skills Funding Agency.

- competition
- investment in infrastructure, including transport and physical development.

> **"Smart Growth** – lifting under performance through increasing the region's stock of businesses; maximising the number of people ready for employment at all skill levels, and ensuring they are equipped to progress in the labour market; increasing the participation of South East businesses (especially small businesses and social enterprises) in tendering for public sector contracts; reducing road congestion and pollution levels by improving travel choice, promoting public transport, managing demand and facilitating modal shifts; ensuring sufficient and affordable housing and employment space of the right type and size to meet the needs of the region and create the climate for long-term investment through efficient use of land resources, including mixed-use developments; and improving the productivity of the workforce and increasing economic activity." *Regional Economic Strategy 2006-2016*

6.26 LDDs and local transport plans should actively seek to support action facilitating /supporting businesses, individuals and communities across the region to be more efficient in their use of resources in performing economic functions. Particular emphasis is needed to facilitate action to lift the prospects of under performing individuals, communities and areas and in making the most efficient as well as effective use of land and premises.

6.27 The RPB will work to develop appropriate plans and monitoring systems to co-ordinate action to support Smart Growth and to evaluate their effectiveness.

6.28 New technologies and new forms of working practices may prompt demand for different types of premises. These opportunities should be realised, not only through ensuring that traditional office developments (both new and existing) are 'future-proofed', but also through the provision of different types of premises to accommodate changing requirements. These may include:

i. telecentres or 'telecottages' in less traditional locations, such as the suburbs
ii. live-work units
iii. more adaptable office and home spaces.

6.29 Emerging new ICT offers the opportunity for both the public and private sectors to deliver services more widely efficiently and effectively and in particularly for the benefit of those in more physically remote communities (e.g. rural areas, the elderly, disabled, and non-English speaking).

Addressing Intra-Regional Economic Disparities

> **POLICY RE6: COMPETITIVENESS AND ADDRESSING STRUCTURAL ECONOMIC WEAKNESS**
>
> Through joint working, national, regional and local partners will actively seek to maintain and enhance the competitiveness of the most economically successful parts of the region and also address structural economic weakness to release the economic potential of those areas which are under performing.
>
> In those parts of the region where the economy is strongest, within a regional and national context, defined as the sub-regions of Milton Keynes and Aylesbury Vale, the Western Corridor and Blackwater Valley, Central Oxfordshire, the London Fringe and Gatwick Area:
>
> i. SEEDA, together with local economic partners, will encourage smart growth which involves maximising the productive value of the sub-regions' resources including human capital, land and natural resources

Sustainable Economic Development

ii. **local partners will promote the economic potential of the international transport hubs at Heathrow and Gatwick, address transport and skills constraints as necessary and be guided by sustainable development principles in facilitating business development in the surrounding areas**

iii. **SEEDA and local partners will promote the take up of ICT to develop remote working practices which will enhance competitiveness and the development of a dynamic knowledge-based economy.**

In the coastal belt, defined as the sub-regions of Kent Thames Gateway, East Kent and Ashford, Sussex Coast, South Hampshire and the Isle of Wight:

i. **local development documents will:**

- **give priority to delivering economic development in allocating land**
- **protect sites for industrial and commercial use where there is a good prospect of employment use**
- **consider whether any upgrading or improvement of existing sites is required.**

ii. **SEEDA and local authorities should work together with other agencies to develop delivery mechanisms to unlock and bring into use sites with economic development potential guided by sustainable development principles, local partners will promote the economic potential of the international gateways of the ports of Southampton, Portsmouth and Dover, the Medway ports, the Channel Tunnel and Southampton Airport to maximise business opportunities in the surrounding areas**

iii. **SEEDA, together with local economic partners and private interests should comprehensively market and target inward investment to employment sites in the sub-region**

iv. **Learning and Skills Councils (and their successors), Local Skills for Productivity Alliance and other key partners will work together to develop training strategies for the local workforce to ensure they benefit from and contribute to structural changes in the area**

v. **SEEDA and local partners will enable and promote the take up of ICT to stimulate increased enterprise and innovation and to transform learning opportunities, as important components of smart growth**

vi. **local and regional partners will address the transport constraints which are an impediment to increased economic performance.**

6.30   Policy SP4 sets out a regeneration policy framework for those parts of the South East with relatively low economic performance and high deprivation.

6.31   There are significant variations in economic performance across the region. While much of the region is performing strongly, there are extensive areas of untapped potential along the South Coast and eastern parts of the region.

6.32   The economically strong areas, defined as the sub-regions of Milton Keynes and Aylesbury Vale, the Western Corridor and Blackwater Valley, Central Oxfordshire, the London Fringe and Gatwick Area, broadly correspond to the Inner South East in the RES. The less prosperous periphery hugging the coast, defined as the sub-regions of Kent Thames Gateway, East Kent and Ashford, Sussex Coast, South Hampshire and the Isle of Wight Special Policy Area, broadly corresponds to the Coastal South East in the RES.

6.33   The current RES sets out the different approaches for these broad but contrasting areas. The emphasis in the economically strong areas, according to the RES, is "on investing in excellence and on harnessing this dynamism to address the untapped potential of pockets of deprivation. New ways of working will be needed alongside appropriate, effective and timely investment in infrastructure, in order to ease the strains associated with economic success and to maintain the benefits of a high quality environment".

Sustainable Economic Development

6.34 In the less prosperous periphery, the RES places an emphasis "on releasing untapped potential, focusing particularly on the economic dynamism generated by the cities and urban areas, and developing new futures for coastal towns that exploit and enhance the advantages of their location".

7 Housing

Introduction

7.1 The Government's key housing policy goal is to ensure that everyone has the opportunity of living in a decent home, which they can afford, in a community where they want to live.

7.2 PPS3: *Housing* requires Regional Spatial Strategies (RSSs) to take a strategic evidence-based approach in setting out the appropriate level of overall housing provision in the regions. The background to housing allocations in this RSS needs to be seen within a historical context. The former Regional Planning Guidance for the South East (March 2001) set out a regional housing provision of 28,050 dwellings per annum (dpa) for the South East. At the time RPG9 indicated that this level of provision applied to the period 2001-2006 and required it to be reviewed before 2006, in the light of monitoring and the findings of the urban capacity and potential growth areas studies. It also stated that a higher rate of provision is likely to be necessary to meet the long term needs in the region and the review would be expected to lead to an increase of about 10 percent.[1] Subsequently, the Government's Sustainable Communities Plan (February 2003) called for an additional 200,000 dwellings in Growth Areas in the South by 2016 and the partial reviews of the strategies for Milton Keynes and Aylesbury Vale, and Ashford, took the implied regional housing level up to about 29,500 dpa.

7.3 The Housing Green Paper – *Homes for the Future, More Affordable, More Sustainable*, published in July 2007 – increased the Government's previous 2005 target of 200,000 net additional dpa in England in 2016 to 240,000 by 2016. Central to this Green Paper were the initiatives to facilitate an increased supply of market and affordable homes in a more sustainable manner.

7.4 Housing provision in the region needs to be considered against this policy background. The South East is a high demand housing area that has to manage the needs arising from and implications of considerable levels of demographic and economic growth whilst respecting environmental constraints. The previous (2004-revised) official projections indicated a population growth of 44,200 and a household growth of about 35,900 per year. The latest sub-national population projections (2006-based) project an annual population growth of about 64,300 and indicate that the recent demographic trends may lead to substantially higher household numbers in the South East than previously understood. Historically, the supply of housing in the South East has not matched demographic-based need and demand, although since 2003 the level of supply began to increase reaching nearly 34,600 in 2006/07. However, the supply of housing still falls short of the demand, and the affordability of housing across the region has been worsening over the years. Although current market conditions indicate that housing completion rates may fall in the short term, there remains a risk that the supply/demand mismatch will increase in the longer time frame that this Plan covers. Both additional market and affordable housing is needed in the South East to meet the demand created by the increase in households. The latest national household projections for England suggest an increase of around 250,000 additional households a year until 2031. The South East's share of this is 39,100 a year.[2]

7.5 Affordability also remains a concern in the rural settlements in the South East. Against a back ground of a 'rural premium' for the price of housing, many rural settlements in the region have been faced with closure of village services and increased reliance on urban settlements for their survival. In seeking to achieve the Government's strategic housing policy objectives, this RSS emphasises the need to create and maintain sustainable communities in all areas, both urban and rural.

---

1 Regional Planning Guidance for the South East (RPG9), DETR, March 2001
2 CLG Housing Statistical Release: Household Projections to 2031, March 2009 available at http://www.communities.gov.uk/documents/statistics/doc/1172154.doc

Housing

Housing Provision

POLICY H1: REGIONAL HOUSING PROVISION 2006 - 2026

Local planning authorities will allocate sufficient land and facilitate the delivery of 654,000 net additional dwellings between 2006 and 2026.

In managing the supply of land for housing and in determining planning applications, local planning authorities should work collaboratively to facilitate the delivery of the following level of net additional dwellings in sub-regions and in rest of the sub-regional areas:

Table H1a

Sub-region / Rest of the sub-regional area	Net Dwelling Completions - Average Annual Provision	Net Dwelling Completions - Total Provision
South Hampshire	4,000	80,000
Sussex Coast	3,465	69,300
East Kent & Ashford	2,835	56,700
Kent Thames Gateway	2,607	52,140
London Fringe	2,394	47,880
Western Corridor & Blackwater Valley	5,105	102,100
Milton Keynes & Aylesbury Vale	3,413	68,250
Central Oxfordshire	2,034	40,680
Gatwick	1,800	36,000
Isle of Wight	520	10,400
Rest of Berkshire	50	1,000
Rest of Buckinghamshire	185	3,700
Rest of East Sussex	330	6,600
Rest of Hampshire	1,220	24,400
Rest of Kent	1,444	28,880
Rest of Oxfordshire	726	14,520
Rest of Surrey	250	5,000
Rest of West Sussex	330	6,600
TOTAL*	32,700	654,000

* sub-regional figures do not add to total due to rounding

Note: The specific housing delivery requirements for districts and/or parts of districts that fall within the above areas are set out in detail in relevant sub-regional and the rest of the sub-regional area chapters.

Local planning authorities will prepare plans, strategies and programmes to ensure the delivery of the annual average net additional dwelling requirement as set out in Table H1b.

Table H1b

District / Strategic Development Area (SDA)	Annual Average	Total	District / Strategic Development Area (SDA)	Annual Average	Total
Adur[1]	105	2,100	New Forest[6]	196	3,920
Shoreham Harbour[1]	500	10,000	New Forest National Park	11	220
Arun	565	11,300	North East/North of Hedge End SDA[7]	300	6,000
Ashford	1,135	22,700	Oxford[8]	400	8,000
Aylesbury Vale[2]	1,345	26,900	South of Oxford SDA[8]	200	4,000
Basingstoke & Deane	945	18,900	Portsmouth	735	14,700
Bracknell Forest	639	12,780	Reading	611	12,220
Brighton & Hove	570	11,400	Reigate & Banstead	500	10,000
Canterbury	510	10,200	Rother	280	5,600
Cherwell	670	13,400	Runnymede[9]	286	5,720
Chichester	480	9,600	Rushmoor	310	6,200
Chiltern	145	2,900	Sevenoaks	165	3,300
Crawley	375	7,500	Shepway	290	5,800
Dartford	867	17,340	Slough	315	6,300
Dover	505	10,100	South Bucks	94	1,880
East Hampshire[3]	260	5,200	South Oxfordshire[8]	547	10,940
East Hampshire[3] (Whitehill/Bordon)	275	5,500	Southampton	815	16,300
Eastbourne	240	4,800	Spelthorne	166	3,320
Eastleigh	354	7,080	Surrey Heath	187	3,740
Elmbridge	281	5,620	Swale	540	10,800
Epsom & Ewell	199	3,980	Tandridge	125	2,500
Fareham[4]	186	3,720	Test Valley	501	10,020
Fareham SDA[4]	500	10,000	Thanet	375	7,500

Gosport	125	2,500	Tonbridge & Malling	450	9,000
Gravesham	465	9,300	Tunbridge Wells	300	6,000
Guildford	422	8,440	Vale of White Horse	578	11,560
Hart	220	4,400	Waverley	250	5,000
Hastings	210	4,200	Wealden	550	11,000
Havant	315	6,300	West Berkshire	525	10,500
Horsham	650	13,000	West Oxfordshire	365	7,300
Isle of Wight	520	10,400	Winchester	612	12,240
Lewes	220	4,400	Windsor & Maidenhead	346	6,920
Maidstone	554	11,080	Woking	292	5,840
Medway	815	16,300	Wokingham[10]	623	12,460
Mid Sussex	855	17,100	Worthing	200	4,000
Milton Keynes[5]	2,068	41,360	Wycombe	390	7,800
Mole Valley	188	3,760	SOUTH EAST TOTAL	32,700	654,000

District housing distribution figures do not add to totals due to rounding.

1) The figure for Adur does not include the interim allocation for the redevelopment of Shoreham Harbour, which is given separately. The Shoreham Harbour allocation may be revised in accordance with the Sussex Coast sub-regional strategy to take account of any new evidence on its potential.

2) The figures for Aylesbury Vale includes some 5,400 related to the expansion of Milton Keynes.

3) The figure for East Hampshire does not include any specific allocation for Whitehill/Bordon. A separate allocation of 5,500 has been made for Whitehill/Bordon as the basis for further study including the implications for the SPA.

4) The figure for Fareham does not include any allocation for the Fareham SDA.

5) The figure for Milton Keynes does not include any adjoining growth in the East of England region which would be subject to testing at future reviews of the RSS for that region.

6) The figure for New Forest does not include any allocations for the parts of the district that fall within the boundaries of the National Park.

7) The allocation for North East/North of Hedge End SDA is to be divided between Eastleigh and Winchester on the basis of further study.

8) The allocation for the south of Oxford SDA is to be divided between Oxford and South Oxfordshire following a selective Green Belt review.

9) The figure for Runnymede includes 2,500 homes for the reuse of the former DERA site at Chertsey to be provided in Runnymede. The precise housing contribution from this site will be tested in accordance with Policy LF6. This allocation will be delivered in the period between 2016-2026. Between 2006-2015 the annual requirement will be 161 dwellings per annum. In the event that the site cannot be released for housing, there is no expectation that the shortfall should be provided elsewhere within Runnymede.

10) The figure for Wokingham includes some 2,500 related to the needs of Greater Reading.

POLICY H2: MANAGING THE DELIVERY OF THE REGIONAL HOUSING PROVISION

Local planning authorities will work in partnership to allocate and manage a land supply to deliver both the district housing provision and the sub-regional and the rest of the sub-regional area housing provision while ensuring appropriate regard to environmental and infrastructure issues.

In planning for the delivery of the housing provision, local planning authorities will also take account of the following considerations:

i. the need to facilitate any proposals that are agreed for Growth Points and eco-towns to be assessed through the next review
ii. ability to accelerate the rate of housing delivery in Growth Areas and New Growth Points
iii. possibility of maximising the scale and the pace of housing delivery on named strategic locations identified in Table H1b
iv. scope to identify additional sources of supply elsewhere by encouraging opportunities on suitable previously developed sites. This includes appropriate opportunities for change of use of non-residential development sites to secure either mixed use residential development or residential development
v. realising opportunities for intensification consistent with criteria in PPS3
vi. providing a sufficient quantity and mix of housing including affordable housing in rural areas to ensure the long term sustainability of rural communities
vii. feasibility of maximising the delivery capacity unlocked by investment in infrastructure at the earliest possible opportunity
viii. the need to address any backlog of unmet housing needs within the housing market areas they relate to, in the first 10 years of the Plan.

In managing the delivery of housing provision, the local planning authorities should plan for an increase in housing completions to help meet anticipated need and demand, and seek to achieve both the district distribution and the relevant sub-regional and rest of the County area provisions. Working together with local planning authorities, the regional planning body should maintain a regional housing trajectory and the sub-regional trajectories.

7.6 The scale of demand and need for housing in the region, together with the importance of the South East to the national economy and its interrelationship with London necessitate that the RSS sets out a housing provision that makes a sufficient response to these strategic needs. This Plan has gone some way towards this goal but at 32,700 dwellings per year, the level that is set here is still significantly below the forecast growth of households and even more so by the more recent 2006-based population projections. The current short term market conditions are not expected to help alleviate the worsening housing affordability in the longer term and the supply range recommended for the South East in the independent advice from the National Housing and Planning Advice Unit (NHPAU) is significantly higher than the level of housing provision set in the Policy H1.

7.7 However, the limitations of the bottom up evidence base on the capacity of sub-regional areas and districts to accommodate a higher level of housing together with a lack of robust economic evidence underpinning this RSS means that it can only provide a limited response at present. Local authorities can test higher numbers through their development plan documents provided that they are consistent with the principles of sustainable development set out in PPS1 and tested through sustainability appraisal and Habitats Regulations Assessment. The review of this RSS will examine the current levels of housing and a rate of provision higher than 32,700 dwellings per annum is likely to be necessary to meet the strategic needs in the region.

7.8 Policy H1 sets out the total amount of housing that is expected to be delivered in the region over the years 2006-26. It includes an annual average figure for each local authority area. These figures should not be regarded as annual targets and are intended to be used in monitoring progress towards achievement of plan objectives, and to inform management of housing supply. The fact that an annual provision or local trajectory number has been met should not in itself be a reason for rejecting a planning application. Decisions should be taken on their merit and local circumstances – including longer term housing needs and affordability in an area. Where delivery is not meeting planned rates, local authorities should work with the regional planning body and partners to investigate and implement action to overcome any obstacles to delivery. Policy IMR1 sets out arrangements for the 'Plan, Monitor and Manage' approach to housing supply.

7.9 Local planning authorities should ensure that there are clear arrangements for managing and monitoring the delivery of the housing provision and the Annual Monitoring Reports must provide housing trajectory data for each part of the districts that fall within each sub-region and/or within a rest of the sub-regional area together with the trajectory for the district as a whole.

7.10 The sub-regional definition as set out in this RSS means that a large part of the region including much of its rural areas fall outside them. Therefore, it is important that housing growth in rural areas is not artificially constrained. The regional planning body and the local planning authorities must plan for and manage the provision of housing to enhance the viability of rural settlements and promote a rural renaissance, and thereby meet the long term needs of the rural communities.

7.11 The Secretary of State expects that as part of the transition to a single Regional Strategy (as part of the Sub-National Review of Economic Development and Regeneration) the review of the RSS will test the scope for any higher levels of growth in the context of Government guidance following the NHPAU advice to the Government. It will also enable the proposals for any confirmed new eco-towns and additional Growth Points to be assessed and brought forward, and identify any additional broad locations to meet longer term needs in the most sustainable way. The review of RSS should also be informed by strategic housing market assessment work, together with the results of monitoring and evaluating the labour market.

Achieving a Mix of Housing

POLICY H3: AFFORDABLE HOUSING

A substantial increase in the amount of affordable housing in the region will be delivered. Local authorities and their partners will work to bring together households in need with funding and new affordable housing stock to support this policy and the Regional Housing Strategy. This will be achieved by:

i. **basing policy and funding decisions on a sound evidence base, gathered through the strategic housing market assessment process. Assessments should examine housing need and demand in relation to both affordable and market housing and where markets cross boundaries should be conducted jointly between authorities**

ii. development and inclusion of targets for the provision of affordable housing, taking account of housing need and having regard to the overall regional target that 25% of all new housing should be social rented accommodation and 10% intermediate affordable housing. Where indicative targets for sub-regions are set out in the relevant sections of this RSS, these should take precedence over the regional target

iii. setting affordable housing targets which are supported by evidence of financial viability and the role of public subsidy in the light of guidance from the regional planning body and the regional housing board

iv. the incorporation of locally set thresholds covering the size of site above which an affordable housing contribution will be required. These may vary across a local authority area depending on the anticipated pattern of new development. Such thresholds will have regard to an assessment of economic viability, scale of need and impact on overall levels of housing delivery

v. working with local communities in rural areas to secure small scale affordable housing sites within or well-related to settlements, possibly including land which would not otherwise be released for development.

Definition of Affordable Housing

Affordable housing is defined as non-market housing, provided to those whose needs are not met by the market, for example homeless persons and key workers. It can include social-rented housing and intermediate housing.

Affordable housing should:

- meet the needs of eligible households, including availability at low enough cost for them to afford, determined with regard to local incomes and local house prices; and

- include provision for the home to remain at an affordable price for future eligible households, or if a home ceases to be affordable, any subsidy should generally be recycled for additional affordable housing provision.

POLICY H4: TYPE AND SIZE OF NEW HOUSING

Local authorities should identify the full range of existing and future housing needs required in their areas working with adjoining local authorities where appropriate. Groups with particular housing needs include older and disabled people, students, black and minority ethnic households, families with children, Gypsies, travellers and travelling showpeople, and others with specialist requirements. Local development documents should require an appropriate range and mix of housing opportunities by identifying:

i. the likely profile of household types requiring market housing
ii. the size and type of affordable housing required.

Local authorities should seek to identify a mix of site allocations in each five year period, preparing development briefs as necessary, to encourage a range of housing types to be provided.

7.12 Housing provision is far more than just a 'numbers game'. It must support the needs of the whole community, and include the provision of both market and affordable housing, as well as reflecting the range of types, sizes and tenures both needed and in demand.

This will include specific groups such as families with children and older and disabled people. Policies H3: Affordable Housing Provision and H4: Type and Size of Housingare included to support this aim.

Affordable Housing

7.13 The cost of housing is a major barrier to continued economic growth, contributing to significant problems in recruitment and retention and longer distance commuting which, in turn, adds to levels of road congestion, pollution and reduced air quality. High housing costs also have potentially serious social consequences. The failure to meet the housing needs of the most vulnerable and lower paid has been shown to affect educational achievement and health.

7.14 Rates of new affordable housing provision in the region have been running well below the rate required to meet existing needs. To address these problems, there needs to be a significant increase in affordable housing provision across the region. The Housing Green Paper sets targets for a substantial amount of additional affordable housing in England – up to 50,000 new social rented homes per year from 2010 and 25,000 new shared equity and shared ownership homes.

7.15 The allocation of public funding for investment in housing reflects advice from the regional housing board. The region's housing strategy identifies provision of additional affordable housing, with improved design and environmental standards as the top priority for the South East. Around £1.2 billion, about 90% of the overall funds, is available for this in the three years from April 2008. The Homes and Communities Agency, which was established in December 2008, is responsible for managing the affordable housing funding programme to deliver national and regional objectives on tenure and dwelling-type mix and the spatial distribution of the affordable housing provided.

7.16 Where administrative boundaries bear little relation to housing markets there is a need for joint working, and in particular the production of joint strategic housing market assessments which are able to look at patterns of housing supply and demand across a wider area. Particular opportunities to provide affordable housing will also be available through the development of Growth Areas, strategic development areas and on major green field sites. Local authorities should work with partners to bring together land, funding and those in need to meet identified community aspirations. Consultation and preparation of area action plans, supplementary planning documents and design briefs can offer a particular vehicle for helping achieve this.

Diagram H1

South East Sub-regional Housing Markets

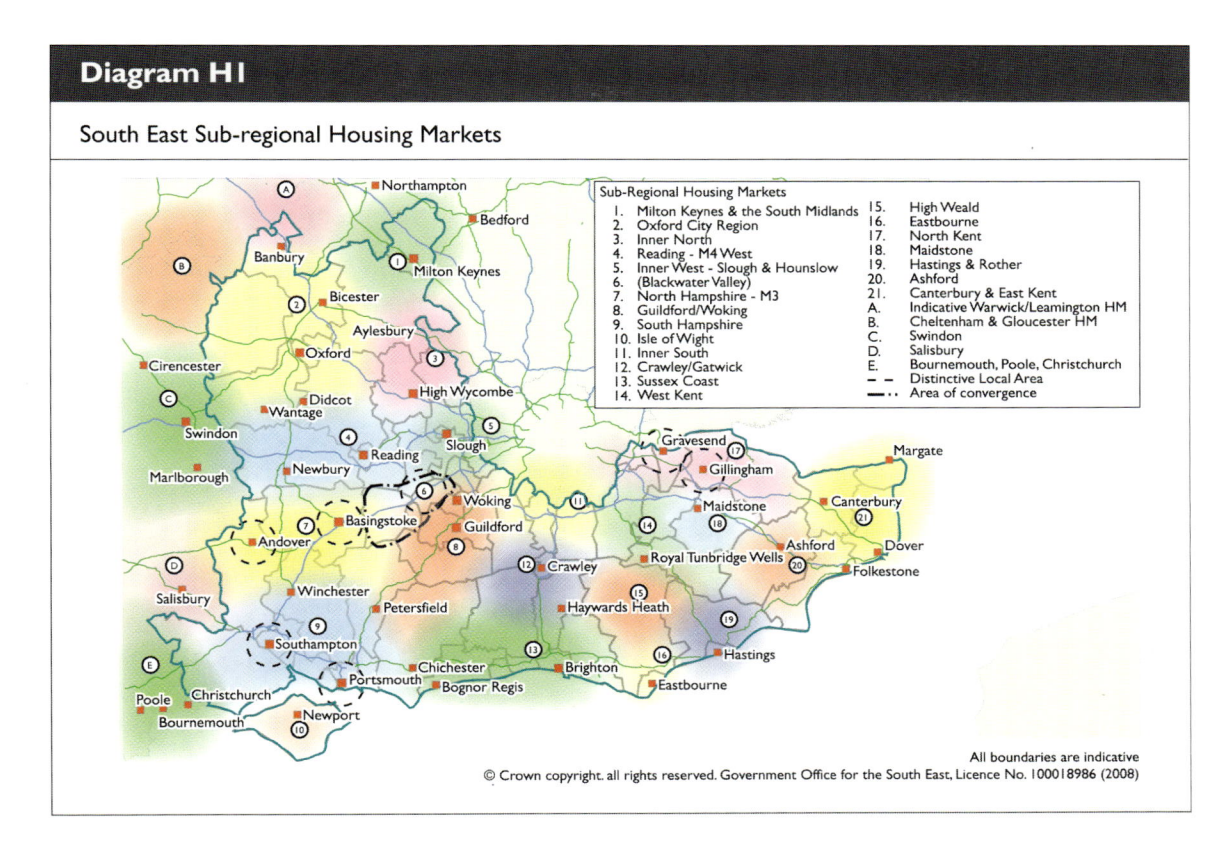

Sub-Regional Housing Markets
1. Milton Keynes & the South Midlands
2. Oxford City Region
3. Inner North
4. Reading - M4 West
5. Inner West - Slough & Hounslow
6. (Blackwater Valley)
7. North Hampshire - M3
8. Guildford/Woking
9. South Hampshire
10. Isle of Wight
11. Inner South
12. Crawley/Gatwick
13. Sussex Coast
14. West Kent
15. High Weald
16. Eastbourne
17. North Kent
18. Maidstone
19. Hastings & Rother
20. Ashford
21. Canterbury & East Kent
A. Indicative Warwick/Leamington HM
B. Cheltenham & Gloucester HM
C. Swindon
D. Salisbury
E. Bournemouth, Poole, Christchurch
– – Distinctive Local Area
—·· Area of convergence

All boundaries are indicative
© Crown copyright. all rights reserved. Government Office for the South East, Licence No. 100018986 (2008)

7.17 The need to provide more high quality affordable homes in the region's extensive patchwork of rural communities is also acute, given high prices and demand, the 'pricing out' of local populations and the need to support essential local services. Paragraph 30 of PPS3 sets out national policy on securing affordable housing in rural communities.

Type and Size of New Housing

7.18 Effective forward planning of housing supply involves an understanding of the sizes, types and tenures of housing that will be needed, and not just the overall numbers. Local authorities should use the findings of Strategic Housing Market Assessments to improve their evidence base on housing mix, by broadening their understanding of the relationship between housing demand and need and housing supply within local housing markets. Assessments should take account of any research or activities undertaken by the regional planning body and housing board to increase consistency and accuracy of local assessments, as well as the ongoing review of the needs of Gypsies and travellers.

7.19 Although much has been made in recent years of the trend towards smaller households (the result of societal and demographic changes), it is by no means the case that only small dwellings, such as one or two-bedroom houses and flats, will be needed in the future. An adequate range of larger properties, suitable for family occupation, will also be required – and with suitable attention to design and layout these can be provided at higher densities than hitherto. Some elderly and disabled people will have specialist needs requiring particular types of provision. The accommodation requirements of Gypsies and travellers should also be addressed.

7.20 Our understanding of the variety of current housing supply and what will be required in the future is evolving. A research project commissioned by the South East England Regional Assembly[3] provided some key pointers in planning for size, mix and tenure in the future:

- in 2005/6 53% of housing completions for the open market were flats. This is a three-fold rise since 1997

---

3 Housing Type and Size in the South East, DTZ Consulting and Research for the South East of England Regional Assembly, April 2007

- the number of houses for sale has declined over the same period
- there has been a marked upward trend in the completion of flats within the public sector since 1997. In 2004/5 70% of dwellings completed by Registered Social Landlords were flats
- the rate of overcrowding in the region is 6% of all households. 15% of social tenants and private rented tenants live in overcrowded conditions

7.21 The research also highlights several techniques that could assist in identifying the size of affordable housing required, such as focusing investment based on the characteristics of those in priority need and negotiating with developers to provide units that meet the requirements of those in priority need. It also points to the need for authorities to pay particular attention to existing stock profiles in particular areas. One example may be rural areas, where a predominance of larger units may mean a policy drive to widen the mix of housing types to cater for all housing need.

Housing Density and Design

> **POLICY H5: HOUSING DESIGN AND DENSITY**
>
> **Positive measures to raise the quality of new housing, reduce its environmental impact and facilitate future adaptation to meet changes in accommodation needs will be encouraged. Local authorities will prepare guidelines for the design of new housing in their areas that encourage the use of sustainable construction methods and address the implications of changing lifestyles for new housing design.**
>
> **In conjunction with the delivery of high quality design and in order to make good use of available land and encourage more sustainable patterns of development and services, higher housing densities will be encouraged, with an overall regional target of 40 dwellings per hectare over the Plan period. Local authorities will reflect this target with appropriate local variations in their local development documents.**

7.22 Higher densities help make the best use of scarce land resources, help support infrastructure and local services and can be successfully achieved with sufficient attention to careful design. Policy BE1 sets out this Plan's approach to promoting and supporting imaginative and efficient design solutions in new development, and aims to increase public acceptance of new housing by making sure that it is of a high quality design that respects local context and confers a sense of place. Design which is inappropriate in its context, or which fails to take the opportunities available for improving the character and quality of an area and the way it functions, should not be accepted. Design also needs to take account of the need to minimise the use of finite resources, adapt to and mitigate against climate change effects and reduce unnecessary pressures on the countryside. Equally, design must address health and safety concerns, including considering how good design can reduce the opportunity for crime and disorder and the fear of crime.[4] Important too, are the implications of changing lifestyles – such as the growing trend towards home working, which can itself have considerable environmental benefits in terms of reducing commuting and office space requirements. New homes should incorporate features that provide built-in flexibility making adaptation easier as people's lives change. Such flexibility benefits the occupiers, but will also allow for reduced expenditure on adaptations in future and reduced need to move people to residential or health care.

7.23 Historically, densities of new residential development in the South East have been some of the lowest in the country. Monitoring data shows that densities have been increasing, to an average of 39 dwellings per hectare net in 2004/05. In accord with the Plan's overall strategy, this trend needs to continue. Policy H5 sets out a density of 40 dwellings per hectare net for the region. It is not expected that this target should be applied uniformly

---

4 For example, by incorporating the principles and standards of *Secured by Design* (ACPO, 2004) and the Secured by Design Award Scheme

to all areas through the production of LDDs, and local authorities should work towards using land efficiently through justification of higher or lower targets based on local development patterns, achievement of the spatial vision for an area, and identification of constraints and opportunities for urban intensification. Policy BE2 sets out the region's strategy for encouraging urban and suburban intensification in areas of high accessibility. Within many urban and suburban areas across the South East there are significant opportunities to provide quality housing development in excess of 50 dwellings per hectare net. Opportunities for higher densities should be identified in the centres of regional hubs, in accordance with the 'living cities' concept used in Policy SP2. Useful advice for local authority members to help them make best use of land when making decisions about development proposals has been published by the South East England Regional Assembly. [5]

Making Better Use of the Existing Stock

POLICY H6: MAKING BETTER USE OF THE EXISTING STOCK

To help meet housing needs and to promote urban renaissance and sustainable use of resources, local authorities should assess the existing housing stock in their areas and implement measures to reduce the number of vacant, unfit and unsatisfactory dwellings. Such measures include:

i. **identifying in local development documents areas that suffer from particular problems of empty and run-down dwellings that would benefit from an action area plan approach to remedying these problems**
ii. **adopting policies and programmes to improve or redevelop areas that are becoming outworn and thus ensure their overall quality and attractiveness as places to live**
iii. **producing empty homes strategies setting out a range of initiatives to bring empty homes back into use**
iv. **considering incentives to encourage smaller households occupying larger properties to move to smaller dwellings**
v. **adopting policies that encourage the conversion of larger houses to flats in appropriate locations where such an approach is consistent with meeting the identified local housing needs.**

7.24 Existing homes will account for over 80% of the homes in the region at the end of the Plan period. It is, therefore, essential that this stock is effectively used and maintained. Living in poor housing can impact significantly on people's health and well-being, and the provision of a decent home for all is a high priority for the region and Central Government. The Government's and Regional Housing Board's target is to bring all social housing into a decent condition by 2010. In line with the Regional Housing Board's advice, additional funding is being provided for improving poor condition private housing occupied by vulnerable households - in parts of the region, mainly in coastal and the more deprived areas, there are significant concentrations of older, predominately pre-1919 properties in poor condition. There is also scope to encourage the adaptation and re-use of existing dwellings across the region to meet changing demographic and social needs and the need to prepare for climate change, provided that this is undertaken in a manner consistent with this Plan's policies on the built environment.

7.25 There also remains scope to bring empty homes back into use and converting existing buildings, in preference to the development of greenfield sites. Although the housing vacancy rate in the South East is the lowest of any region there are parts of the region where vacancy rates are high and where action may help to reduce these rates.

7.26 Empty homes strategies can include such initiatives as:

---

5   Councillor's Toolbox: Making the Best Use of Land, South East England Regional Assembly, 2004

i. setting up a register of empty homes, identifying empty properties and establishing the reasons why they remain empty and the measures which would bring the property back into use
ii. renovation grants (to bring an unfit property up to modern habitable standards)
iii. imposing a high level (e.g. 90%) of council tax on empty properties
iv. encouraging use of accommodation above shops
v. working in partnership with housing associations on leasing schemes (providing for the owner to lease the empty property to a housing association that will guarantee a reasonable rent and the return of the property in good condition at the end of the lease) or identifying empty homes that the housing association can buy and bring back into use, subject to the availability of funding
vi. carrying out enforcement measures, compulsory purchase orders or enforced sale procedures on empty properties that are creating nuisances in terms of decay, infestation or crime
vii. working with the private sector and potential tenants to ensure the maximum occupation of private sector rented housing.

Provision for Gypsies and Travellers: Interim Statement

7.27 DCLG Circular 01/2006 *Planning for Gypsy and Traveller Caravan Sites* sets out the policy and legislative framework for the Government's aim of reducing tensions between Gypsies and Travellers and the settled community, through sustainable site provision and effective enforcement. The Circular requires regional spatial strategies, on the basis of local authority Gypsy and Traveller Accommodation Assessments, to determine a strategic view of needs across the region and identify the number of pitches required for each local planning authority. It also requires local authorities to allocate suitable sites within their local development documents to meet the identified need set out in regional spatial strategies. The Department for Communities and Local Government's Circular 04/2007 – *Planning for Travelling Show People* provides further guidance.

7.28 The regional planning body are currently (April 2009) undertaking a single issue review of Gypsy and traveller accommodation needs in the region. As part of the review, local authorities in the South East have now completed their Gypsy and Traveller Accommodation Assessments in accordance with the Housing Act 2004.

7.29 The accommodation assessments will provide for the first time comprehensive, robust and credible data relating to the needs and requirements of the Gypsy and traveller community.

7.30 Circular 01/2006 states that where there is a clear and immediate need, local planning authorities should bring forward development plan documents containing site allocations in advance of regional consideration of pitch numbers, and completions of the Accommodation Assessments.

Transport

8 Transport

Context

8.1 This Transport chapter forms the Regional Transport Strategy (RTS) for South East England to 2026. It is based on and replaces the existing RTS, published by the Government in July 2004, and takes into account the subsequent stream of national policies and announcements impacting on it; for example, the White Papers on Aviation and the Future of Rail, and the Delivering a Sustainable Transport System (DaSTS) initiative. In setting out the long-term regional framework for the development of the transport system in the region, the RTS provides the context within which other relevant regional strategies, including those of the South East England Development Agency (SEEDA), the Highways Agency (HA) and the rail industry, will be developed. It also provides the context within which local authorities (transport and/or planning) will review their local transport plans (LTPs) and local development frameworks (LDFs).

8.2 From evidence presented by the Regional Assembly at the 2006/2007 examination-in-public (EiP), the key challenges faced by the region's transport system are understood to be:

 i. to provide consistently good access between the United Kingdom and the world through gateway ports and airports
 ii. to maintain high quality radial connectivity to London, and develop orbital routes around London
 iii. to deliver transport measures which address severe deprivation
 iv. to address unpredictable journeys in buoyant areas
 v. to reduce the impact of the transport system on the environment.

8.3 Monitored travel information for the South East shows an increase in overall travel per person since 2004, including an increase in travel by car. Some of these changes are capable of being positively influenced by the South East Plan, the clearest example of this being the concentration of movement and development at a number of urban locations. Evidence suggests that pressure on the transport system is increasing and the urban focus can best support the re-balancing of the transport system toward more sustainable modes, while maintaining, and indeed improving, overall levels of accessibility. In so doing it will assist in reducing the impact of the transport system on both the natural and built environment.

8.4 The need to re-balance the transport system in favour of sustainable modes is recognised throughout this Plan, accepting that it is unrealistic to achieve an absolute reduction in traffic within the life of the Plan.

8.5 The RTS sets out to deliver the following: "Our vision is a high quality transport system to act as a catalyst for continued economic growth and provide for an improved quality of life for all in a sustainable and socially inclusive manner; a regional transport system that progressively reaches the standard of the best in North West Europe."

8.6 Translating this vision into a set of regionally specific objectives that integrate spatial and transportation planning at the regional level, the RTS seeks:

 i. to facilitate urban renaissance and foster social inclusion by re-balancing the structure and use of the transport system. In particular, bringing forward measures that encourage modal shift to more sustainable modes and significantly improve the attractiveness of local public transport services, walking and cycling
 ii. to reduce the wider environmental, health and community impact associated with the transport system, by bringing forward management measures that reduce our reliance on single occupancy car use
 iii. to maintain the existing transport infrastructure as an asset
 iv. to develop road and rail links that improve inter and intra-regional connectivity
 v. to improve and develop transport connections to the region's international gateways (ports, airports and international rail stations)

Transport

vi. to improve transport management and infrastructure within and to the Thames Gateway to maximise regeneration potential and encourage economic potential
vii. to support economic regeneration in East Kent through investment in improved accessibility
viii. to take forward transport management and infrastructure proposals required to support development in the Growth Areas of Milton Keynes and Aylesbury Vale, Ashford and the designated new growth points
ix. to improve road and rail links along the South Coast to improve spatial connectivity and realise economic opportunities to reduce disparities within the region
x. to improve strategic road and rail links within and to the Western Corridor and Blackwater Valley to maintain economic success.

8.7 The transport strategy and policies are focused on a set of core principles:

i. managing and investing
ii. mobility management
iii. road pricing and charging
iv. communications technology
v. the rural dimension
vi. regional hubs and spokes
vii. the gateways, airports and ports
viii. freight.

Manage and Invest

> **POLICY T1: MANAGE AND INVEST**
>
> **Relevant regional strategies, local development documents and local transport plans should ensure that their management policies and proposals:**
>
> i. **are consistent with, and supported by, appropriate mobility management measures**
> ii. **achieve a re-balancing of the transport system in favour of sustainable modes as a means of access to services and facilities**
> iii. **foster and promote an improved and integrated network of public transport services in and between both urban and rural areas**
> iv. **encourage development that is located and designed to reduce average journey lengths**
> v. **improve the maintenance of the existing transport system**
> vi. **include measures that reduce the overall number of road casualties**
> vii. **include measures to minimise negative environmental impacts of transport and, where possible, to enhance the environment and communities through such interventions**
> viii. **investment in upgrading the transport system should be prioritised to support delivery of the spatial strategy by:**
>
> a. **supporting the function of the region's international gateways and inter-regional movement corridors (see Diagram T1 at the end of the chapter)**
> b. **developing the network of regional hubs and spokes (see Diagram T2 at the end of the chapter)**
> c. **facilitating urban renewal and urban renaissance as a means of achieving a more sustainable pattern of development**
> d. **improving overall levels of accessibility.**

8.8 Achieving a more sustainable pattern of development is dependent upon accepting that the transport system within the region is a resource that has a finite capacity at any point in time. While this capacity will increase as a consequence of the investment already programmed, the RTS reflects the simple fact that it is not possible to build our way out of the problem. Future investment in the transport system must play its proper role in tackling climate change as well as supporting people's desire for mobility. DfT's publication Delivering a Sustainable Transport System (DaSTS) sets out how this can be achieved and is in line with an approach of rebalancing the transport system, building on recent changes in travel patterns and applying a spatial approach to planning in which decisions on investment in the transport system are more closely integrated with economic, environmental and social objectives.

8.9 This approach is the key principle underpinning the "Manage and Invest" strategy that defines the RTS.

The key components of 'manage' are:

- influencing the pattern of activities and specifically new development, so that more people have the opportunity to work and shop etc. closer to their home location
- seeking greater utilisation of capacity on the existing transport system, e.g. more active management of the road network and intelligent transport systems, and route capacity utilisation
- managing demand on the transport system, particularly on the road network, e.g. re-allocating capacity, promoting sustainable modes, parking policy, travel planning and possible fiscal measures.

8.10 Realising the full potential offered by the opportunities to rebalance the transport system provided by the spatial strategy requires the concept of mobility management to be embraced as an integral element of this RTS. Mobility management encourages an approach that embraces the need to develop the transport system in a way that considers more positively the inter-relationship between all elements of the transport system. It creates an integrated approach to managing the demand for movement that capitalises on the opportunities created through the spatial strategy by seeking to adjust, over time, people's pattern of travel in a way that increases the use of sustainable modes while maintaining overall levels of access to services and facilities. Climate change is one of the greatest challenges facing the UK and transport has an important role to play. Economic growth and reducing CO_2 are not incompatible and the right balance between management and investment in infrastructure at local, regional and national level will be critical in achieving that balance.

Mobility Management

POLICY T2: MOBILITY MANAGEMENT

The policies and proposals set out in local development documents and local transport plans should include policies to achieve a rebalancing of the transport system in favour of sustainable modes based on an integrated package of measures drawn from the following:

i. the allocation and management of highway space used by individual modes of travel
ii. the scale of provision and management (including pricing) of car parking both off and on-street
iii. the scope and management of public transport services
iv. an integrated and comprehensive travel planning advice service
v. improvements in the extent and quality of pedestrian and cycle routes
vi. charging initiatives
vii. intelligent transport systems including the use of systems to convey information to transport users
viii. incentives for car sharing and the encouragement of car clubs
ix. local services and e-services to reduce the need to travel
x. changes in ways of working that alter the extent and balance of future demand for movement

xi. demand responsive transport and other innovative solutions that increase accessibility

xii. measures that increase accessibility to rail stations.

Plans will need to reflect the fact that low delivery from any one of these elements will require a compensatory increase in delivery from one or more of the others.

8.11 The adoption of an integrated approach to investment in, and management of, the transport system will enable the link between economic growth and the growth in car-based traffic to be gradually uncoupled, while at the same time increasing the overall level of accessibility to goods and services. Where proposals to increase the capacity of the transport system are brought forward, these should be accompanied by measures that seek to sustain the benefits of that investment. This approach requires a high level of co-ordination between delivery agencies. It also requires integration with decisions in other policy areas.

8.12 This RTS places a strong and particular need to bring forward demand management measures that should, over time, achieve a significant change in the overall pattern of movement, with a higher proportion of journeys being undertaken on foot, by cycle or public transport (bus, rail and rapid transit or, where car based, using car clubs or car sharing). The likely mix of demand management measures in individual sub-regions will be indicated in each sub-regional strategy. Any future review of this RTS should consider regional standards for public transport accessibility.

Road Pricing and Charging

POLICY T3: CHARGING

Local transport authorities and particularly those responsible for the hubs should consider using the powers available under the Transport Act 2000 and Local Transport Act 2008, and Government funding, to test new charging initiatives. This may be done, where appropriate, jointly with other authorities. Road user charging should be considered as part of an integrated approach to support delivery of the regional strategy. In addition to being consistent with national guidance, any scheme within the region should be matched with promotion of sustainable alternatives to vehicle use, and be designed so as to avoid disadvantaging regeneration areas dependent on road access.

8.13 The results of the Government's Road Pricing Feasibility Study were published in support of the White Paper, *The Future of Transport* in 2004. The Government has subsequently indicated a willingness to lead the debate on national road pricing.

8.14 The Government has committed itself to work alongside forward-looking authorities and areas to help them put in place packages of measures that tackle local congestion problems, with resources from the Transport Innovation Fund being made available to support packages that combine road pricing, modal shift and better public transport services. In addition, the Government is exploring the technology that would be required for any future widespread system of road pricing that varied charges according to time of day, place and distance travelled.

8.15 Further work is required to understand the potential implications that local, and any future widespread, road pricing system might have for the balance of investment proposals (including management measures) required to facilitate delivery of the spatial strategy set out in the South East Plan. Local authorities should consider road pricing and charging in identifying the mix of interventions, particularly at a sub-regional level.

Parking

POLICY T4: PARKING

Local development documents and local transport plans should, in combination:

i. adopt restraint-based maximum levels of parking provision for non-residential developments, linked to an integrated programme of public transport and accessibility improvements
ii. set maximum parking standards for Class B1 land uses within the range 1:30 m^2 and 1:100m^2
iii. set maximum parking standards for other non-residential land uses in line with PPG13: *Transport*, reducing provision below this in locations with good public transport
iv. include policies and proposals for the management of the total parking stock within regional hubs that are consistent with these limits
v. apply guidance set out in PPS3: *Housing* on residential parking, reflecting local circumstances
vi. support an increase in the provision in parking at rail stations where appropriate
vii. ensure the provision of sufficient cycle parking at new developments including secure cycle storage for new flats and houses which lack garages.

8.16 Planning Policy Guidance Note 13: *Transport* (PPG13) requires development plans to set maximum levels of car parking for broad classes of development.

8.17 The region exhibits a wide range of social and economic circumstances that necessitates a flexible approach to identifying appropriate levels of car parking provision. Such an approach should provide a level of accessibility by private car that is consistent with the overall balance of the transport system at the local level. Nevertheless, the constraints that will continue to exist in terms of the capacity of the transport system, when coupled with the need to re-balance the use of the transport system, means that overall local authorities should seek a level of parking provision that is tighter than that set out in PPG13. Local authorities adjoining other regions must also liaise with the appropriate authorities to ensure a consistent approach to the level of parking provision. Particular attention should be given to the relationship with London in this respect.

8.18 Proposals to increase the provision of car parking at railway stations should be considered favourably, particularly at rail stations associated with regional hubs. Local authorities should consider safeguarding land specifically to accommodate an increase in car parking at rail stations. However, any increase in parking at a rail station should be part of a package of measures that also seeks to enhance access by bus, cycling and walking.

8.19 Parking policy is currently under review and a consultation has taken place on draft PPS4: *Planning for Sustainable Economic Development*, which allows local authorities to develop their own car parking policies for non-residential development, setting maximum standards based on certain criteria. Policy T4 will need to be viewed in light of the outcome of the PPS4 consultation.

Travel Planning and Information

POLICY T5: TRAVEL PLANS AND ADVICE

Local authorities must ensure that their local development documents and local transport plans identify those categories of major travel generating developments, both existing and proposed, for which travel plans should be developed.

Local transport authorities should also consider piloting the concept of transport planning advice centres for regional hubs in their local transport plans.

8.20 Research commissioned by the Government and published as *Smarter Choices* has served to emphasise the important role that travel planning plays as part of delivering the mobility management approach. Travel plans can be a positive measure in enabling economic activity and growth in the region.

8.21 Local authorities should implement their own travel plan as a priority. They should also put in place mechanisms to monitor the outcomes of travel plans in order that the measures set out within them might be amended in light of practical experience.

8.22 Local authorities can also play a leading role in engaging the public, business community, health sector, education sector and transport industry in a meaningful partnership that promotes the co-ordinated development and implementation of travel plans. Local authorities should actively support travel plan initiatives taken by private sector companies and other organisations.

Communications Technology

> **POLICY T6: COMMUNICATIONS TECHNOLOGY**
>
> **Investment in communications technology that increases access to goods and services without increasing the need to travel should be actively encouraged and taken into consideration in identifying future transport needs.**

8.23 Improvements in communications technology have the potential to reduce the need to travel significantly. Such technology can increase access to services for rural communities and support economic activity more generally through improved access to services and international markets. In bringing forward proposals to manage, and/or develop, the use of the existing transport system, the opportunities created through the application of such technology should be constructively explored and realised.

The Rural Dimension

> **POLICY T7: RURAL TRANSPORT**
>
> **Local transport plans covering areas that are not wholly urban should:**
>
> i. **take a co-ordinated approach to encouraging community-based transport in areas of need**
> ii. **include a rural dimension to transport and traffic management policies, including looking for opportunities to improve provision for cyclists and pedestrians between towns and their nearest villages**
> iii. **develop innovative and adaptable approaches to public transport in rural areas that reflect the particular and longer-term social and economic characteristics of the region.**

8.24 In the South East over 20% of the population lives in rural areas, and with an above average level of car ownership in rural areas, the car will continue to provide the primary mode of travel. Improving travel choice in rural areas is to be encouraged, while accepting that there is unlikely to be a single model for delivering the flexible and responsive transport services required to meet the diverse needs of rural communities. Targeted and innovative schemes will therefore need to be developed, making creative use of available resources.

Gateways, Hubs and Interchanges

8.25 The gateway function of the South East, in providing connectivity to the rest of Europe and the rest of the world, has shaped the transport networks that are seen today. These are shown on Diagram T1 along with the corridors of international and inter-regional importance. This highlights the location of international gateway ports and airports which are of both national and regional importance.

8.26 Policy SP2 (Chapter 4) establishes the concept of regional hubs as centres where the provision of (or potential to provide) a range of multi-modal transport services supports the concentration of land uses and higher order economic, cultural and service activity. These are fundamental to the way in which the region's transport services operate, and will need to be planned to operate into the future.

8.27 In some instances a high level of public transport accessibility does not in itself warrant identification of the location as a regional hub, but a high level of accessibility and interchange is of regional significance. The role of these transport interchanges should be protected and enhanced where possible. The pattern of gateways, hubs and interchanges are set out in Diagram T1.

Regional Spokes

POLICY T8: REGIONAL SPOKES

Relevant regional strategies, local development documents and local transport plans will include policies and proposals that support and develop the role of regional spokes by:

i. providing a level of service that supports the role of regional hubs as a focus of economic activity
ii. delivering improvements in journey time reliability that support the rebalancing of the transport system in favour of non-car modes
iii. developing a complementary and integrated network of rail and express bus/coach services along spokes and inter-regional corridors
iv. addressing identified bottlenecks
v. improving access to international gateways.

8.28 In order that the full potential of the regional hubs as centres of economic activity within a more polycentric structure might be realised, they must be supported by a network of regional spokes (transport designed to support the regional hubs through appropriate linkages that enhance accessibility primarily by public transport). It should be noted that not only corridors with an existing rail link qualify as spokes. Where there is no rail infrastructure or a parallel road corridor, consideration should be given to provision for alternative public transport modes on the highway network. The regional significance of these corridors of movement should be reflected in management priorities and investment proposals brought forward by the responsible delivery agencies. The national and European significance of those regional spokes that provide access to the region's key international gateways should be taken into account where appropriate. The pattern of spokes is set out in Diagram T2.

Airports

POLICY T9: AIRPORTS

Relevant regional strategies, local development documents (LDDs) and local transport plans (LTPs) will include policies and proposals that:

i. support the development of Gatwick and Heathrow Airports and safeguard land at Gatwick for a possible new runway after 2019 as set out in the 2003 Air Transport White Paper and subsequent Government statements
ii. encourage Southampton Airport to sustain and enhance its role as an airport of regional significance
iii. support an enhanced role for Kent International Airport as an airport of regional significance
iv. take account of airport operator masterplans produced in accordance with the Air Transport White Paper.

Priority should be given in Airport Surface Access Strategies:

i. to reduce the environmental impact of surface access
ii. to increase modal share in favour of public transport and sustainable modes
iii. to set and monitor targets that are consistent with the aims of LDDs and LTPs.

8.29 The Air Transport White Paper (ATWP) sets out the Government's policy for a second runway at Stansted, a third runway and additional terminal capacity at Heathrow provided that stringent environmental limits can be met, and the need to safeguard land for a new runway at Gatwick. Following the public consultation on the future development of Heathrow Airport, in early 2009 the Government confirmed a new runway and additional terminal at Heathrow as the bestway forward. Until a final planning decision is made about the future of Heathrow, and since there is a strong case on its own merits for a new wide-spaced runway at Gatwick after 2019, land should continue to be safeguarded for this.

8.30 The Air Transport White Paper highlighted the important role that small airports can play in providing access to air services that reduce the pressure on the main airports, particularly in the period before a new runway in the South East is built. In addition to the potential previously identified for Southampton Airport, the potential of Kent International Airport to fulfil an enhanced role as a regional airport is also acknowledged. Other smaller airports could play a valuable role in meeting local demand and contributing to regional economic development. Subject to relevant environmental considerations, their development should be supported, and regional and local planning frameworks should consider policies which facilitate growth at these airports.

8.31 The White Paper supported the production or updating of masterplans by Airport operators to set out the development of airports up to 2015. The appropriate planning and transport bodies will need to take account of these new or revised airport masterplans.

8.32 Heathrow, Gatwick and Southampton Airports are locations of substantial modal interchange and traffic generators attracting a range of related and non-related developments. The concentration of this economic activity and high level of accessibility means that it is vital that their surface access strategies ensure multi-modal access to airports and help reduce the environmental impact of surface access. The development of connecting coach services will be of major importance, particularly in the period before new rail routes such as Crossrail can be delivered.

Ports

POLICY T10: PORTS AND SHORT SEA SHIPPING

Relevant regional strategies, local development documents and local transport plans will include policies and proposals for infrastructure that maintain and enhance the role of the following ports:

i. gateway ports – Southampton, Dover, Portsmouth, Medway (Sheerness), Medway (Thamesport) and Port of London
ii. regionally significant ports – Newhaven, Ramsgate and Shoreham.

> The major ports should give priority to the preparation of port masterplans as a means of identifying future infrastructure requirements.
>
> Encouragement should be given to investment in infrastructure that supports short sea shipping connections linking the region into the wider European network via these ports.

8.33 The region's ports play a vital role in supporting the UK economy. The ports are, however, dependent upon the quality of the infrastructure providing effective connections. It will remain for the port sector to bring forward and justify proposals for future investment in individual port infrastructure, with proposals for investment in infrastructure that support existing port operations and, where justified, their expansion, being promoted in the light of future National Policy Statement for Ports. In this context, the Port of Southampton is recognised as a major international deep-sea port with significant global and economic importance, and its infrastructure and development needs, both short and long term, require further consideration. The geographical location and network of port infrastructure in the region provides the opportunity to encourage the development of short sea shipping services as a real alternative to land transport.

8.34 The Interim Report of the Ports Policy Review (July 2007) confirmed the broad market led approach for the development of ports, including encouragement for major ports (those handling more than 1 million tonnes annually) to produce port masterplans. Major ports in the South East are Southampton, Dover, Portsmouth, Medway (Thamesport), the Port of London, Newhaven, Ramsgate and Shoreham. Masterplans enable better planning for transport interventions and ports with development needs should consider producing masterplans in accordance with Government guidance. The identified transport requirements should then be taken into account in relevant national strategies, local development documents and LTPs.

Freight Movements

> **POLICY T11: RAIL FREIGHT**
>
> The railway system should be developed to carry an increasing share of freight movements. Priority should be given in other relevant regional strategies, local development documents, and local transport plans, providing enhanced capacity for the movement of freight by rail on the following corridors:
>
> i. Southampton to West Midlands
> ii. Dover/Channel Tunnel to and through/around London
> iii. Great Western Main Line
> iv. Portsmouth to Southampton/West Midlands.

> **POLICY T12: FREIGHT AND SITE SAFEGUARDING**
>
> Relevant regional strategies, local development documents and local transport plans should include policies and proposals that:
>
> i. safeguard wharves, depots and other sites that are, or could be, critical in developing the capability of the transport system to move freight, particularly by rail or water
> ii. safeguard and promote sites adjacent to railways, ports and rivers for developments, particularly new intermodal facilities and rail related industry and warehousing, that are likely to maximise freight movement by rail or water
> iii. encourage development with a high generation of freight and/or commercial movements to be located close to intermodal facilities, rail freight facilities, or ports and wharves.

Transport

> **POLICY T13: INTERMODAL INTERCHANGES**
>
> The regional planning body should work jointly with DfT Rail, Network Rail, the Highways Agency, the Freight Transport Association and local authorities to identify broad locations within the region for up to three inter-modal interchange facilities. These facilities should have the potential to deliver modal shift and be well related to:
>
> i. rail and road corridors capable of accommodating the anticipated level of freight movements
> ii. the proposed markets
> iii. London.

8.35 The efficient movement of freight through the region is a key issue arising from its gateway function. Freight movement within the region is also a key consideration in facilitating continued economic success. The majority of freight movements are made by road and this will continue to be the case due to the mode's flexibility and general suitability to accommodate a wide range of movements and consignments. Journey time reliability is a key consideration for business, and appropriate provision for freight should be given consideration in the design of major road schemes.

8.36 Rail freight has an important role to play in a number of markets, with the railway system offering a lower impact alternative to road freight for many journeys. There is a need to protect routes on the rail network that benefit freight movements and to address bottlenecks on the network that adversely affect rail freight.

8.37 Work undertaken by the former Strategic Rail Authority identified the need for between three and four inter-modal interchange terminals to serve London and South East England. Areas of search for potential sites should be identified in partnership between rail and road network operators, local authorities and the logistics industry. Potential sites for new inter-modal interchange terminals will need to meet a number of criteria. In particular they must:

- be of sufficient size and configuration to accommodate an appropriate rail layout, transfer operation and value added activities
- be already rail connected or capable of rail connection at a reasonable cost
- have adequate road access or the potential for improved road access
- be situated away from incompatible land uses.

8.38 Suitable sites are likely to be located where the key rail and road radials intersect with the M25 motorway.

Management and Investment Proposals

> **POLICY T14: TRANSPORT INVESTMENT AND MANAGEMENT PRIORITIES**
>
> The regionally significant transport investment currently programmed for delivery in the South East is set out in Appendix A: Strategic Transport Investment Priorities.
>
> Regional partners, led by the regional planning body, should work together to produce an Implementation Plan to clarify the partnerships, policy links, timing, scale and cost of the interventions necessary to support the spatial strategy within this Plan.
>
> The regional planning and development bodies should work with the Government Office, DfT Rail, Network Rail, the Highways Agency, local authorities, public transport operators, statutory environmental bodies, the business community and other key stakeholders to deliver and keep under review investment proposals of regional or sub-regional significance.

> In developing schemes additional to current commitments, priority should be given to stronger demand management measures, including those that make the best use of the existing infrastructure asset, promote sustainable travel and reduce demand by behavioural change.
>
> Development plans should include policies that safeguard delivery of:
>
> i. the specific investment proposals set out in Appendix A
> ii. other major projects where they are required to support delivery of the regional spatial and transport policy frameworks, or of the Communities Plan growth agenda.
>
> As far as possible, the location, design and construction of all new transport infrastructure projects should enhance the environment and communities affected.

8.39 The management and investment intervention proposals required will vary with each area and should be developed for the sub-regions and across the region to enable the transport system to play its role in facilitating delivery of the spatial strategy. The extent of certainty about the contents of the mix varies, and will need to be developed further in all areas.

8.40 Delivering a Sustainable Transport System (DaSTS) recommends that Government policies focus on improving the performance of existing transport networks in congested and growing city catchments; and on key inter-urban corridors and key international gateways that are showing signs of increasing congestion and unreliability. In carrying out long-term transport planning, goals and challenges should be defined non-modally and a full range of solutions should be considered to identify those which offer the highest returns. This consideration should include behavioural change, getting better use out of existing infrastructure, pricing signals, changes to public transport services, and small and large infrastructure schemes.

8.41 Regional partners are taking forward work on the Implementation Plan for the South East, with the intention of producing a document that gives a comprehensive picture of strategic infrastructure requirements for the region, to be used and developed as a valuable planning tool to take forward the delivery of strategic policies. Interventions in the Implementation Plan will be derived from committed schemes, the output of regional DaSTS work, Regional Transport Board prioritisation, the EiP Panel's views of priority schemes and local views.

8.42 Investment in transport should be prioritised according to its contribution to the RTS objectives and policies and be in line with the outcomes of DaSTS work. Reviews of LTPs and future prioritisation exercises should reflect this. The Implementation Plan programme of investment should be regularly reviewed to ensure it continues to deliver the infrastructure and services necessary to support the RSS.

8.43 Appendix A lists the regionally significant transport investment currently programmed for the region and as submitted in the February 2009 Regional Funding Advice from the South East to Government. These are the major schemes which are most certain to be delivered, while acknowledging that all Government supported schemes are subject to value for money and affordability tests and most are also subject to the completion of statutory procedures. Specific transport infrastructure projects will be developed through a balanced appreciation of economic, environmental, and social considerations, in line with the principles of sustainable development.

8.44 Further details of these and other sub-regional projects should be included in the Implementation Plan, the requirements of which are set out in Planning Policy Statement 11: *Regional Spatial Strategies*. The Implementation Plan should set out for each policy and priority proposal:

- the appropriate implementation mechanisms
- the organisations responsible for delivery

- the current status of proposals in terms of priority for implementation
- the timescales for key actions to deliver policies, including any output targets.

8.45 An associated section of the Implementation Plan should be kept under review as an evolving non-statutory region-wide document that is regularly updated, preferably as part of the annual monitoring process.

8.46 The following locations have been identified as priority transport links likely to come under increasing transport pressure as a result of underlying traffic growth and the development strategy of the RSS, and where further work should be focused to identify the interventions needed:

- West of Reading to London. Particularly to address unreliability of the strategic road network, to include consideration of M4 management and capacity measures, Thames Valley bus and coach network, and Berkshire sub-regional mobility management measures
- A34 in Oxfordshire. Taking account of development options including adequate land use/transport scenario testing such as a detailed Green Belt transport study, and building on the Access to Oxford study
- A2/A282/M2 corridor (including Thames Crossing options).

8.47 In addition to the three locations above, further work should be undertaken in the following areas:

- assessing the main features of the transport system in the region including an assessment of the problems to be addressed by the transport strategy, and the underlying causes of those problems, set in a DaSTS context
- understanding the potential for reducing demand at a regional and sub-regional level through interventions that focus on behavioural change, including pricing mechanisms
- the transport implications of new growth and development, covering eco-towns and the second round of New Growth Points, and including development proposals in Canterbury, Herne Bay and Whitstable, the Thanet urban area, Shepway, Medway, Sittingbourne & Sheppey, south Oxford, Milton Keynes and Crawley
- further development of a cross-modal regional freight strategy, with a greater locational specificity for inter-modal interchanges and lorry parking and rest areas
- access to international gateways (including surface access to Heathrow and Gatwick, and improvements to Southampton Airport interchange facilities)
- public transport improvements (including Winchester-Southampton transport corridor improvements, Brighton strategic interchange facilities, and a north-south and east-west inter-urban coach network in the Western Corridor and Blackwater Valley)
- rail improvements (including Southampton-Midlands rail improvements, East-West Rail, Reading Station improvements, Route Utilisation Strategy rail schemes, North Downs rail line, and bottlenecks on Brighton Main Line, Kent Railways, South London Railways, South West Main Line, Sussex Coast and Great Western Main Line
- inter-regional link improvements.

8.48 Plans, strategies, investment decisions and programmes should take forward and secure delivery of the transport investment and management priorities of regional significance outlined in Appendix A and, as a secondary priority in transport terms, other projects in the region's Implementation Plan.

8.49 In developing interventions additional to current commitments, priority should be given to stronger demand management in areas of high road network pressure and to proposals which:

- fully explore opportunities to make the best use of existing infrastructure by improving management and maintenance before recommending investment in new infrastructure

- are based on a multi-modal approach
- adopt a general presumption against increasing highway capacity except where it is a specific regional priority or a localised improvement essential to regeneration or delivering environmental enhancement.

8.50 LDFs should take account of the transport priorities set out in Appendix A and in the regional Implementation Plan, both in terms of their land use strategy and proposals, and by including appropriate policies to help ensure the delivery of the priorities in their area.

8.51 Other specific transport proposals of local significance that support the delivery of the sub-regional area policies should be included in LTPs and development plan documents and be taken forward by local authorities, transport delivery and other relevant bodies.

Appendix A: Strategic Transport Infrastructure Priorities

8.52 This appendix lists regionally significant investment in transport infrastructure that has been completed recently, is currently under construction, or is currently programmed for delivery. There are, and will be, other schemes not listed here that are important in a local context.

Table 1 – Schemes Completed since April 2001

Sub-Region	Scheme	Date Completed
Sussex Coast	A22 Dualling Nightingale Farm Polegate	Apr-01
Sussex Coast	A27 Polegate Bypass	Jun-02
South Hampshire	Eastern Road	Mar-03
Kent Thames Gateway	A206 South Thameside Dev. Route 4 (STDR4)	Jun-03
Kent Thames Gateway	A2/M2 Widening	Jul-03
Milton Keynes & Aylesbury Vale	A41 Aston Clinton Bypass	Oct-03
Milton Keynes & Aylesbury Vale	Provision of 12 car length platforms at all stations on the West Coast Main Line between London and Northampton	Sept-04
Western Corridor & BlackwaterValley	A34 Chieveley/M4 Jct 13 improvements	Aug-04
Rest of Kent	A21 Lamberhurst Bypass	Mar-05
Kent Thames Gateway	A2 Bean to Cobham Phase 1	Apr-05
Kent/Sussex/Surrey/Hants	Southern New Trains project	Jun-05
Kent Thames Gateway	A228 Main Road to Ropers Lane	Jul-05
London Fringe	M25 Jct 12-15 Widening	Nov-05
Kent Thames Gateway	Fastrack Phase 1	Mar-06
South Hampshire	Copnor Bridge Replacement Scheme	Mar-06
Gatwick Area	Crawley Fastway	Jun-06
Kent Thames Gateway	A249 Iwade Bypass to Queensborough	Jul-06
Rest of Kent	A228 Leybourne & West Malling Corridor Improvement	Oct-06
Western Corridor & BlackwaterValley	M40 Jct 4/1404 Handy Cross Jct improvements	Mar-07
East Kent & Ashford	East Kent Access Phase 1	Sep-07
Milton Keynes & Aylesbury Vale	A4146 Stoke Hammond/Linslade Western Bypass	Sep-07
Kent Thames Gateway	New Ebbsfleet International Station	Nov-07
Kent Thames Gateway	A2/A282 Dartford Improvement	Dec-07
Kent Thames Gateway	Fastrack Thames Way	Mar-08
Kent Thames Gateway	M25 J1b - 3 Widening	Jun-08
Kent Thames Gateway	Fastrack Everard's Link Phase 2	July 08
Sussex Coast	A27 Southerham – Beddingham Improvement	August 08
South Hampshire	M27 J3 - 4 Widening	Sept-08

South Hampshire	A3 Integrated Bus Priority Corridor	Nov-08
South Hampshire	M27 J11-12 Climbing Lanes	Dec-08
Kent Thames Gateway	A2 Bean – Cobham Widening Phase 2	Feb-09

Table 2 – Schemes Currently Under Construction

Sub-Region	Scheme	Funding Source	Core Policy Delivery
MK & AV	Aylesbury Vale Parkway new Station	CIF	T1, T2, T8
MK & AV	Aylesbury Vale Public Transport Hub & Southcourt Bridge	CIF	T1, T2, T8
MK & AV	M1 J14	CIF	T1, T2, T8, SP2
MK & AV	Milton Keynes Central Station incremental capacity upgrade	CIF	T1, T2, T8
Rest of Surrey	A3 Hindhead Improvement	PMS – R	T1, T2, T8, SP2
WC&BV	M4 J11 (Green Park Improvements) & Mereoak Roundabout	LTP/Other	T1, T2, T8

Table 3 – Interventions Currently Programmed to Start by end 2013/14

Sub-Region	Scheme	Funding Source	Core Policy Delivery
EKA	Sittingbourne Northern Relief Road	LTP/Other	T1, T8
EKA	East Kent Access Phase 2	LTP	T1, T8, T10, SP4, RE2, RE6, TSR1
EKA & KTG	High speed domestic commuter services - Kent to St Pancras	Rail	T1, T2, T8
Isle Of Wight	Ryde Public Transport Interchange	LTP/Other	T1, T2, T8
KTG	Rushenden Link Road	HCA	T1, T8
KTG	Medway Bus Corridor	CIF	T1, T2, T6, T7, T9, T10
KTG	A228 Ropers Lane – Grain	CIF	T1, T2, T4, T7, T8
KTG	Dartford Station	CIF	T1, T2, T8
KTG	Northfleet Station	CIF	T1, T2, T8
KTG	Gillingham Railway Station	CIF	T1, T2, T8
London Fringe	A244 Walton Bridge	LTP	T1, T8
Sussex Coast	Bexhill to Hastings Link Road	LTP/Other	T1, T8, H1, RE3, RE65
WC&BV	Green Park Multi-Modal Interchange	Dev	T1, T2, T8
WC&BV	Reading Station Incremental Capacity Upgrade	Rail/LTP	T1, T2, T8, T11, SP2
WC&BV/Central Oxon/S Hants/ Rest of Hants/ Rest of Oxon	Southampton – West Midlands Gauge Upgrade	TIF	T1, T8, T10, T11, SP2
National	Crossrail	Rail	T1, T2, T8, SP2
National	Thameslink	Rail	T1, T2, T8, SP2
National	M25 J5 – 7 Widening	PMS – N	T1, T8
Regional	Additional peak passenger capacity on all rail routes to London (HLOS 2009-14)	Rail	T1, T2, T8
EKA	M20 J10A	PMS – N/Other	T1, T2, T8
Gatwick Area	A23 Handcross to Warninglid Widening	PMS - R	T1, T8
London Fringe/WC&BV	Airtrack - rail services from Waterloo/Reading/ Guildford to Terminal 5	Public/ Private	T1, T2, T8, CC8b
Sussex Coast	A21 Baldslow Junction Improvements	PMS - R	T1, T8, RE6

| Rest of Kent | A21 Tonbridge Bypass to Pembury Dualling | PMS – R | T1, SP2, RR2, RR3 |
| Rest of Kent | A21 Kippings Cross to Lamberhurst Bypass | PMS - R | T1, SP2, RR2, RR3 |

Table 4 – Interventions over £5m in the RFA programme or within the February 2009 RFA Regional Recommendations, not yet approved by DfT (for start by end 2013/14)

Sub-Region	Scheme	Funding Source	Core Policy Delivery
South Oxon	A34 / Access to Oxford Package	LTP/Other	T1, T2, T8, SP2
S Hants	Access to Strategic Development in Portsmouth and South-East Hampshire; Tipner Interchange	LTP/Other	T1
WC&BV	Thames Valley Strategic Coach & Bus Network (High Wycombe Coachway)	LTP/Other	T1, T2, T8
EKA	Ashford Smartlink Bus Rapid Transit	LTP/Other	T1, T2, SP2, H1, RE3
KTG	A2 Bean Junction	PMS – R/Other	T1, T8
London Fringe	Guildford Hub Transport Improvement Scheme	LTP	T1, T2, SP2
MKAV	A421 Milton Keynes to M1	LTP	T1, T2, T8, SP2
Rest of W Sussex	A24 Ashington to Southwater	LTP	T1
S Hants	Northern Bridge Portsmouth	LTP	T1
Sussex Coast	Improved access along the Sussex Coast (Brighton and Hove Bus Rapid Transit)	LTP/Other	T1, T2, SP2

Key

- LTP   Local Transport Plan
- CIF   Community Infrastructure Fund
- PMS – R   Programme of Major Schemes – Regional Roads
- PMS – N   Programme of Major Schemes – National Roads
- Dev   Developer Funded
- HCA   Homes and Communities Agency

Footnote

8.53   Interventions beyond 2013/2014 will be determined by the DaSTS transport programme plan, the regional programme of investment priorities for the period beyond 2013/2014, and the guidance provided by paragraphs 8.46 and 8.47.

80 Transport

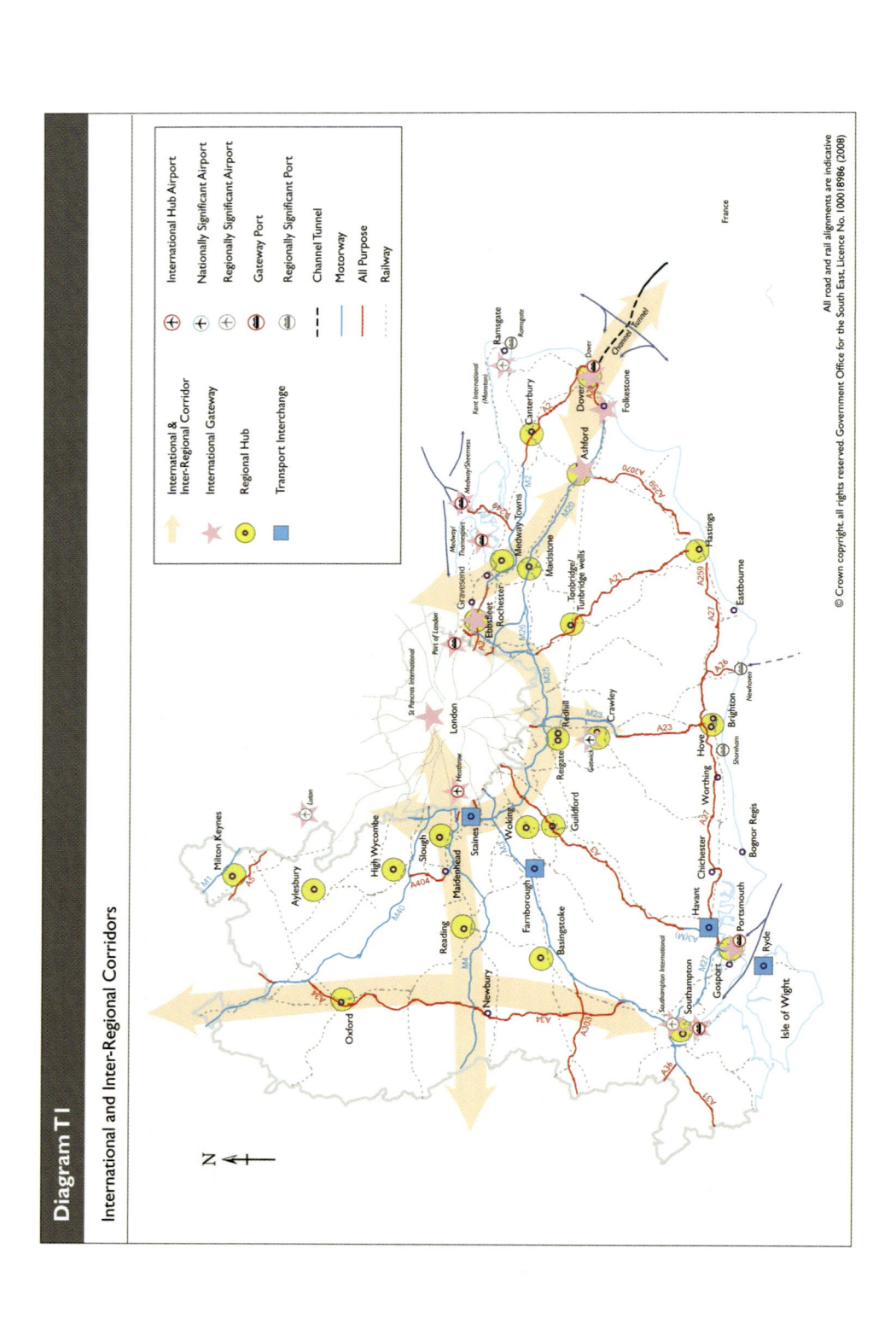

8

The South East Plan - Regional Spatial Strategy for the South East

Diagram T1
International and Inter-Regional Corridors

Legend:
- International Hub Airport
- Nationally Significant Airport
- Regionally Significant Airport
- Gateway Port
- Regionally Significant Port
- Channel Tunnel
- Motorway
- All Purpose
- Railway
- International & Inter-Regional Corridor
- International Gateway
- Regional Hub
- Transport Interchange

© Crown copyright, all rights reserved. Government Office for the South East, Licence No. 100018986 (2008)

All road and rail alignments are indicative

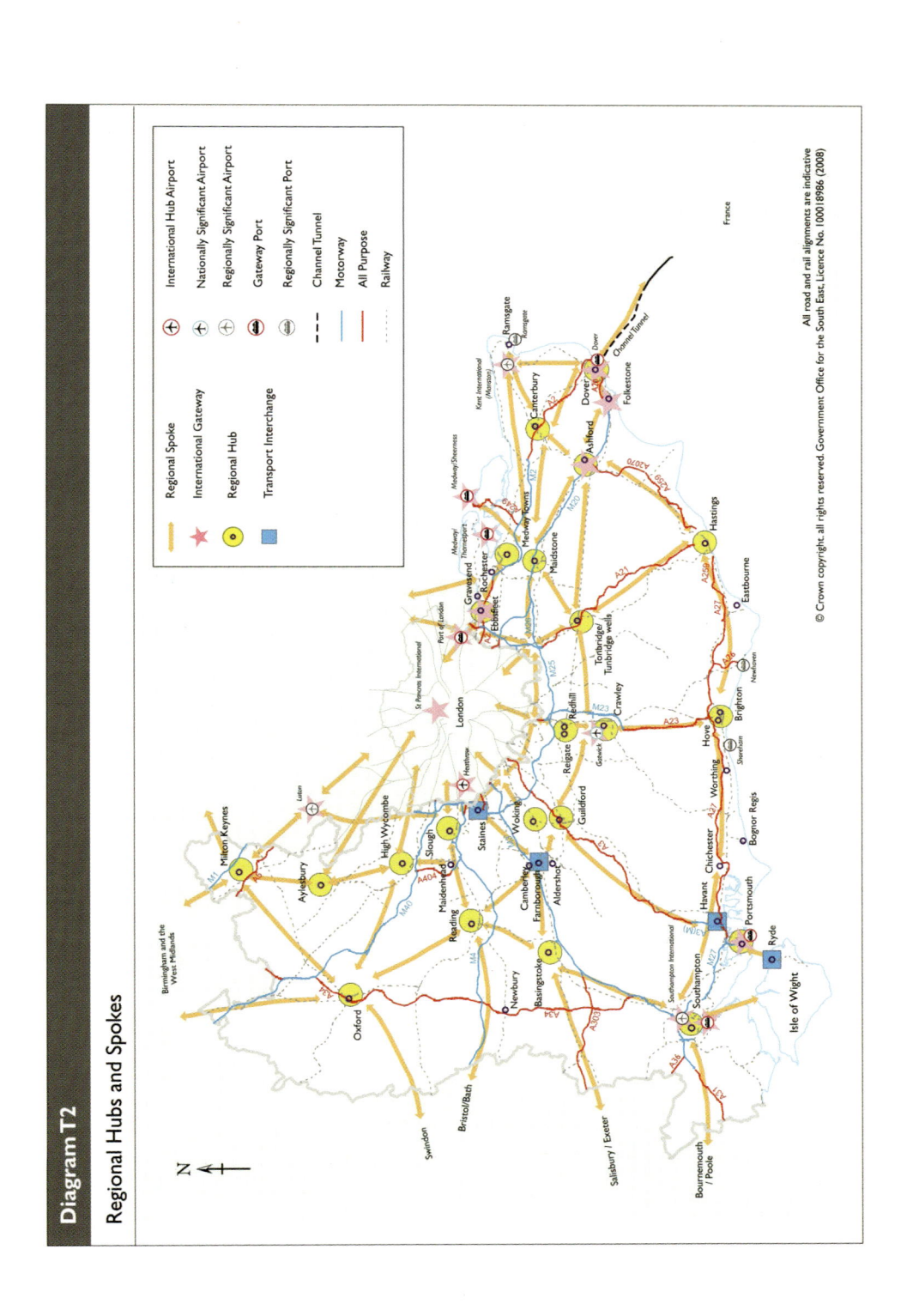

Transport 81

Diagram T2

Regional Hubs and Spokes

8 Transport

9 Natural Resource Management

Context

9.1 Residents of the South East live in one of the most beautiful regions in England, and benefit from a strong economy and healthy environment. The quality and variety of the environment is one of the region's defining characteristics, with a large proportion of the South East recognised to be of international and national importance in terms of nature conservation and landscape value. The environment is also a major economic asset, estimated to contribute around £8 billion to the region's economy.[1]

9.2 Sustainable natural resource management is a key theme of the Plan. This means ensuring mitigation of climate change impacts, greater efficiency in the use of natural resources, the reduction of pollution and waste, and ensuring that features of importance are protected and enhanced, including wildlife and landscapes. These aims are reflected in the cross-cutting policies of the Plan (CC1, CC2, CC3, CC4) and set out in detail in this section.

The Region's Key Environmental Challenges are identified as:

Challenge	Issue	Response	Core Policy
WATER RESOURCES	Maintaining an adequate supply and encouraging water efficiency whilst meeting EU Directives	• Protect aquifers and surface waters from over-abstraction and pollution • Increase efficiency of use • Develop new sources of supply	NRM1 NRM3 CC1 CC3 CC4
WATER QUALITY	Maintaining and improving quality, meeting EU Directive standards and objectives	• Avoidance and management of household, business and agricultural effluent discharge into receiving waters and systems • Improvements to existing and provision of new wastewater infrastructure	NRM2 CC1
FLOODING	Increased risk of flooding due to development in flood plains, changing patterns of rainfall, extreme weather, storms, rising sea levels and agricultural run off	• Avoid an increase in flood risk through appropriate location and design of new development in line with PPS25 sequential test and strategic flood risk assessments	NRM1 NRM4 CC2

---

1   SEEDA (2002) *The Environmental Economy of South East England*

Natural Resource Management

		•	Protect existing flood defences	
		•	Incorporate sustainable urban drainage and flood storage measures into new development.	
BIODIVERSITY	Protecting and improving the diversity of habitats and species across the South East, particularly sites and species of national and international importance, to contribute to quality of the environment and quality of life	•	Avoid or mitigate development pressure on sites	NRM5
				NRM6
				NRM7
		•	Maintain and expand important wildlife assets	CC2
		•	Better management of habitats	CC8
		•	Establish, connect and maintain green infrastructure	
COAST	Maintaining coastline as an environmental, economic and recreational resource, responding to climate change pressures and rising sea levels Avoiding instability, erosion and flooding	•	Ensure sensitive amounts and types of development	NRM7
				CC1
		•	Reinforce links with Shoreline Management Plans, Estuary Management Plans and Coastal Habitat Management Plans	
AIR QUALITY	Tackling areas of poor air quality, avoiding deterioration in existing air quality	•	Influence movement, mode and management of transport	NRM8
				CC1
		•	Guide the location of development away from areas of poor air quality	
NOISE	Maintaining tranquil areas, preventing nuisance from noise	•	Guide development away from noisy activity	NRM10
		•	Manage traffic noise	
		•	Sound proofing and screening in new development	
SUSTAINABLE DESIGN AND CONSTRUCTION	Reducing resource use in construction and lowering environmental impacts of new development	•	Sensitive and forward thinking design in new development	NRM1
				CC2
		•	Encourage high standards under the Code for Sustainable Homes	CC3
				CC4
		•	Encourage local and renewable materials	

Natural Resource Management

ENERGY	Reducing greenhouse gas emissions and other pollutants, improving security and diversity of supply	• Reduce energy demand through efficiency gains • Adopt interim regional targets • Deploy renewable energy schemes • Incorporate renewable energy into new development • To maintain supply, develop conventional energy generating schemes	CC1 CC2 CC3 NRM 11-16
WASTE	Tackling increasing waste output, lack of landfill capacity	• Reduce waste production • Increase re-use and recycling • Develop new waste facilities, including energy from waste	CC1 CC3 CC4 W1-W17
MINERALS	Ensuring adequate supply, impacts arising from extraction, processing and transport	• More efficient use of resources • Increase recycling • Re-use of construction and demolition waste • Use of secondary aggregates	CC1 M1-M5

Sustainable Water Resources and Water Quality Management

> **POLICY NRM1: SUSTAINABLE WATER RESOURCES AND GROUNDWATER QUALITY**
>
> Water supply and ground water will be maintained and enhanced through avoiding adverse effects of development on the water environment. A twin-track approach of demand management and water resource development will be pursued.
>
> In preparing local development documents, and determining planning applications, local authorities will:
>
> i. assist the UK in achieving the objectives of the Water Framework Directive by delivering appropriate actions set out in River Basin Management plans. [2]

---

2   River Basin Management Plans (RBMP) set out the practical steps to allow the UK to met Objectives of the European Water Framework Directive (WFD) in distinct River Basin Districts. Objectives of the WFD include: (i) no deterioration in the status of water bodies (ii) all water bodies to have achieved good ecological status (or equivalent) by 2027. There are 11 River Basin Districts in the UK, and the SE region is covered by two: Southern and Thames, for which RBMPs will be adopted in December 2009. These plans will last until 2015, and will then be followed by two further six year planning periods. For more information please go to the environment Agency web-site at: www.environment-agency.gov.uk/wfd

Natural Resource Management

ii. identify any circumstances under which new development will need to be supported by water efficiency standards exceeding extant Building Regulations standards
iii. set out the circumstances under which sustainable drainage solutions should be incorporated into new development
iv. encourage winter water storage reservoirs and other sustainable land management practices which reduce summer abstraction, diffuse pollution and runoff, increase flood storage capacity and benefit wildlife and recreation
v. direct new development to areas where adequate water supply can be provided from existing and potential water supply infrastructure. In addition ensure, where appropriate, that development is phased to allow time for the relevant water infrastructure to be put in place in areas where it is currently lacking but is essential for the development to happen.

Water Quality Management

POLICY NRM2: WATER QUALITY

Water quality will be maintained and enhanced through avoiding adverse effects of development on the water environment.

In preparing local development documents, and determining planning applications, local authorities will:

i. take account of water cycle studies, groundwater vulnerability maps, groundwater source protection zone maps and asset management plans as prepared by the Environment Agency, water and sewerage companies, and local authorities
ii. ensure that the environmental water quality standards and objectives as required by European Directives are met
iii. ensure that the rate and location of development does not breach either relevant 'no deterioration' objectives or environmental quality standards
iv. not permit development that presents a risk of pollution or where satisfactory pollution prevention measures are not provided in areas of high groundwater vulnerability (in consultation with the Environment Agency and Natural England).

Local authorities will work with water and sewerage companies and the Environment Agency to:

i. identify infrastructure needs, allocate areas and safeguard these for infrastructure development
ii. ensure that adequate wastewater and sewerage capacity is provided to meet planned demand
iii. ensure that impacts of treated sewage discharges on groundwater, inland and marine receiving waters do not breach environmental quality standards or 'no deterioration' objectives
iv. ensure that plans and policies are consistent with River Basin Management Plans
v. ensure that water cycle studies are carried out, prior to development sites being given planning permission, where investigations by the Environment Agency indicate that water quality constraints exist
vi. ensure that Sustainable Drainage Systems are incorporated in a manner to reduce diffuse pollution.

Local authorities should promote land management initiatives to reduce diffuse agricultural pollution.

9.3 The South East is one of the driest parts of the country and experiences high levels of water demand. In some areas the existing balance of supply to demand is very sensitive, with demand close to exceeding currently available sustainable supply. The ecological

Natural Resource Management

quality of some streams, rivers and wetlands is being adversely affected as a result. The region also has the highest dependence on groundwater for public supply in the country, with over 70% of the region's public water supply coming from groundwater. Climate change will also impact on the capacity of rivers to dilute treated sewage effluent as a result of reduced river levels in the summer months.

9.4 A twin-track approach to water management is required. Firstly, we must increase the efficiency with which we use existing infrastructure, whilst moderating demand through education and behavioural change, increased water efficiency, leakage management and the use of metering. Secondly, sustainable new water infrastructure needs to be planned and provided in step with the development it serves. This will include the timely provision of new strategic resources (such as reservoirs and waste water treatment works requiring long lead in times) as well as more local infrastructure. Early engagement of local authorities, the Environment Agency, the Water Services Regulation Authority (Ofwat), developers and water companies in the planning process is therefore imperative. The regional planning body will work with Government, the Environment Agency, Ofwat and regional stakeholders to ensure that development provided for in the Plan is matched with substantial improvements in water efficiency. Savings should be monitored against a per capita per day consumption target that will be set out in the regional planning body's monitoring framework.

9.5 Water resources and water quality have been taken into account in development of the Plan, and also through the Sustainability Appraisal and Habitats Regulations Assessment process. Studies will also be required to inform local development frameworks.

9.6 *Water quality* assessments have taken account of water quality, physical capacity and ecological considerations and have identified seven locations where water quality constraints mean that a limit should be placed on additional housing. Analysis identified a further nine sites where further work needs to be carried out.[3] The Habitats and Birds Directives already place constraints on the capacity of some receiving waters within European sites. Future growth and the Water Framework Directive have further implications for both these and undesignated areas, and further work and monitoring will be required. In addition, further investigations are required into the extent of infiltration into some sewerage networks which, if addressed, could increase the capacity of existing works in high constraint locations such as in/near sites of international importance. The need to maintain and improve water quality should be taken into account at LDF level, and in the light of any new information available. The timely provision of waste water treatment works and other sewerage infrastructure is essential and will require early engagement of local authorities, the Environment Agency, infrastructure providers and other key stakeholders.

9.7 Although new water resources can be developed to meet projected demand, the extent to which new resources are provided should take into account social, environmental and economic costs and benefits. Development should be phased so that supporting infrastructure (such as that required to avoid an adverse effect on Special Areas of Conservation, Special Protection Areas and Ramsar sites) can be put in place before development commences.

Strategic Water Resources Development

POLICY NRM3: STRATEGIC WATER RESOURCES DEVELOPMENT

There is a demonstrable need for new water resource schemes and increased demand management over the period of the Plan to cater for water supply needs of current and future development and the protection of the environment.

---

3 Initial assessments did not take into account the implications of the Water Framework Directive standards. It should be noted that ongoing work into the implications of growth and the Water Framework Directive will need to inform future development in areas where water quality has already been identified as an issue. In locations where water quality constraints are identified as a result of ongoing investigations this will need to be reflected in LDFs and future reviews of the RSS.

Natural Resource Management

> Strategic new water resource options that may be required to be operational over the Plan period include:
>
> i. Upper Thames reservoir, Oxfordshire
> ii. Enlargement of Bewl reservoir, Kent
> iii. Broad Oak reservoir, Kent
> iv. Clay Hill reservoir, East Sussex
> v. Havant Thicket reservoir, Hampshire.
>
> Local authorities should work with the water companies and the Environment Agency in assisting in the timely delivery of schemes. Local development documents should allocate and safeguard sites identified for the reservoir schemes identified in this policy and others that are identified by the companies and Environment Agency as being required to deliver necessary water infrastructure.
>
> Other options being considered include enlargement of Darwell reservoir, a strategic option in north-west Sussex, effluent re-use schemes, desalination schemes and bulk transfer pipelines in a number of locations.
>
> In considering applications for new water resource schemes, consideration should be given to:
>
> i. need at local, sub-regional, regional, and inter-regional scales
> ii. water companies working together to find the most optimal (economic) solutions
> iii. presence of alternative options including water efficiency in new and existing homes and businesses
> iv. environmental impacts and potential to deliver social and environmental benefits
> v. improving overall resilience and flexibility.

9.8 A small number of strategic new water reservoirs are likely to be required in the region over the lifetime of the Plan, and are already included as options in statutory water company plans. Some reservoir schemes have gained support for initial stages of design and planning from Ofwat, including the Upper Thames reservoir in Oxfordshire.

9.9 Reservoirs will require a long lead time to go through planning, assessment, funding and construction phases before they become operational. Some resources are of intra-regional and inter-regional significance, providing water resources across the South East and to adjacent regions, notably London and South West England.

9.10 Major strategic schemes have been identified in Policy NRM3 reflecting those identified in water company plans and included in regional modelling of water supply-demand balance. Not all schemes listed as options will necessarily come forward but safeguarding of sites in local development documents (LDDs) is required so as not to foreclose these options, and ensure that planning for these schemes is facilitated. In addition to these major schemes smaller-scale water resource developments will also be required.

Sustainable Flood Risk Management – Making Space for Water

> **POLICY NRM4: SUSTAINABLE FLOOD RISK MANAGEMENT**
>
> The sequential approach to development in flood risk areas set out in PPS25 will be followed. Inappropriate development should not be allocated or permitted in flood zones 2 and 3 (Diagram NRM1), areas at risk of surface water flooding (critical drainage areas) or areas with a history of groundwater flooding, or where it would increase flood risk elsewhere, unless there is over-riding need and absence of suitable alternatives.
>
> Local authorities, with advice from the Environment Agency, should undertake a Strategic Flood Risk Assessment (SFRA) to provide a comprehensive understanding of the flood risk and put in place a framework for applying the PPS25 sequential approach. This will

Natural Resource Management

> facilitate allocating sites in a decreasing probability of flood risk. The SFRA would assess future climate change and identify appropriate types of development in accordance with the PPS25 sequential test and flood vulnerability of different land uses.
>
> Existing flood defences will be protected from development. Where development is permitted in appropriately defended floodplains it must be designed to be resilient to flooding (to minimise potential damage) and to allow for the future maintenance, realignment or management of the defences to be undertaken.
>
> In the preparation of local development documents and considering planning applications, local authorities in conjunction with the Environment Agency, should also:
>
> i. take account of River Basin Management Plans, Catchment Flood Management Plans, Shoreline Management Plans and Surface Water Management Plans in developing local development documents and other strategies. Where locationally specific flood risk and land management options such as flood storage, managed realignment and set back from coastal defences are identified, land should be safeguarded for these purposes and appropriate land use and land management practices should be encouraged
>
> ii. consider the associated social and environmental costs and benefits to fisheries, biodiversity and the built and historic environment in assessment of new flood management schemes
>
> iii. require incorporation and management of Sustainable Drainage Systems (SuDS), other water retention and flood storage measures to minimise direct surface run-off, unless there are practical or environmental reasons for not doing so
>
> iv. take account of increased surface water drainage on sewage effluent flows on fluvial flood risk.

9.11 The South East has a particularly wide ranging flood risk management challenge with an extensive area at risk of flooding, due to coastal, tidal, fluvial, groundwater and surface run-off flood risk. The probability of flooding can be reduced through the management of land, river systems and flood defences, and the impact reduced through influencing the type of development in flood risk areas, flood warning and emergency responses.

9.12 To adapt to climate change we must design and locate new development with flood risk in mind, and we must plan to make more space for water through better management of land for water storage and flood protection.

9.13 Over 208,000 properties in the South East have been identified as being within an area where there is high probability of flooding. [4] Zones are defined in Planning Policy Statement 25: *Development and Flood Risk* and are set out on the Environment Agency's Flood Zone map (see Diagram NRM1). This information will be used as a starting point to develop strategic flood risk assessments and inform local development decisions. The Environment Agency has also produced a flood map that takes account of the presence and standard of flood defences in these flood zones.

---

4 Environment Agency, *State of the Environment Report, South East England*, 2007

Natural Resource Management

Diagram NRM1
Indicative Flood Zones

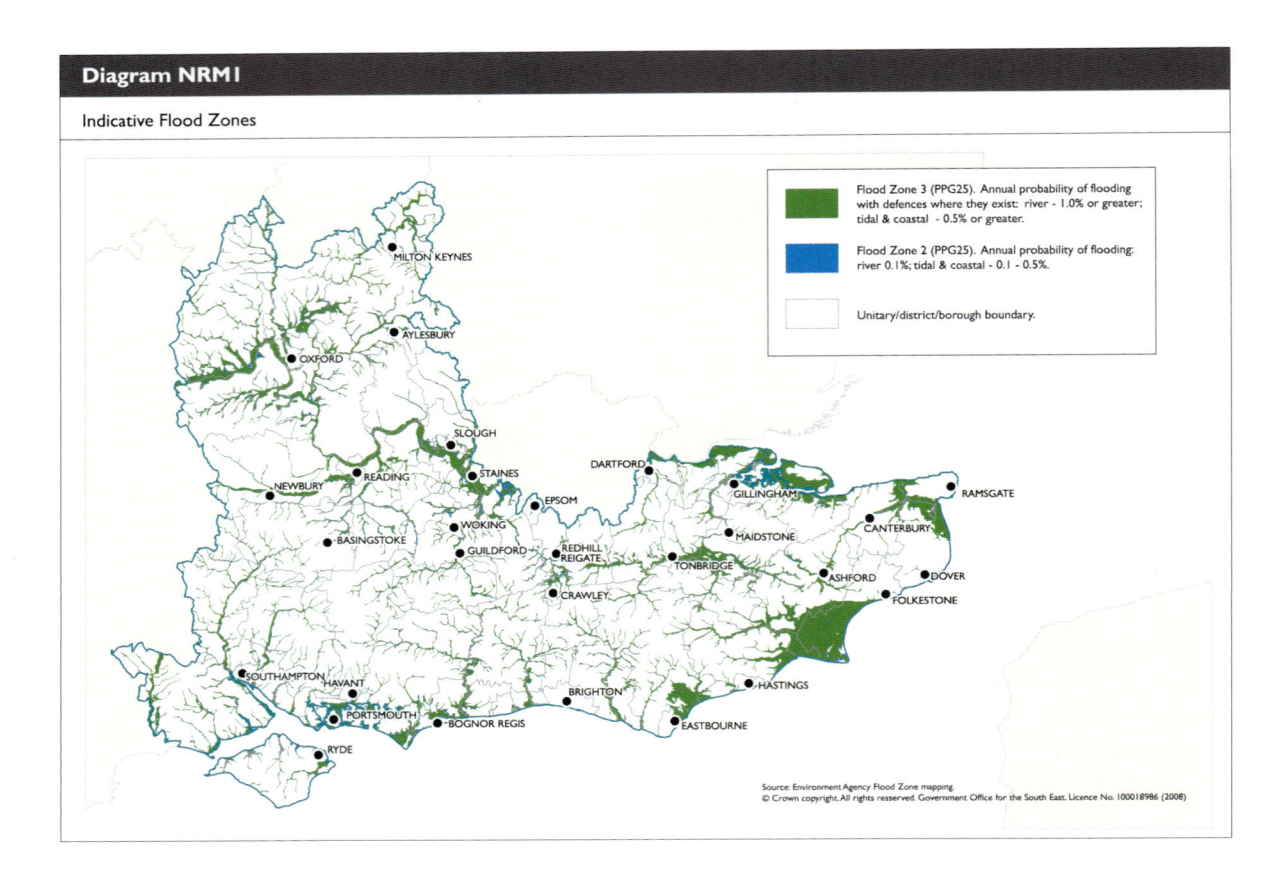

Flood Zone 3 (PPG25). Annual probability of flooding with defences where they exist: river - 1.0% or greater; tidal & coastal - 0.5% or greater.

Flood Zone 2 (PPG25). Annual probability of flooding: river 0.1%; tidal & coastal - 0.1 - 0.5%.

Unitary/district/borough boundary.

Source: Environment Agency Flood Zone mapping.
© Crown copyright. All rights reserved. Government Office for the South East. Licence No. 100018986 (2008)

9.14   PPS25 recommends a precautionary sequential approach to allocation and permitting of sites for development, avoiding areas of highest risk (zone 3) where possible. However, a degree of flexibility will be needed to consider the relative severity of flood risk and, in some instances, accepting the need to live with some level of flood risk, designing development to reduce the risk and minimise the impact of flooding.

9.15   The probability and impacts of flooding can be reduced through:

i. applying the sequential test set out in PPS25
ii. ensuring that an appropriate Strategic Flood Risk Assessment (SFRA) is carried out for developments or plan allocations in flood zones 2 and 3. This includes those areas benefiting from defences of an appropriate standard. The assessment must also address impacts of climate change and the policies of Catchment Flood Management Plans (CFMPs) or Shoreline Management Plans (SMPs), and avoid foreclosing options for realignment and management of defences to reinstate natural floodplains. Further guidance on flood resilience is available from sources including the Association of British Insurers. [5]
iii. ensuring development does not worsen flooding in its surroundings, through use of appropriate sustainable drainage systems (SuDS) to help reduce the likelihood of flooding and pollution by controlling surface water run off. Where possible multiple benefits, including for recreation and wildlife, should be delivered. In considering SuDS solutions, the need to protect ground water quality must be taken into account, especially where infiltration techniques are proposed. Proposals must include an agreement on the future management, maintenance and replacement of these structures. A range of SuDS techniques is listed in the box below. Further guidance is available from the National SuDS Working Group
iv. encouraging positive flood risk management by changing farming and forestry land management practices. This is especially important where it would directly contribute to the delivery of CFMP objectives, enhance biodiversity and amenity, or mitigate the impact of urban development on the water environment.

5   www.abi.org.uk

9.16 CFMPs aim to achieve the most effective management of flood risk (probability and/or consequence), against a background of increasing flood probability. They provide broad policies and provide prioritised actions which take a whole river catchment approach to flood risk management and should be reflected in LDDs.

Sustainable Drainage Systems

- permeable surfaces – allowing infiltration of rainwater into the underlying construction or soil
- filter drains/strips – linear features which store and conduct water but may also permit infiltration
- swales – shallow vegetated channels constructed to conduct or store rainwater, often from roads/paved areas, possibly also allowing infiltration
- basins, ponds and wetlands – providing storage for surface water run off and infiltration. These may be designed to be dry at some points of the year
- soakaways – below ground structures designed to promote the infiltration of surface water to ground
- Infiltration trenches – linear structures, usually filled with granular material designed to promote the passage of surface water to ground. These techniques may not be appropriate in certain areas due to the vulnerability of groundwater
- rainwater re-use – the harvesting/collection of rainwater from roofs and hard standing for non-potable uses. Unlike greywater, rainwater may not require treatment to allow it to be stored
- green roofs – planted roof areas where the vegetated area provides a degree of retention and treatment of water and promotes evapotranspiration

---

Conservation and Improvement of Biodiversity

POLICY NRM5: CONSERVATION AND IMPROVEMENT OF BIODIVERSITY

Local planning authorities and other bodies shall avoid a net loss of biodiversity, and actively pursue opportunities to achieve a net gain across the region.

i. They must give the highest level of protection to sites of international nature conservation importance (European sites [6]). Plans or projects implementing policies in this RSS are subject to the Habitats Directive. Where a likely significant effect of a plan or project on European sites cannot be excluded, an appropriate assessment in line with the Habitats Directive and associated regulations will be required.

ii. If after completing an appropriate assessment of a plan or project local planning authorities and other bodies are unable to conclude that there will be no adverse effect on the integrity of any European sites, the plan or project will not be approved, irrespective of conformity with other policies in the RSS, unless otherwise in compliance with 6(4) of the Habitats Directive.

iii. For example when deciding on the distribution of housing allocations, local planning authorities should consider a range of alternative distributions within their area and should distribute an allocation in such a way that it avoids adversely affecting the integrity of European sites. In the event that a local planning authority concludes that it cannot distribute an allocation accordingly, or otherwise avoid or adequately mitigate any adverse effect, it should make provision up to the level closest to its original allocation for which it can be concluded that it can be distributed without adversely affecting the integrity of any European sites.

iv. They shall avoid damage to nationally important sites of special scientific interest and seek to ensure that damage to county wildlife sites and locally important wildlife and geological sites is avoided, including additional areas outside the boundaries

---

6 'European sites' is the term used to encompass sites that have the highest level of protection in the UK either through legislation or policy. These are Special Areas of Conservation (SACs), candidate SACs (cSACs), Special Protection Areas (SPAs), proposed SPAs (pSPAs) and Ramsar sites.

> of European sites where these support the species for which that site has been selected.
>
> v. They shall ensure appropriate access to areas of wildlife importance, identifying areas of opportunity for biodiversity improvement and setting targets reflecting those in the table headed 'Regional Biodiversity Targets - Summary for 2010 and 2026' below. Opportunities for biodiversity improvement, including connection of sites, large-scale habitat restoration, enhancement and re-creation in the areas of strategic opportunity for biodiversity improvement (Diagram NRM3) should be pursued
>
> vi. They shall influence and applying agri-environment schemes, forestry, flood defence, restoration of mineral extraction sites and other land management practices to:
>
> - deliver biodiversity targets
> - increase the wildlife value of land
> - reduce diffuse pollution
> - protect soil resources.
>
> vi. They shall promote policies that integrate the need to accommodate the changes taking place in agriculture with the potential implications of resultant development in the countryside.
>
> vii. They shall require green infrastructure to be identified, developed and implemented in conjunction with new development.

9.17 The South East contains significant areas of importance for nature conservation, including sites designated for their international importance (see map NRM2). There have been major losses of habitats and species populations in the region over recent decades, due to inappropriate management, agricultural practices, development and fragmentation. In spite of this, the region still supports a high proportion of UK habitats and species. Further fragmentation of habitats will compromise functionality of the environment, impacting on economic and social objectives, as well as the ability of species to move and respond to the effects of climate change.

9.18 This Plan responds by setting out a policy approach to ensure the conservation and, where appropriate, enhancement of biodiversity of valuable wildlife sites across the region. Policy NRM5 also reflects the highest level of protection that exists for European sites.

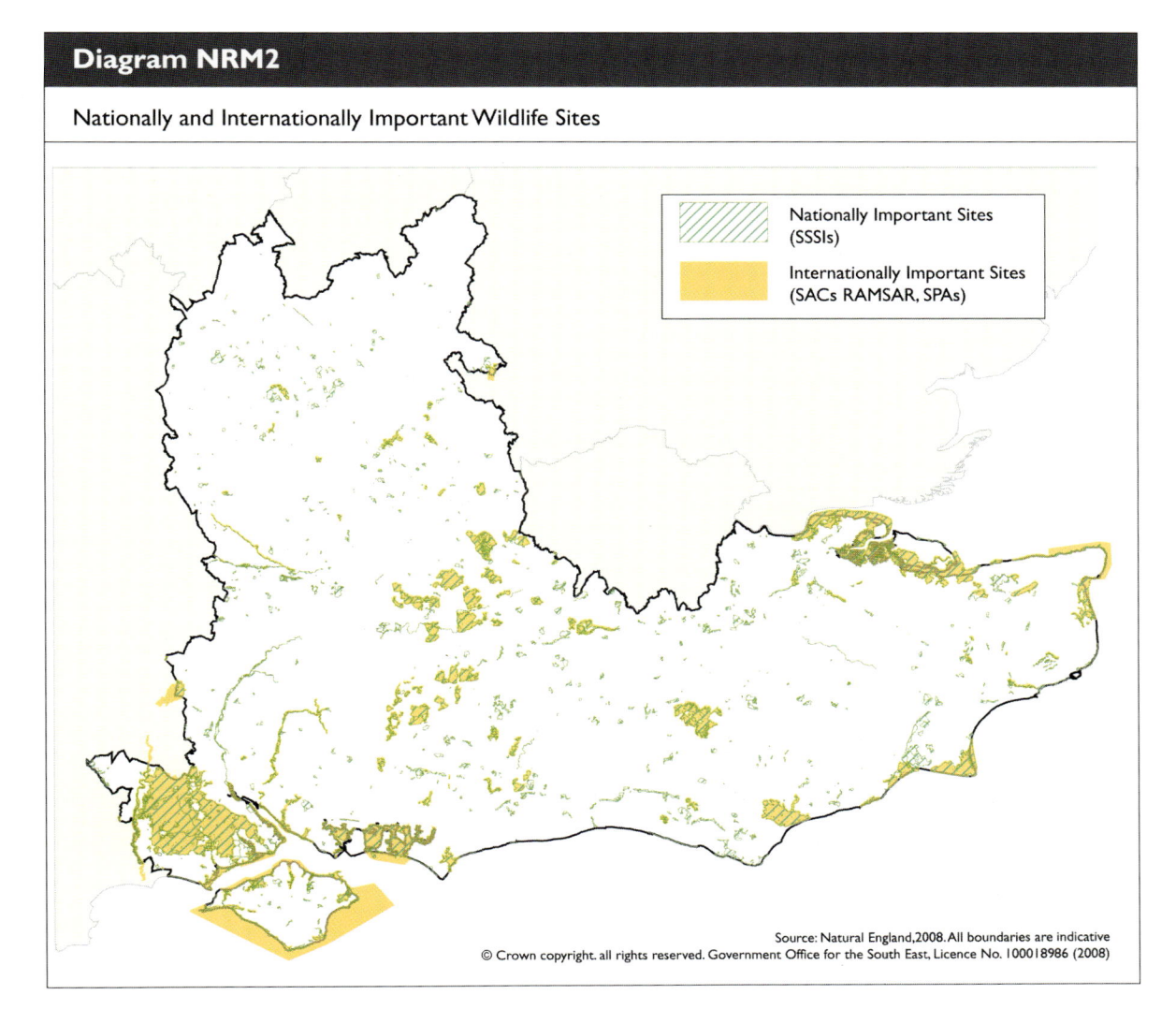

Diagram NRM2

Nationally and Internationally Important Wildlife Sites

Legend: Nationally Important Sites (SSSIs); Internationally Important Sites (SACs RAMSAR, SPAs)

Source: Natural England, 2008. All boundaries are indicative
© Crown copyright. all rights reserved. Government Office for the South East, Licence No. 100018986 (2008)

9.19　As a non-site specific strategic regional plan, implementation (including the more locationally specific distribution of housing allocations) will be determined through local plans and projects. It is vital therefore that the requirements of the Conservation (Natural Habitats, &c) Regulation 1994 are met in relation to such local plans and projects (including granting of planning permission).

9.20　Local planning authorities should avoid in the first instance and mitigate where necessary for identified effects on European sites. Where necessary, local planning authorities will need to identify opportunities for avoidance and mitigation when testing proposed plans and projects, including the options for the spatial distribution of housing allocations. In some circumstances, this may require an approach to be developed and implemented across administrative boundaries.

9.21　All local planning authorities are required to consider in-combination effects as part of the Habitats Regulations Assessment of plans and projects including cross-boundary issues.[7] To assist local planning authorities in drawing up plans that are compliant with the Habitats Directive, Natural England will work with the Secretary of State to identify those circumstances where there is a high risk of cross-boundary implications for European sites. Where these areas are identified the Secretary of State and Natural England will provide guidance for the development of avoidance and mitigation strategies to protect the integrity of European sites.

7　Cross-boundary issues refer to those issues that may cross one or more local planning authority boundaries and that may require a cooperative approach in considering the effects on European sites.

9.22 Where, in accordance with Policy NMR5iii, a local planning authority's development plan documents make provision for less than they are allocated in this RSS (such as fewer housing numbers than those set out in Policy H1), they will need to demonstrate at independent examination that this is the only means of avoiding or mitigating any adverse impacts on European sites. This will involve clearly showing that they have attempted to avoid adverse effects through testing different distribution options and that the mitigation of impacts would be similarly ineffective.

9.23 **Conserving Biodiversity** -Biodiversity protection and enhancement in the region will be achieved by:

  i. conserving and enhancing the extent and quality of designated conservation sites, especially those afforded the highest levels of protection under international and national legislation (the locations of these sites are illustrated in Diagram NRM2)
  ii. conserving and enhancing the diversity and distribution of habitats and species, as designated sites only represent the best examples of their kind
  iii. recognising the importance of green networks and open green space within urban and suburban areas and taking steps to protect and enhance their provision
  iv. recognising the particular nature of urban wildlife (including those on previously developed land). These may be of local importance for wildlife and for the provision of quality green-spaces
  v. conserving soil resources to help protect below ground ecosystems which help retain above ground biodiversity.

9.24 **Improving Biodiversity** – Opportunities for biodiversity and habitat enhancements at a range of scales need to be identified and realised. The South East England Biodiversity Forum (SEEBF) has identified regional biodiversity targets that set out the contribution the region can make towards national targets in the UK Biodiversity Action Plan. These focus on habitats for which the region is particularly important and for which there are significant opportunities. These are set out in the following table:

Regional Biodiversity Targets - Summary for 2010 and 2026

Regional Habitats Grouping	Broad Habitat (BAP)	Existing habitat resource (ha or km) [8]	Target for habitat improvement [9]		Area of Strategic Opportunity
			2010 [10]	2026 [11]	
Heath/ Acid grass/ Mire	Acid Grasslands Dwarf Shrub Heath	27000	3200	6400	New Forest Thames Basin Heaths Ashdown Forest, North Hampshire Western Greensand

9 Improvement" includes the "enhancement", "restoration", "creation" and "re-creation" as defined in SEEBF August 2004 rationale paper
8 South East England Biodiversity Forum. *Action for Biodiversity in the South East* (1999). Figures for Berkshire area unavailable
11 These aspirational targets are based on doubling the 2010 targets. There is currently insufficient local data for more accurate targets.
10 2010 targets are built up from recommendations by Local Biodiversity Action Plan Partnerships based on best available information

Natural Resource Management

					Emer Bog
Calcareous Grassland	Calcareous Grassland	9000	4400	8800	North Downs
					South Downs
					Chilterns
					Berkshire Downs escarpment
					North Wessex AONB
					Isle of Wight
					Cranbourne Chase AONB
					Mole Gap to Reigate Escarpment
Coastal and Floodplain Grazing Marsh	Coastal and Floodplain Grazing Marsh	32000	950	1900	North Kent Marshes
					East Kent
					Ashford
					Romney Marshes
					Pevensey Levels
					South Coast rivers
					Manhood Peninsula
					Chichester and Langstone Harbour
					Test, Itchen and Avon
					Upper Thames tributaries
					River Kennet and tributary
					West Hampshire coast
					Brading Marshes

Meadows/ Neutral grass/ Hay Meadows/ Purple Moor Grass	Neutral Grassland	5200	2050	4100	Upper Thames tributaries Others not identified
Ancient and Native Woodland/ Pasture Woodland/ Parkland	Broad-leaved, mixed and Yew Woodland Coniferous Woodland	247000 [12]	30,350 [13]	111,300	Blean North Downs Weald West Weald Woodlands Chilterns Bernwood Windsor Forest Wychwood Tytherly Woods Forest of Bere Harewood Forest New Forest Isle of Wight Woodlands
Fen/Reed	Fen, marsh, swamp	700 (reedbeds) 200 sites (fens)	950	1900	Not identified
Rivers	Rivers and Streams	1500 km (chalk rivers)	400	800	East Kent Romney Marshes SouthCoast rivers Test, Itchen and Avon Upper Thames tributaries River Kennet and tributaries

---

13 Target provided by SEEBF
12 This total provided by Forestry Commission. See SEEBF Rationale Paper August 2004 for more information

Natural Resource Management

Lakes/ Ponds/ Open Water	Standing Open Water and Canals	Incomplete data	500	1000	Not identified
Intertidal	Saltmarsh Estuaries, inlets and enclosed bays	23000	700	1400	North Kent Marshes East Kent Romney Marshes South Coast Rivers Manhood Peninsular Chichester and Langstone harbours West Hampshire coast Brading Marshes
Shingle/ Dunes/ Lagoons	Saline lagoons, Shingle above high tide mark	3800	30	60	East Kent Romney Marshes Chichester and Langstone harbours Manhood peninsular West Hampshire coast Brading Marshes
Cliffs and Slopes	Maritime Cliff and Slope	150 km	Incomplete data		Not identified
Littoral/ sub-littoral chalk	Open Coast	77km	Incomplete data		Not identified

9.25   The indicative diagram (NRM3) shows areas of greatest strategic opportunity for the enhancement, restoration and re-creation of key wildlife habitats. It is not a map of formal designations and constraints, although the areas of strategic opportunity do include protected sites with statutory designations including those identified in Diagram NRM2. It does not illustrate all local opportunities for improvement, including those that may occur outside of these areas, nor identify areas of importance for protected species.

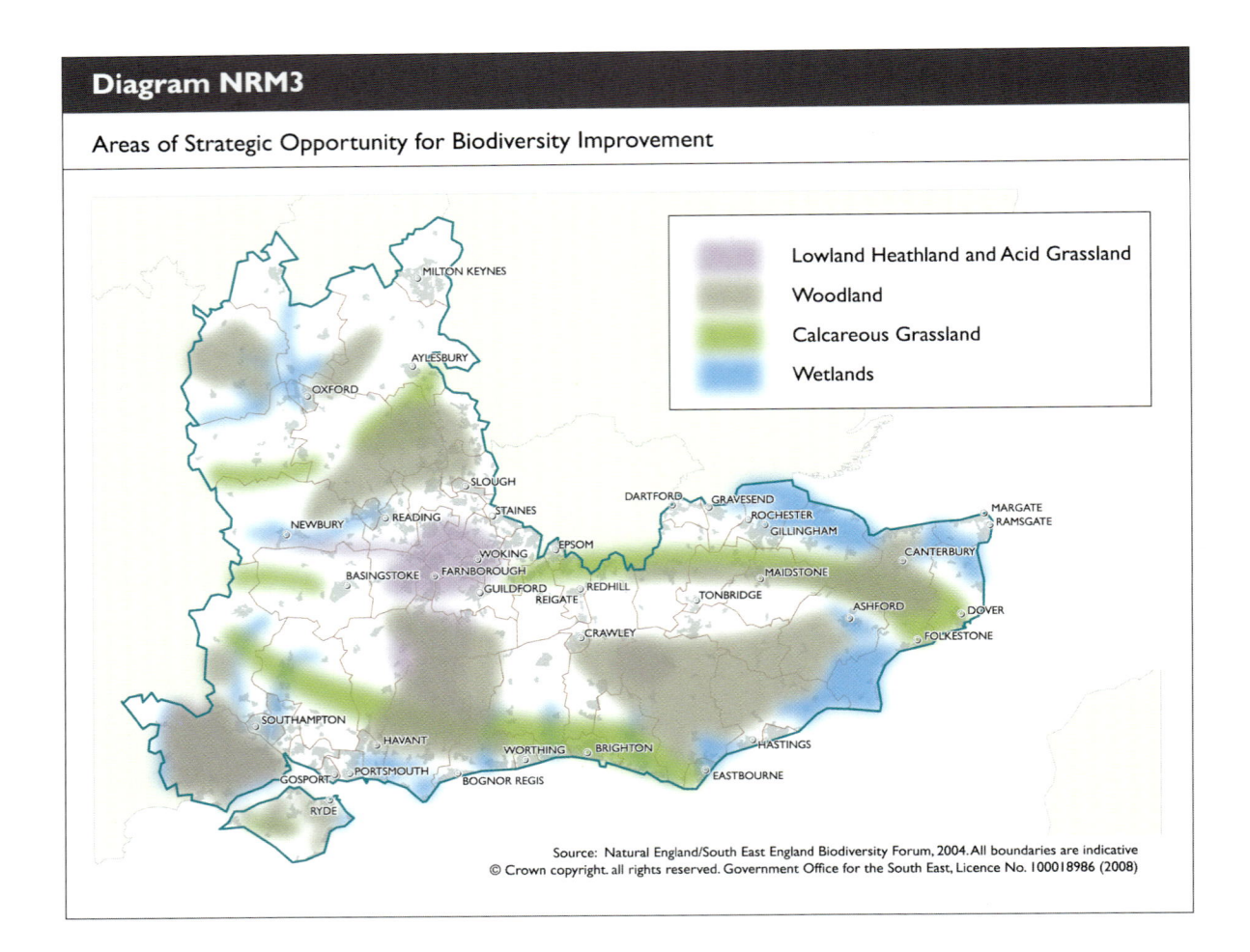

Natural Resource Management

Diagram NRM3

Areas of Strategic Opportunity for Biodiversity Improvement

Legend:
- Lowland Heathland and Acid Grassland
- Woodland
- Calcareous Grassland
- Wetlands

Source: Natural England/South East England Biodiversity Forum, 2004. All boundaries are indicative
© Crown copyright. all rights reserved. Government Office for the South East, Licence No. 100018986 (2008)

9.27 Planning has an important and positive role to play in protecting and enhancing the region's biodiversity, and helping natural systems to adapt to climate change impacts. Local authorities, government agencies and other organisations should work together to achieve biodiversity targets by:

i. identifying areas of opportunity for biodiversity improvement in LDDs, community strategies and other strategies affecting land-use and management including Shoreline Management Plans, Catchment Flood Management Plans, the Regional Forestry Framework
ii. putting in place long-term management policies and monitoring procedures
iii. ensuring that opportunities for biodiversity improvement are sought and realised as part of development schemes, including regeneration and development of previously developed land, and that where possible these contribute to creation and enhancement of green corridors and networks [14]
iv. pursuing joint projects on areas that cross administrative boundaries, particularly where this enables a more strategic approach to restoration of habitats and reconnection of fragmented sites
v. identifying and securing measures to help implement biodiversity improvement including, for example, developer contributions and targeting of agri-environment schemes.

9.28 Areas of strategic opportunity for biodiversity improvement have been identified (Diagram NRM3). These are broad indicative areas of greatest regional-scale potential for enhancement, restoration and re-creation of given habitats. Their identification was informed by assessments of existing habitats, the nature and location of designated sites (including international sites, SSSIs, county wildlife sites) and underlying geology and topography.

---

14   See www.englishnature.org.uk/pubs/publication/pdf/tcpabiodiversityguide.pdf

Natural Resource Management

9.29 These areas do not represent the only areas in the region where habitat enhancement will be feasible, and does not preclude habitat enhancement and creation where this would meet local targets and other benefits, such as green space in urban areas.

9.30 The areas of strategic opportunity for biodiversity improvement in Diagram NRM3 are based on key habitat types, but within each area the distribution and nature of existing habitats and designated sites must be taken into account. The key strategic habitats comprise:

   i. lowland heath and acid grassland, where there are major opportunities for restoration and re-creation of habitats on sand and gravel including heathland, acid grassland, acid woodland and bog
   ii. chalk downs where there are opportunities to restore, re-create and manage chalk grassland, chalk woodland and species-rich scrub
   iii. woodland, where there are concentrations of important woodland habitats which could be restored, enhanced and re-connected and where other key habitats including grassland, wetland and heath could be restored
   iv. wetlands (including coastal and floodplain grazing marsh, reed beds, inter-tidal mudflats and saltmarsh) where wet grassland, reed bed, fen, open water and wet woodland habitats could be restored and re-created and where coastal realignment could help to re-create inter-tidal habitats.

Thames Basin Heaths Special Protection Area

POLICY NRM6: THAMES BASIN HEATHS SPECIAL PROTECTION AREA

New residential development which is likely to have a significant effect on the ecological integrity of Thames Basin Heaths Special Protection Area (SPA) will be required to demonstrate that adequate measures are put in place to avoid or mitigate any potential adverse effects. Such measures must be agreed with Natural England.

Priority should be given to directing development to those areas where potential adverse effects can be avoided without the need for mitigation measures. Where mitigation measures are required, local planning authorities, as Competent Authorities, should work in partnership to set out clearly and deliver a consistent approach to mitigation, based on the following principles:

i. **a zone of influence set at 5km linear distance from the SPA boundary will be established where measures must be taken to ensure that the integrity of the SPA is protected**

ii. **within this zone of influence, there will be a 400m "exclusion zone" where mitigation measures are unlikely to be capable of protecting the integrity of the SPA. In exceptional circumstances, this may vary with the provision of evidence that demonstrates the extent of the area within which it is considered that mitigation measures will be capable of protecting the integrity of the SPA. These small locally determined zones will be set out in local development frameworks (LDFs) and SPA avoidance strategies and agreed with Natural England**

iii. **where development is proposed outside the exclusion zone but within the zone of influence, mitigation measures will be delivered prior to occupation and in perpetuity. Measures will be based on a combination of access management, and the provision of Suitable Accessible Natural Greenspace (SANG).**

Where mitigation takes the form of provision of SANG the following standards and arrangements will apply:

iv. **a minimum of 8 hectares of SANG land (after discounting to account for current access and capacity) should be provided per 1,000 new occupants**

v. **developments of fewer than 10 dwellings should not be required to be within a specified distance of SANG land provided it is ensured that a sufficient quantity of**

> SANG land is in place to cater for the consequent increase in residents prior to occupation of the dwellings
> vi. access management measures will be provided strategically to ensure that adverse impacts on the SPA are avoided and that SANG functions effectively
> vii. authorities should co-operate and work jointly to implement mitigation measures. These may include, inter alia, assistance to those authorities with insufficient SANG land within their own boundaries, co-operation on access management and joint development plan documents
> viii. relevant parties will co-operate with Natural England and landowners and stakeholders in monitoring the effectiveness of avoidance and mitigation measures and monitoring visitor pressure on the SPA and review/amend the approach set out in this policy, as necessary
> ix. local authorities will collect developer contributions towards mitigation measures, including the provision of SANG land and joint contributions to the funding of access management and monitoring the effects of mitigation measures across the SPA
> x. large developments may be expected to provide bespoke mitigation that provides a combination of benefits including SANG, biodiversity enhancement, green infrastructure and, potentially, new recreational facilities.
>
> Where further evidence demonstrates that the integrity of the SPA can be protected using different linear thresholds or with alternative mitigation measures (including standards of SANG provision different to those set out in this policy) these must be agreed with Natural England.
>
> The mechanism for this policy is set out in the TBH Delivery Framework by the TBH Joint Strategic Partnership and partners and stakeholders, the principles of which should be incorporated into local authorities' LDFs.

9.31   The Thames Basin Heaths Special Protection Area (SPA) is designated under European Directive 79/409/EEC because of its populations of three heathland species of birds – Dartford Warbler, Nightjar and Woodlark. This designation covers parts of 15 local authority areas and three counties and is likely to have a major impact upon the potential for development within these areas and others adjoining it. See following diagram showing local authority boundaries, 400m and 5km zones:

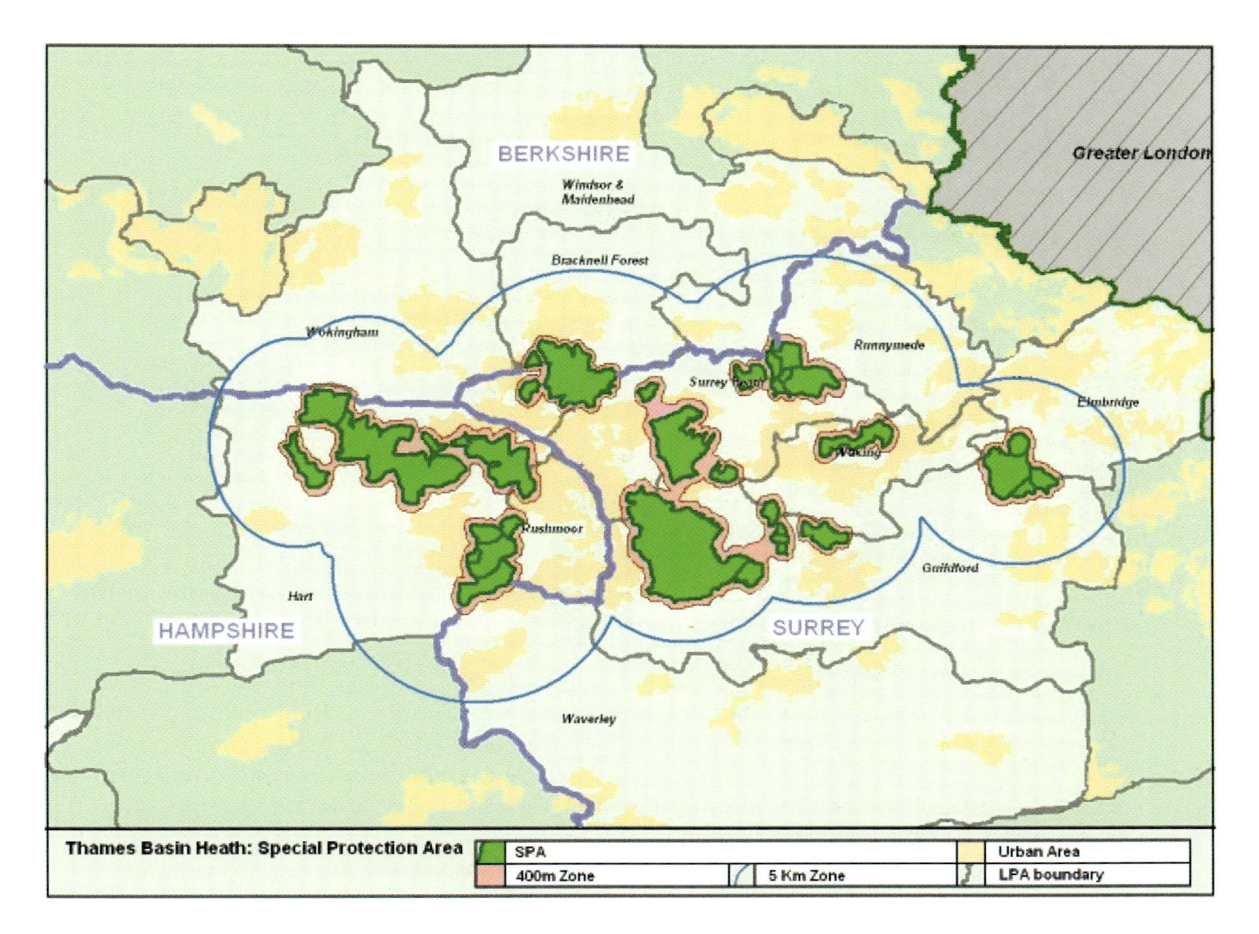

Natural Resource Management

Thames Basin Heath: Special Protection Area
- SPA
- 400m Zone
- 5 Km Zone
- Urban Area
- LPA boundary

9.32 Natural England has identified that net additional housing development (residential institutions and dwellings) up to 5km from the designated sites is likely to have a significant effect (alone or in combination with other plans or projects) on the integrity of the SPA. Initial advice from Natural England is that an exclusion zone of 400 metre linear distance from the SPA is appropriate. The district level housing allocations for the sub-region presuppose that an effective approach to dealing with the effects of development on the SPA can be found. Local authorities that are affected by the designation should deal, in their LDDs, with the issue of the effects of development on the SPA, and put forward a policy framework to protect the SPA whilst meeting development requirements. The focus of this policy is on avoidance and mitigation of the effects of residential development. This does not obviate the need for possible Habitats Regulation Assessment on other forms of development.

9.33 Nor do the provisions of this policy exclude the possibility that some residential schemes (and, in particular, relatively large schemes) either within or outside the 5k zone might require assessment under the Habitats Regulations due to a likely significant effect, alone or in combination with other plans or projects, and subject to advice from Natural England.

9.34 Applications for all non-residential development will need to be subject to Habitats Regulations Assessment where they are likely to have a significant adverse impact on the integrity of the Thames Basin Heaths SPA.

9.35 To assist local authorities in the preparation of LDDs and to enable development to come forward in a timely and efficient manner, Policy NRM6 sets out the extent of mitigation measures required, based on current evidence. The evidence available indicates that effective mitigation measures should comprise a combination of providing suitable areas for recreational use by residents to buffer the SPA and actions on the SPA to manage access and encourage use of alternative sites. Such measures must be operational prior to the occupation of new residential developments to ensure that the interests of the SPA are not damaged. Local Authorities and Natural England will need to co-operate so that the effect of mitigation measures can be monitored across the SPA.

9.36   Where developers propose a bespoke solution, this will be assessed on its own merits under the Habitats Regulations. The SANG requirement for bespoke solutions may vary according to the size and proximity of development to the SPA; early consultation with Natural England and the local planning authority is encouraged.

9.37   Should it become apparent during the lifetime of this Plan that alternative arrangements may need to apply, these must be brought forward with the agreement of Natural England.

9.38   One route would be the publication of supplementary guidance to this Plan by Natural England to set out alternative arrangements or further details.

Woodlands

> **POLICY NRM7: WOODLANDS**
>
> In the development and implementation of local development documents and other strategies, local authorities and other bodies will support the implementation of the Regional Forestry and Woodland Framework, ensuring the value and character of the region's woodland are protected and enhanced. This will be achieved by:
>
> i.   protecting ancient woodland from damaging development and land uses
> ii. promoting the effective management, and where appropriate, extension and creation of new woodland areas including, in association with areas of major development, where this helps to restore and enhance degraded landscapes, screen noise and pollution, provide recreational opportunities, helps mitigate climate change, and contributes to floodplain management
> iii. replacing woodland unavoidably lost through development with new woodland on at least the same scale
> iv. promoting and encouraging the economic use of woodlands and wood resources, including wood fuel as a renewable energy source
> v.   promoting the growth and procurement of sustainable timber products.

9.39   The region is the most wooded in England, with almost 275,000 hectares covering around 15% of the land area (the area of woodland having increased over recent years), although coverage varies around the region. This provides many social and environmental benefits for its inhabitants. The management of a substantial proportion of this resource is, however, inadequate and many woodlands are neglected.

9.40   The Regional Forestry and Woodlands Framework [15] highlights how trees, woodlands and forestry can contribute to the sustainable development of the region and sets out the steps needed to secure the future of its woodland. This framework is the regional expression of the England Forestry Strategy.

9.41   In order to ensure that woodlands continue to contribute towards the sustainable development of the region and the quality of life, we need to:

   i.   protect and enhance the value and character of the region's woodland, promoting appropriate woodland planting in association with major areas of development to restore and improve degraded landscapes
   ii. realise the economic, environmental and social benefits that woodland management and tree planting can provide
   iii. promote higher standards of management of existing woodlands, and seek new markets for woodland produce
   iv. support the implementation of the Regional Forestry and Woodland Framework
   v.   manage woodland in light of the impact of climate change.

---

15   *Seeing the Wood for the Trees,* Forestry Commission (2004)

Natural Resource Management

Coastal Management

POLICY NRM8: COASTAL MANAGEMENT

An integrated approach to the management and planning in coastal areas will be pursued. Appropriate social, economic and environmental objectives should be taken into account in relevant plans. The dynamic nature and character of the coast should be managed through enhanced collaboration between organisations and across administrative boundaries. In the development and implementation of local development documents and other strategies, local authorities and other agencies should:

i. plan for climate change and forecast effects on the coastal zone
ii. promote and establish cross-border and cross-sectoral arrangements to facilitate an integrated approach to coastal management. This will include the conservation and enhancement of the most valuable habitats and environments (natural and built), the development and management of public access, recreation and tourism potential, and identification and management of development and commercial opportunities. This will be within the context of flood risk management and coastal protection measures contained in Catchment Management Plans, Shoreline Management Plans, Coastal Defence Strategies, Catchment Flood Management Plans, Estuary Management Plans, Harbour Management Plans and River Basin Management Plans
iii. identify opportunities for, and ensure that development does not prejudice options for managed realignment, significantly affect sediment inputs and transport, lead to an increase in flood risk or preclude the delivery of sustainable flood risk management solutions in the future
iv. avoid built development on the undeveloped coastline unless it specifically requires a rural coastal location, meets the sequential test set out in Planning Policy Statement 25: *Development and Flood Risk* and does not adversely affect environmental, cultural and recreational resources. In particular, development must not compromise the ability to preserve the interest features of Natura 2000 sites through managed retreat of coastal habitats in response to sea level rise
v. prevent development on unstable land or areas at risk of erosion, as identified in Shoreline Management Plans
vi. realise opportunities for sustainable coastal defences which enhance the region's wildlife, and fisheries, especially where this will contribute to the achievement of regional and national biodiversity targets and help meet the requirement of the Habitats Directive
vii. consider whether permission for development should be time-limited to ensure the minimisation of risk to life and property in the long term but allow economic and social benefits to be gained in the short term.

9.42 The extensive coastline of the region is an important environmental, economic and recreational resource. However, it is characterised by a legacy of human intervention. Considerable lengths of the region's coast have been developed with 90 – 95% of its frontage defended against erosion and/or flood risk. [16] This represents a considerable investment both in terms of built assets and economic activity. The coast also contains a significant share of the region's designated wildlife sites, possesses nationally designated landscapes and is home to some of the South East's, and the country's most iconic images.

9.43 The financial and cultural investment made in the coast has determined a continued policy of intervention over the last 200 years which attempts to 'hold the line'. Areas of the undeveloped coast have been designated as 'Heritage Coast' reflecting their landscape, cultural and recreational importance. Locations of the region's Heritage Coasts are indicated on Diagram CLM1 in Chapter 11.

16 Scoping Study: A Strategic Approach to the Management of the Coast in the South East – WS Atkins May 2001

9.44 Although a vital necessity in some locations, holding the line works against the dynamic nature of coastal processes. This can lead society into an unsustainable policy of coastal defence, ignoring that the coastline has and will continue to change and evolve. The impacts of climate change, including increased storminess and frequency of extreme events, combined with a continuing trend of rising sea levels and insufficient sediment supply, render traditional coastal defence practices inappropriate as the sole tool of risk management.

9.45 A range of responses, based upon the principle of risk management rather than defence, will be necessary for sustainable shoreline management in the future, especially when responding to the impacts of climate change. When considering shoreline management, the location of development, opportunities for imaginative management options to reduce erosion and flood risk, benefit to wildlife and improvement of the landscape all need full consideration. Better integration of coastal protection, flood defence and land use planning is required.

9.46 As a result, securing the sustainable management of the coastal zone extends beyond matters of coastal defence. The wider context of development pressures facing the coastal environment must be considered.

9.47 The land use planning system has acted as the predominant regulatory tool to control development above mean low water, governing a variety of sectoral interests. The nature of the physical and chemical relationships between catchments, coastal waters and the marine environment are also such that impacts of activities seemingly removed from the coastal environment may significantly and adversely affect this valuable resource.

9.48 The need for an integrated approach to the management of these issues in coastal areas has been the subject of European-wide studies leading to a EU recommendation to all Member States on the implementation of Integrated Coastal Zone Management (ICZM) [17] Good practice on ICZM already exists in the region, for example the Solent Forum, the emerging Kent Coastal Forum, Arc Manche, and by national bodies such as the Local Government Association's Coastal Special Interest Group [18] and CoastNet, promoting ICZM at a sub regional, national and international level.

9.49 The objectives of ICZM are:

i. a more naturally functioning coastline which accommodates habitats and species
ii. the effective management of risk to life and property from coastal erosion and flooding within the context of rising sea levels and climate change
iii. the sustainable growth and regeneration of coastal communities and settlements.

9.50 Much of the South East coast is highly developed and options for management of coastal processes are often constrained by historic patterns of development. However, the planning system must enable, where possible, important environmental features and habitats to respond to environmental change through creating and re-creating habitats threatened by climate change and sea level rise. This is consistent with the review of the National Strategy for Flood and Coastal Erosion Risk Management in England and thinking emerging from the second round of Shoreline Management Plan (SMP) reviews (currently piloted in two SMP frontages in the South East) which will identify options for coastal protection and management, including any opportunities for managed realignment and more natural and sustainable coastal defence options. Policy development (as well as implementation) between coastal groups and coastal planning authorities should be better integrated. The very long term horizon of Shoreline Management Plans (up to 100 years) extends a long way beyond the time frame of this Plan. This means that they aid the development of long-term spatial strategies and decisions about land use for years to come. The next round of SMPs will therefore inform the next review of this Plan, and will also need to be taken into account in the production of LDDs.

---

17 EU Recommendation on the Integrated Management of Coastal Zones May 2002.
18 http://www.coastalsig.lga.gov.uk/info_pack.htm

Natural Resource Management

9.51 A SMP is a high level document that forms an important element of the strategy for flood and coastal erosion risk management. Shoreline Management Plans are being prepared for the following areas of the South East:

Shoreline Management Plans, as at March 2009

Flood Risk Management Plan	Area	Stage (Lead Authority)
SMP	Medway & Swale Estuary	Due to be completed April 2009 (EA)
SMP	Isle of Grain to South Foreland	Due to be completed April 2009 (Canterbury)
SMP	South Foreland to Beachy Head	Appropriate Assessment to be finalised. SMP due to be completed June 2009 (Shepway)
SMP	Beachy Head to Selsey Bill	Due to be completed March 2009 (Arun)
SMP	Selsey Bill to Hurst Spit	Draft report near completion. Expected to be completed March 2010 (Solent Operating Authorities)
SMP	Isle of Wight	Draft report near completion. Expected to be completed March 2010 (Isle of Wight + EA)
SMP	Hurst Spit to Durlston Head	Draft report consultation scheduled August 2009. (Bournemouth)

Air Quality

POLICY NRM9: AIR QUALITY

Strategies, plans, programmes and planning proposals should contribute to sustaining the current downward trend in air pollution in the region. This will include seeking improvements in air quality so that there is a significant reduction in the number of days of medium and high air pollution by 2026. Local development documents and development control can help to achieve improvements in local air quality through:

i. ensuring consistency with Air Quality Management Plans
ii. reducing the environmental impacts of transport, congestion management, and support the use of cleaner transport fuels
iii. mitigating the impact of development and reduce exposure to poor air quality through design, particularly for residential development in areas which already, or are likely to, exceed national air quality objectives
iv. encouraging the use of best practice during construction activities to reduce the levels of dust and other pollutants
v. assessing the potential impacts of new development and increased traffic levels on internationally designated nature conservation sites, and adopt avoidance and mitigation measures to address these impacts.

Natural Resource Management

9.52   The primary driver for national, regional and local air quality management is the protection of human health, although the impact of certain pollutants on wildlife habitats and vegetation is also a concern. Air quality has generally improved over recent years although the region still contains some of the worst air pollution locations in the UK where action is needed. This is therefore an issue of regional significance. Guidance on development control and planning for air quality is provided in advice published by the National Society for Clean Air (NSCA).

9.53   Emissions from industrial sources are well regulated and are relatively minor compared to those from motor vehicles and aviation, although the overall background levels of some pollutants are high. Influencing patterns, mode and individual choice of transport (for example through implementation of the transport policies in this Plan) will be important in achieving further improvements in air quality, as will using trees to trap pollution, particularly in urban areas. Emissions from forecast growth in aviation are a particular concern in this region.

9.54   The Air Quality Strategy (AQS) 2000 for England, Scotland, Wales and Northern Ireland sets out the Government's policies aimed at delivering cleaner air in the UK. Where it is considered one or more of the objectives within the AQS are unlikely to be met, local authorities must declare Air Quality Management Areas (AQMAs) and develop action plans setting out how they intend to improve air quality. As a result 14 local authorities have declared larger AQMAs. Other smaller ones comprising only a few roads, typically in town centres also operate. Local authorities have produced draft or final Air Quality Action Plans that have investigated options to reduce emissions. These relate to Nitrogen Dioxide (NO_2) and Particulate Matter (PM10) primarily from road transport, and Sulphur Dioxide at Dover (from ships manoeuvring in the harbour).

Noise

POLICY NRM10: NOISE

Measures to address and reduce noise pollution will be developed at regional and local level through means such as:

i.   **locating new residential and other sensitive development away from existing sources of significant noise or away from planned new sources of noise**
ii. **traffic management and requiring sound attenuation measures in major transport schemes**
iii. **encouraging high levels of sound-proofing and screening as part of sustainable housing design and construction.**

9.55   Noise can have a serious effect on the quiet enjoyment of property and places, reducing quality of life. Ambient noise and neighbour noise can have significant impacts on quality of life. Planned new residential development must take these factors into account, in accordance with the guidance in PPG24: *Planning and Noise*.

9.56   For existing dwellings, other statutory instruments (such as the Environmental Protection Act 1990) should be used where necessary to ensure noise annoyance does not become a significant impediment to achieving a good quality of life for all residents in the region. Building Regulations set standards for ensuring resistance to the passage of sound in building fabric.

9.57   The European Directive on Environmental Noise (2002/49/EC) aims to avoid, prevent or limit the effects of exposure to environmental noise. It applies to larger cities, major roads, railways and airports. The Environment Agency has now produced noise maps which nationally cover 23 major urban areas (including Brighton, Portsmouth, Reading and Southampton), as well as 80,000 km of roads within urban areas, 28,000 km of major road networks and almost 5,000 km of railways. Action plans to reduce noise pollution are now being developed.

9.58 Although the role of spatial planning in relation to other controls is relatively limited, it can influence exposure to environmental noise primarily through design and location of new development, and influencing traffic and its management.

Energy Efficiency and Renewable Energy

9.59 Careful use and creation of energy supplies is a key challenge for the region. Policies to engender more efficient use of energy in new development have already been included in Chapter 5 (Cross Cutting Polices), and in particular Policy CC4. A more detailed policy on energy efficiency and renewable energy in new development is also set out below. In addition, an effective regional spatial strategy can also play a wider co-ordinating role in securing safer, cleaner and more renewable forms of energy supply for future generations, including Combined Heat and Power. The remainder of this chapter therefore provides further policy, guidance and targets for renewable energy deployment. Their effective implementation is imperative if we are to combat climate change, reduce fuel poverty and deliver a more diverse and secure energy supply through reducing reliance on traditional forms of power generation.

9.60 The Climate Change Act 2008 introduced a legally binding target of at least an 80% cut in greenhouse gas emissions by 2050, to be achieved through action in the UK and abroad, plus a reduction in CO_2 emissions of at least 26% by 2020. Both these targets are against a 1990 baseline. At the time of publication of this plan, the 2020 target was being reviewed to reflect the move to all greenhouse gases, and the increase in the 2050 target to 80%. Policy CC2 of the Plan sets a carbon reduction target for the region and identifies the critical importance of energy efficiency and renewable energy in mitigating climate change.

9.61 The principal national targets of relevance are:

   i. to meet 10% of UK electricity generation from renewable sources by 2010. The UK will also contribute to a binding EU target of 20% of energy consumption to come from renewable sources by 2020. The UK share of the target is 15%. Consultation in 2008 on a new renewable energy strategy sought views on how to drive up the use of renewable energy in the UK, as part of the Government's overall strategy for tackling climate change and to meet our share of the EU target [19]
   ii. to increase installed capacity of combined heat and power (CHP) generation to 10,000 MW by 2010
   iii. to reduce domestic energy consumption by 30% by 2010
   iv. to ensure that all new homes are built to zero carbon standards by 2016 [20]
   v. to eradicate fuel poverty among vulnerable households across the UK by 2016-18.

9.62 The targets are supported by a range of fiscal measures and regulations in place to encourage improved energy efficiency in new and existing buildings, uptake of combined heat and power and to create more favourable conditions for development of renewable sources of energy. These include:

   i. capital grants and tax breaks for energy efficiency improvements and CHP
   ii. provision of energy efficiency advice to households and business
   iii. minimum energy efficiency standards set by Building Regulations (which are being progressively tightened in 2010, 2013 and 2016)
   iv. the Renewables Obligation, which requires all licensed electricity suppliers to supply part of their electricity from eligible renewable energy sources increasing from 3% in 2002-2003 to 15.4% in 2015-16
   v. the Climate Change Levy, which is charged on all energy supplied to industry and commerce, agriculture and public administration and services.

---

19 Renewable Energy Consultation, Department for Business, Enterprise and Regulatory Reform, June 2008
20 *Building a Greener Future: Towards Zero Carbon Development.* Department for Communities and Local Government, December 2006

Natural Resource Management

9.63 A significant amount of technical work underpins the policies and targets for renewable energy set out in this RSS. Regional assessments of renewable energy potential have been made, based upon the capacity, opportunities and constraints of the region to accommodate renewable energy. [21]

9.64 Although the primary purpose of the policies set out in this Plan is to promote renewable energy and energy efficiency through new development it should also be recognised that there remains scope to encourage further prudent use of energy (for example by using excess heat from electricity generation and industrial processes). In addition there are opportunities associated with the development of renewables in other policy areas, such as rural development (particularly biomass), transport (use of biofuels), economic development (opportunities for new markets, industries and employment) and improving the quality of built environment and urban renaissance (energy efficiency as part of high quality design).

Development Design for Energy Efficiency and Renewable and Low Carbon Energy

---

POLICY NRM11: DEVELOPMENT DESIGN FOR ENERGY EFFICIENCY AND RENEWABLE ENERGY

Local authorities should:

i. **promote and secure greater use of decentralised and renewable or low-carbon energy in new development, including through setting ambitious but viable proportions of the energy supply for new development to be required to come from such sources. In advance of local targets being set in development plan documents, new developments of more than 10 dwellings or 1000m^2 of non-residential floorspace should secure at least 10% of their energy from decentralised and renewable or low-carbon sources unless, having regard to the type of development involved and its design, this is not feasible or viable**

ii. **use design briefs and/or supplementary planning documents to promote development design for energy efficiency, low carbon and renewable energy**

iii. **work towards incorporation of renewable energy sources including, in particular, passive solar design, solar water heating, photovoltaics, ground source heat pumps and in larger scale development, wind and biomass generated energy**

iv. **actively promote energy efficiency and use of renewable and low carbon energy sources where opportunities arise by virtue of the scale of new development including regional growth areas, growth points and eco-towns.**

Local authorities and other public bodies, as property owners and managers, should seek to achieve high levels of energy efficiency when refurbishing their existing stock.

9.65 Policies CC2, CC3 and CC4 (Chapter 5) set out cross-cutting policies on resource use and sustainable design and construction. These two policies, together with Policy NRM11 are vital tools in preparing the region for the effects of climate change and the need to reduce the consumption of resources. Policy NRM11 requires local authorities to set ambitious and deliverable targets for the use of decentralised and renewable or low-carbon energy to supply new development. In drawing up and testing local targets and associated thresholds local authorities may wish to consult the technical work developed alongside this Plan. [22]

---

21 *Development of a Renewable Energy Assessment and Targets for the South East*, Government Office for the South East, 2001, *Regional & Sub-regional Assessment to 2010, 2016 & 2026*, South East of England Regional Assembly & AEAT/FPD Savills, 2002

22 *The Evidence Base for Sustainable Energy Policies in the South East* (September 2006), Future Energy Solutions and Savills for the South East of England Regional Assembly.
http://www.southeast-ra.gov.uk/southeastplan/publications/research/evidence_base_for_sustainable_energy_policies_v4_sep06.pdf

9.66 Local targets should be set out in development plan documents (DPDs), supplementary planning documents (including design briefs) may be used to help implement and support adopted policies in DPDs.

Combined Heat and Power

> **POLICY NRM12: COMBINED HEAT AND POWER**
>
> **Local development documents and other policies should encourage the integration of combined heat and power (CHP), including mini and micro–CHP, in all developments and district heating infrastructure in large scale developments in mixed use. The use of biomass fuel should be investigated and promoted where possible.**
>
> **Local authorities using their wider powers should promote awareness of the benefits of mini and micro-CHP in the existing build stock.**

9.67 As well as encouraging the use of efficient design and layout and renewable energy technology in new development, this Plan encourages the use of combined heat and power (CHP) and district heating in new buildings. For the purposes of this guidance, district heating should be interpreted as including cooling, and that the term 'cooling' includes absorption cooling.

9.68 The Government has set a target for the installation of 10,000 MW of CHP generation by 2010. CHP and district heating systems use excess heat from electricity generation (including from renewable fuels) or industry to heat or cool buildings in the locality. Traditional CHP is highly fuel efficient (70-90% compared to 30-50% for conventional heating and electricity generation) and can result in savings in energy use and expenditure. Mini-CHP is applicable at a street scale or for large buildings, and micro-CHP is a replacement for conventional domestic boilers. This uses normally wasted heat to generate electricity. Every 1,000 MW of CHP capacity decreases carbon emissions in the range 0.48 – 0.95 million tonnes a year. CHP plants can be powered by a range of fuels and can vary in size.

9.69 CHP deployment will be most effective where the generation plant is relatively close to the users of the heat, where this includes a mix of uses to even out the pattern of demand for electricity and heat through the day and where the density and layout of development reduces costs of installation of the necessary infrastructure and distribution of heat.

9.70 There is scope, therefore, to encourage provision of CHP (preferably certified as 'good quality' under the CHP quality assurance scheme) in association with new and existing developments and, in particular, large scale regeneration or mixed use schemes. It may also have the potential for use in remote rural areas that do not have access to mains gas supplies.

Renewable Energy

9.71 Most renewable energy developments will require planning permission as they will be below 50 MW. Above this threshold, consent is required from the Department for Energy and Climate Change under Section 36 of the Electricity Act 1989.

9.72 To date, the South East has experienced a very low level of renewable energy development. This situation is likely to change. The introduction of measures such as the Renewables Obligation and the Climate Change Levy are providing strong financial stimulus for the development of markets for renewable energy. Capital grants also encourage the development of a range of renewable energy resources and technologies, particularly biomass, offshore wind and photovoltaics. In addition, it can be expected that the UK will continue to face increasingly demanding carbon reduction targets which will be met in part through improving efficiency and an increasing contribution to energy supplied from renewables.

9.73 The assessments of renewable energy potential in the region indicate what is possible and could be delivered. However, technological, planning and commercial considerations will guarantee that the actual pattern of deployment will vary.

9.74 LDDs and other strategies should reflect this potential and provide a framework for renewable energy development, anticipating the likely range and scale of developments which may come forward over the short, medium and longer terms and encouraging appropriate development.

Regional Renewable Energy Targets

POLICY NRM13: REGIONAL RENEWABLE ENERGY TARGETS

The following minimum regional targets for electricity generation from renewable sources should be achieved by the development and use of all appropriate resources and technologies:

Year/ timescale	Installed Capacity (MW)	% Electricity Generation Capacity
2010	620	5.5
2016	895	8.0
2020	1,130	10.0
2026	1,750	16.0

The renewable energy resources with the greatest potential for electricity generation are onshore and offshore wind, biomass, and solar. The renewable energy resources with the greatest potential for heat generation are solar and biomass.

9.75 Regional targets, reflecting the assessment of potential for renewable energy, have been established to ensure that the region contributes towards the UK targets for renewable energy.

9.76 Although only illustrative of what is possible, the targets identify the potential mixture and relative scale of different resources that have the best prospects of coming forward and providing synergies with other policy areas.

9.77 The potential for generation of electricity from renewable energy sources is presented in the targets in Policy NRM13 as installed capacity in MegaWatts (MW) and as a percentage of total capacity. The percentages are based on current installed electricity generation capacity, with an assumption that any growth in demand or consumption of electricity is met by additional generation capacity in the region from renewables only or by imports to the region, and no increase in conventional generation capacity in the region. Improvements in efficiency will help to reduce the growth in demand and consumption.

9.78 It is estimated that by 2026, if the target is met, renewable sources would provide enough electricity for one million homes. This would result in an annual saving of almost two and a half million tonnes of carbon dioxide through displacing generation from conventional fossil fuel sources. The use of renewably generated heat would result in even greater savings. Almost 12% of electricity output would be generated from renewable sources by 2026. It should be noted that this measure of output will be different to figures for installed capacity due to some fluctuations in inputs (for example, varying wind speeds).

9.79 The targets relate only to electricity generation, reflecting the national targets. However, heat generation (from biomass, solar and geothermal/ground source) and use, and the development and use of liquid biofuels in transport, although not quantified in the targets, will also be important in offsetting fossil fuel energy generation and should be encouraged. Heat generation and use is also often the most efficient and cost-effective means of using renewable energy.

9.80 The assessments of renewable energy potential identify offshore wind, onshore wind, and biomass as presenting the greatest opportunities for the generation of electricity and heat over the short to medium terms. In the longer term (between 2016 and 2026), solar generated electricity (photovoltaics), wave and tidal stream energy are identified as having increasing potential.

9.81 With the proviso that the waste hierarchy will be applied the targets include energy derived from biomass waste and from thermal treatment and anaerobic digestion. Biomass waste includes discarded woody waste, including waste from gardens and parks, paper and card, kitchen and food wastes and textiles. Non-waste biomass includes wood, agricultural and forestry residues and energy crops. The assessment of potentially available biomass waste has taken account of the priority afforded to recycling and composting in national and regional waste management policy, including the draft Regional Waste Management Strategy. Therefore it is expected that the targets will be largely met and exceeded through the use of non-waste resources.

9.82 Waste management decisions will be taken on the basis of waste policy and need to consider the waste hierarchy (prioritising reduction, re-use and recycling) and the management technique representing the Best Practicable Environmental Option. Waste management decisions should not be driven by the renewable energy targets but can contribute towards their delivery.

9.83 Landfill gas also contributes to the achievement of the Renewable Energy target although energy from this technology may reduce in the long-term as a result of waste policy.

Spatial Implications – Sub-regional Targets

POLICY NRM14: SUB-REGIONAL TARGETS FOR LAND-BASED RENEWABLE ENERGY

Development plans should include policies, and development proposals as far as practicable should seek, to contribute to the achievement of the following regional and indicative sub-regional targets for land-based renewable energy (see Diagram NRM4):

Sub-region	2010 Renewable Energy Target (MW)	2016 Renewable Energy Target (MW)	Champion
Thames Valley and Surrey	140	209	TV Energy
East Sussex and West Sussex	57	68	ECSC
Hampshire and Isle of Wight	115	122	Hampshire CC & Isle of Wight Council
Kent	111	154	Kent Energy Centre

Local authorities should collaborate and engage with communities, the renewable energy industry and other stakeholders on a sub-regional basis to assist in the achievement of the targets through:

i. **undertaking more detailed assessments of local potential**
ii. **encouraging small scale community-based schemes**
iii. **encouraging development of local supply chains, especially for biomass**
iv. **raising awareness, ownership and understanding of renewable energy.**

Natural Resource Management

9.84 Sub-regional targets provide an indication of the relative potential for development of different resources at sub-regional level. These indicate that the distribution of resources and potential for development is reasonably even throughout the region with significant opportunities for the deployment of all of the major resources – wind, biomass and solar – in all parts of the region.

9.85 The clear implication is, therefore, that there is potential for the development of all major resources and technologies (apart from those requiring coastal or offshore locations) throughout the region and that all local authorities should include policies in their development plans to contribute to the regional targets through supporting the development of all renewable energy resources.

9.86 Overall, Kent, Hampshire and the Isle of Wight, and the Thames Valley and Surrey appear to have the greatest potential for onshore wind development and also for the installation of photovoltaics reflecting the likely rate of new development. The Thames Valley and Surrey sub-region appears to have the greatest potential for biomass fuelled electricity generation, reflecting the existing woodland resource and the potential for coppice in the sub-region and in adjoining counties and regions. Unlike other resources that may only be exploited where they occur, such as wind, biomass fuel can be transported some distance and so the location of electricity and/or CHP plants is more flexible than other resources and difficult to specify.

9.87 The potential and targets for each sub-region are illustrated in Diagram NRM4. These are based on the broad regional assessments of resource availability.

9.88 More detailed local consultation and assessments of potential should be undertaken to refine these indicative targets and define more specific local targets, as has been undertaken, for example, by the Isle of Wight Council. This should involve identification of the technical availability as well as with the practicability of development of the full range of renewable energy technologies, the opportunities, and constraints to their development.

Diagram NRM4

Indicative sub-regional Land-Based and Offshore Potential, 2010-2016

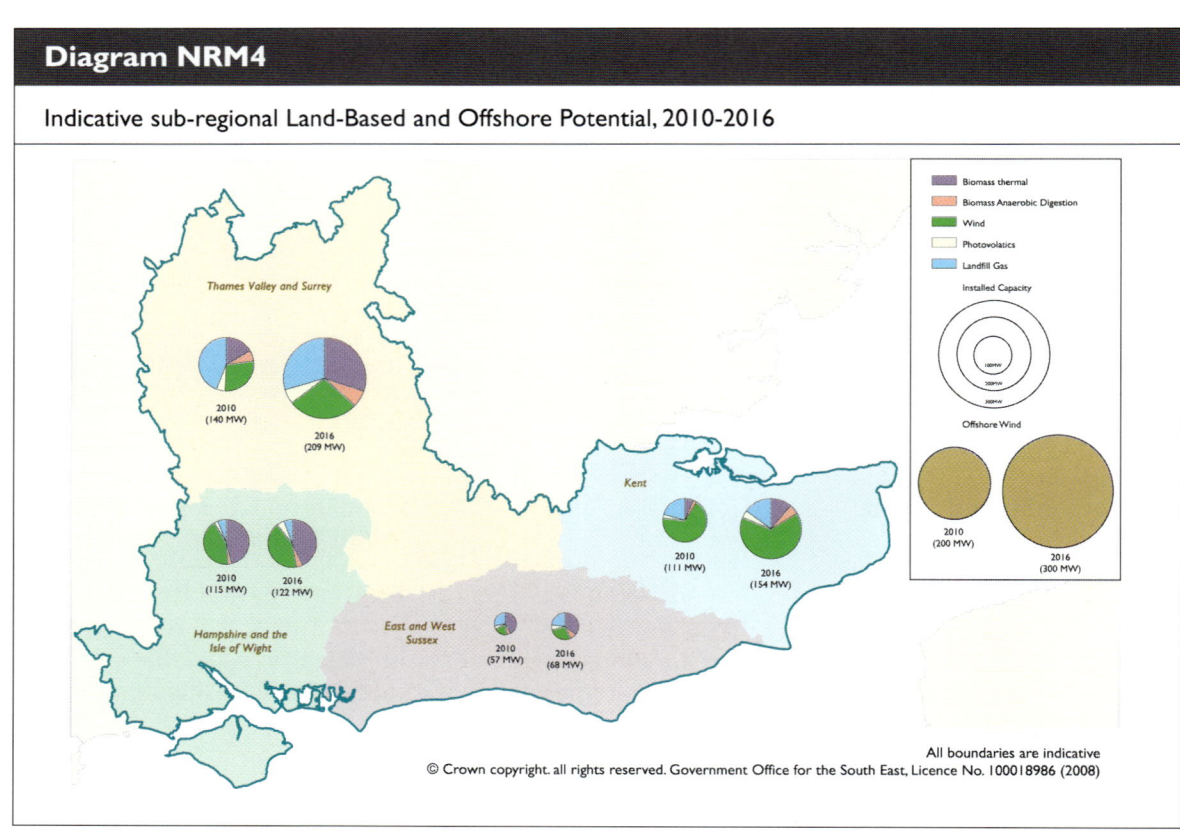

Natural Resource Management

9.89 Offshore wind, tidal stream and wave power have not been included in the sub-regional targets as development will be outside of normal local authority planning jurisdiction. For offshore wind, the consenting and leasing process is managed by the Crown Estate and BERR. This involves the identification of strategic areas for development and strategic environmental assessment. Local authorities will, however, be consultees in the process. The Thames Estuary is one of the three strategic areas in England identified for offshore wind development in the short term as future developments will be expected in this part of the region. Onshore infrastructure, such as sub-stations, may require planning permission. The assumed contribution to the regional targets from offshore wind/marine technologies is 200MW at 2010 and 300MW at 2016.

9.90 Sub-regional champions have been identified to take forward work on compiling more detailed assessments in each of the sub-regions. It is expected that the results of this work will allow a more detailed geographical breakdown of targets and relative potential of different renewable energy resources. Delivery will be monitored through See-Stats (www.see-stats.org).

Planning for Renewable Energy Resources

> **POLICY NRM15: LOCATION OF RENEWABLE ENERGY DEVELOPMENT**
>
> **Local development documents should encourage the development of renewable energy in order to achieve the regional and sub-regional targets. Renewable energy development, particularly wind and biomass, should be located and designed to minimise adverse impacts on landscape, wildlife, heritage assets and amenity. Outside of urban areas, priority should be given to development in less sensitive parts of countryside and coast, including on previously developed land and in major transport areas.**
>
> **The location and design of all renewable energy proposals should be informed by landscape character assessment where available. Within areas of protected and sensitive landscapes including Areas of Outstanding Natural Beauty or the national parks, development should generally be of a small scale or community-based. Proposals within or close to the boundaries of designated areas should demonstrate that development will not undermine the objectives that underpin the purposes of designation.**

9.91 Given the distribution of renewable resources and potential across the region, it is expected that renewable energy developments of all types will also come forward throughout the region. The region's potential will most likely be realised through a mixture of developments of different types and scales and integration of technologies into buildings. This could translate into a total of around 140 individual schemes (plus photovoltaic installations) by 2010, increasing to around 250 schemes (plus photovoltaics) by 2016 and 2026. This implies development of up to three wind energy clusters and four single large turbines per county area over the next 20 years plus at least one larger scale wind farm. Similarly, it may imply construction of one large biomass plant in each county area over the same time period and a larger number of smaller scale developments.

9.92 District councils and unitary authorities will be the planning authorities for the majority of land-based renewable energy schemes. LDDs, together with supplementary planning documents should reflect the availability of different resources and include guidance on the circumstances in which renewable energy developments will be acceptable in principle and be most likely to be permitted, taking into account the need to adapt to changing technologies.

9.93 Development of renewable energy infrastructure, particularly wind turbines, should be located and designed so as to avoid conflict with landscape and wildlife conservation, as set out in PPS7: *Sustainable Development in Rural Areas* and PPS9: *Biodiversity* and *Geological Conservation*. The scale and number of developments forecast in the assessments indicates that this should be achievable. Civil aviation and military requirements may also constrain wind development in certain areas.

9.94 Wind energy may only be exploited where it is sufficiently strong. An average wind speed of 6.5 metres per second (14.5 mph) has been generally regarded as the cut-off point for commercially viable developments although development at lower wind speeds (6 m/s) is likely to become more feasible with technological advances and price support provided by the Renewables Obligation.

9.95 Many of the areas with the highest wind speeds are on higher ground, within sensitive and protected countryside, including Areas of Outstanding Natural Beauty (AONBs) and the national parks in the New Forest and proposed in the South Downs. However, there are large parts of the region where there are no nationally important landscape or wildlife designations and wind speed is relatively high. It is expected that all local authorities in the region will accommodate at least one wind energy development over the next two decades.

9.96 Priority should be given to the development of renewable energy schemes, particularly larger scale ones, in less sensitive areas including previously developed and industrial land and areas where there is already intrusive development or infrastructure, for example major transport corridors. This could help to reduce the potential for conflict and delay in determining applications on visual impact and amenity grounds.

9.97 However, wind and other renewable energy development should not be precluded in AONBs and the national parks as there will be locations where small scale construction e.g. a wind development of between one and four turbines not generating more than 5MW, can be accommodated where conflict with statutory landscape protection purposes set out in PPS7 can be avoided or minimised through careful siting and design, including reducing the cumulative impact of a number of individual schemes.

9.98 The application of landscape character assessment, drawing on advice from Natural England, may help in identifying and developing guidance on location, scale and design of developments, particularly in areas of sensitive landscape. Renewable energy developments should not necessarily conflict with the objectives of Green Belt.

9.99 For biomass, issues to consider include the transportation of biomass fuel to the plant, the scale and design of buildings and the feasibility of combined heat and power. Operation of such plants, including monitoring and control of emissions, will be regulated by the Environment Agency to strict standards. Co-firing of conventional fossil fuel plants with biomass is likely to contribute to the achievement of the targets, at least in the short term, and should help create a market for, and stimulate, further development of biomass fuels.

9.100 Use of biomass fuel sourced close to the plant should be encouraged to maximise benefits in terms of carbon savings and rural development and reduced transport distances. Planting of energy crops has the potential to change landscape character and affect biodiversity, positively or negatively, depending on location. This is outside of planning control but the source of fuel, and location of plant in relation to this (its proximity) should be a consideration in determining proposals.

9.101 Community-based and owned projects, in which communities develop and operate projects and in which economic benefits are retained within a locality, will be important in improving understanding and acceptance, and enabling a steady build up of renewables in the region. In particular, such projects can demonstrate the wider benefits that may result from renewable energy projects, including employment creation and diversification and landscape management, and may be appropriate in more sensitive areas of countryside.

Renewable Energy Development Criteria

> **POLICY NRM16: RENEWABLE ENERGY DEVELOPMENT CRITERIA**
>
> Through their local development frameworks and decisions, local authorities should in principle support the development of renewable energy. Local development documents should include criteria-based policies that, in addition to general criteria applicable to all development, should consider the following issues:
>
> i. **the contribution the development will make towards achieving national, regional and sub-regional renewable energy targets and carbon dioxide savings**
> ii. **the potential to integrate the proposal with existing or new development**
> iii. **the potential benefits to host communities and opportunities for environmental enhancement**
> iv. **the proximity of biomass combustion plant to fuel source and the adequacy of local transport networks**
> v. **availability of a suitable connection to the electricity distribution network.**

9.102 All proposals should be considered on their individual merits with regard to scale, location, technology type and cumulative impact. Identification of criteria may aid decision-making when assessing proposals coming forward.

9.103 However, it is essential that such criteria are phrased in a positive way and are seen as supporting other policies that generally encourage renewable energy development. The provisions and criteria of other policies, for example for protection of biodiversity, landscape and amenity will apply to all developments and should be considered in addition to those set out below. In addition, these issues will be part of environmental assessments undertaken for such developments.

9

The South East Plan - Regional Spatial Strategy for the South East

10 Waste and Minerals

Waste Management – The Need for Change

10.1 One of the most significant issues facing the Region is the growing amount of waste and how to manage it. The most recent statistics are as follows :

- in 2006, approximately 23.6 million tones (mt) of waste was managed at permitted waste management facilities in the South East. Approximately 12mt was sent to landfill (of which almost 2.3mt was imported into the region from London), nearly 6.1mt went to transfer facilities, approximately 3.7mt went to treatment facilities, approximately 1.1mt went to metal recycling sites, and the throughput of permitted waste incineration facilities was approximately 700,000 tonnes
- the total included 4.6mt of Municipal Solid Waste (MSW – collected by local authorities) of which almost 54% was landfilled and 34% was recycled or composted
- in addition, approximately 36,000 tonnes of agricultural waste was managed in the South East during 2006. (This figure is considerably lower than previously reported, as it does not include organic wastes such as manure and slurry, which are not defined as wastes when applied to land for agricultural or ecological benefit.)
- the Environment Agency estimated that in 2002/03 the South East produced approximately 8.9mt of Commercial and Industrial (C&I) waste, of which just under half was landfilled
- a Construction, Demolition and Excavation waste (C&D) survey conducted by the Department for Communities and Local Government estimated that the South East received approximately 14.2mt of C&D waste, 6.6mt of which was recycled as aggregates or soil
- between 2001 and 2006, inputs to landfill have decreased by approximately 20% whilst waste through transfer and treatment facilities increased by 12% and 57% respectively. However between 2005 and 2006, waste sent to landfill increased by approximately 5%. In the same year inputs to transfer facilities decreased by 1%, and waste sent through treatment facilities increased by 14%.

10.2 If this continues, landfill capacity will be used up within a decade, valuable resource potential will be wasted and waste management and environmental problems created for the future. European and national policies demand that the proportion of waste from which we recover value is increased, and that the proportion of waste sent to landfill is decreased.

A Resource Management Approach

10.3 A new approach is needed. To achieve the necessary change this Plan adopts a resource management approach reflecting the waste hierarchy which prioritises reduction, re-use, recycling and recovery of value before disposal is considered, and the concept of 'zero waste' which takes as its long-term aspiration the elimination of waste through changes in product design, behaviour management and changes in the economy. This means treating materials that are currently perceived as waste as a resource, with value. It also means taking account of the use of resources as a whole, particularly energy, in managing waste. In addition, new restrictions on the types of waste that can be accepted at landfill sites are creating a need for increased capacity in alternative management methods.

10.4 Together these policies require an urgent and rapid development of a significant amount of new infrastructure, the delivery of which is a key objective for this Plan. Through technological innovation and investment in new facilities and systems, coupled with the potential increase in profits from best practice in waste minimisation and waste re-used, or sold, as recovered materials, this also represents an economic development opportunity for the region, consistent with the policy of smart growth.

10.5 This shift in emphasis will not be easy and will not be achieved immediately or through regional spatial policy alone. The key actions needed in taking a resource management approach include:

- engagement at all points of the design/production/consumption/waste management chain to achieve waste avoidance and minimisation at all stages, recovering and returning materials back into the production system and being efficient in the use of resources
- establishing resource recovery systems which will require new infrastructure to recover, reprocess and transform waste material into useful products. This requires a focus on key material streams (e.g. aggregates, food waste, paper and metals), rather than waste origins i.e. household/commercial/construction, segregation as far as possible, and the most appropriate methods to maximise recovery. The creation of a more commercial environment would help; one in which operators are encouraged and prepared to invest in the collection and treatment of C&I wastes
- facilitating delivery of many more facilities and sites on the ground through the planning system. Achieving the vision requires a switch to industrialised waste reception, storage and processing, including a range of facilities and activities such as Materials Recovery Facilities (MRFs), aggregates processing, composting, anaerobic digestion and other energy recovery plants. There will also be a need for dis-assembly plants and a range of other new industries. Resource parks, where related resource management activities are clustered together, would facilitate synergies between activities thus maximising the potential for recovery.

POLICY W1: WASTE REDUCTION

The regional planning body, SEEDA, the Environment Agency and other regional partners will work together to reduce growth of all waste to 1% per annum by 2010 and 0.5% per annum by 2020 by:

i. **encouraging waste reduction in all regional and local strategies**
ii. **identifying and disseminating examples of good practice and encouraging local authorities and businesses to implement waste minimisation programmes**
iii. **establishing a regional working group to identify opportunities and priorities for waste reduction in relation to supply chains, product design, manufacture, labelling, retailing, procurement, consumption and resource recovery**
iv. **developing enhanced regional information and awareness programmes to alter individual and corporate behaviour.**

10.6 The waste hierarchy requires **reduction** as the first stage of resource management. The levels of waste to be managed in the other policies in this chapter are based on a significant slowing in the growth rate so that by the end of the period of the Plan the amount of waste produced will have largely stabilised. Policy W1 provides the framework for regional partners to work with consumers, industry and all tiers of local government to raise awareness of the need to reduce waste and achieve the minimisation and reduction rates necessary. Monitoring of growth rates will be essential and forecasts will be regularly reviewed. It is important not to make overly optimistic assumptions about reduction as these may diminish the focus on the scale of new waste management infrastructure that needs to be delivered.

10.7 Reducing the growth in waste requires measures other than spatial planning, such as fiscal, and a combination of producer responsibility legislation, raised awareness and behavioural changes by both consumers and industry. Successful initiatives rely on changing people's attitudes and behaviour, through education or encouragement. The Government is committed to a number of initiatives to create opportunities for the reduction, re-use, recycling and energy recovery of waste, such as:

- increasing the landfill tax escalator so that the standard rate of tax will increase by £8 per year from 2008 until at least 2010/2011 to give greater financial incentives to businesses to reduce, reuse and recycle waste (from £24 now to £48 in 2010).

- consulting on removing the ban on local authorities introducing household financial incentives for waste reduction and recycling
- introducing enhanced capital allowances for investment involving the use of secondary recovered fuel for combined heat and power facilities.

10.8 To help reduce C&I waste generation, and thus the cost to industry, through resource efficiency, design, packaging and labelling, a number of local, regional and national networks and initiatives exist where good practice is promoted and exchanged by the private and public sectors. For example Sustainable Business Partnerships, the Envirowise programme, Egeneration and the South East England Development Agency's (SEEDA) sustainable business awards schemes, which now has a waste minimisation category. There is significant scope for SEEDA to extend its role further, for example in promoting innovation in waste minimisation.

10.9 The regional planning body, with the South East Regional Technical Advisory Body for waste (SERTAB) where appropriate, will continue to review and disseminate best practice, raise awareness, encourage changes in practice and inform advocacy of changes required in legislation and support. Compliance with this Plan, the sustainability appraisal process and guidance provided in the South East Regional Sustainability Framework applied to waste and local development frameworks, and waste management plans, will ensure that reduction and the resource management approach become key elements in policy formulation and implementation.

POLICY W2: SUSTAINABLE DESIGN, CONSTRUCTION AND DEMOLITION

Development plan documents will require development design, construction and demolition which minimises waste production and associated impacts through:

i. **the re-use of construction and demolition materials**
ii. **the promotion of layouts and designs that provide adequate space to facilitate storage, re-use, recycling and composting.**

In particular, development in the region's strategic Growth Areas, Growth Points and strategic development areas should demonstrate and employ best practice in design and construction for waste minimisation and recycling.

10.10 Building activity is a significant contributor to waste production and improved waste management in this sector is a key dimension for advocacy and action. Fortunately there is already a relatively high degree of re-use of C&D waste on-site and 36% of the managed waste stream is also currently re-cycled. This could be further encouraged through the selection of materials and techniques used in construction, and the design of buildings to accommodate space which will facilitate recycling and re-use.

10.11 The large-scale proposals in the region's Growth Areas and Growth Points, the strategic development areas, Regional Hubs and areas that may be developed as eco-towns present major opportunities to implement this policy and demonstrate best practice.

10.12 The Government's Code for Sustainable Homes includes a requirement for Site Waste Management Plans and contains other proposals which will contribute to the aims of this policy.

POLICY W3: REGIONAL SELF-SUFFICIENCY

Waste authorities and waste management companies should provide management capacity equivalent to the amount of waste arising and requiring management within the region's boundaries, plus a declining amount of waste from London. Provision of capacity for rapidly increasing recycling, composting and recovery should be made reflecting the targets and requirements set out in this chapter.

Provision for London's exports[1] will usually be limited to landfill in line with the Landfill Directive targets and, by 2016, new permissions will only provide for residues of waste that have been subject to recycling or other recovery process. Waste planning authorities (WPAs) should provide landfill capacity for the following apportionment of London's exported waste:

Landfill Provision to be Made for London Waste

Waste Authority Area	2006-2015		2016-2025	
	Apportionment %[2]	Million tonnes	Apportionment %[2]	Million tonnes
Berkshire Unitaries	9.3	1.12	8.6	0.63
Buckinghamshire	17.6	2.12	16.2	1.18
East Sussex, Brighton and Hove	8.8	1.06	8.1	0.59
Hampshire, Portsmouth, Southampton and New Forest National Park	0	0	7.8	0.57
Kent & Medway	13.1	1.58	12.1	0.88
Milton Keynes	10.8	1.30	10	0.73
Oxfordshire	18.7	2.26	17.2	1.26
Surrey	11.5	1.39	10.6	0.77
West Sussex	10.2	1.23	9.4	0.69
SE TOTAL	100	12.1[1]	100	7.30[3]

(1) Estimated imports of MSW and C&I from London in 2006 is 1.21 million tonnes (Source: Environment Agency note for Inter Regional Waste Forum, March 2008).

(2) From 'Towards a Methodology for Apportionment of London's Exported Waste', Alternative Apportionment Options: Revision for EiP, page 15, option 2f, Jacobs Babtie report, January 2007. For 2006-2015 these have been amended based on advice from SEERA to reflect the Hampshire M&W Core Strategy.

(3) Reduced to reflect Policy W5 MSW/C&I diversion targets.

Provision for recovery and processing capacity for London's waste should only be made where there is a proven need, with demonstrable benefits to the region, including improving the viability of recovery and reprocessing activity within the region, and in the nearest appropriate location. A net balance in movements of materials for recovery and reprocessing between the region and London should be in place by 2016.

The regional planning body will continue to work closely with all neighbouring regions to monitor and review waste movements and management requirements.

The figures in the above table should be used as a benchmark for the production and testing of development plan documents, but WPAs should use more recent data where this is available in order to assess and plan for capacity. Any major changes to the figures may dictate a need to reconsider the apportionment through a review of the RSS.

10.13   The South East is a major importer of waste, mostly from London, with a smaller amount from the South West. London currently has limited capacity for waste processing and recovery and very little landfill and planned capacity falls well short of its current and future management requirements. To address this shortfall the London Plan sets targets for recovery, composting and increasing self-sufficiency, and proposes a large increase in capacity and a number of new facilities. However London will continue to be reliant on capacity in surrounding regions well into this Plan period.

10.14 Net regional self-sufficiency will be achieved by providing for capacity equivalent to the waste forecast to require management within its boundaries (Policy W7), plus an allowance for disposal of a declining amount of waste from London for landfill. Imports from London to the South East of municipal, C&I waste are currently estimated to be approximately 1.2 million tonnes per year.

10.15 A methodology to apportion these exports has been developed taking into account existing landfill voidspace, geology and environmental constraints to development of new landfill, proximity to London, and sustainable transport. The resulting apportionment is set out in the table in Policy W3 and should be used as the basis for further testing in production of waste development frameworks, taking into account more detailed information about site suitability and availability. There will inevitably be a transition period where materials accommodated will be a function of existing contracts. Although C&D waste is not covered in Policy W3, London exports of this material contribute to more specialised needs, such as for the treatment of contaminated soils (Policy W15), and for recycling facilities (Policy M2).

10.16 Beyond 2016, new provision for landfill to accept London's waste will be limited to residues. In addition, it is assumed that London's exports to landfill in the region will gradually decline (at a rate comparable to the region's own reduction in reliance on landfill as set out in Policy W13), reflecting the achievement of greater self-sufficiency in London. It is anticipated that exports of municipal and C&I waste for disposal in landfill will gradually decline to 0.7mt in 2026. The regional planning body will continue to work with the Greater London Authority and the regional planning body for the East of England to monitor inter-regional waste movements and coordinate development and implementation of respective policies.

10.17 There may be situations where the use of facilities within the region for recovery or processing of waste materials from London, or other regions, would also be appropriate. For example, where the facility is the nearest available to the source of materials, where there are good sustainable transport links, and where this would make provision of recovery or reprocessing capacity more viable. Conversely, London might be able to provide facilities for waste from the South East. The overall objective is of a net balance in the flows of materials for recovery and reprocessing. The reference to 'recovery' in Policy W3 as an element of the net balance, but only in this instance, excludes incineration with energy recovery.

Definitions

Residues

Residues of waste are defined as "waste where further value cannot be recovered", although there are economic and market limitations on how this is interpreted at any one time.

Recovery

Throughout this chapter the terms 'recover' and 'recovery' are used consistently (with one exception) to comply with the following definition in Waste Strategy 2000, para 2.36, page 21:

" 'Recovery' means to obtain value from wastes through one of the following means:
- *recycling*
- *composting*

- *other forms of material recovery (such as anaerobic digestion)*
- *energy recovery (combustion with direct or indirect use of the energy produced, manufacture of refuse derived fuel, gasification, pyrolysis or other technologies)."*

The European Court of Justice Judgement (C-458/2000) ruled that energy obtained from packaging waste through a dedicated municipal incinerator may no longer be called recovery.

The exception is in Policy W3 where recovery, as an element of a net balance in movements between the South East and London, does <u>not</u> include incineration with energy recovery.

POLICY W4: SUB-REGIONAL SELF-SUFFICIENCY

Waste planning authorities (WPAs) will plan for net self-sufficiency through provision for management capacity equivalent to the amount of waste arising and requiring management within their boundaries. A degree of flexibility should be used in applying the sub-regional self-sufficiency concept. Where appropriate and consistently with Policy W3, capacity should also be provided for:

i. waste from London
ii. waste from adjoining sub-regions (waste planning authority area within or adjoining the region).

WPAs should collaborate in the preparation of plans, including identifying and making provision for potential flows across the regional and sub-regional boundaries, and identifying possible sites that could be served by sustainable transport modes. Co-operation will be encouraged between county councils and unitary authorities at the sub-regional level, particularly in respect of meeting the needs of the region's strategic growth areas.

10.18　Sub-regional self-sufficiency will be sought, while accepting that movement of waste between sub-regions will occur and is often necessary to reduce long distance transport. The level of self-sufficiency capable of being achieved will depend principally on:

　　i. the characteristics of the sub-region e.g. the extent to which there are major settlements close to its boundaries, and opportunities for use of sustainable transport modes
　　ii. the nature of the waste stream, with greater control being capable of being influenced over MSW than C&I and C&D
　　iii. the type of facility, with wider catchment areas necessary to justify more specialised reprocessing facilities such as MRFs.

10.19　Sub-regions will generally be based on combinations of waste planning authority areas where management is more effective on a cross boundary basis. Joint working, particularly in Growth Areas and the provision of larger facilities serving cross-border catchments, will be required between Kent and Medway; Hampshire, Portsmouth, Southampton and the New Forest National Park; West Sussex, East Sussex and Brighton and Hove; the unitary authorities of Berkshire; and between Buckinghamshire and Milton Keynes.

POLICY W5: TARGETS FOR DIVERSION FROM LANDFILL

A substantial increase in recovery of waste and a commensurate reduction in landfill is required in the region. Accordingly, the following targets for diversion from landfill of all waste need to be achieved in the region (Policy W6 targets are a component of these):

Year	Municipal Solid Waste (MSW)	Commercial and Industrial (C&I)	Construction and Demolition (C&D)	All Waste	
	mt/yr	mt/yr	mt/yr	mt/yr	%
2008	2.0	5.2	10.0	17.2	68
2010	2.5	5.8	10.1	18.4	71
2015	3.9	7.4	10.4	21.7	79
2020	4.7	8.7	10.7	24.0	84
2025	5.1	9.4	10.9	25.5	86

Regional Targets for Diversion from Landfill.

Source: Regional Waste Management Capacity: Survey, Methodology and Monitoring, Updated Final Report, 2008 (modelled Scenario 1)

Note: Percentage targets for diversion from landfill in the year 2008 have been interpolated.

Waste planning authorities (WPAs) should ensure that policies and proposals are in place to contribute to the delivery of these targets, and waste management companies should take them into account in their commercial decisions. The optimal management solution will vary according to the individual material resource streams and local circumstances and will usually involve one or more of the following processes:

- re-use
- recycling
- mechanical and/or biological processing (to recover materials and produce compost, soil conditioner or inert residue)
- thermal treatment (to recover energy)
- priority will be given to processes higher up this waste hierarchy.

WPAs should continue to provide sufficient landfill capacity to process residues and waste that cannot practicably be recovered.

10.20 The targets in Policy W5 incorporate the assumed scale of recycling and composting in Policy W6. They refer to overall diversion from landfill, which includes recovery but also treatments that may be excluded from this definition.

10.21 Compared with the national targets in Waste Strategy for England 2007, the MSW recovery element of Policy W5 is 35% in 2005 (compared with the national target of 40%) 52% in 2010 (compared with 53% nationally) and 74% in 2015 (compared with 67% nationally). The targets take in to account the following:

  i. landfill directive targets for diversion of biodegradable municipal waste
  ii. waste strategy for England 2007 targets for recovery of municipal solid waste, and for recycling /composting (treated as one component) of household waste
  iii. best value targets for recycling and composting of household waste
  iv. analysis of waste composition and assessment of practicable levels of recycling and composting.

POLICY W6: RECYCLING AND COMPOSTING

The following targets for recycling and composting should be achieved in the region:

Waste and Minerals

Year	Municipal Solid Waste		Commercial and Industrial		Construction and Demolition		All Waste	
	mt/yr	%	mt/yr	%	mt/yr	%	mt/yr	%
2008	1.6	36	3.9	46	5.8	48	11.3	45
2010	1.9	40	4.5	50	6.1	50	12.9	50
2015	2.6	50	5.5	55	6.1	50	15.0	55
2020	3.1	55	6.4	60	7.3	60	17.1	60
2025	3.6	60	7.3	65	7.3	60	19.1	65

Regional Recycling and Composting Targets

Source: Regional Waste Management Capacity: Survey, Methodology and Monitoring, Updated Final Report, 2008 (modelled Scenario 1)

Note: Percentage targets for diversion from landfill in the year 2008 have been interpolated.

Waste authorities should adopt policies and proposals to assist delivery of these targets and waste management companies should take them into account in their commercial decisions.

10.22 The regional targets in Policy W6 require a large increase in the amount of all waste recycled and composted from around nine million tonnes in 2002/3 (35% of all waste) to over 15 million tonnes by 2015 (55%) and almost 20 million tonnes by 2025 (65% of all waste).

10.23 To ensure that sufficient facilities are developed, development plan documents will identify specific sites to allow for recycling, composting, reprocessing and transfer facilities, and safeguarded to protect them from other development since high land prices can hinder the development of waste recycling facilities. Sites should generally be located in or near to urban areas, close to the main sources of waste, although a range of facilities will also be needed to serve rural areas.

10.24 Consideration should be given to upgrading or expanding existing sites, on the presumption that these sites are suited to community needs, have an established waste management use, may have necessary infrastructure, and may be more likely to gain planning permission. Co-location of facilities will enable a more integrated approach to all wastes to be developed, assisting reprocessing and development of markets for recycled materials.

10.25 Inert waste recycling facilities will also be required as most existing facilities are situated at landfill sites and have temporary consents. Inert waste recycling facilities can be acceptable on some employment sites particularly if the site is in close proximity to sources of waste. In these cases, they will need to operate to higher environmental standards if in proximity to homes and business.

10.26 Until 2015, the targets for recycling and composting of municipal solid waste exceed national targets because of the current high levels of recycling in the region and because its settlement pattern and general levels of prosperity suggest that these higher levels are achievable. Longer-term targets are more aspirational, setting a direction for continuing innovation and improvement.

POLICY W7: WASTE MANAGEMENT CAPACITY REQUIREMENTS

Waste planning authorities (WPAs) will provide for an appropriate mix of development opportunities to support the waste management facilities required to achieve the targets set out in this strategy. The annual rates of waste to be managed as shown in the table below provide benchmarks for the preparation of development plan documents and annual monitoring.

Waste Authority Area	Waste Type	2008-2010	2011-2015	2016-2020	2021-2025
Berkshire Unitaries	MSW	441	480	522	563
	C&I	845	919	999	1061
Buckinghamshire	MSW	272	296	322	347
	C&I	993	1080	1175	1247
East Sussex, Brighton & Hove	MSW	391	426	463	499
	C&I	446	485	527	560
Hampshire, Southampton, Portsmouth and New Forest National Park	MSW	910	990	1077	1160
	C&I	1785	1942	2113	2242
Isle of Wight	MSW	97	105	115	123
	C&I	147	160	174	185
Kent & Medway	MSW	958	1042	1133	1221
	C&I	2120	2307	2509	2663
Milton Keynes	MSW	123	134	146	157
	C&I	27	29	32	34
Oxfordshire	MSW	319	347	377	406
	C&I	630	685	745	791
Surrey	MSW	638	694	755	813
	C&I	830	903	982	1042
West Sussex	MSW	473	514	559	603
	C&I	943	1026	1116	1185

Average Tonnages to be Managed (thousand tonnes)

Waste and Minerals

> Source: Regional Waste Management Capacity: Survey, Methodology and Monitoring, Updated Final Report, 2008 (modelled Scenario 1)
>
> Note: MSW and C&I data used excludes both intra and inter-regional waste movements.
>
> In bringing forward and safeguarding sites for waste management facilities, WPAs should consider the type, size and mix of facilities that will be required, taking into account:
>
> - activities requiring largely open sites, such as aggregate recycling and open windrow composting
> - Activities of an industrial nature dealing with largely segregated materials and requiring enclosed premises, such as materials recovery facilities, dis-assembly and re-manufacturing plants, and reprocessing industries
> - activities dealing with mixed materials requiring enclosed industrial premises, such as mechanical-biological treatment, anaerobic digestion and energy from waste facilities
> - hybrid activities requiring sites with buildings and open storage areas, including re-use facilities and enclosed composting systems.
>
> In areas of major new developments consideration should be given to identifying sites for integrated resource recovery facilities and new resource parks accommodating a mix of activities where they meet environmental, technical and operational objectives.
>
> The figures in the above table should be used as a benchmark for the production and testing of development plan documents, but WPAs should use more recent data where this is available in order to assess and plan for capacity. Any major changes to the figures may dictate a need to reconsider the apportionment through a review of the RSS.

10.27 There is an immediate and acute shortfall in the capacity required to achieve the ambitious targets for recycling, composting and other forms of recovery, including energy recovery, and the overall diversion of waste from landfill. There needs to be a rapid increase in management capacity, and the mixture of facilities, and regional waste planning authorities must start to address this shortfall now. The urgency for this is compounded by the long lead-time for many facilities and difficulties in obtaining planning permission.

10.28 To deliver this additional capacity and as the basis for the preparation of waste development documents, Policy W7 provides targets for the tonnages to be managed in each sub-region. These targets should be considered alongside the overall tonnages requiring management, and the apportionment of London's waste, in Policies W3, W5, W6 & W13. In addition to the provision of facilities in waste development documents, it is essential that sites are also safeguarded in local development frameworks. In two tier areas authorities should work together to achieve site identification and safeguarding.

10.29 To illustrate the scale of the need, the following table provides an illustration of the additional capacity required to meet the management requirements of the Strategy at 2015.

Illustrative Additional Capacity Required by 2015 (million tonnes)

Waste Authority Area	MSW/C&I Recycling and Composting*	MSW/C&I Recovery	C&D Recycling
Berkshire unitaries	0.060	0.049	- 0.836
Buckinghamshire	0.015	- 0.299	0.014
East Sussex, Brighton and Hove	- 0.020	0.488	- 0.185

Hampshire, Southampton, Portsmouth and New Forest National Park	- 0.119	1.024	0.136
Isle of Wight	- 0.078	0.060	- 0.085
Kent	- 0.761	0.440	1.084
Medway	0.293	0.034	1.034
Milton Keynes	0.158	0.035	- 0.031
Oxfordshire	0.206	- 0.102	0.191
Surrey	- 0.482	- 0.155	0.322
West Sussex	- 0.339	- 0.324	- 0.561
SOUTH EAST	- 1.069	1.252	1.083

Source: Regional Waste Management Capacity: Survey, Methodology and Monitoring, Updated Final Report, 2008 (modelled Scenario 1)

Note: Negative figures represent deficits/shortfall while positive figures represent surplus capacity.

* Data used for MSW/C&I Recycling and Composting capacity assumes that 20% of total waste transfer capacity delivers recycling.

POLICY W8: WASTE SEPARATION

Waste collection authorities and waste management companies should provide separate collections of recyclable and compostable materials as widely and as soon as practicably possible. Householders and small and medium-sized businesses should be encouraged to separate waste for collection by such schemes through information and promotional campaigns. Civic amenity sites should be organised to encourage separation of materials for re-use and recycling.

10.30   Best practice in Europe indicate that high recycling rates are being achieved through the application of a range of measures, including:

- incentives to participate e.g. kerbside collection and mandates to separate at source
- charging schemes or quotas to encourage source separation
- education and awareness raising
- producer responsibility measures that channel financial support to local authorities to collect the materials covered by legislation
- facilities to process recycled materials or recover materials from mixed waste, including mechanical and biological treatment.

10.31   In the UK, the highest recycling rates of municipal waste are achieved where regular kerbside collections of separated recyclable and compostable material are provided, together with provision of bins to encourage materials separation at civic amenity sites. Extension of current best practice in the UK could achieve recycling and composting rates of household waste between 27% and 36%, increasing to around 60% with extended separate collections.

10.32   There is scope for better integration of collections of recyclables from municipal and C&I waste, particularly given the relative size of the C&I waste stream and the ability to separate materials at source.

Waste and Minerals

10.33 There is scope for better integration of collections of recyclables from municipal and commercial and industrial waste, particularly given the relative size of the commercial and industrial waste stream and the ability to separate materials at source.

> **POLICY W9: NEW MARKETS**
>
> **The regional planning body, SEEDA, Waste Resources Action Programme (WRAP) and other partners will work together to establish regional and local programmes to develop markets for recycled and recovered materials and products.**

10.34 The development of markets for recycled materials is essential to ensure that materials collected for recycling have a value and are used effectively. Encouraging appropriate investment in the region would help reduce the transport of materials over long distances, provide economic opportunities and also encourage greater self-sufficiency in management. The potential for business development and job creation in recycling should be fully exploited. An important means of developing markets will be public sector procurement practices that require use of recycled materials.

> **POLICY W10: REGIONALLY SIGNIFICANT FACILITIES**
>
> The regional planning body will work with waste authorities, the Environment Agency, SEEDA, industry and WRAP to encourage provision of appropriate new or expanded regional and pan-regional scale recovery and processing facilities, supported by a sub regional network of bulking and sorting facilities. This should include two strategic resource recovery parks located at or with good access to ports.
>
> The material streams requiring regional or pan-regional facilities are:
>
> - paper and card
> - plastics
>
> Those requiring sub-regional facilities are:
>
> - glass
> - wood
> - tyres
> - electrical and electronic equipment
> - end of life vehicles

10.35 Greater resource recovery requires a small number of large scale specialist facilities serving larger catchments than waste planning areas or even the region as a whole. Waste planning and disposal authorities should encourage and set criteria for the determination of these facilities using the guidance in Policy W17. An initial analysis suggests that it may be appropriate to plan for specialist facilities for the following materials:

- **paper and card** - The current rate of approximately 4.4 million tonnes per year will rise as overall waste and recycling rates grow. The region already has major paper and cardboard recycling capacity in Kent that draws material from outside of the region, particularly London and there is potential for expansion in the South East. This requires large amounts of fresh water and plant is very capital-intensive so expansion of the existing facilities may present the greatest opportunity.
- **plastic** - Regional generation of recyclable plastics is estimated at approximately 1.6 million tonnes per year but the sector is very fragmented and a third of collected materials are exported. Processing plastic waste materials back to basic feedstock through pyrolysis may become viable and support development of new facilities.
- **glass** - Glass recycling is well-established but most is processed beyond the region. Current recyclable glass generation in the region is approximately 0.5 mt pa.

Manufacture of high value products may present opportunities for reprocessing investment in the region and lower value uses for glass are being developed including production of concrete, road surfacing material, construction aggregates, bricks, tiles and pipes.

- **tyres** -Approximately 50,000 tonnes of tyres are produced in the region each year, with the amount forecast to rise to 67,000 tonnes in 2012. There is an existing processing capacity shortfall that is forecast to worsen. There are several alternatives to landfill, all producing material that has potential for use. Much of the region's waste tyre production could be used as a fuel in cement kilns.
- **electrical equipment** -Regional generation of waste electrical and electronic equipment (WEEE) is estimated as 140,000 tonnes pa. There will be a need for several dismantling, disassembly and re-manufacturing facilities at the sub-regional level and facilities for batteries.
- **end of life vehicles** -Estimated regional generation is 330,000 vehicles and 310,000 tonnes per year. The Directive relating to end of life vehicles requires dismantlers to be authorised and sets out environmental treatment standards which may result in the closure of many existing facilities. A small number of new facilities (up to ten facilities with 30,000 unit capacity) may therefore be required throughout the region.

POLICY W11: BIOMASS

Waste collection, planning and disposal authorities should encourage the separation of biomass waste, as defined in the Renewables Obligation, and consider its use as a fuel in biomass energy plants where this does not discourage recycling and composting.

10.36   Approximately 45% of material currently collected at amenity sites and/or kerbside collections is green or wood waste which has the potential for use as a biomass fuel. Together with other biodegradable materials this qualifies as biomass under the Renewables Obligation and could play an important role in generating renewable energy. Ensuring that the material is uncontaminated with plastics – as required by the Renewables Obligation - will depend on separate collection of these materials, or adequate separation at a MRF. Use as a fuel will help change perception, away from a waste to a resource with value, however the definition needs to be clarified to reduce association with incineration of mixed waste.

10.37   Policies NRM13 and 14 contain targets for renewable energy generation. However the Plan is clear that renewable energy targets should not drive waste management decisions, which should be made in the context of the waste hierarchy and assessment of the optimal management solution. The targets also assume that as much biomass waste as practicably possible will be recycled and composted rather than used for energy generation.

POLICY W12: OTHER RECOVERY AND DIVERSION TECHNOLOGIES

The regional planning body, SEEDA, the Environment Agency and the regional partners will promote and encourage the development and demonstration of anaerobic digestion and advanced recovery technologies that will be expected to make a growing contribution towards the delivery of the regional targets for recovery, diversion from landfill, and renewable energy generation over the period of the Plan.

Waste development documents and municipal waste management strategies should only include energy from waste as part of an integrated approach to management. All proposed waste facilities should:

i.   **operate to the required pollution control standard**
ii. **include measures to ensure that appropriate materials are recycled, composted and recovered where this has not been carried out elsewhere.**

> Proposed thermal facilities should, wherever possible, aim to incorporate combined generation and distribution of heat and power.

10.38   Anaerobic digestion of biodegradable waste converts up to 60% of organic matter into biogas which can be burned to generate electricity and/or heat. The residue is inert and may be used as a soil improver or landfill cover, or further treated to improve its qualities as compost. There are a number of advantages over other recovery methods and this could be considered akin to composting in the hierarchy. There are a number of small plants in the region, including some for the treatment of sewage, but potential for much greater use of this technique.

10.39   Mechanical-Biological Treatment (MBT) where recyclables recovered from sorted or mixed waste are used to produce Refuse-Derived Fuel (RDF) or inert residue, is also a technology that can reduce landfill.

10.40   However markets for the residues from biological treatment are currently limited. For example suitable rural land for spreading improved digestate is difficult to find due to issues such as water quality, drainage and landscape character. In parallel with further research, improvement and promotion of the technologies there is also need for further work to provide market outlets for residues. This challenge should not be underestimated.

10.41   Energy generated from incineration of mixed waste is not eligible under the Renewables Obligation Order. However the biomass fraction of mixed waste that has been processed by an advanced technology (where gas or liquid fuel is produced using gasification or pyrolysis) qualifies under the Order and this may provide a stimulus to the development of these technologies.

10.42   Incineration of mixed waste with energy recovery represents a proven technology and there are a number of existing and planned plants in the region. It is often opposed locally due to fears about environmental, amenity and health impacts. However, incinerators are increasingly strictly regulated, emission of pollutants has declined, and the health effects of waste management have been the subject of recent research which did not highlight any adverse effects of incinerator emissions.

10.43   There are concerns that incinerators are inflexible and stifle other forms of recycling and recovery. Energy recovery, recycling and composting need not be mutually exclusive and contracts can, and should, be formulated to ensure that incineration will not compromise recycling and composting. Energy recovery should always be part of an integrated approach that allows for the highest levels of recycling and recovery practicable. This is a further advantage of the co-location of a mix of facilities.

10.44   Advanced thermal technologies, such as pyrolysis and gasification, are often regarded as a more acceptable and efficient means of recovering energy. These are currently not proven on a large scale in the UK. The development and piloting of new and advanced thermal technologies in the region will be supported if these prove to have demonstrated benefits over other technologies. However, it is not prudent to wait for technologies to develop before taking action to increase recovery and diversion of waste from landfill, and these technologies are considered unlikely to make a major contribution to the management of the region's waste management and recovery and diversion targets in the short-term.

POLICY W13: LANDFILL REQUIREMENTS

Waste development documents should provide for continuing but declining landfill capacity. Non-inert landfill capacity should be husbanded to provide for disposal of residual non-inert waste. At regional level there should be provision for at least the following landfill capacity:

Regional Landfill Requirements (mt/yr) 2008-2025

Year	MSW Landfill	C&I Landfill	C&D Landfill	SE Sub-Total	London Imports	SE inc. London Imports
2008	2.5	3.4	2.2	8.00	1.21	9.21
2010	2.3	3.1	2.1	7.48	1.03	8.51
2015	1.4	2.5	1.7	5.54	0.73	6.27
2020	1.0	2.0	1.5	4.44	0.55	4.99
2025	1.0	1.8	1.2	3.98	0.53	4.51

Source: Regional Waste Management Capacity: Survey, Methodology and Monitoring, Updated Final Report, 2008 (Modelled Scenario 1)

Landfill gas collection and energy recovery should be standard practice at all non-inert landfill sites.

10.45   If the proposed increases in recovery and diversion from landfill are achieved there is, in overall terms, sufficient landfill capacity to manage the region's waste, plus a declining amount of waste exported from London (see Policy W3), until approximately 2013-2014. Therefore there will be a continuing need for some additional landfill capacity for waste, including residues of recovery processes at sub-regional level. Non-inert landfill capacity should be managed as a limited resource and increasingly become the means of disposal of residues of other recovery and materials that would not benefit from, or cannot practicably be subject to, recovery processes.

10.46   Although the Landfill Directive will cause an increasing amount of biodegradable waste to be diverted from landfill, some biodegradable waste will continue to be disposed of and degrade to release methane-rich landfill gas. This powerful greenhouse gas can be captured and burned to generate power and/or heat through proven and economically feasible technology.

POLICY W14: RESTORATION

Development plan documents will secure high quality restoration and, where appropriate, aftercare of waste management sites so as to help deliver the wider environmental and social objectives of this Plan.

10.47   Where waste management operations or facilities are temporary, restoration and management to protect and enhance the environment, is required. Although landfill has often been used to restore worked out minerals sites, in future the opportunity for more imaginative restoration should be explored and delivered. Restoration can assist in delivering other regional and national environmental objectives, such as habitat re-establishment and biodiversity targets, new woodland and the provision of public amenity and recreational space. The South East England Biodiversity Forum is identifying opportunities and priorities for habitat re-establishment and the potential for restoration of minerals and waste sites to help achieve regional biodiversity targets.

POLICY W15: HAZARDOUS AND OTHER SPECIALIST WASTE FACILITIES

The regional planning body, and the South East Regional Technical Advisory Body for waste, through the Hazardous Waste Task Group will maintain guidance on regional hazardous waste management requirements. Current priority needs include:

> i. hazardous waste landfill capacity, particularly to serve the needs of the south and south-east of the region
> ii. treatment facilities for air pollution control residues (from combustion facilities)
> iii. treatment/de-manufacturing plant for waste electronic and electrical equipment, supported by a network of transfer facilities
> iv. a sub-regional network of contaminated C&D waste treatment facilities
> v. a sub-regional network of landfill cells for stabilised non-reactive hazardous wastes.
>
> **Waste development documents will :**
>
> vi. identify and safeguard sites for storage, treatment and remediation of contaminated soils and demolition waste
> vii. identify criteria for the determination of large scale specialist hazardous waste facilities
> viii. assess available landfill provision and, where necessary, encourage the creation of a protective cell for stable hazardous waste.

10.48 Hazardous waste deposits in the South East are dominated by oil and oil/water mixtures – 160,000 tonnes, approximately 33% of hazardous waste – and C&D waste, including contaminated soils, and asbestos - 170,000 tonnes, 35% of hazardous waste. The majority is landfilled.

10.49 Management of hazardous waste will change significantly over the next few years. European legislation directs hazardous waste away from landfill, imposes greater requirements for waste treatment and requires stricter pollution control. The European Hazardous Waste List will define many more types of waste as hazardous for the first time, and energy from waste will result in the generation of hazardous residues that require disposal.

10.50 Provision will be required for a small number of large-scale specialist facilities for hazardous waste streams. There is also a need for facilities for large volumes of source separated material, merchant recycling, complex phase separation, plasma/vitrification, and solidification.

10.51 Waste development documents should identify a range of sites and/or identify criteria for the determination of large-scale specialist facilities. These should be located and designed to make use of rail or water transport to reduce the environmental impact. Bulking facilities may also be needed located to enable inter-modal transfer.

10.52 The Regional Assembly and SERTAB have established a Hazardous Waste Task Group which has identified the priorities listed in Policy W15. The Group will continue to keep requirements and the effects of legislation under review.

> **POLICY W16: WASTE TRANSPORT INFRASTRUCTURE**
>
> **Waste development documents should identify infrastructure facilities, including sites for waste transfer and bulking facilities, essential for the sustainable transport of waste materials. These sites and facilities should be safeguarded in local development documents. Policies should aim to reduce the transport and associated impacts of waste movement. Use of rail and water-borne transport with appropriate depot and wharf provision should be encouraged wherever possible, particularly for large facilities.**

10.53 All waste management has transport implications. There is a need for facilities, such as bulking and transfer stations, to minimise travel by smaller waste collection vehicles, serve larger, more cost-effective waste treatment facilities and make use of more sustainable transport modes. Appropriate location of facilities such as at inter-modal terminals where materials can be transferred from road to rail or water, can reduce transport.

> **POLICY W17: LOCATION OF WASTE MANAGEMENT FACILITIES**
>
> Waste development documents will, in identifying locations for waste management facilities, give priority to safeguarding and expanding suitable sites with an existing waste management use and good transport connections. The suitability of existing sites and potential new sites should be assessed on the basis of the following characteristics:
>
> i. good accessibility from existing urban areas or major new or planned development
> ii. good transport connections including, where possible, rail or water
> iii. compatible land uses, namely:
>
> - **active mineral working sites**
> - **previous or existing industrial land use**
> - **contaminated or derelict land**
> - **land adjoining sewage treatment works**
> - **redundant farm buildings and their curtilages**
>
> iv. be capable of meeting a range of locally based environmental and amenity criteria.
>
> Waste management facilities should not be precluded from the Green Belt. Small-scale waste management facilities for local needs should not be precluded from Areas of Outstanding Natural Beauty and National Parks where the development would not compromise the objectives of the designation.

10.54   Policy W7 identifies the urgent need for a wide range of new waste management facilities which, with the emphasis on recycling and recovery rather than landfill, will increasingly need to be situated in permanent locations. If new facilities are to be developed in time for meeting the challenging targets in this Plan, it is essential that waste and local development documents are site-specific wherever possible, but also specify locational criteria to provide the basis for considering other proposals.

10.55   Many facilities will need to be developed close to the source of waste and will therefore generally be close to urban areas. Development in the countryside, particularly the urban fringe and where there are rural waste management needs, will also be required and may represent the most appropriate location for certain activities, such as composting.

10.56   Waste management facilities should not be precluded from designated areas such as Green Belt, Areas of Outstanding Natural Beauty (AONBs) or National Parks, if the objectives of more environmentally sustainable forms of waste management are to be met. This is particularly important in the South East because of the proportion of land covered by such designations and the pattern of high-density development. It is essential that waste facilities proposed in such areas are assessed in the light of local circumstances and national/regional policy, and are subject to good design and landscape character appraisal. Within Green Belts major developed sites may provide suitable locations (PPG2, Annex C).

10.57   The types of facility that might be considered cannot be specified and will depend on local circumstances. It is also important not to stifle technological innovation and advance by referring to lists of types of facility that may be treated as exclusive. However the types of facility likely to be justified in Green Belts, where the lack of suitable alternative sites, and proximity to urban areas and the source of waste may be important factors, are likely to be different to those likely to be justified in AONBs and National Parks where facilities will probably be smaller in scale and associated with rural communities.

10.58   The co-location of waste management facilities, for example in recovery parks on sites offering good transport links, can provide significant environmental benefits and enable economies of scale by allowing flexible, integrated facilities to be developed. Co-location can also assist the separation of waste for different types of recovery on one site. Waste and local development plan documents should identify sites that would be suitable for co-location, taking advantage of the opportunities available in major areas of new development.

Minerals

10.59   The South East is the most populous English region and subject to significant growth pressures. The maintenance of a healthy regional economy will require an adequate supply of minerals and minerals related products to support a major housing programme, deliver key infrastructure projects and provide the everyday products that we all use. However, planning policy also has to balance the essential requirements of the regional economy for minerals and manufactured products with the environmental impact arising from their extraction, processing and transport.

10.60   This Plan provides a set of policies and proposals to strike that balance. It replaces chapter 11 of existing Regional Planning Guidance for the South East (RPG9, June 2006).

Policy Framework

10.61   Regional minerals policies are guided by sustainable development as a key principle. This means that while delivering the minerals that the region and the nation needs, extraction and processing should:

- safeguard the region's naturally occurring minerals and encourage the use of suitable alternative construction materials where appropriate
- protect the environment and local amenity
- minimise the adverse impacts of the transport of minerals and construction materials.

10.62   Development proposed in this Plan will impose considerable demands on the provision of minerals and construction materials across the region. This applies particularly to construction aggregates which also have to make a contribution to the needs of London, as the capital has only limited primary resources and, in recent years, a generally static supply of traditional sea-borne materials. Extraction of aggregates at a high rate over the decades has now exhausted some reserves. Consideration of more difficult and sensitive sites in the region is now required along with a degree of reliance on other sources such as marine aggregates.

10.63   The management of transport demand is an important issue for the South East where much of the primary road network operates at, or above, capacity and because there is a shortage of freight paths on the rail network. As local minerals production concentrates on fewer, larger sites, it is likely that distances to markets will increase and, with the region largely dependent on hard rock imported over long distances, pressures on the transport network could intensify. Regional policy is therefore to encourage a modal shift to increase the proportion of minerals and manufactured products transported into and within the region by rail and sea. To achieve this capacity, constraints will need to be overcome, and existing and new depot and wharf sites to handle materials in bulk will need to be safeguarded.

10.64   Mineral working and processing can have an adverse impact on the environment and local amenity and, as a consequence, extensive mineral resources will remain unavailable for working. Mineral development frameworks should include policies to manage specific impacts such as noise and dust and encourage good site management and effective restoration.

10.65   Only exceptional circumstances would permit extraction or processing in locations of special landscape importance such as the Areas of Outstanding Natural Beauty, or internationally or nationally designated areas of nature conservation importance, such as Special Areas of Conservation, Special Protection Areas or Sites of Special Scientific Interest. However, the growth in the number of specially designated areas, notably the shortly to be designated South Downs and recently established New Forest National Parks, and the extent of environmental constraints generally is likely to cause difficulties in maintaining some minerals reserves across the region. Accordingly, the potential for mineral extraction to take place as carefully considered exceptions to national policy in areas subject to these constraints should be kept under review, especially if provision for land-won aggregates is to be maintained in line with national guidance.

Current Regional Minerals Supply

10.66   Supply patterns for the region's significant minerals are essentially national with the exception of sand and gravel and, to a lesser degree, clay. Quantitatively, the most important regional mineral, construction aggregates, is mainly used for the manufacture of concrete, as coated and uncoated roadstone and as a fill material. The main sources of supply in the South East are:

- **primary aggregates** – there are extensive deposits of sharp sand and gravel and to a lesser extent soft sand in the region, which generally enables local sources to supply nearby urban markets over short distances. Regional sources of crushed rock include Kentish ragstone, limestone and ironstone (for aggregate use) in Oxfordshire, and small quantities of sandstone in West Sussex.
- **secondary aggregates and recycled materials** – materials include construction, demolition and mineral waste, and other minerals such as chalk that can be used as a fill material.
- **imports** – marine-dredged aggregates from licensed extraction sites, mainly in the Channel, are an increasingly important source of supply, being landed at wharves on the Thames, in East and West Sussex and Hampshire. There are very limited indigenous reserves of hard rock in the region. Some hard rock is imported into the region by sea from distant sources such as Scotland and mainland Europe, and much of the remainder travels by rail from Somerset, Leicestershire and elsewhere. Inter-regional movements of land-won sand and gravel largely balance, but the lack of primary reserves in London attracts exports from the South East.

10.67   Other regionally or nationally significant minerals worked in the South East are clay, chalk, silica sand, and gypsum. Fuller's earth, previously of some importance regionally, is now only worked in small quantities in Oxfordshire and, following an examination of existing reserves and the extent to which the mineral has been replaced by other materials, is not considered to warrant further attention, subject to periodic review. There are other mineral resources in the region which have also been assessed but none of these is considered to be of regional significance in the period to 2016. For example, with the closure of the Kent coalfield, energy minerals are insignificant although hydrocarbons are exploited in modest quantities in West Sussex, Surrey and Hampshire.

10.68   The structure and distribution of the minerals industry in the South East is changing, reflecting national trends which are likely to affect future patterns of supply. Overall, the number of extraction sites is declining and the manufacture of products such as cement, bricks and plasterboard is becoming concentrated in fewer, bigger plants which supply larger areas, often on a regional or national scale. Some minerals are increasingly being imported for use in the region while manufactured products are also being imported from abroad to supply regional needs. The use of alternatives to natural minerals and the availability of synthetic materials may also influence future regional demand.

Future Supply of Minerals – the Overall Approach

10.69   The approach is to meet identified and justified needs for mineral supply in the region, but to do so by making significantly more efficient use of natural resources, including so-called 'waste' products, with a reduced overall environmental impact. This natural resource management approach mirrors the line taken for waste.

10.70   The core strategy for minerals therefore seeks to:

- encourage more efficient use of minerals in construction and manufacture, so as to reduce, and eventually eliminate, growth in demand
- make significantly more use of recycled materials

- meet the regional guideline for land-won primary aggregates and an appropriate proportion of the demand for other minerals from sites in the region, subject to demanding extraction, transport and restoration standards, wider environmental considerations and any available government guidance
- make use of an anticipated increase in aggregate resources from the English Channel, provided that this extraction is consistent with sustainable resource use
- import into the region sufficient hard rock and other minerals to meet those industrial and construction needs that cannot be supplied from indigenous regional minerals resources.

10.71 The supply of construction aggregates in the South East should be met from a significant increase in supplies of secondary and recycled materials, a reduced contribution from primary land-won resources and an increase in imports of marine-dredged aggregates.

10.72 The identification and approval of mineral sites, their working and their subsequent re-use/restoration cannot be seen in isolation. Minerals make a crucial contribution to wider economic and development activity. Workings and the transport of minerals have health and other social impacts, such as noise and dust, as well as more obvious environmental effects. Local extraction often has special significance for rural areas, whereas the import of material via wharves and depots impacts more in urban areas. Some parts of the region have particularly significant development needs, notably the regional growth areas, but cannot be adequately supplied from available local mineral resources, necessitating intra or extra-regional imports. Substantial areas of the region were largely excluded from consideration for mineral extraction as a result of their special character and designation.

10.73 Over the Plan period, it is expected that there will be a gradual change in the mix of these elements of supply, as construction efficiencies and recycling play an increasing part. It is anticipated that the demand for minerals will be gradually uncoupled from economic growth. In the longer term, any increase in consumption will be made up through increased use of alternative materials.

10.74 Mineral planning authorities should ensure that provision is made for sufficient supplies of aggregates, clay, chalk, silica sand and gypsum to be extracted and processed to meet regional and, where appropriate, national needs. This extraction process should be consistent with achieving the environmental protection and enhancement, and transport policies of this Plan. Although self-sufficiency of supply is in theory desirable, in practice it is unachievable at either regional or local level in the South East for minerals such as aggregates or gypsum.

Sustainable Construction and Environmental Management

POLICY M1: SUSTAINABLE CONSTRUCTION

The regional planning body, the South East England Development Agency, the construction industry, and other stakeholders will work to encourage the development of sustainable construction practices, and to promote good practice, reduce wastage and overcome technical and financial constraints, including identifying sustainable supply routes and seeking to reduce delivery distances. The long-term aspiration is that annual consumption of primary aggregates will not grow from the 2016 level in subsequent years.

Local development documents should promote the use of construction materials that reduce the demand for primary minerals by requiring new projects to include a proportion of recycled and secondary aggregates wherever practicable.

10.75 The promotion of environmentally sustainable design can reduce the demands placed on the region's natural resources by encouraging construction practices which use alternatives to primary minerals and increase energy efficiency. The construction industry is already developing alternative building products using synthetic materials or C&D

waste; examples include the manufacture of building blocks from ash, clinker and other waste materials, the use of desulphurgypsum in plasterboard manufacture and the development of new techniques in the manufacture of brick panels. There is also scope for reducing the demand for primary construction materials by cutting the amount of waste on construction sites, greater use of modern off-site building techniques and by more effective quality control and auditing of building projects, to ensure that wastage and the use of inappropriate materials is avoided. This can best be achieved through the regional planning body working with relevant organisations to encourage a sustainable approach to construction, to overcome technical and financial constraints and by promoting best practice.

10.76 The regional planning body will disseminate good practice on positive and creative planning needed in considering the use of mineral sites once extraction has ceased. After-use should be considered when determining an application and appropriate conditions should be attached to permissions to facilitate an appropriate after-use. In some cases, restoration to an agricultural or equivalent use would be appropriate; in other cases, another positive alternative use may be appropriate. Whatever the after-use, it will be essential that it is established to a high standard with appropriate aftercare and management. Best practice should also include effective communication with local communities throughout the planning, operation and restoration of mineral sites, including setting out clear timescales for the operation and restoration phases and adhering to these as far as possible. In addition, the regional planning body will work with the South East England Regional Development Agency and others to provide better signposting of advice on sustainable construction and disseminate good practice, for example, by making Growth Areas exemplars of best practice.

Recycling and Re-use

POLICY M2: RECYCLED AND SECONDARY AGGREGATES

The use of secondary aggregates and recycled materials in the South East should increase from 6.6mtpa (29% of the guidelines for primary aggregate production in the region) to at least 7.7mtpa (34%) by 2016 so as to reduce the need for primary aggregates extraction. To enable this target to be met, and where possible exceeded, mineral planning authorities (MPAs) should ensure that their mineral development frameworks enable provision to be made for the following:

Mineral Planning Authority Area	Apportionment of recycled and secondary aggregate provision (million tonnes per annum) by 2016
Berkshire Unitaries	0.7 mtpa
Buckinghamshire	0.6 mtpa
East Sussex/Brighton and Hove	0.5 mtpa
Hampshire/Portsmouth/Southampton/New Forest	1.7 mtpa
Isle of Wight	0.1 mtpa
Kent	1.4 mtpa
Medway	0.2 mtpa
Milton Keynes	0.2 mtpa
Oxfordshire	0.9 mtpa
Surrey	0.8 mtpa

West Sussex	0.8 mtpa

MPAs should identify sites to contribute to such provision in minerals development frameworks. Local planning authorities should safeguard these sites through their local development frameworks.

Policy W17: Location of Waste Management Facilities applies to all proposals for mineral recycling facilities. Where temporary recycling facilities are to be proposed in the Green Belt, Areas of Outstanding Natural Beauty or National Parks, they should be sited at existing minerals or waste sites wherever possible.

Note

The reference to mineral development frameworks should be taken to embrace mineral, waste or combined mineral and waste development frameworks.

10.77　National policy is to increase the use of secondary and recycled materials as substitutes for natural minerals, placing considerable emphasis on increasing the use of secondary aggregates in the construction industry as an alternative to dwindling reserves of primary aggregates. This is reflected in the waste policies, which set challenging targets for the recycling of construction and demolition (C&D) waste (see Policy W6: Recycling and Composting Targets). It is therefore a prime objective of regional minerals policy to increase supplies of secondary aggregates and encourage a greater use of mineral waste in the construction industry in accordance with the principles of sustainable development.

10.78　Recycled aggregate is principally derived from C&D waste, whilst recycled road planings also play a part. Secondary materials in the region come from spent rail ballast, pulverised fuel ash, waste glass and scrap tyres. The target set out in Policy M2 should be regarded as a minimum and the upper figure of 7.7mpta should have been exceeded by the end of the period.

10.79　Additional minerals recycling facilities will be required in the region to process C&D waste, as specified by Policy W15: Hazardous Waste, including provision for 'hub sites' to deal with the off-site remediation of contaminated soils.

10.80　To meet national and regional targets and the apportionment in Policy M2 above, mineral planning authorities should identify sufficient sites for recycling plants, primarily on brownfield sites or within new employment developments, to ensure that there is an increase in the recycling of C&D and other waste for use as secondary aggregates in the region. In identifying sites, mineral planning authorities should take into account:

　i.　the need for recycling operations to be located within a viable catchment area close to the origins of the waste material and to the subsequent markets. For construction and demolition materials, this will generally mean the main urban areas. Different considerations will apply to highways and railway depots, and more specialist facilities for recycling materials, such as pulverised fuel ash from power stations
　ii.　the ability for such recycling operations to be enclosed in an industrial building, although acknowledging that at present most are sited in the open
　iii.　the need to provide an indication of typical site sizes, acknowledging the need for materials storage before and after processing.

10.81　Since recycling facilities are concerned with the re-use of already extracted primary materials and will prevent the unnecessary exploitation of finite reserves, this should be regarded as a waste management activity. Policy W17: Location of Waste Management Facilities (and its supporting text) will therefore be relevant in translating this guidance into mineral development documents.

10.82   Given uncertainties in relation to data, and the fact that not all recycling requires dedicated facilities because of the use of mobile equipment on construction sites, the demand aspects of the apportionment in Policy M2 should be tested in preparing mineral or waste development frameworks.

Primary Aggregates

POLICY M3: PRIMARY AGGREGATES

The supply of construction aggregates in the South East should be met from a significant increase in supplies of secondary and recycled materials, a reduced contribution from primary land-won resources and an increase in imports of marine-dredged aggregates. Mineral planning authorities should plan to maintain a landbank of at least seven years of planning permissions for land-won sand and gravel which is sufficient, throughout the Plan period, to deliver 13.25 million tonnes (mt) of sand and gravel per annum across the region, based on the following sub-regional apportionment:

Berkshire Unitaries	1.57mtpa
Buckinghamshire	0.99mtpa
East Sussex/Brighton& Hove	0.01mtpa
Hampshire/Southampton/Portsmouth	2.63mpta
Isle of Wight	0.05mtpa
Kent/Medway	2.53mtpa
Milton Keynes	0.12mtpa
Oxfordshire	1.82 mtpa
Surrey	2.62mtpa
West Sussex	0.91mtpa

and 2.2 million tonnes of crushed rock per annum across the region, based on the following sub-regional apportionment:

Kent	1.2mtpa
Oxfordshire	1.0mtpa

10.83   The National and Regional Guidelines for Aggregates Provision in England, 2001- 2016, published by the former Office of the Deputy Prime Minister in June 2003, set a total aggregate supply figure for the region of 570mt over the period, a substantial reduction from the 1994 figure. They assumed an increased contribution from secondary and recycled materials (118mt) and included a guideline requirement for primary aggregates of 247mt. Imports of primary aggregates to the region from all sources (excluding marine sand and gravel) would remain significant at 85mt.

Waste and Minerals

10.84 Marine-dredged sand and gravel supplies should increase to 120mt for the period between 2001 and 2016, making a significant contribution to regional requirements. This will largely be dependant on the granting of additional dredging licences under the 'Government View' procedure, in particular to exploit new resources in the East English Channel, which are also likely to supply the near continent.

10.85 Local sand and gravel extraction cannot meet all the requirements of the South East. Construction also requires crushed rock but the geology of the region is such that hard rock resources are very limited. National guidance states that the regional supply of land-won sand and gravel (which was set at 16.5mtpa) should reduce to 13.25mtpa over the period. The supply of crushed rock should increase by 10% to a total of 2.2mtpa. An element of regional primary production should be used to supply London where natural resources are limited, but the capital would be expected to increase significantly supplies from recycling and secondary sources. Sand and gravel exports, including to London, are broadly balanced by imports from adjoining regions. In planning to meet the overall national guidelines figure, it is assumed that these constituent elements of that supply will also be met. Thus, for the period 2001-2016, it is assumed that 118mt will come from alternative materials, 212mt from land-won sand and gravel, 35mt from crushed rock, 120mt from marine sand and gravel, and 35mt from net imports. The National and Regional Guidelines for Aggregates Provision are in the process of being revised for the period 2005- 2020. The amount of sand, gravel and crushed rock that the South East will be expected to plan for is likely to be reduced.

10.86 The regional supply figure has been apportioned initially to mineral planning authorities or groups of mineral planning authorities on the basis of average sales over the last seven years (1995-2001), discounting years with the highest and lowest sales in each county to avoid exceptional demands (for example, arising from a major development project) distorting the longer term average production figure. The apportionment is considered a more accurate basis for distribution than a simple pro-rata reduction for each area. It has, however, been modified to take into account two exceptional factors: first, a particular peak of production in Buckinghamshire caused by two very large extraction programmes; secondly, the high level of overall production that would result in Oxfordshire and Surrey, relative to their geography and future housing needs.

10.87 The establishment of the New Forest National Park created a new minerals planning authority, as will the designation of the South Downs National Park, with the consequent need for a revised apportionment. No apportionment is proposed for the New Forest on the basis of the boundaries now established, but there is a commitment to working out the existing landbank of permitted reserves of sand and gravel in the one active extraction within the Park.

10.88 Although the apportionment is based on a logically and reasonably robust analysis, it is recognised that it is essentially derived from past rates of production, rather than an appraisal of future needs and the likely availability of materials, taking into account a more detailed analysis of environmental and other constraints. The regional planning body is therefore in the process of undertaking a review of the apportionment.

10.89 Mineral development documents should include policies that reflect the sub-regional apportionment figures for primary aggregates production. They should also set criteria against which planning applications for quarries, processing plants and wharves and depots for imports can be assessed and ensure that adequate facilities are available to meet future demand.

Other Minerals

POLICY M4: OTHER MINERALS

Future provision should be made in local development documents for clay, chalk, silica sand and gypsum as regionally significant minerals of national importance. Where practicable, substitute and recycled waste materials should be used to conserve natural

Waste and Minerals

resources, high quality reserves should be safeguarded for appropriate end uses, and new handling facilities developed where this would increase the quantity of minerals and manufactured products being transported by rail or water.

Mineral planning authorities should plan for:

- a permitted reserve of clay for brick and tile product manufacture, sufficient to last for at least 25 years at current production rates, should be maintained to supply individual works throughout the Plan period, and new manufacturing capacity developed if this would replace older plants or reduce net imports to the region; for small-scale manufacture, a long-term landbank of a lesser period than 25 years may be appropriate
- a permitted reserve of chalk for cement manufacture, sufficient to last for at least 25 years at current production rates, should be maintained throughout the Plan period in Kent and Medway
- a permitted reserve of silica sand should be maintained throughout the Plan period in Surrey and Kent, equivalent at current production rates, to at least 10 years at existing sites and at least 15 years at new sites
- a permitted reserve of gypsum, sufficient to last at least 20 years at current production rates, should be maintained throughout the Plan period in East Sussex to support the building product and cement industries, and the use of desulphurgpsum imported by rail over the shortest practicable distance should be encouraged.

10.90 Some non-aggregate minerals worked and processed in the South East have regional or national importance. They are clay for brick and tile production, chalk for cement manufacture, silica sand which has a number of industrial applications and gypsum which is used in plasterboard and cement manufacture. Mineral development documents should direct where and how future provision should be made for regional requirements, while future supplies need to be safeguarded.

10.91 It is recognised that there are other minerals worked in the region which contribute to the local economy and character, but which are worked on a smaller scale and have less impacts than those to which the policies apply in this strategy (such as brickearth or energy minerals); or which have no significant workings but provide a geological resource (notably fuller's earth). The contribution of these minerals should be dealt with appropriately in mineral development documents.

10.92 **Clay** -Unlike other non-aggregate minerals, clay occurs widely throughout the South East, its most significant use being in the manufacture of bricks, tiles and related construction materials. Brick is a durable, versatile and sustainable construction material that can be re-used or recycled, and which contributes greatly to local architectural styles.

10.93 The Weald and Wadhurst clays of the High Weald and the gault of the Low Weald are the principal regional clay resource, with most brick production taking place at works in East and West Sussex and Surrey. In Kent, most brick manufacture has been historically based on local supplies of brickearth and the majority of sites identified as suitable for extraction have now been worked out. The Lower Oxford Clays have been extensively exploited in Buckinghamshire but the Fletton brick plants in the north of the county were closed by 1994.

10.94 The region has significant deposits of brick clay with substantial permitted reserves which overall are sufficient to maintain local supplies to the brick and tile industry and meet regional requirements over the Plan period. Only in Hampshire, and possibly in Kent, is it likely that further reserves need to be identified. Mineral planning authorities should reassess those extensive areas covered by planning permissions for clay extraction which now have little or no commercial value for that purpose and old clay permissions that are now dormant. In order to maintain brick and tile manufacture within the region, it is important to maintain the high quality clay reserves for this use rather than for other uses such as for engineering landfill.

Waste and Minerals

10.95 **Chalk** -Although chalk is worked for a range of end-uses, its regional significance is as the major raw material (together with smaller quantities of clay and gypsum) for the manufacture of cement. Given the anticipated future supply patterns, there is unlikely to be any need to secure substantial new production capacity or reserves in the South East. However, producers will become increasingly reliant upon importation by sea (from European operations) and by road/rail from their other UK core works. Therefore suitable wharves and rail distribution sites should be protected from inappropriate development, which may constrain their future use. The limited number of producing plants in the UK and the growth in imports suggest that maintenance of regional cement manufacturing capacity and the safeguarding of associated mineral supplies are of importance to both the national economy and the delivery of the regional development strategy.

10.96 **Silica Sand** -Silica sand, or industrial sand, is a sparsely distributed and valuable mineral resource which is an essential raw material in many UK manufacturing industries. The major markets for silica sand from the South East are in high specification glass manufacture, a reflection of its purity and low alumina content, in the foundry industry and in other industrial processes. Silica sand is quarried from the Lower Greensand in Kent and Surrey. Future silica sand production in the region is likely to be confined to these counties, with the major extraction site located between Bletchingley and Godstone, where there are substantial reserves of high quality silica sand. These resources are potentially large enough to satisfy regional needs for high specification requirements in the Plan period.

10.97 **Gypsum** -Gypsum is exploited commercially in East Sussex and is an important raw material for the construction industry. It is used in the manufacture of plasterboard and other plaster-based products in the cement industry and in other industrial applications. Gypsum is mined and processed near Robertsbridge, where there is a plasterboard plant with a rail link and a purpose-built road access. The Robertsbridge works and its associated mine at Brightling have national importance as the only resource in southern England, with access to reserves expected to last for at least 30 years. It is unlikely that an alternative location for mining and processing would be needed in the South East.

10.98 **Others** -Oil is currently being extracted under Hampshire and Surrey. With regard to fuller's earth, the only permitted reserve remaining in the UK, other than that left at Woburn, Bedfordshire, is at Moor Mill (Baulking) in Oxfordshire where the dry reserve is estimated at 294,000 tonnes. While there is no specific regional policy regarding hydrocarbons or fuller's earth, it is important that mineral planning authorities with such resources within their area consider these as part of their preparation of mineral development documents.

Safeguarding of Wharves, Rail Depots and Mineral Reserves

> **POLICY M5: SAFEGUARDING OF MINERAL RESERVES, WHARVES AND RAIL DEPOTS**
>
> **Mineral planning authorities should assess the need for wharf and rail facilities for the handling and distribution of imported minerals and processed materials, and identify strategic sites for safeguarding in their minerals development frameworks. These strategic facilities should be safeguarded from other inappropriate development in local development documents. Existing mineral sites, and proposed sites and 'areas of search', should be identified in mineral development documents for the extraction and processing of aggregates, clay, chalk, silica sand and gypsum. These should then be safeguarded in local development documents.**

10.99 Mineral planning authorities should undertake assessments of the need for wharves and depots and, to assist the identification of those sites to be safeguarded, the following strategic criteria should be used:

  i. capacity to supply imported material to the region
  ii. proximity to markets

iii. value of the specialist infrastructure
iv. adequacy of existing or potential environmental safeguards.

10.100 Existing mineral workings and processing plants which have regional significance should also be protected from other development and further consideration given to extending safeguarding arrangements to larger known resources which are not specifically allocated in mineral development documents. All partners must work towards the aim of achieving a modal shift in the transport of minerals. Mineral development documents should include a requirement that any applicants for the development of alternative uses on wharf or depot sites must demonstrate that there is no realistic prospect of a transport use continuing or being reintroduced on the site.

Countryside and Landscape Management

11 Countryside and Landscape Management

11.1 The South East region is blessed with a diverse and, in many areas, high quality natural environment and countryside, including a particularly high proportion of nationally designated landscapes (covering 35 per cent of the region - higher than any other region). At the same time, the demand for new development in the region brings with it both risks to precious environments and opportunities to plan for growth in a way that protects and cherishes the countryside and landscapes that make up the region.

11.2 The importance of protecting and supporting the countryside is a fundamental objective for this Plan, as the countryside performs various functions that contribute to quality of life in the region. It is valuable:

- *Environmentally* - through its provision of key habitats, as a flood management resource and carbon sink, and as a provider of renewable energy sources and food
- *Economically* - through the jobs it creates, the millions of visitors it attracts and by helping the region retain and attract high value employees and businesses
- *Socially* - through the enjoyment and tranquillity it provides its users, and by providing recreational opportunities and supporting more healthy lifestyles.

11.3 Around two-thirds of the region is farmland or farm woodland. Agriculture, horticulture and forestry have essential roles to play in management of landscape and biodiversity, as well as commercial production. The strengthening of these land-based industries, and their ancillary industries, should be encouraged to enable them to effectively undertake these functions and support and maintain incomes and commercial viability. This will be particularly important in the light of changes occurring as a result of Common Agricultural Policy (CAP) Reform. The decoupling of payments from direct production to subsidies strongly linked to rural development, environmentally friendly farming systems and more modern farming methods will gradually be phased in during a transition period to 2012. While there is considerable uncertainty as to the effect of these changes on landscape and countryside management in the South East, CAP reform does offer substantial opportunities for the future of agriculture and the protection of the landscape through its new focus on agri-environmental schemes.

The New Forest National Park

POLICY C1: THE NEW FOREST NATIONAL PARK

High priority will be given to conserving and enhancing land and its specific character within the New Forest National Park. The local planning authority and other partners should also develop supportive sustainable land management policies, both inside the National Park and within the zone of 'New Forest commoning activity', including protection of grazing land outside the National Park which is needed to support National Park purposes.

In considering proposals for development, the emphasis should be on small-scale proposals that are sustainably located and designed. Proposals which support the economies and social well-being of the Park and its communities, including affordable housing schemes, will be encouraged provided that they do not conflict with the purposes for which the Park has been designated. Planning decisions should also have regard to the setting of the Park.

11.4 The Countryside Agency (now Natural England) designated the New Forest National Park in 2002 and the Government formally confirmed the new National Park in March 2005. The New Forest is located between the conurbations of Southampton to the east, and Bournemouth and Poole to the west, the latter being located within the South West region. Most of the National Park lies within Hampshire, with a small area in Wiltshire. A National Park Authority was established in April 2005 with a limited range of statutory powers and functions, and it became fully operational on 1 April 2006.

Countryside and Landscape Management

11.5 The Strategy for the New Forest 2003, prepared by the New Forest Committee, has been modelled on a National Park Plan with significant stakeholder input. The overall aim is to sustain and enhance the beauty and richness of the New Forest as a living, working landscape, with special recognition of the importance of commoning. It acknowledges that there are issues to be addressed that arise from the proximity of urban development to its boundaries, and its accessibility to visitors. As far as possible the area should therefore become a model for sustainability.

11.6 The Government recognises that each National Park is different, so although the overarching policy framework needs to uphold generic National Park standards and objectives, these need to be informed by more locally specific issues. There are special circumstances in the New Forest that warrant a tailor-made policy approach, due to the fact that it has the highest proportion of area in international nature conservation designations of any National Park; it is the smallest National Park; and is under intense pressure. There is also a need to protect areas outside the National Park for 'back-up' commoning land to sustain grazing in the open forest. Further work needs to be undertaken (perhaps by the New Forest National Park Authority) to provide advice to local planning authorities with regard to protecting the setting of the Park and safeguarding land with a functional relationship to it.

The South Downs National Park

> **POLICY C2: THE SOUTH DOWNS**
>
> **Pending the final approval of the proposed South Downs National Park, the purposes of its designation should be a material consideration in the making of any planning decision that may significantly affect the Park.**

11.7 On 31 March 2009, the Secretary of State for the Environment, Food and Rural Affairs announced that a South Downs National Park will be designated. The Designation Order for the National Park will be confirmed once a consultation on the proposed inclusion of six additional areas of land has concluded. It is expected that a National Park Authority will be established from April 2010 and will take on its full range of statutory powers and functions from 1 April 2011. Once the National Park is designated, the existing East Hampshire and Sussex Downs Areas of Outstanding Natural Beauty will be revoked.

Areas of Outstanding Natural Beauty

> **POLICY C3: AREAS OF OUTSTANDING NATURAL BEAUTY**
>
> **High priority will be given to conservation and enhancement of natural beauty in the region's Areas of Outstanding Natural Beauty (AONBs) and planning decisions should have regard to their setting. Proposals for development should be considered in that context. Positive land management policies should be developed to sustain the areas' landscape quality. In drafting local development documents, local planning authorities should have regard to statutory AONB Management Plans.**
>
> **In considering proposals for development, the emphasis should be on small-scale proposals that are sustainably located and designed. Proposals which support the economies and social well being of the AONBs and their communities, including affordable housing schemes, will be encouraged provided that they do not conflict with the aim of conserving and enhancing natural beauty.**

11.8 There are eleven designated Areas of Outstanding Natural Beauty (AONB) in the region, an indication of the landscape quality of the South East. The AONBs make a significant contribution to the distinctiveness of the South East, as well as helping support and sustain the region's high quality of life and economic success. The character of the

Countryside and Landscape Management

region's AONBs is influenced by the pressures on them, stemming from their accessibility to a large and mobile population, including those travelling from London to enjoy the region's countryside. In planning terms they require the same focus on protection and positive land management as National Parks. Within the AONBs statutory Management Plans provide a policy and action framework which should influence and help determine planning, decision making, advice and resource allocation priorities for local authorities, government agencies and statutory undertakers. In particular, they should provide an underpinning for the development of AONB specific policy in local development frameworks (LDFs).

11.9 Some AONBs in the region abut the coastline and coincide with stretches of Heritage Coast. Some current AONB designations extend to the high water mark, whereas planning law extends to the low water mark, leaving stretches of land on the coast which are not afforded the higher levels of protection afforded to AONBs. Local authorities should work to protect the setting of nationally designated landscapes down to the low water mark.

11.10 The South East's AONBs are shown on Diagram CLM1.

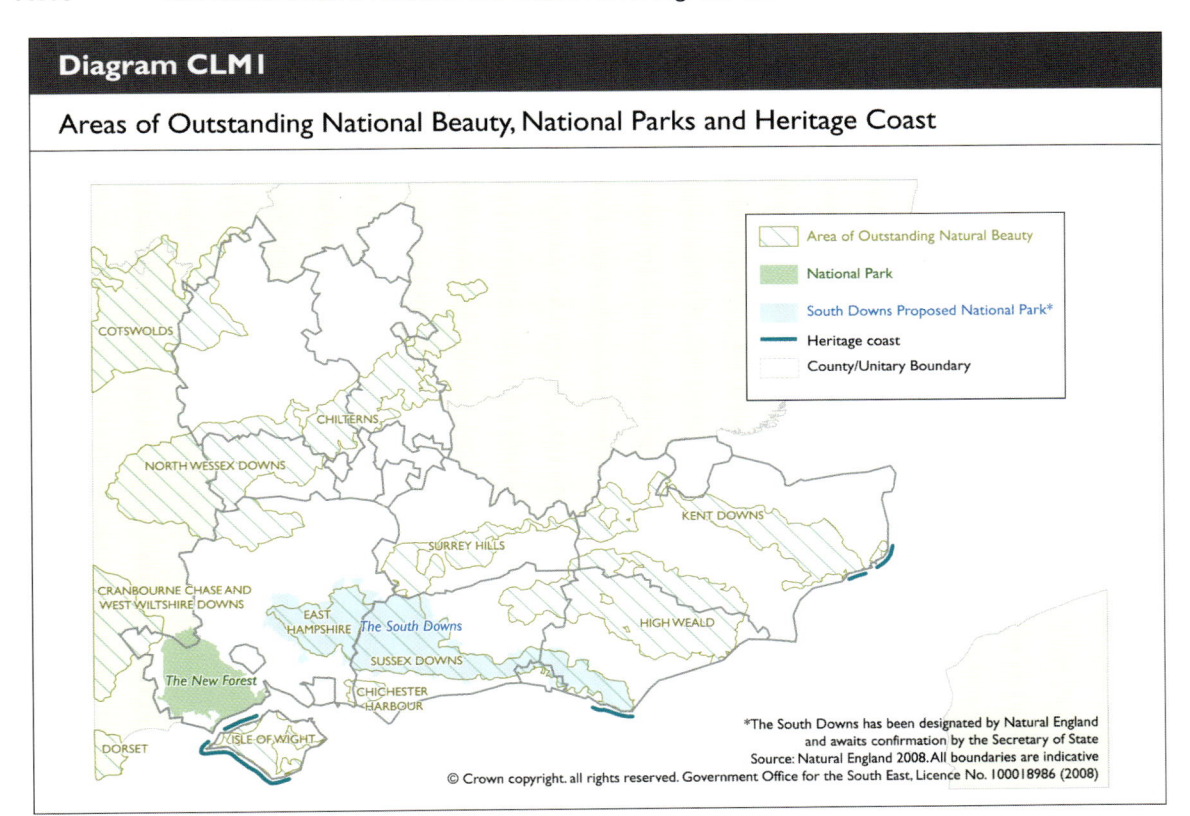

Diagram CLM1

Areas of Outstanding National Beauty, National Parks and Heritage Coast

*The South Downs has been designated by Natural England and awaits confirmation by the Secretary of State
Source: Natural England 2008. All boundaries are indicative
© Crown copyright, all rights reserved. Government Office for the South East, Licence No. 100018986 (2008)

Landscape and Countryside Management

POLICY C4: LANDSCAPE AND COUNTRYSIDE MANAGEMENT

Outside nationally designated landscapes, positive and high quality management of the region's open countryside will be encouraged and supported by local authorities and other organisations, agencies, land managers, the private sector and local communities, through a combination of planning policies, grant aid and other measures.

In particular, planning authorities and other agencies in their plans and programmes should recognise, and aim to protect and enhance, the diversity and local distinctiveness of the region's landscape, informed by landscape character assessment.

Countryside and Landscape Management

> **Positive land management is particularly needed around the edge of London and in other areas subject to most growth and change. In such areas long-term goals for landscape conservation and renewal and habitat improvement should be set, and full advantage taken of agri-environmental funding and other management tools.**
>
> **Local authorities should develop criteria-based policies to ensure that all development respects and enhances local landscape character, securing appropriate mitigation where damage to local landscape character cannot be avoided.**

11.11 The Government's overall aim is to promote a multi-purpose, inclusive and thriving countryside which respects local distinctiveness and protects our valued landscapes. The very high quality of the South East's countryside, coupled with its accessibility and productivity mean that a careful approach to landscape management is vital to its future protection and success. In practice this will mean developing two key areas of understanding:

   a. why the South East's landscapes are unique, and how future changes can support their environmental, cultural and economic value. Key to help develop this are an understanding of the capacity of the landscape to provide the ecosystem services required to support growth and the use of Landscape Character Assessment.

   b. how planning policy, land management practices and funding initiatives can best be used in unison to achieve the objectives of this Plan. In particular, given that the landscape character in the south east is to a large extent determined by farming practices, how the agricultural sector can continue to manage the countryside in a way that supports farming enterprise whilst preserving the unique character of local landscapes. Agricultural practices also offer potential to help combat climate change. Further policy is set out in Policies NRM5 and NRM15. Policy RE3 also offers policy to support farm enterprise. A key tool in achieving this is the Environmental Stewardship Scheme, managed by the Department for Environment, Food and Rural Affairs (Defra), which is designed to provide subsidy from CAP for environmental management. Defra's Rural Development Programme for England also provides a framework for distributing funds from CAP, with the new programme covering both environmental stewardship and socio-economic issues. Natural England, the Forestry Commission and the South East of England Development Agency remain key delivery agents for this programme.

Managing the Urban Rural Fringe

> **POLICY C5: MANAGING THE RURAL-URBAN FRINGE**
>
> **Local development documents should:**
>
> i. **identify issues and opportunities that require action to deliver a sustainable multi-functional rural-urban fringe, using the key functions set out in Box BE1 (see Chapter 12) as a checklist**
>
> ii. **plan positively for facilities connected with the sustainable management of urban areas**
>
> iii. **identify any parts of the rural-urban fringe around settlements that are currently or potentially subject to dereliction.**
>
> **To ensure action will be taken local authorities should:**
>
> i. **ensure better management of the rural-urban fringe, including where applicable Green Belt, by working with neighbouring planning authorities and partners in developing and implementing strategies and action plans for rural-urban fringe areas**

Countryside and Landscape Management

> ii. **target positive management on areas where urban extensions are planned including engaging local communities and landowners to ensure early consideration is given to landscape and biodiversity enhancement, woodland management, recreation provision and access routes.**

11.12   There are more than 170 small rural towns and 1,400 villages in the region. Given the large number and complex pattern of settlements in the South East, the rural-urban fringe is a particularly important asset and serves functions for both urban and rural areas. It is often an area of mixed land use, rapid change and, particularly in some parts of the South East, many competing pressures for land. In some places it is subject to poor maintenance, neglect and vandalism. There is potential to make better use of these areas in order to meet the wider objectives of the Plan.

11.13   Integrated policies, implementation plans and delivery mechanisms need to be brought together to secure the benefits available to the people of the South East region from the urban rural fringe. A combination of policy development, careful management and leverage of funding sources (for example developer contributions, environmental stewardship funds, and woodland grant schemes), can realise many opportunities available, and minimise any problems of deterioration. Opportunities also exist to link management of the rural-fringe with creation of new green infrastructure. Policy CC8 sets out this Plan's approach to green infrastructure.

11.14   Research[1] has shown that the urban rural fringe serves an important role both functionally and structurally in the South East. The Countryside in and Around Towns Vision[2] identifies ten key functions which should be pursued through greater interaction and integration between the functions (see the following box):

Ten key functions of the urban rural fringe

1. A bridge to the country

Networks of new and improved parks, woodlands and other green spaces are linked to the urban centre and wider countryside by footpaths, bridleways, rivers and their valleys, canals and cycle ways. Urban parks, country parks and other green spaces are joined up to form continuous green corridors between town and country.

2. A gateway to the town

As a gateway to the urban area the quality of the countryside creates a powerful first impression to visitors and possible investors.

3. A health centre

A more accessible and attractive countryside and green space infrastructure close to where most people live and work provides an invaluable recreational resource.

4. A classroom

The countryside in and around towns provides hands-on learning opportunities in a variety of 'outdoor classrooms'. This supports all parts of the national curriculum with a particular relevance to environmental education and rural studies.

5. Recycling and renewable energy centre

The countryside in and around towns is recognised as playing an important part in the sustainable management of the waste, water and pollution generated in urban areas.

---

1   *Unlocking the potential of the rural urban fringe*, Groundwork and the Countryside Agency, 2004
2   *The Countryside in and Around Towns*, Groundwork and the Countryside Agency, 2005

Countryside and Landscape Management

> **6. A productive landscape**
>
> Farmers operating close to urban areas take full advantage of their proximity to large urban markets, supplying consumers with high quality local produce through direct marketing and farmers markets as well as supermarkets.
>
> **7. A cultural legacy**
>
> The countryside in and around towns contains many imprints of the history of our towns and communities, their development and expansion or sometimes even their disappearance.
>
> **8. A place for sustainable living**
>
> Careful decisions have been taken about where to accommodate the need for new development, especially for affordable homes. Those decisions have followed an examination of the pros and cons of increasing housing densities in existing urban areas, expanding market towns and villages, allowing the selective expansion of cities, and creating new settlements.
>
> **9. An engine for regeneration**
>
> Strategies for local regeneration use the countryside on the urban edge to help communities develop their own confidence, skills and prospects.
>
> **10. A nature reserve**
>
> The countryside in and around towns contains historic and newly established woodlands, wetlands, meadows and a broad array of other natural habitats.

11.15   Further guidance on Rural-Urban Fringe Management is also available from Natural England.[3]

11.16   Within the South East examples of co-ordinated action already exist, and provide an opportunity for more joined-up approaches in their respective areas. Three Groundwork Trusts operate within the region (Kent and Medway, Solent and Thames Valley). Two specific 'Green Arc' initiatives also work on rural-urban fringe management - the South West Green Arc is focused on the area between London and the Surrey Hills AONB and the North West Green Arc covers the area between London and the Chilterns AONB, including parts of the River Thames Corridor. These particular initiatives offer opportunities to help better manage the urban-rural fringe around the capital, including cross boundary working to help improve accessibility, biodiversity and recreation in these areas. Local authorities in areas covered by 'Green Arc' initiatives should support and deliver the objectives of the relevant initiative when preparing LDFs.

Countryside Access and Rights of Way Management

> **POLICY C6: COUNTRYSIDE ACCESS AND RIGHTS OF WAY MANAGEMENT**
>
> **Through Rights of Way Improvement Plans and other measures, local authorities should encourage access to the countryside, taking full advantage of the Countryside and Rights of Way Act 2000, particularly by:**
>
> i.   **maintaining, enhancing and promoting the Public Rights of Way system, and permissive and longer distance routes, to facilitate access within, to and from the countryside for visitors and all members of the local community**
>
> ii. **identifying opportunities and planning for routes within and between settlements, seeking to reduce car use for shorter journeys**

---

3   *Urban Fringe Action Plans: Their Role, Scope and Mechanisms for Implementation*, Entec for the Countryside Agency, 2003

Countryside and Landscape Management

iii. where possible, making new routes multi-functional to allow for benefits for multiple users and contribute to the wider objectives of green infrastructure

iv. on Natura 2000 and Ramsar wetland sites with an identified risk of adverse impact from recreational use or other urbanisation impact (including air pollution), promote appropriate access and other management measures (both pedestrian and vehicle), to avoid such risks.

11.17 The region has a well-used public rights of way network, which provides a major opportunity to improve the well-being of individuals through exercise and access to countryside. This should be maintained and enhanced, recognising the need of visitors and local communities, to enable people to visit and enjoy the region's countryside and ensure that it can be enjoyed by all, as well as providing opportunities to enhance green infrastructure networks and reduce car use for shorter journeys within or between settlements. Rights of Way Improvement Plans should be used to establish the needs of an area to access both rural and urban areas. These plans will be integrated into local transport plans by 2010. Policies TSR6, S2 and those in Chapter 8 (transport) are also relevant to countryside access and rights of way management.

The River Thames Corridor

POLICY C7: THE RIVER THAMES CORRIDOR

Riparian local authorities should work together, and with other stakeholders, to establish a coordinated policy framework for the river and its valley corridor through their local development frameworks to reflect their environmental, heritage and recreational value through both rural and urban areas,

Taking account of the Thames River Basin Management Plan, local authorities should work together with other agencies to:

i. maintain and enhance the landscapes and waterscapes of the River Thames Corridor, in terms of their scenic and conservation value and their overall amenity

ii. conserve and enhance the nature conservation resources of the River Thames Corridor through the protection and management of its diverse plant and animal species, habitats (including wildlife networks) and geological features

iii. provide accessible facilities and opportunities for countryside and river-related recreation

iv. take account of the setting of the river in exercising their normal development control duties.

Where the river passes through urban areas, local authorities should, working together where necessary:

i. make provision for riverside open spaces and access routes

ii. protect and improve scenic views of the river and from the river, especially where they contain significant natural or built heritage features

iii. ensure a high quality of sympathetic design of new developments within sight of the river

iv. seek the conservation and improvement of the historic built environment that is part of the river's heritage and setting.

Local authorities should:

i. ensure that new development does not restrict or endanger navigation on the river

ii. seek to secure the protection and improvement of existing river-related infrastructure that is necessary for the sustainable development and use of the river

> iii. **guard land for river-related businesses that support sport and leisure use of the river**
> iv. **encourage the sustainable use of the river.**

11.18   The River Thames remains a major natural asset to the region, and is of regional and inter-regional significance. This Plan therefore contains specific policy guidance on the River Thames, which replaces previous guidance covering the Windsor to Hampton section, as set out in RPG3B/9B.[4]

11.19   Local policy and principles should be guided by the following objectives:

- For the built environment:
    - to secure high quality development on the river and riverside, which is appropriate to its context
    - to protect and enhance historic building sites, structures, landscape, skylines and views of importance
    - to make the best use of the river's potential attraction for a range of uses, including regeneration of redundant land and buildings, and promotion of recreational opportunities
    - to protect important archaeological remains.

- For the natural environment:
    - to improve the quality and provision of open space along the river
    - to conserve and enhance the ecology of the river
    - to respect green belt, open land and areas of ecological, conservation and landscape importance.

- To promote, protect and enhance the use of the river:
    - for transport use
    - for recreation
    - for public access.

11.20   Available tools to help co-ordinate action to manage the River Thames include the Thames River Basin Management Plan, Landscape Character Assessment (see Policy C4), the production of joint supplementary planning documents, focusing LDF spatial policies and guidance on the River Thames and the co-ordination of local landscape designations. One example of joint action is the Thames Landscape Strategy. This was created through a partnership of local councils and national agencies and presents a two tiered approach to the management of the river between Hampton and Kew. The first part covers main issues such as tourism, recreation, nature conservation and access, and the second covers specific projects and management proposals, dividing this section of the river into twelve 'character reaches'. Policies TSR7, KTG2 and KTG7 also cover aspects of policy for the River Thames.

---

4   RPG3B/9B - Strategic Planning Guidance for the River Thames, Government Office for London, February 1997

12 Management of the Built Environment

Introduction

12.1 The built environment of the region has a profound influence on the quality of life for residents of the South East. Our cities, towns and villages provide the main source of employment opportunities, access to essential services, leisure opportunities and, most importantly, a home to the vast majority of the citizens of the region. It is essential that they are managed and developed in a way that reinforces and enhances all these roles. Policies in this chapter develop the principles of Policy SP3: Urban Focus and Urban Renaissance), and complement and expand Policy CC6: Sustainable Communities and Character of the Environment. The chapter also contains specific policies relating to neighbourhood management, suburbs and small market towns.

Management for an Urban Renaissance

POLICY BE1: MANAGEMENT FOR AN URBAN RENAISSANCE

Local authorities and their partners will use opportunities associated with new development to help provide significant improvements to the built environment. They will:

i. **through their community strategies and local development frameworks, set out an overall strategy for enhancing the quality of life in each urban area which reflects a vision developed in consultation with local communities**

ii. **work closely with key service providers to ensure that physical, community, cultural and green infrastructure is planned and phased in accordance with planned development**

iii. **in partnership with other public agencies, the private sector and the local community, establish innovative management arrangements for town centres, business parks, and residential neighbourhoods**

iv. **develop and implement public realm and open space strategies**

v. **promote and support design solutions relevant to context and which build upon local character and distinctiveness and sense of place, including the sensitive reuse of redundant or under-used historic buildings**

vi. **support and identify opportunities for appropriate higher density and mixed-use development schemes**

vii. **draw up design-led supplementary planning documents to help implement development briefs, design codes and master plans for key sites in consultation with key stakeholders.**

12.2 The concept of urban renaissance is a building block for the South East Plan. Urban renaissance goes far beyond the simple notion of concentrating the majority of development in urban areas. It is about making our towns and cities places where people will choose to live, work and spend their leisure time.

BOX BE1

Research has identified five pillars of urban renaissance, all of which should reinforce each other within the overall objective of raising quality of life.[1] Each applies equally to settlements of all sizes, from small market towns to suburban neighbourhoods and large cities. These principles should be reflected in local management of urban renaissance initiatives. They are:

Good Governance – Bringing together the local community, their elected representatives, businesses and developers to deliver an agreed vision for an area. This vision should be established through community strategies and delivered through the local development framework. Good governance requires co-ordinating agencies and investment to work towards common

---

1   *Living Places: Urban Renaissance in the South East*, URBED for Government Office for the South East, 2000

goals. This includes co-ordinating the timely delivery of key infrastructure and services to support new development, such as health care, education, public open space, community safety, public transport and affordable housing. It also means pooling and developing design, delivery and management skills and sharing good practice wherever possible. A current good practice example of a local authority working with local people and businesses to deliver an agreed vision is Bracknell Forest Council's work with its Regeneration Partnership to redevelop the town centre.

Achieving Design Excellence – Pursuing creative solutions to respect the character and charm of our unique and historic settlements, and by working to improve the existing urban fabric. This means a design-led approach to new development so that it complements and supports the area around it, and results in varied, attractive, safe and accessible towns, suburbs and villages where people and businesses want to be. The revitalisation of the historic dockyards at Chatham and Portsmouth are just two current examples of this in action within the region.

Promoting Economic Strength - Attracting investment, through improvements to the appeal and accessibility of the built environment. Initiatives can include developing attractions and amenities in town centres, refurbishing and redeveloping existing buildings and land, supporting the evening economy, encouraging public/private partnership and supporting job creation. A current good example of new development bringing economic and other benefits to an area through a partnership of private and public bodies is the development of the Oracle Centre in Reading, which has provided a mix of uses on a derelict site in the town centre.

Environmental Responsibility - Appreciating the contribution which high quality public realm, private gardens, open spaces, streets, squares and green corridors can make to urban areas, reducing land take, managing traffic in a way that puts people before cars and creating and protecting safe, tranquil and accessible streets and open space. Environmental responsibility also results in new buildings which meet high environmental standards and initiatives to plan for the efficient use of energy – for example, Woking Borough Council's recent initiatives to install green energy systems and combined heat and power plant in the town.

Social Well-being and Inclusion - Developing spaces to meet the needs and aspirations of everyone, particularly in the parts of the region suffering from decline. This requires steps to ensure that communities engage with, influence and manage the delivery of local services and green infrastructure in a way that widens opportunities for all, and concerted effort to plan for a mix of housing types and tenures and tackle problems of existing unfit housing stock. Promoting inclusion and well being into the design of services and infrastructure in new development considers the need to help reduce crime and encourage healthy living. A current example of an area working successfully to change its role and image is Brighton, which has prevented the threat of decline by improvements to its environment and the careful planning of complementary new development, attracting people, business and visitors.

BOX BE2: Sources of guidance and good practice available to help practitioners deliver urban renaissance objectives

- **Councillor's Toolbox: making the best use of land**, South East England Regional Assembly
- **In Suburbia: Delivering Sustainable Communities**, South East of England Regional Assembly
- **Neighbourhood Revival: towards more sustainable suburbs in the South East**, URBED
- **PPS1 – Delivering Sustainable Development**, DCLG
- **Living Places – Cleaner, Safer Greener & Living Places, Caring for Quality**, DCLG
- **Achieving Quality of Design in Local Plans**, RIBA
- **Protecting Design Quality in Planning**, CABE
- **By Design, better places to live. A Companion Guide to PPG3**, DTLR/CABE
- **By Design, urban design in the planning system, towards better practice**, DETR/CABE
- **Building in Context**, English Heritage/CABE
- **Urban Design Compendium**, English Partnerships and Housing Corporation

Management of the Built Environment

- **Creating Successful Masterplans, CABE**
- **Design Codes, English Partnerships**
- **Safer Places: The Planning System and Crime Prevention, Home Office/ODPM**
- **Green Space Strategies: a good practice guide, CABESpace**

Managing Neighbourhood Change

> **POLICY BE2: SUBURBAN INTENSIFICATION**
>
> Local development frameworks should identify locations where intensification could assist wider planning objectives. Such locations could include areas of high accessibility immediately around public transport nodes in predominantly residential neighbourhoods, underutilised industrial estates and low density retail parks. Clear planning and design guidance should be included for such intensification opportunities. This guidance, which may take the form of local development document policies, should be based on local character appraisal and clearly set out the basis on which proposals for the intensification of existing residential areas will be assessed.

12.3   Policies SP2: Regional Hubs and SP3: Urban Focus and Urban Renaissance also contain policy relevant to suburban intensification.

12.4   The South East is especially characterised by its suburban settlement structure. These suburbs vary widely in terms of their physical, social and environmental make up. They range from the most affluent to some of the most deprived neighbourhoods and vary in character from mixed use inner suburbs to executive residential areas on the urban-rural fringe. Although traditionally considered inherently stable, economic, social and behavioural change has placed new pressures on many of these areas. Some are experiencing the loss of their original purpose, to support industries that no longer exist. Others are experiencing considerable pressures for development which threatens to change their character, but which may also present opportunities for more sustainable forms of development.

12.5   **Suburban Intensification** - Many suburban areas in the South East are facing considerable pressure for new development. The scale of the pressures for development and intensification over the foreseeable future and their impact on quality of life is a strategic issue for the region.

12.6   At present much of the infill and intensification taking place in suburban neighbourhoods is viewed in a negative way, and dealt with on an incremental and piecemeal basis, thereby placing undue pressure on local infrastructure and services. The result is often characterised by:

   i. ad-hoc, incremental (and often poorly designed) intensification and backland development that can lead to the loss of wildlife habitats and corridors
   ii. a failure to provide adequate housing choice for all sections of the community
   iii. increasingly unsustainable patterns of travel leading to increasing congestion and pollution, and in many cases a decline of local centres
   iv. a loss of employment land and lost opportunities for more mixed use development.

12.7   There is a need for a positive and planned approach to intensification, with clear guidance set out in local development documents and/or supplementary planning documents, based upon neighbourhood assessments of character and capacity with the full involvement of the local community and key service providers. One example of such an approach is a supplementary planning document on Housing Intensification, produced by Wycombe District Council in December 2005. A quick and simple 'healthcheck' of social, physical and environmental capital can be a useful starting point for identifying priorities.[2] Some useful criteria for assessing proposals for intensification might include:

---

2   See *Neighbourhood Revival: towards more sustainable suburbs in the South East*, URBED, 2004

Management of the Built Environment

   i. the need for and potential impacts associated with different types, tenure and occupancy of new development
   ii. impact on the availability or potential availability of community resources (e.g. schools, health centres etc)
   iii. accessibility of the neighbourhood by means of transport other than the car (e.g. on foot, cycle, bus, train)
   iv. contribution to local sense of place/character
   v. impact on open space / biodiversity
   vi. effect on car usage and parking.

12.8 **Areas of Opportunity** - Part of the overall spatial strategy seeks to make the best use of all urban land in the region. This includes suburban land. To this end sub-regional strategies and local development frameworks (LDFs) should seek to identify neighbourhoods at risk or which may present significant development opportunities.

12.9 For neighbourhoods that are highly accessible by public transport, local authorities should seek to strengthen the range of facilities and services at and around existing or potential transport nodes. In addition potential opportunities for planned intensification may exist on highly accessible but under-utilised industrial estates or retail parks in suburban areas. In some cases, particularly where an increased mix of uses is a policy objective, this may require local authorities to take a more proactive approach to land assembly or enter into joint ventures with development institutions to achieve their planning objectives. [3] Area action plans could provide a useful framework for taking forward this approach. It will be essential that these establish clear mechanisms for securing funding for local community infrastructure through land value capture, and that the funds accrued are reinvested within the neighbourhood in accordance with clearly identified priorities.

POLICY BE3: SUBURBAN RENEWAL

Local authorities should identify neighbourhoods, especially in suburban areas, in need of renewal, which would benefit from a proactive and integrated approach to area management.

For those neighbourhoods identified local authorities should work with their partners to develop Neighbourhood Management Plans (NMPs).

NMPs should set out a clear framework for the integrated development, management and delivery of community services, environmental quality and infrastructure provision. They should be developed through partnership working with residents, service providers, employers and developers.

12.10 **Neighbourhoods at Risk** - In many suburbs, local retail, health and education facilities may be of poor quality or absent, leading to social and economic deprivation and long term decline. Such neighbourhoods can demonstrate characteristics more commonly associated with inner urban areas. Where this is the case there is a need for a more integrated approach to neighbourhood management, whereby local service providers (e.g. health, education, housing, crime & disorder reduction partnerships etc) work together to maximise opportunities to provide co-ordinated services in ways which meet local needs and assist regeneration. The Government's Neighbourhoods Charter seeks to support the setting up of voluntary partnerships between communities, their local authority and service providers. Active neighbourhood management will be particularly important in those neighbourhoods, including through the production of Neighbourhood Management Plans to facilitate this process. In areas experiencing associated physical decline, for example some poorly designed housing estates, partial demolition and restructuring, combined with creation of new useable green space could significantly help transform the image of a neighbourhood, support mixed communities and contribute towards meeting housing need. One example of a community-led partnership is the

---

3 *Suburban Property Markets* (FPD Savills, 2004)

Management of the Built Environment

"Leigh Park Creating Quality Places" project in Havant which has brought together the local community and stakeholders in the area, assisted by a professional team, to develop solutions to regenerate the local neighbourhood.

The Role of Small Rural Towns ('Market' Towns)

> **POLICY BE4: THE ROLE OF SMALL RURAL TOWNS ('MARKET' TOWNS)**
>
> Local planning authorities should encourage and initiate schemes and proposals that help strengthen the viability of small rural towns, recognising their social, economic and cultural importance to wider rural areas and the region as a whole. Local planning authorities, through their local development documents and other means, should:
>
> i. support and reinforce the role of small rural towns as local hubs for employment, retailing and community facilities and services
> ii. encourage community-led local assessments of need and action planning
> iii. provide for sufficient housing development (especially for affordable housing) in small rural towns where this would reinforce and develop the distinctive character and role of the town and meet identified needs
> iv. protect and enhance the character and appearance of individual small rural towns
> v. develop public transport networks which meet the needs of both the market towns and their surrounding rural area.

12.11   Small rural or 'market' towns play a key part in the economic and social functioning of the region, and in contributing to its character and built form. In identifying small rural market towns in LDFs, local authorities should take account of the function and size of a town. Such towns should generally be up to 20,000 population. They often act as a focal point for trade and services for a rural hinterland, and such towns can have a variety of backgrounds – they are not just limited to those which have a traditional agricultural market or strong historic character.

12.12   In recent years small rural towns have been relatively successful in economic and social terms. They have seen substantial economic and housing growth. The spatial strategy set out in this Plan does not envisage them as a main focus for development, but as local hubs they will complement the role of regional hubs. As key service centres they will still need to foster economic vitality and appropriate development including the provision of affordable housing. This local character and identity should be reinforced and enhanced. Individuality is the key to the success of market towns, which will depend on their appeal as a commercial business and retail centre, an attractive residential location and visitor destination. Guidance in the Town Centres Chapter (Chapter 13) stresses the need for local authorities to set out the other towns, villages and local centres to complete the network of town centres in their area.

12.13   Some small rural towns also have social problems and here community engagement and capacity building, and the management and resourcing of community initiatives (such as Market Town Health-checks and SEEDA's Market Town programmes) can help address disadvantage and social isolation, linked with LDFs, local transport plans and community strategies. Consideration should also be given to extending the role of small rural towns as centres for education and training, and to a more innovative approach to the multiple use of existing infrastructure, such as schools and libraries to develop this role.

Management of the Built Environment

Village Management

POLICY BE5: VILLAGE MANAGEMENT

In preparing local development documents (LDDs), local planning authorities should positively plan to meet the defined local needs of their rural communities for small scale affordable housing, business and service development, taking account of changing patterns of agriculture, economic diversification, and continued viability of local services. LDDs should define their approach to development in villages based on the functions performed, their accessibility, the need to protect or extend key local services and the capacity of the built form and landscape setting of the village. All new development should be subject to rigorous design and sustainability criteria so that the distinctive character of the village is not damaged.

To assist this, local planning authorities should encourage community-led local assessments of need and action planning to inform decision making processes.

12.14   Villages form an important part of the network of settlements in the region, and are often the subject of pressures arising from their location in a highly dynamic region, but also from stagnation or exclusion, in some cases resulting from a loss of services or changing community structure. Villages are defined in this Plan as settlements with populations less than 3,000. Limited small-scale development can help meet the specific local housing, business and service needs of individual rural settlements, preferably informed by community led mechanisms such as parish plans and village design statements. Development must be guided by strong design requirements which respect the character of the settlement. Community and service needs may be partially met through joint services, co-location and information technology. In some cases, development may serve a group of villages.

Management of the Historic Environment

POLICY BE6: MANAGEMENT OF THE HISTORIC ENVIRONMENT

When developing and implementing plans and strategies, local authorities and other bodies will adopt policies and support proposals which protect, conserve and, where appropriate, enhance the historic environment and the contribution it makes to local and regional distinctiveness and sense of place. The region's internationally and nationally designated historic assets should receive the highest level of protection. Proposals that make sensitive use of historic assets through regeneration, particularly where these bring redundant or under-used buildings and areas into appropriate use should be encouraged.

12.15   The historic environment includes the physical evidence of past human activity. It is all around us as part of everyday life, and it is therefore dynamic and continually subject to change. It is not limited to the built environment and archaeological sites, but includes landscapes, both urban and rural and as an example of its great diversity, marine heritage sites around the coast. These environments are fragile and require protection, but also have an enormous potential to contribute to a sense of place and identity and add to the quality of our daily lives through understanding and appropriate management and access.

12.16   It is widely recognised that the South East has a rich and diverse historic environment.[4] This is a tremendous asset, a precious and irreplaceable expression of our history, heritage and culture, visibly so, where it lies at the heart of local and regional character and sense of place. The historic buildings and landscapes that characterise the region add much to the quality of life that underpins the region's economy. Both the rural

---

4   See for example *Heritage Counts: the State of the South East's Historic Environment*, English Heritage

Management of the Built Environment

landscape and the historic urban fabric influences investment decisions of individuals and businesses. The historic environment is part of the wider environment of the region that is a 'draw' for those investing in the area.

12.17 Regionally significant historic features and sites in the South East include:

1. historic cities of Canterbury, Chichester, Oxford, Rochester, Southampton and Winchester
2. maritime heritage relating to the Thames Estuary, Solent, the Channel Coast including naval dockyards of Chatham, Portsmouth and Sheerness, Regency Brighton and the seaside built heritage of the Kent and Sussex coasts
3. an historic countryside of varying character reflecting both Midlands Enclosure on top of open field systems and more organically developed landscapes of Kent and Sussex
4. an outstanding archaeological heritage from the Palaeolithic sites of Boxgrove and the Thames gravels, through a rich prehistory reflecting the development of agriculture, through Roman centres of Canterbury, Chichester and Silchester and the wider network of smaller towns, villages and other rural settlements, through major Saxon and medieval ecclesiastical and urban centres
5. the network of historic market towns and villages with their medieval churches and other historic buildings
6. the stately homes and historic parks and gardens ringing London from Oxfordshire to Kent
7. the defence heritage of the region which has always been in the front line of the defence of England.

Historic Environmental Designations in the South East

- more than 76,000 listed buildings (> 5,500 Grade I and Grade II*) including more than 200 buildings at risk (more than any other region)
- almost 2,000 conservation areas
- about 2,600 scheduled monuments
- more than 350 registered historic parks and gardens and six registered battlefields
- two inscribed World Heritage Sites (and three on the Tentative List)
- finds recorded in 22 Historic Environment Records maintained by local authorities

12.18 Apart from the designations referred to in the above box, account needs to be taken of the wider historic environment including Historic Environment Records that currently provide information on some 130,000 features in the region.

12.19 Sustainable management of the historic environment through the planning system and other plans and strategies should be based upon an understanding of its significance and vulnerability to change. This is critical given that the pace and scale of change faced by the region. The standardisation of some new development can lead to a dilution of local character, and should be discouraged. Local character assessment, for example historic landscape and urban characterisation, can be a useful tool to inform policy development.

12

The South East Plan - Regional Spatial Strategy for the South East

13 Town Centres

Introduction

13.1 The Government's key objective for town centres, as set out in Planning Policy Statement 6 (PPS6): *Planning for Town Centres*, is to promote their vitality and viability. This will be done by planning for the growth and development of existing centres through focusing development in the centres and encouraging a wide range of services in a good environment, accessible to all.

13.2 In this chapter the term town centre is used to cover both city and town centres. The policies in this chapter apply to all development in town centres, including business accommodation, residential, leisure, arts, culture, tourism and retail.

13.3 Reference should also be made to policies on management of the built environment, sustainable economic development and tourism and related sports and recreation (Chapters 12, 6 and 14 respectively). South East England's town centres are vital elements of the regional economy and provide for a mixture of uses including residential, business accommodation, service provision, retail, leisure and tourism. The South East has a complex pattern of town centres and the relationships between centres vary throughout the South East and into adjoining regions.

13.4 By far the biggest external influence on the South East's town centres is the relationship with London. In addition to the importance of central London as a centre of employment, retail, culture and other services, the outer metropolitan centres of Hounslow, Kingston, Sutton, Croydon, Bromley and Uxbridge compete with towns in the London Fringe.

13.5 Also of importance are links to other regions. Town centres to the west of the region are linked to the South West through the M4 corridor to Swindon, while Southampton is only 30 minutes away from Bournemouth/Poole. Central Milton Keynes and Banbury in the north of the region are integrated into the economy of the East Midlands. There are regional shopping centres in Kent in the South East and Thurrock in the East of England (Bluewater and Lakeside respectively).

Development of Town Centres

13.6 The development of dynamic and successful town centres is central to the achievement of sustainable development in the South East. While the most significant growth is expected in the Primary Regional Centres, particularly the Centres for Significant Change indicated with an asterisk in Policy TC1, the policies aim to distribute growth to middle and lower order centres to create a balanced network of centres not overly dominated by the largest centres. Local centres are likely to be a focal point for some but not necessarily all development and should develop their distinctive features and nature. Reference should also be made to policy BE4: The Role of Small Rural Towns ('Market' Towns).

13.7 Growth and development needs to be supported in appropriate urban centres in the South East which include the Growth Areas at Milton Keynes, Ashford and the Thames Gateway and existing major centres. In planning for growth, the special relationship with the metropolitan centres in west, south and east London needs to be particularly addressed so as to create networks of urban centres which complement each other whilst being self-sufficient in terms of employment provision, retail, leisure and culture. In other areas the polycentric nature of the settlement pattern needs to be taken into account in planning for the sustained growth of centres.

13.8 Reference should also be made to the distinctive character of particular centres whether planning for growth or change. For example, in Oxford new development will need to build on the architecture and cultural amenity, as well as the value of new services to the local community and tourists alike. New investment of an appropriate level and scale should be promoted, in particular in vulnerable centres in need of regeneration. In accommodating new growth, best practice in urban design and development needs to be encouraged along with quality in the public realm and better access by public transport, cycling and walking. Town centre regeneration offers a real opportunity to achieve exemplar developments, demonstrating the highest standards of sustainable construction and energy efficiency (further guidance is provided in Policy CC4: Sustainable Design and Construction). This will be achieved through the development of effective town centre management, partnerships and strategies.

13.9 Regional hubs provide the opportunity to focus the development of quality transport services in a way that supports urban communities and urban renaissance while maintaining the levels of accessibility to goods and services.

13.10 **Management and maintenance** – Some of the issues relating to the maintenance of a centre can be addressed through preventing the problem in the first place. Local authorities should ensure that a budget is allocated for on-going maintenance of the town centre, and should support and encourage management and maintenance through strategies and partnerships.

13.11 The Government has now passed legislation that allows Business Improvement Districts (BIDs) to be introduced in England. These are only possible where a gap in the services provided has been identified and agreed, and where the businesses of a designated area determine by vote to fund the provision of the missing services.

Strategic Network of Town Centres

13.12 Policy TC1 summarises the strategic network of town centres (see Diagram TC1).

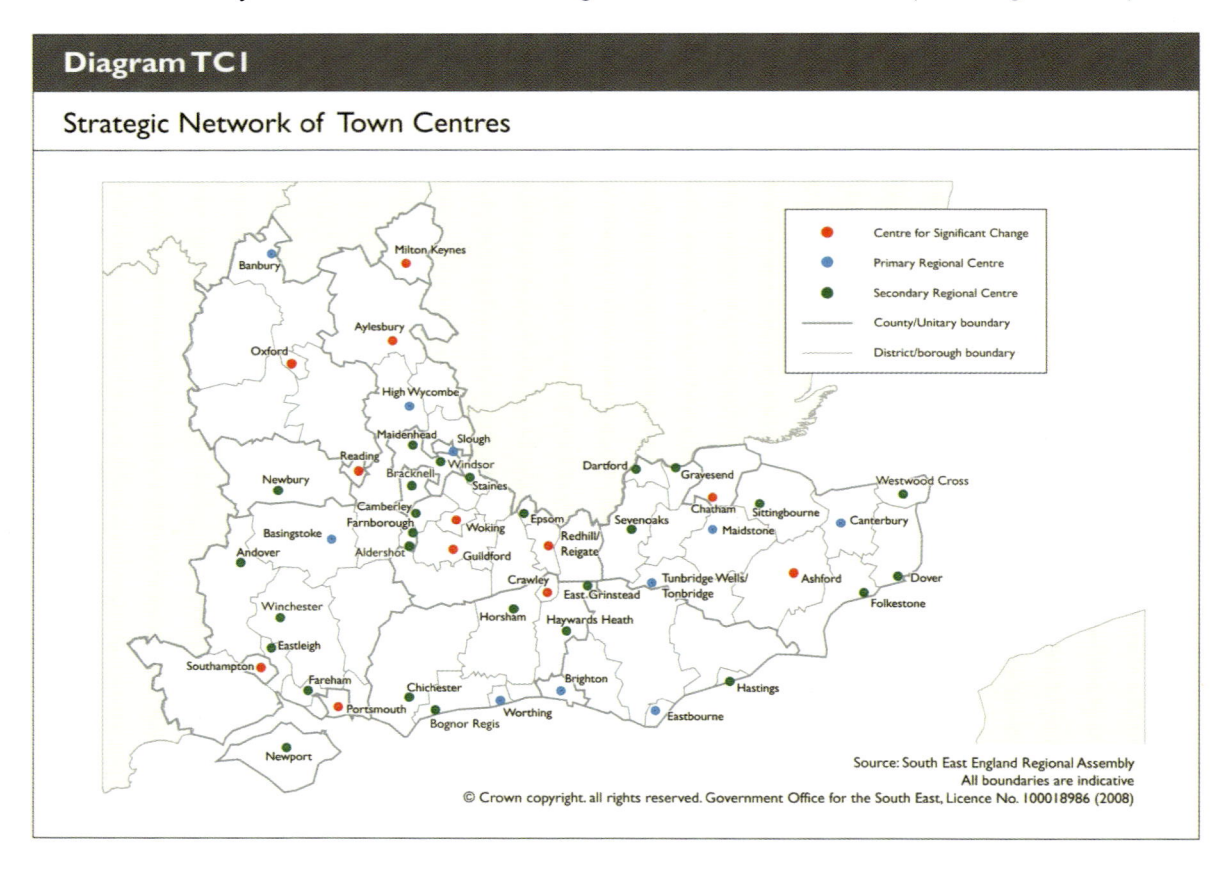

Diagram TC1

Strategic Network of Town Centres

Legend:
- Centre for Significant Change (red)
- Primary Regional Centre (blue)
- Secondary Regional Centre (green)
- County/Unitary boundary
- District/borough boundary

Source: South East England Regional Assembly
All boundaries are indicative
© Crown copyright, all rights reserved. Government Office for the South East, Licence No. 100018986 (2008)

13.14 This network has been developed by firstly developing a rank of town centres in the South East based on a number of individual indicators covering both retail and non-retail uses[1]. The rank was then revised through sensitivity testing against rental, employment and further floorspace data and in line with the overall spatial strategy. This is, however, a flexible process and a centre's role will be tested through regular town centre assessments.

---

1   See technical note 2 – Strategic Network of Town Centres

13.15 The 22 Primary Regional Centres include all the centres designated as regional hubs except Hastings and Ebbsfleet. The list of primary regional centres also includes a further three centres identified as major regional centres from the research. The secondary regional centres include a further 27 centres identified as being of sub-regional importance from the research. The policy takes into account developments, trends and proposed changes and sets out a network of town centres for 2026. The network will be the focus for large scale developments. However, growth will not be restricted to these centres. The full network of town centres in the South East includes other towns which provide the main retail and other services in a local area as well as villages and local centres, which typically comprise a smaller range of services serving a smaller catchment. Local authorities should set out the other towns, villages and local centres to complete the network of town centres in their area and they should review their needs using robust data and analysis to provide a strategy for their future development.

POLICY TC1: STRATEGIC NETWORK OF TOWN CENTRES

A network of strategic town centres will be developed across the region as set out below. This is intended to be a dynamic network of centres which will be kept under review. Local planning authorities should carry out regular assessments of town centres in the network.

Primary Regional Centres	Secondary Regional Centres
Ashford (Kent)*	Aldershot
Aylesbury*	Andover
Banbury	Bognor Regis
Basingstoke	Bracknell
Brighton	Camberley
Canterbury	Chichester
Chatham*	Dartford
Crawley*	Dover
Eastbourne	East Grinstead
Guildford*	Eastleigh
High Wycombe	Epsom
Maidstone	Fareham
Milton Keynes (Central)*	Farnborough
Oxford*	Folkestone
Portsmouth*	Gravesend
Reading*	Hastings
Redhill/Reigate*	Haywards Heath
Southampton*	Horsham
Slough	Maidenhead
Tonbridge-Tunbridge Wells	Newbury
Woking*	Newport (Isle of Wight)

Worthing	Sevenoaks
	Sittingboune
	Staines
	Westwood Cross (Thanet)
	Winchester
	Windsor

* Centres for Significant Change

This network of town centres will be a focus for those town centre uses set out in PPS6.

Guidance on the implementation of this policy is set out in Policy TC2.

New Development and Redevelopment in Town Centres

13.16 Regional Priorities for Retail Development – A regional study into Town Centre Futures (November 2004) and addendum (April 2005), showed very substantial growth in residual retail expenditure and development in the period to 2026, even when the model's assumptions were sensitivity tested through reducing levels of expenditure growth and increasing levels of turnover efficiency and growth of e-commerce. The consultants advised that around £20 billion residual expenditure for new comparison retail floorspace should be used for planning at a regional level over the period to 2026. Taking into account floorspace proposals, assuming an average sales density for modern comparison goods floorspace of c.£5,000 per m^2, and assuming that all spend generated by non-town centre retailing is accommodated in town centres first, this results in the floorspace capacity forecast of around 4 million m^2 gross. The forecasts indicate a doubling of the existing floorspace stock in the leading 50 town centres by 2026. However, for the rest of this decade there is no significant forecast capacity when the current proposals in the South East are taken into consideration.

13.17 In determining where the residual expenditure should be directed, policy in Planning Policy Statement 6 should be taken into account.

13.18 At a regional level the study also concluded that:

  i.   there is increasing concern in relation to the homogeneity of our high streets and a need to promote and market the individuality of retail centres
  ii. planning and managing change on the high street due to the impact of the Internet and new technological advances represents a major challenge to all town centres in the future. There is a need to monitor the growth of e-commerce and its impact on high street performance
  iii. quantitative forecasts should be supplemented by a wider assessment of each centre's role as a focus for employment, leisure and recreation.

13.19 The consultants identified a 'buffer zone' (10 mile zone) around the South East regional boundary to examine the impact of larger surrounding centres on shopping patterns in the South East region (see Diagram TC2).

Town Centres

Diagram TC2
Retail Catchments

Legend:
- Centre for Significant Change
- Primary Regional Centre
- Secondary Regional Centre
- Adjoining Regional Centre
- Buffer Zone catchment boundary
- South East Region
- Core catchment
- Secondary catchment
- Outer catchment

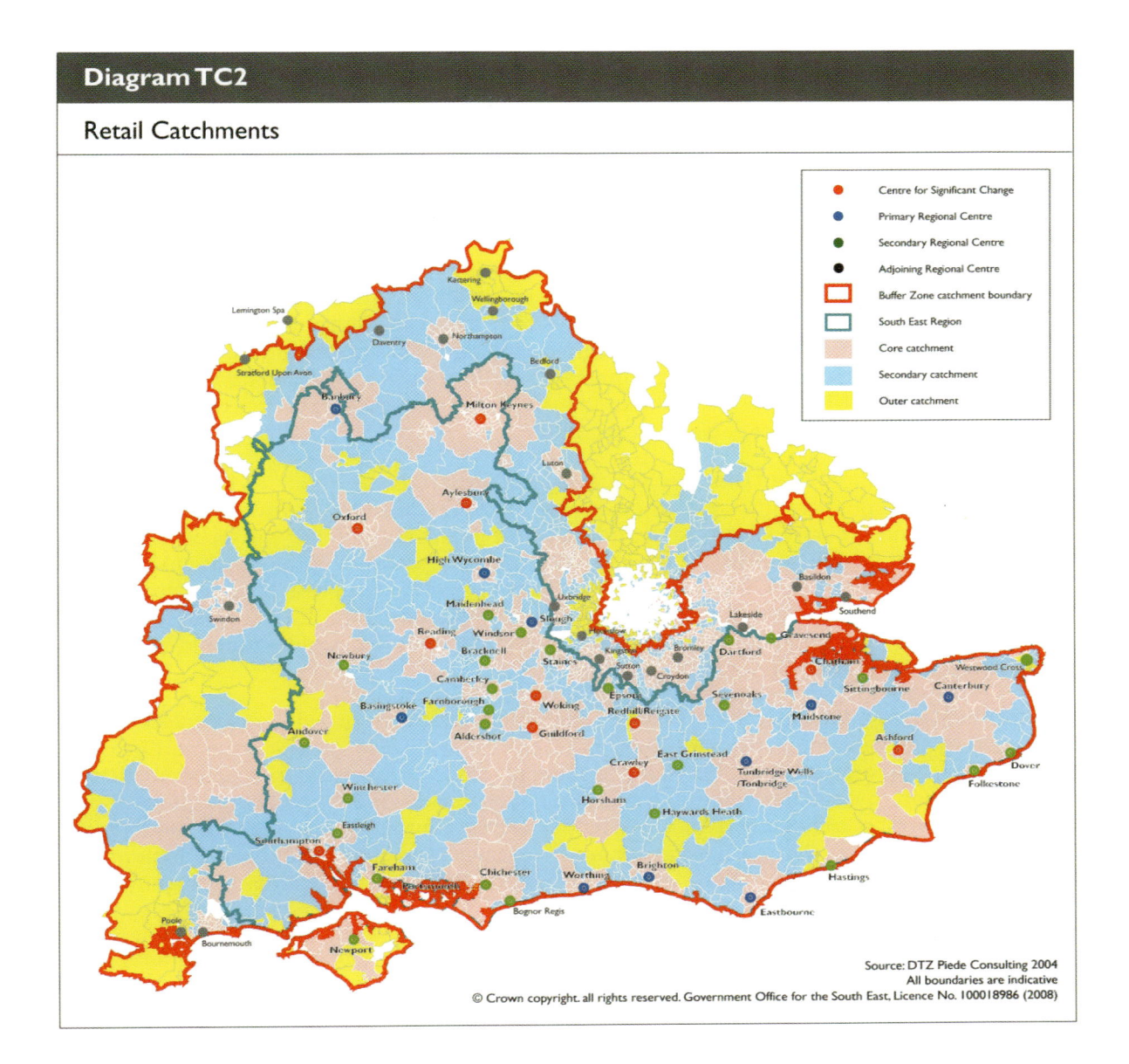

Source: DTZ Piede Consulting 2004
All boundaries are indicative
© Crown copyright, all rights reserved. Government Office for the South East, Licence No. 100018986 (2008)

13.21 The map shows the extension of the catchment areas of the outer London centres into the South East region as well as the secondary and outer catchments of Milton Keynes, Banbury, Oxford and Southampton extending into adjoining regions.

- **Regional priorities for office and leisure development in town centres** – In line with advice in PPS6, the regional planning body, as part of the review of this guidance will develop more regionally specific guidance on the regional strategy for leisure and office uses in town centres.
- **Strategy for the development of the network of centres** – The regional study into town centre futures has helped inform the strategy for the development of a balanced network of centres for each sub-regional strategy area. Details about specific centres are set out in the sub-regional chapters (16 - 24 and Chapter 25). Reference is also made to links across the regional boundary and relationships to the five centres in the strategic network which do not fall within the sub-regions (Maidstone, Tonbridge-Tunbridge Wells, Banbury, Winchester and Andover).

Town Centres

POLICY TC2: NEW DEVELOPMENT AND REDEVELOPMENT IN TOWN CENTRES

Until advice is available, via a review of this RSS, about the broad quantum of growth expected in the strategic network of town centres, local planning authorities, in preparing their development plan documents (DPDs), should be guided by the following considerations.

Local authorities should carry out further work, including joint working where there are issues that are common to two or more local authority areas, to assess the need for further floorspace in town centres and set out a vision and strategy for the network and hierarchy of centres within their area. This work should include other centres not listed in Policy TC1 as these centres may have an important role in meeting local needs. This should take account of the important inter-relationships between centres within and beyond the region's boundaries and especially with London.

The Centres for Significant Change, indicated with an asterisk in Policy TC1 are expected to undergo the most significant change across the range of town centre uses during the plan period and proactive, integrated strategies for their development will be particularly important. All of the Centres for Significant Change are identified as Regional Hubs. These town centres will be the focus for significant growth, along with areas where there are particular regeneration needs or a specific growth area focus. Major retail developments, and other town centre uses of a large scale, should be located in these Centres for Significant Change.

After the Centres for Significant Change, the most significant growth is expected to be needed in the remaining Primary Regional Centres, with less growth expected in the Secondary Regional Centres. However, as local planning authorities draw up their DPDs, they will need to consider whether there is a need to re-balance the network of centres to ensure that it is not overly dominated by the largest centres. Authorities will also need to consider whether there are areas where investment should be stimulated, including town centres with deficiencies, deprived areas, or areas that will undergo significant housing and employment growth.

Plans and strategies prepared by local authorities and other stakeholders should have regard to the following:

i. the need to support the function and viability of pre-eminent town centres to accommodate change and growth within each sub-regional strategy area
ii. the need to assess the capacity to accommodate change and growth in such areas
iii. the need to respect the historic character, environment and cultural value of existing town centres
iv. the need to ensure safe, secure and attractive environments for people to live, shop and work
v. the need to promote new investment of an appropriate scale, in particular in vulnerable centres in need of regeneration
vi. the need to support sustainability objectives, including the role of regional hubs, taking account of the impact on traffic and the need to minimise reliance on the car/lorry and promote public transport accessibility
vii. the potential impact on the vitality and viability of town centres.

POLICY TC3: OUT-OF-CENTRE REGIONAL/SUB-REGIONAL SHOPPING CENTRES

No need has been identified for any further out-of-centre regional or sub-regional shopping centres or large-scale extensions to such existing centres during the period to 2026. The role and regeneration of town centres should not be undermined by an intensification of such development.

13.22 There will need to be a review of the chapter on town centres, and the relevant parts of the sub-regional strategies to take account of further work that is required to assess the need for additional floorspace in the region. This information will be used to inform where growth can and should be accommodated in the network of town centres. This work will need to take account of the likely growth of e-commerce and home shopping, and the impact this may have on future floorspace requirements.

13 Town Centres

14 Tourism and Related Sports and Recreation

Context

14.1 South East England comprises the largest tourism market in the UK, outside Greater London. This is a result of many factors including:

  i. the diversity of the region's environment (including attractive countryside, historic towns and coastal resorts)
  ii. the strength of its economy (as a driver of significant business tourism)
  iii. its geographical location (as the gateway to the UK from North West Europe via the Channel Tunnel and the passenger ferry ports)
  iv. its proximity to London (the UK's primary international tourist destination and the source of an unrivalled potential domestic visitor market).

14.2 Together these and other characteristics combine to make the South East a unique visitor destination with significant untapped potential for further tourism related growth. However, it is essential that any such growth be managed in a sustainable way.

14.3 The contribution of tourism to the overall vision for quality of life in the South East can be significantly enhanced by:

  i. delivering a high quality and rewarding experience for all visitors, accessible to all
  ii. providing a greater variety of jobs and opportunities for training over a wide range of skill levels
  iii. providing stronger support for urban renaissance and regeneration, especially in the South Coast resorts and the Thames Gateway
  iv. helping to diversify and develop further the rural economy
  v. underpinning and promoting environmental quality and local distinctiveness in town and country
  vi. generating community benefits to enhance quality of life for all social groups in the region
  vii. encouraging travellers passing through the region's international gateways to spend time within the South East.

14.4 Delivery of these objectives at the regional level will fall on a wide range of partners at the regional, sub-regional and local levels. At the regional level SEEDA and Tourism South East will play the leading role, particularly in relation to skills development, marketing, communications and research. The overall framework for the development of the tourism sector in the South East is set out in the Regional Tourism Strategy[1].

14.5 At the local level it is important to establish a comprehensive, long-term vision for the role of tourism and related activities within a locality. The vision needs to be sufficiently explicit and embedded in the community strategy, the local cultural (or tourism) strategy and the local development framework (LDF) in order to shape investment and decisions. In seeking to implement the vision an integrated approach is needed to ensure that tourism objectives are reflected in local activities such as town centre management and regeneration, open space strategies, heritage enhancement initiatives, countryside management and environmental stewardship.

14.6 Predicted changes in temperatures and increased volatility in weather patterns brought about by climate change are likely to have a particularly significant impact on the tourism sector in the region. Long-term planning of tourism in the region will need to be undertaken with an understanding of how changes may present opportunities and threats to the industry. Maintaining and enhancing the South East's attractiveness as a tourism destination will rely upon a planned response to the challenges presented. Opportunities for the tourism sector may include:

---

1 *Tourism ExSEllence*: The Strategy for Tourism in the South East (Tourism South East)

i. increased appeal of the region for visitors as a result of generally warmer summers and milder winters, and also a preference to overseas destinations suffering more severe effects of climate change

ii. increased opportunities for environmental tourism as new habitats are created

iii. niche opportunities as a result of lifestyle changes in a new climate.

14.7 Planning for tourism and recreation will need to take account of the different characteristics and qualities of areas in the South East. Tourism and related activities are considered as having a particularly important role to play in the following areas:

14.8 **The South Coast –** The coastal strip and the Isle of Wight comprise a particularly diverse landscape, including the traditional coastal resorts, major urban centres for which tourism may or may not be a key economic driver, dramatic coastline, attractive rural hinterlands and high quality natural landscapes (including parts of the South Downs and New Forest). It also accommodates a huge diversity of tourism-related activity from short activity breaks (land and sea-based) to traditional seaside holidays, business conferences and numerous day visits to visitor attractions (e.g. museums, aquariums, etc.).

14.9 **Tourism hotspots -** Tourism hotspots are identified as Oxford, Windsor and surrounds, Canterbury and Brighton and Hove. These parts of the region experience very high levels of tourism and day visitor activity, which makes a significant contribution to the local economy. They contain important built and cultural heritage resources, and are popular with overseas tourists and business tourists. However, large visitor numbers also bring impacts, such as traffic congestion and pressure on local services, which require careful management in order to maximise the benefits of tourism to the local and regional economies.

14.10 **National Parks –** The South East contains two national parks - the New Forest and the South Downs (subject to final designation). Both are nationally significant visitor destinations. The latter, with an estimated 30 million leisure visits annually, would be the most visited national park in the UK.

14.11 **River Thames –** The River Thames is of considerable importance to tourism. The river provides high quality landscapes along its length and is widely used for a range of informal leisure activities, bringing direct economic benefits to its surrounding area. It receives 14 million tourism visitors a year from walkers, canoeists, rowers and boaters, day-trippers and holidaymakers.

14.12 **Gateways –** The South East's tourism industry benefits from strong linkages to North West Europe through its international gateways. A substantial proportion of international passenger movements transit the region's major airports and ports, including Gatwick (Heathrow is just beyond the regional boundary), the ports of Dover, Portsmouth and Southampton and the Channel Tunnel, which provides direct access to North West Europe.

Coastal Resorts

POLICY TSR1: COASTAL RESORTS

Opportunities will be sought to diversify the economic base of the region's coastal resorts, while consolidating and upgrading tourism facilities in ways which promote higher value activity, reduce seasonality and support urban regeneration. To meet these objectives:

i. local strategic partnerships (LSPs) and marketing partnerships covering coastal resorts are encouraged to establish a vision and strategy for the future of tourism in their area and its contribution to wider regeneration objectives. Where appropriate, this should be undertaken in co-operation with neighbouring LSPs which together form an integrated tourism market

> ii local development frameworks should address the spatial dimensions of an agreed vision for tourism and identify 'core areas' and associated policies for tourism in coastal resorts to which specific tourism related planning policies apply for the purposes of:
>
> - controlling inappropriate development
> - co-ordinating management and environmental initiatives
> - setting environmentally sustainable development objectives
> - identifying land for particular types of tourism related development
> - identifying necessary infrastructure investments.
>
> iii. SEEDA should work proactively with other members of LSPs covering coastal resorts in the sub-regions of Kent Thames Gateway, East Kent and Ashford, Sussex Coast, South Hampshire and the Isle of Wight in the coastal belt to facilitate the development and implementation of regeneration strategies
>
> iv local authorities, in collaboration with the regional tourist board, should act strategically to develop complementary approaches to the marketing and development of the coastal resorts to enhance their overall competitiveness.

14.13 The traditional coastal seaside resorts have been hit hardest by the decline in long stay holidays by domestic tourists in the UK. Most will need to diversify and some will need to move away from tourism altogether. This will involve identifying and developing new markets alongside their traditional holiday base, and strengthening the product to attract visitors. This could include a diversity of product offers in relation to arts, entertainment, health, sport and fitness. It will also include the diversification of the local economy into other non-tourism related activities. A comprehensive strategy should be developed based upon a holistic vision for the resort as an area to live, work and visit. The type of facilities and associated investment required to deliver the vision may differ significantly from those traditionally provided. Higher value-added tourism should be the overall objective, with the emphasis on quality of visitor experience as opposed to the number of visitors.

14.14 Where appropriate, local planning authorities covering resorts should consider identifying 'core areas' which encompass the key visitor attractions and facilities (e.g. accommodation) within their LDFs. As a planning tool, this concept can help define the management priorities for the core area. For example, tourism investment can be prioritised within the identified boundary while other forms of development can have priority outside it.

14.15 Within these core areas attention should be given to:

i. improving the general environment and making it special and distinctive place within the resort
ii. maintaining architectural distinctiveness and promoting high quality design by highlighting their special character, whether it is vernacular building style or introducing public/environmental art.
iii. controlling inappropriate development which may be detrimental to the overriding objectives for the core area and encouraging appropriate re-investment
iv. establishing and co-ordinating area management initiatives, including mobility management, involving retailers and other commercial interests
v. addressing the implications of coastal flooding
vi. controlling the gradual reduction of bed stock on the core tourism areas
vii. encouraging the conversion of unviable or outdated accommodation stock for complementary tourism-related uses such as holiday apartments, which are unlikely to harm the tourism character of the area.
viii. use of land assembly powers where these are required to facilitate the regeneration/redevelopment of key seafront sites.

Tourism and Related Sports and Recreation

14.16 Appropriately managed, most resorts can absorb large numbers of visitors with little adverse impact. Other destinations within their hinterlands, such as areas with high landscape value or small villages, are more susceptible to damage and erosion of character. Therefore, resorts can act as a reservoir of demand for the surrounding rural hinterland through the promotion of a resort as a town by the sea, as well as a base for exploring the surrounding countryside. This is particularly pertinent along the coastal strip because of the difficulties of developing additional accommodation in inland areas covered by the environmental designations. Where this is the case, neighbouring coastal and inland authorities should work together in developing their respective tourism strategies and LDFs to ensure complementarity. An integrated cross border approach to the provision of public transport and visitor management would be particularly beneficial. In the case of the Isle of Wight, it is important that there is close collaborative working with the mainland on these issues. However, formal joint working between the island's local strategic partnership (LSP) and those on the mainland is not considered appropriate.

Tourism Related Rural Diversification and Development

> **POLICY TSR2: RURAL TOURISM**
>
> **Opportunities to promote tourism and recreation-based rural diversification should be encouraged where they provide jobs for local residents and are of a scale and type appropriate to their location.**
>
> **Local planning authorities in formulating planning policies and taking decisions will:**
>
> i. **support proposals which seek to develop the tourism opportunities associated with all types of rural development initiatives**
>
> ii. **protect access to, and support proposals for upgrading, inland waterways and associated facilities for recreational use in accordance with relevant management strategies**
>
> iii. **in surrounding countryside areas with significant tourism potential, local authorities should identify actions to strengthen linkages between market towns and their hinterlands through the provision of integrated sustainable transport and complementary product development, investment and marketing, including the promotion of locally produced products, such as food and crafts.**

14.17 Tourism, recreation and leisure activity in rural areas can bring significant economic, social and environmental benefits if carefully managed and, in many instances, will serve to underpin the continued viability of local services, including village shops, country pubs and agricultural enterprises. Other forms of rural diversification, such as woodland initiatives, the marketing of locally branded farm produce or country sports activities can also be mutually supportive of tourism activity and opportunities to develop linkages should be actively identified and pursued. Maintenance and enhancement of landscape character through good farming practices can also increase the potential in rural areas to attract tourism. However, the potentially significant environmental impacts associated with tourism and recreational-related development warrants the inclusion of specific criteria in development plan documents, against which the development applications for these uses should be considered. In this respect, tourism and related uses may provide particular benefits in terms of assisting with the retention or re-use of historic buildings contributing to the character of the countryside.

14.18 The River Thames and other inland waterways provide further opportunities for sustainable tourism, if suitably planned and provided for: Although recreational boating facilities are generally small and widely dispersed, there are a large number of recreational boats within the region, of which over half have accommodation and catering facilities. A shortage of moorings throughout the region, however, prohibits growth. Proposals for additional moorings should ensure they address any potential impacts they may have upon natural habitats. Local authorities should seek to positively address this issue through development plans. In developing additional moorings for the river it is important to ensure that local environment and habitat needs are taken into account and appropriately mitigated. The River Thames Alliance has prepared a Thames Waterway Plan for the period 2006-2011 which provides a strategic framework for reinvigorating leisure and tourism along the river corridor. Further policy on the River Thames is set out in Policy C7.

14.19 Rural market towns experiencing visitor pressure should adopt integrated visitor management strategies alongside town centre management to ensure they can adapt positively to changing travel habits, retail patterns and lifestyles more generally. It is important that growth in visitor numbers is managed in such a way that it does not undermine intrinsic environmental qualities. In a similar way to coastal resorts, market towns can provide the base from which visitors explore the rural hinterland. Similarly, the tourism and related linkages between market towns and the surrounding countryside will be strengthened by an integrated approach to transport management, marketing and promotion and product development. This will also help encourage longer stays.

Provision for Regionally Significant Sports Facilities

POLICY TSR3: REGIONALLY SIGNIFICANT SPORTS FACILITIES

Opportunities will be sought to protect, upgrade and develop new regionally significant sports facilities, particularly in Thames Gateway, Milton Keynes/Aylesbury Vale and Ashford.

i. **Local development documents should make adequate provision for new or expanded regionally significant sporting venues to redevelop or expand to meet future demands and requirements of the sport and of the spectator, taking into account sports governing bodies' needs strategies as they become available.**

ii. **Sport England should be proactive in advising the regional planning body and local authorities on the need for new or expanded regionally significant sporting venues.**

iii. **local authorities should be proactive in maximising the benefits to local communities of any major or expanded sporting facilities.**

iv. **regional partners, including Sport England, SEEDA and the regional planning body, should in partnership with the Greater London Authority identify and promote opportunities for new investment in sports facilities in the region associated with the London Olympics in 2012.**

14.20 Sport England has identified facilities of regional or national importance as:

i. facilities for national or international events. Many examples exist in the region, including tennis at Eastbourne, horse racing at royal Ascot and sailing in the Solent (Cowes week) and along the River Thames (Henley Regatta)

ii. UK Sports Institute facilities – two of the nine UK Sports Institutes centres are in the South East. The Lawn Tennis Association has an important presence at Bisham Abbey

iii. facilities identified in the strategies of the national governing bodies of sport. Examples include national rowing facilities at Caversham Lakes and regional yachting facilities in the Solent

iv. stadia with sub-regional implications. An example is Southampton Football Stadium, which also caters for a wide range of community and educational initiatives.

Tourism and Related Sports and Recreation

14.21 Within its Planning Policy Statement and its National Lottery Strategy, Sport England seeks large-scale investment on new and improved sports facilities. Many governing bodies for sport have now produced their own facility strategies, identifying the need for new or upgraded facilities that are of regional or national significance. Sport England will play a valuable role in advising individual local authorities on the need to provide for these facilities through the development plan process. Well managed sporting facilities of this scale and/or quality can also provide considerable benefits to local communities as well as the sports clubs they serve.

14.22 Consultation with key stakeholders (such as the police and other emergency services) should be undertaken as soon as possible to ensure that appropriate measures are put in place and facilities are provided to ensure any development is safe, secure and inclusive to all.

Tourism Attractions

POLICY TSR4: TOURISM ATTRACTIONS

Priority should be given to improving the quality of all existing attractions to meet changing consumer demands and high environmental standards in terms of design and access.

i. Local authorities and partners will:

- **encourage the enhancement and upgrade of existing visitor attractions**
- **include policies in development plans for determining applications for all new and changes to existing visitor attractions that are likely to have a significant impact locally.**

In developing such policies local authorities should consider the following criteria:

a. do they help reinforce the distinctiveness of a locality?
b. are they accessible by public transport and accessible to all (Disabled Discrimination Act compliant)?
c. do they provide wet weather facilities and help extend the season?
d. will they facilitate regeneration?
e. are they complementary to existing attractions (or will they displace existing activity)?

ii. New, regionally significant tourism attractions should only be developed where they will expand the overall tourism market and can be easily accessed by public transport. A sequential approach to site identification should be adopted for all new regionally significant attractions (those generating more than 250,000 visitors per annum) unless there are overriding requirements related to that site or sectoral reasons linked to cluster development. A suitable location should be sought:

- **within the sub-regions of Kent Thames Gateway, East Kent and Ashford, Sussex Coast, South Hampshire and the Isle of Wight in the coastal belt or the Milton Keynes and Aylesbury Vale Growth Area.**
- **only where it can be demonstrated that no suitable sites are available in the above areas should other locations be considered.**

14.23 A visitor attraction is defined by the tourism industry as a permanently established excursion destination, a primary purpose of which is to allow public access for entertainment, interest or education, rather than being a primary retail outlet or a venue for sporting, theatrical or film performance.

14.24 Within the South East, further provision of large attractions is unlikely to significantly expand the overall volume of tourism and may have adverse implications for existing attractions. 'Regionally significant' attractions (defined as those attracting at least 250,000 visitors per annum on the basis of their likely traffic impact, given the seasonal nature of demand) should only be encouraged in exceptional circumstances. One such exception

Tourism and Related Sports and Recreation

is the Thames Gateway – an area with an absence of any major attractions but one for which major population and employment growth is planned with significant improvements in transport accessibility. The overall market for tourism could therefore significantly expand in this area and other Growth Areas. Development within the regeneration areas would also be in accordance with the overall spatial strategy.

14.25 For new, regionally significant attractions, the onus will be on developers to demonstrate that they have assessed all potential development locations within the Kent Thames Gateway, Sussex Coast, East Kent and Ashford, and South Hampshire sub-regions or the Growth Areas of Milton Keynes and Aylesbury. Only if it can be demonstrated that a suitable site/location for the attraction cannot be found within these areas should other locations be considered, other than in exceptional circumstances. Exceptional circumstances might include, for example, where the location of a particular attraction is dependent upon the intrinsic physical or built environmental characteristics of a particular site or where attractions are linked to particular local themes or clusters of activity. In this case, local planning authorities should be prepared to consider the possibility of one-off visionary projects (e.g. the Eden Project in Cornwall). In such cases, a proposal should be treated on its merits, taking account of the potential economic benefits to the area and the region, the impact on the environment locally and more widely and the extent of 'fit' with other plans and policies already in place.

Visitor Accommodation

POLICY TSR5: TOURIST ACCOMMODATION

The diversity of the accommodation sector will be positively reflected in tourism and planning policies.

i. In formulating planning policies and making decisions local planning authorities should:

- consider the need for hotel developments to be in the proposed location, including links with the particular location, transport interchange or visitor attraction, and seek measures to increase access for all by sustainable transport modes
- provide specific guidance on the appropriate location for relevant accommodation sub-sectors. This should be informed by their different site requirements and market characteristics and how these relate to local planning objectives
- encourage the extension of hotels where this is required to upgrade the quality of the existing stock to meet changing consumer demands.
- include policies to protect the accommodation stock where there is evidence of market demand
- strongly encourage the provision of affordable staff accommodation as part of new and existing accommodation facilities in areas of housing pressure. The criteria for the application of such a requirement should be clearly set out in the development plans
- facilitate the upgrading and enhancement of existing un-serviced accommodation, including extensions where this will not harm landscape quality or identified environmental assets. Particular attention should be paid to identifying suitable sites for the relocation of holiday parks under threat from coastal erosion or flooding.

ii Tourism South East and local authorities should, working together, undertake active monitoring of the demand for and supply of tourism accommodation on a regional and sub-regional basis.

14.26 The visitor accommodation sector has become increasingly demanding and sophisticated, with a wide range of provision catering for specific visitor markets. The sector includes not only many different types of serviced accommodation (bed and breakfast, motels, hotels and guesthouses) but also self-catering accommodation (static caravan parks and touring caravan sites, holiday flats, camp sites, farm based accommodation etc).

Tourism and Related Sports and Recreation

Local development framework policies for visitor accommodation should be based upon a thorough understanding of the needs and characteristics of the many different accommodation subsectors required to meet the demands of varied consumer markets. Sub-sectors include:

i. hotels (guesthouses, hotels, country inns, motels)
ii. paying guest (e.g. bed & breakfast)
iii. rented house (cottages, farms)
iv. caravan and camping parks (static, touring and mixed)
v. holiday villages/camps
vi. group accommodation (e.g. hostels).

14.27 Policies should be built on an ongoing dialogue between local authority planners and representatives of the accommodation industry and supported by regular monitoring and assessments of demand and supply across the region, both quantitatively and qualitatively. In a number of areas of the South East the hotel stock is failing to meet changing consumer expectations in terms of standards of service. In many cases the existing stock will require extension to meet these expectations and, without upgrade, many accommodation providers go out of business and the stock is converted to other uses (e.g. residential). Local authorities, to inform planning decisions, should monitor the cumulative impact of small losses of accommodation stock.

14.28 Hotels are an important component in encouraging sustainable tourism. By providing accommodation for longer tourist visits, the presence of hotels can generate expenditure in an area and increase linkages to other tourism opportunities. As town centre locations offer access from a range of transport modes, ideally new hotel development should be located in town centres, preferably as part of mixed use developments where development can complement other town centre uses. However, hotel developers find it difficult to compete for land in many urban areas due to high land values. In accordance with national planning guidance on retail and town centres and transport, local authorities should assess applications for new hotel developments outside town centres (and not associated with major transport hubs or gateways) in terms of the extent to which the proposal needs to be in the proposed location. Proposals should also be assessed against the likely impact of the proposed development on existing town centre accommodation providers, Disabled Discrimination Act compliant accessibility by public and other modes of transport and impact on travel and car use. Assessments should specifically take account of the quality (i.e. service level) as well as the size of the proposed development as this will have a significant influence on the impacts on existing providers. Limited service provision is particularly suited to town centre locations as it can complement other town centre uses by providing a larger market for their services (e.g. bars and restaurants).

14.29 There continues to be an ongoing need for staff accommodation in association with hotels and unserviced accommodation in the South East, due to the problems of securing affordable housing. The availability of staff housing is critical for many operators to attract and retain staff and should be encouraged by local authorities where appropriate.

14.30 Unserviced accommodation (e.g. camping and caravan sites, holiday parks, self catering units, farmhouses and youth hostels) is a popular and vital component of the leisure accommodation offer in the region and provides a particularly valuable role in supporting longer stay/higher value rural tourism. This may include an increasing need to provide facilities for the winter storage of caravans given the increased trend for apartment living in the South East. Many self-catering units in rural parts of the region are under pressure to convert to residential uses to secure quick and substantial financial returns. Local planning authorities should seek to protect good quality accommodation in rural areas where there is evidence of market demand.

14.31 As visitor expectations change, it is likely that there will be increased demand for improvements to many existing holiday and caravan parks throughout the region, notably in the coastal areas. Significant expansion of existing sites may be required to facilitate the provision of new facilities and meet higher amenity standards. Applications to upgrade

Tourism and Related Sports and Recreation

facilities should be considered favourably by local authorities where there is evidence of existing or untapped demand subject to environmental policies set out elsewhere in this Plan.

Visitor Management and Access

> **POLICY TSR6: VISITOR MANAGEMENT**
>
> i. **Local development frameworks (LDFs) and tourism or cultural strategies will identify areas which would benefit from the development and implementation of visitor management. Where different local authority areas form part of a single tourism destination or market, opportunities should be taken to coordinate or integrate the development and implementation of visitor management plans**
> ii. **LDFs and local transport plans will address the management of tourism-related travel demand in an integrated way as part of a wider visitor management approach to managing tourism pressures and reflecting the priorities in the regional transport strategy. Depending on the nature of the tourism offer, this should include:**
>
> - **promoting a multi-modal approach to access to attractions and large events. Local authorities should facilitate this by encouraging operators to establish travel plans for attractions and events generating large numbers of trips**
> - **developing a range of travel planning approaches to specifically address transport impacts associated with urban and rural tourism.**

14.32   The potential environmental pressures associated with high levels of visitor activity are intensified as a result of poor visitor management. An integrated, inter-agency approach to visitor management is required to improve the experience of visitors whilst ameliorating:

   i. visitor congestion during peak months in many of the region's historic towns and cities
   ii. damage and disruption in areas of high landscape and environmental value such as the South Downs and New Forest.

14.33   This can and has been achieved in many areas through the introduction of area wide visitor management plans. In many cases, visitor management plans could usefully be complemented by strategic initiatives to disperse visitor pressure away from identified 'tourism hotspots'. For example, the provision of opportunities for leisure and recreation in the countryside, which enhances its character through maximising the use of highly managed areas (e.g. country parks) and directing activities to the most sustainable locations that are accessible by all.

14.34   Larger tourism, sport and recreation attractions/destinations, for example theme parks, are important generators of trips. Many one-off major events such as concerts, festivals or annual sporting events can also create significant, albeit short term, pressures on local environments. More effective management of access to these large scale facilities and events can reduce adverse transport impacts associated with them without undermining the benefits of the event to the local economy and visitor experience. An integrated approach to managing visitor access to major tourism sites, both permanent attractions and single events, is essential in providing better links to public transport networks, improved parking arrangements (including coach parking) and trips by walking and cycling.

Priority Areas for Tourism Development and Management

> **POLICY TSR7: PRIORITY AREAS FOR TOURISM**
>
> Local development frameworks, tourism/cultural strategies and transport plans will seek to emphasise and implement the following sub-regional priorities:

i. **The Coastal Strip and the Isle of Wight** – seeking complementary approaches to the development and management of tourism so as to upgrade facilities, promote diversity, and reduce seasonality and improve access, whilst retaining and enhancing the natural character of the area and having regard to issues of capacity and environmental sensitivity. This includes making use of the attraction of Canterbury and Brighton to encourage longer stays through linked trips to surrounding areas

ii. **Windsor and surrounds** – Cross-border working to manage the pressures associated with existing high levels of business and leisure tourism activity, through improved visitor management, enhanced public transport access, including coach travel to larger attractions, and strategic planning of visitor accommodation

iii. **Oxford** – Joint working with neighbouring authorities to encourage longer stays and to provide improved visitor management

iv. **River Thames** – Joint working to achieve the potential for informal recreation and sporting uses, within the wider uses of the working river, improved management and access in appropriate locations

v. **Thames Gateway** – Realising the potential for growth in business, sporting, environmental and attraction based tourism as part of the wider regeneration strategy for the Gateway, which includes the port and logistics sectors, adding value to the existing tourism market

vi. **Milton Keynes/Aylesbury Vale and Ashford** – Joint working to make appropriate provision for tourism, sport and recreation within the context of their identification as regional Growth Areas for the delivery of sustainable communities

Local authorities, the regional planning body and the regional tourism board should pursue an inter-regional approach to co-ordination and management in the following tourism areas:

- **The Thames Gateway (London and South Essex)**
- **Oxford (Cotswolds)**
- **New Forest (Dorset)**
- **Windsor and surrounds (London)**
- **Chilterns AONB (East of England)**
- **Milton Keynes/Aylesbury Vale (South Midlands).**

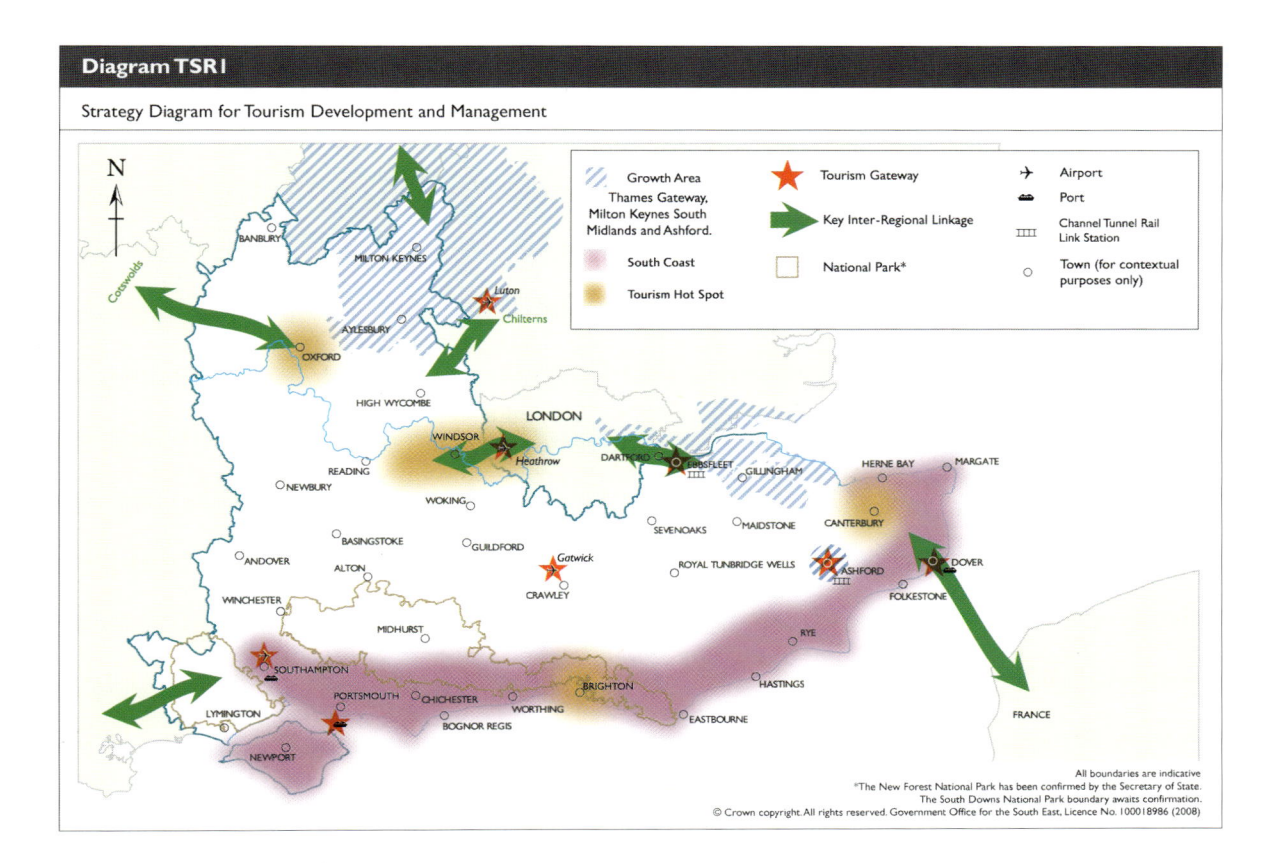

Tourism and Related Sports and Recreation

Diagram TSR1

Strategy Diagram for Tourism Development and Management

14.35 The priority areas for tourism development and management are shown on Diagram TSR1. Policy for these areas is set out in TSR7. Areas have been selected as they exhibit one of more of the following characteristics:

i. tourism as a major driver of the sub regional economy
ii. significant growth being planned over the South East Plan period, where tourism and/or large scale sport and recreation activity could be important to the development strategy
iii. areas where a cross boundary approach would benefit the planning and management of tourism and related activities
iv. areas where inter-regional cooperation would be beneficial.

14.36 **Coastal strip and the Isle of Wight** – Major new investments in tourism facilities and infrastructure in key resorts should be appraised in a sub-regional context, in terms of the added value they bring to the coastal strip as a whole. Complementary approaches should work towards the improvement of access to and within the area, and ensure that the upgrading of facilities retains and enhances the natural character of the area.

14.37 The wider area includes the tourism hotspots of Canterbury and Brighton and Hove, which contain important built and cultural heritage assets. Scope exists to make use of these assets to increase visitor numbers, particularly from overseas or the business sector, and to increase visitor spend whilst reducing impact through encouraging longer stays through linked trips to surrounding areas.

14.38 Tourism generates almost one quarter of the Isle of Wight's GDP, the highest proportion in the region. There is a need to maintain close working with mainland authorities in order to, for example, secure the accessibility improvements required to underpin the future success of its tourism industry.

14.39 **Windsor and surrounds** – A co-ordinated and integrated approach (between planning, transport and tourism authorities and operators) to the strategic planning and management of tourism-related activity in this sub-region is urgently required. This should include a concerted action in relation to visitor management for existing attractions and events and a requirement for all new attractions to be accessible by public transport. Cross boundary cooperation (including outer London boroughs) should also be actively pursued in the context of planning for new hotel developments in the area, given the pressure on land resources from competing uses.

14.40 **Oxford** - A regionally significant destination for overnight as well as day visits. However, many of the visitor pressures faced in the city are a result of the high proportion of day visits, particularly from London. Stronger integration of the city's tourism market with the surrounding countryside and inland waterways would help to encourage longer stays, perhaps as the starting point for visits into the Cotswolds and the West Country.

14.41 **New Forest and South Downs** - The majority of land area covered by the national parks is of special interest for nature conservation, including areas designated under international and national designations. Within the New Forest considerable work has been undertaken on promoting links between sympathetically managed countryside, reinstating traditional agricultural practices, environmental benefits, quality local produce and green tourism and access issues. These integrated approaches to rural development will also be a priority for the South Downs National Park once the Authority is operational in 2011 in partnership with other bodies.

14.42 **River Thames** - The River Thames represents a major recreational resource and there remains a need to further recognise and expand its potential. The river basin is subject to competing land use pressures, with the threat of losses to tourism infrastructure such as public open spaces, car parks, moorings and access points risking undermining its role in providing a tourism and recreation resource. Opportunities should be taken to support further co-ordination of access, management and land use planning to prevent this occurring.

14.43 **Thames Gateway** - The anticipated economic growth and planned transport improvements should provide the opportunity to develop a valuable business tourism market, provided suitable quality accommodation and conference/exhibition facilities are made available. Similarly, hosting the 2012 Olympics in east London will provide significant opportunities for high quality sports-related and ancillary development activity in the area and attract significant visitor numbers. The legacy of this could be particularly beneficial for the sub-region. The area also benefits from environmental assets, including internationally designated wildlife habitats. This could provide additional opportunities for tourism activity, if appropriately managed.

14.44 **Milton Keynes/Aylesbury Vale and Ashford Growth Areas** – The scale of growth in these areas will be regionally significant both in terms of population and employment. As a consequence, it will be important that opportunities for tourism, sport and recreation-related development are identified and fully integrated into the development plans for these areas.

14.45 **Inter-regional linkages** – In these areas, particular emphasis should be given to cross boundary working. There is considerable scope for exploiting the tourism opportunities associated with international gateways.

15 Social and Community Infrastructure

Context and Purpose

15.1 The Region's strategic vision for 2026 is for a socially and economically strong, healthy and just South East that respects the limits of the global environment. To achieve this the region must facilitate the development of health, education, cultural and leisure amenities, necessary to meet the needs of a growing population and manage the implications of demographic and settlement change.

15.2 The South East is a diverse society that is undergoing significant change. High levels of migration that may need to be accommodated within the South East communities during the life of this Plan will bring both economic and cultural benefit, but also potential risks to community cohesion. Working with Local Strategic Partnerships (LSPs), the local planning authorities should take a lead role in tackling barriers to cohesion and promoting integration between existing and new communities. In those parts of the region where significant growth is proposed, integrating place shaping with community cohesion should be a particular priority.

15.3 Key challenges for the South East may also emerge from:

   i. the specific needs of an ageing population
   ii. persistent poverty among certain groups of the population and in certain geographic areas
   iii. worklessness and polarisation of access to work and skills
   iv. polarisation in health outcomes
   v. an increasing digital divide
   vi. the increasing prevalence of obesity and its impact, life choice and health outcomes
   vii. the impact of the current economic downturn on mental well-being.

15.4 LSPs should play a key role, bringing together the different parts of the public, private, community and voluntary sectors to tackle priority issues including health, education/lifelong learning, community safety, housing and transport/infrastructure, and access to social/leisure/cultural activities.

Addressing Social Needs in the South East

POLICY S1 : SUPPORTING HEALTHY COMMUNITIES

Local development documents should embrace preventative measures to address the causes of ill health by reflecting the role the planning system can play in developing and shaping healthy sustainable communities, including:

i. **community access to amenities such as parks, open spaces, physical recreation activity, and cultural facilities**
ii. **mixed and cohesive communities, with a particular focus on access to housing for socially excluded groups**
iii. **healthier forms of transport, by incorporating cycle lanes and safe footpaths in planned developments.**

15.5 The living environment has a fundamental impact on the health of a population, often by providing opportunities for healthy lifestyles. There are two main areas where health interfaces with planning:

   i. the health implications of spatial planning decisions - including impacts such as those of transport planning on physical activity, travel to schools and places of work, noise and air pollution, access, climate change, and social networks
   ii. the spatial aspects of planning for health services – including the requirement for health services and infrastructure (and related issues such as access).

Social and Community Infrastructure

15.6 The Government strategy *Healthy Weight, Healthy Lives* (2008) sets a commitment to tackle rising rates of obesity by promoting healthy eating, encouraging active lifestyles and supporting weight management programmes. Local planning authorities should work with Strategic Health Authorities, Primary Care Trusts, transport authorities, education authorities and other service providers to tackle health problems such as obesity that have multiple causation and require action through several policy sectors.

> **POLICY S2 : PROMOTING SUSTAINABLE HEALTH SERVICES**
>
> **Local planning authorities should work closely with the NHS across its delivery bodies to ensure the provision of additional and reconfigured health and social care facilities to meet the anticipated primary care and capacity needs of local communities. Where need is identified, land should be made available for additional community, social and primary care facilities.**
>
> **Local authorities and the various NHS Trusts should work closely together to facilitate joint planning and to influence NHS estate strategies. Health Impact Assessments should become an integral part of the decision-making process.**

15.7 Joint strategic needs assessments are a systematic approach by PCTs and local authorities to identify the current and future health and well being needs of local populations and to inform commissioning and planning of services, and to inform the local Sustainable Communities Strategy.

15.8 Local area agreements are an important mechanism for joint action on improving the health and well being of local populations and to reduce inequalities in health. Health services can make a significant contribution to a sustainable region. *Saving Carbon, Improving Health*, the NHS carbon reduction strategy for England, published in January 2009, sets out an ambition for the NHS to reduce carbon and improve sustainability and it is vital that the NHS works more closely with local authorities to ensure that changes to the configuration of health and social care provision are delivered in a sustainable manner.

15.9 The NHS *High Quality Care For All* Next Stage Review Final Report by Lord Darzi (June 2008) sets the agenda for providing high quality personalised care. Both Strategic Health Authorities in the South East have produced local responses to this review which include focusing on prevention and providing care closer to home.

15.10 With the third highest sickness absence rates in England, work-place health is a significant challenge to the wellbeing of the South East economy and to region's aim to achieve Smart Growth. Sickness absenteeism and implications of ageing population are particularly problematic areas for Small and Medium Enterprises. There is good evidence that being in work has a positive effect on health and the Department for Health and Department for Work and Pensions joint strategy *Health, Work and Wellbeing* aims to increase access to work and to reduce dependency on benefits. The current Regional Economic Strategy (RES) also aims to embrace new ways of working that support businesses and develop a diverse and healthy workforce which will improve the region's competitiveness.

15.11 The local planning authorities should work with the relevant stakeholders including business community and Occupational Health services to ensure that the health implications of spatial planning decisions are fully considered and provided for. They should make use of Health Impact Assessments where appropriate to facilitate evidence-based recommendations about practical ways to enhance the positive impacts of a proposal, and to remove or minimise any negative impacts on health, well-being and health inequalities that might arise or exist.

Education and Skills

> **POLICY S3: EDUCATION AND SKILLS**
>
> Local planning authorities, taking into account demographic projections, should work with partners to ensure the adequate provision of pre-school, school and community learning facilities. Policies should advocate the widening and deepening of participation through better accessibility, reflecting the role the planning system can play in developing and shaping healthy sustainable communities. Policies should:
>
> i. **take account of the future development needs of the economy and the community sector**
> ii. **encourage mixed use approaches, that include community facilities alongside 'formal' education facilities**
> iii. **seek to ensure access for all sections of society to education facilities at locations with good public transport access.**

15.12 While the qualification profile of the South East workforce is higher than in many other English regions, it remains lower than that of international competitors, particularly in terms of intermediate (level 2-3) skills and qualifications. The highest proportions of individuals without basic skills tend to be concentrated in the Thames Gateway and along the coast but with some exceptions such as Slough and Crawley.[1] However, even in the higher achieving areas there are still considerable numbers of individuals lacking basic skills.

15.13 Achieving a substantial improvement in qualifications for both adults and young people will require an increased focus on reducing basic skills problems, which affect more than one in five (22 per cent) people in the South East, and this is being topped up by approximately 6,000 young people each year leaving schools in the South East lacking basic skills.[2] Poor basic skills in the current and potential workforce significantly restricts the supply of people into intermediate level training and education.

15.14 Increasing the levels of employment and addressing skills needs among socially excluded populations (including ex offenders and substance mis-users, those with disabilities, the elderly and other vulnerable groups) and increasing the economic activity levels amongst those in incapacity benefit are common aims for the RES, the South East England Health Strategy and this Plan. The Regional Health Strategy promotes action to secure physical and mental health and wellbeing of children in special circumstances are identified (including looked after children, children with disabilities, young offenders).

15.15 A real step-change in delivery is required and local authorities and others responsible for these services need to increase efforts to break through the barriers to delivery, with adequate resources and effective flexible delivery mechanisms.

15.16 Government departments, local authorities and other public landowners should also recognise the need for additional schools and colleges at an early stage of major new development. The phased provision of primary and secondary education, along with early years and lifelong learning, will be needed throughout the region, to accommodate population growth and behavioural changes. The changing work and life styles will also add to the demand for pre-school facilities. The locations of facilities must be accessible to the communities they serve. Consideration should be given to the use of school and college buildings after hours, to support learning among the wider community.

---

1 Skills Insight Annual Skills Review 2003/2004 (Skills Insight)
2 Spending Review 2004: South East Regional Emphasis Document

Social and Community Infrastructure

Higher and Further Education

> **POLICY S4: HIGHER AND FURTHER EDUCATION**
>
> Local authorities should work with the Learning and Skills Council, the Higher Education Funding Council for England, SEEDA and the higher and further education sectors to ensure that these sectors' needs are addressed in local development frameworks.

15.17 The Higher and Further Education sectors in the region are critical to the South East's productive capacity and are powerful drivers of technological change and to local and regional economic development.

15.18 In 2005 there were 25 Universities or Higher Education Colleges in the South East region hosting some 200,000 full-time students, and employing about 64,000 staff. Although in many parts of the region participation levels in higher education are above the national average, reflecting the social mix, there remain significant pockets of low participation. Widening and deepening participation is important for both the economic and social development of the region.

15.19 Moreover, the Higher and Further Education providers are:

i. an important economic entity in their own right - a major source of high quality and stimulating employment, bringing a substantial and stable stream of national funding into the region, with associated local expenditure, which has a strong economic multiplier effect on the local economy

ii. a direct support to the development of industry and the regional economy - attracting national and regional funding and improving the competitiveness and effectiveness of businesses and public services in the region

iii. a cultural and recreational resource - resources are often available to the wider public, with libraries, galleries and other facilities open to the community as audience and for participation.

15.20 The higher education providers should play their full role in helping the region to achieve the aims of Smart Growth as set out in Policy RE5 of this Plan and in the RES. This means helping to raise the level of innovation, creativity and global competitiveness in the region and working towards assisting more people to join the labour force by removing barriers to work and enhancing skills levels.

15.21 A framework for an effective and efficient higher education offer would need to recognise the importance of ancillary services for higher education establishments; including student accommodation, sports facilities, incubator units suitable for small spin-off businesses from universities and the need to give particular encouragement to developments that maximise the potential of a university by siting it as part of a multi-use development to include employment, healthcare, leisure and other community uses.

15.22 Regional and local partners should work flexibly with Higher Education funding providers to address the expected increase in demand for Higher Education places in the region arising as a result of the growing propensity for students to live in the parental home whilst studying.

Cultural and Sporting Activity

> **POLICY S5: CULTURAL AND SPORTING ACTIVITY**
>
> Increased and sustainable participation in sport, recreation and cultural activity should be encouraged by local authorities, public agencies and their partners through local development documents and other measures in order to improve the overall standard of fitness, enhance cultural diversity and enrich the overall quality of life.

Social and Community Infrastructure

> **Provision for cultural and sporting activity should:**
>
> i. be based on an up to date strategy for the selected provision which should cover aspects such as the arts, heritage, the museums, libraries and archive sectors and sporting activity
> ii. be based on an audit of current supply and an assessment of this supply against estimated demand/growth. The audits should cover the quantitative, qualitative and accessible nature of provision. Authorities should encourage formal partnership working to put in place effective programmes of provision and management.
>
> **Local development documents should include policies relevant to local needs designed to:**
>
> i. encourage participation by disadvantaged and socially excluded persons/groups
> ii. locate facilities sustainably where they can be accessed by a range of modes of transport particularly healthy forms of transport i.e walking and cycling
> iii. make joint service provisions where appropriate
> iv. give special attention to cultural provision in supporting economic growth and urban regeneration, which may be the subject of area action plans
> v. include policies encouraging workplace and other everyday provision for increased physical activity.

15.23 The cultural agenda in the region runs broad and deep. It includes, for example, the arts (theatres, community arts centres and work space for artists), sport and physical activity (including playing fields, other outdoor playing space, sports centres and swimming pools) as well as open space for informal activities. It also includes libraries and archive facilities, museums and galleries, and the built heritage (including historic buildings, landscapes and sites). The activities of the cultural and creative sectors permeate many of the key concerns of the South East Plan. 13% of the region's workforce is employed in cultural and creative industries (with the sector experiencing significant growth over recent years) and the sport-related activities alone employ around 75,000 people in the region. South East residents spend £2.1bn annually on sports-related goods and services and around 863,000 people participate in organised sports clubs, which have an annual income of around £550m.[3]

15.24 A rich and varied cultural 'landscape' is a contributor to 'Smart Growth' and is essential to delivering a competitive information-led economy. Research has shown that successful cultural policies can also help regeneration and urban renaissance. At a personal level, cultural activities promote health, including physical and mental well-being. To successfully engage people in cultural activities it is vital that a wide range of opportunities are available and easily accessible, for example in single mixed-use locations.

15.25 Although the South East has high levels of participation in cultural activities and in sport there are also groups and communities cut off from these opportunities due to lack of education, transport or other resources. Education and economic status have a high correlation with physical activity. Despite substantial achievements much of the region's cultural potential goes untapped,[4] and unlocking some of the unrealised possibilities would have benefits for improved health and wider social inclusion.

15.26 Cultural and community facilities – such as libraries, community and sports centres along with village halls – can provide lifelong learning and skills development in an environment that may be more suitable to groups excluded from, or less able to access, mainstream services. The provision of mixed use facilities (encompassing sport and cultural activity) and the activities they support offer a method of bringing together existing and new communities in areas of growth.

---

3 Source: *The Value of the Sports Economy in the Regions* – A Study on Behalf of Sport England by Cambridge Econometrics: The Case of the South East. June 2003
4 *The Cultural Agenda – Realising the Cultural Strategy of the South East Cultural Consortium* (South East England Cultural Consortium, November 2002)

15.27 This Plan supports Sport England's national strategy, and the focus on creating a world leading community sports system which will ensure that a substantial, and growing, number of people from across the community play sport. Consequently there is a need for local authorities to support the promotion of sport, along with health and well-being by increasing physical activity in their areas. This required support is consistent with:

i. the Government's White Paper *Choosing Health: Making Healthy Choices Easier* (2004)
ii. the publication by the South East Physical Activity Co-ordinating Team (SEPACT) entitled *A Framework for Physical Activity in the South East* (2004) which makes links between the health and physical activity agendas in the region
iii. the need for good physical accessibility to cultural and sports facilities, reflecting statements in the regional cultural strategy, the *Cultural Cornerstone* (2001).

15.28 Local authorities should consider developing supplementary planning documents for providing cultural and sporting infrastructure, to meet existing needs and those arising from new development. Consideration should also be given to the importance of promoting sport and recreation within the workplace by local authorities and businesses.

Community Infrastructure

> **POLICY S6: COMMUNITY INFRASTRUCTURE**
>
> **The regional planning authority and regional partners, including SEEDA, will work with Government and other agencies to increase investment in physical and social infrastructure and secure co-ordination between development and essential infrastructure provision.**
>
> **Where appropriate, the mixed use of community facilities should be encouraged by local authorities, public agencies and other providers, through local development documents and other measures in order to make effective use of resources and reduce travel and other impacts.**
>
> **Local planning authorities, in consultation with those delivering services using community infrastructure (including the Third Sector and Faith organisations), will ensure facilities are located and designed appropriately, taking account of local needs and a whole life costing approach.**
>
> **Policies should also ensure that:**
>
> i. **community infrastructure supports economic growth and regeneration, with particular priority for health and education provision**
> ii. **creative thinking and action on new mixes of cultural and community facilities is encouraged**
> iii. **appropriate facilities are made accessible to all sections of the community, in both urban and rural settlements.**

15.29 Sustainable communities depend on the effective delivery of community infrastructure. Given the expected growth in the region's population, there will inevitably be a need for additional investment in community infrastructure - childcare, community centres, village halls, places of worship, fire and rescue stations, leisure centres, libraries, police stations, prison provision, social services facilities, and waste and recycling facilities.

15.30 Mechanisms to ensure and enhance community infrastructure need to take account of the flexible use of buildings and spaces as well as the traditional 'single use building' approach. Provision of community infrastructure is essentially a matter for local action although local assessments of need should be informed by national and regional guidance for assessment, where they are available, and should be utilised to identify gaps that can be addressed through the development process.

Social and Community Infrastructure

15.31 Access to this community infrastructure is also vital. For those who are reliant on the availability of key services, access to such facilities (taking account of health issues and the time and cost) can be a key determinant of the quality of life.

15.32 This is of particular concern for those living in rural areas where the dispersed nature of the resident population, combined with a broad reliance on use of the private car, can lead to difficulties for service delivery.

16 South Hampshire

Diagram SH1: South Hampshire Sub-regional Strategy Area

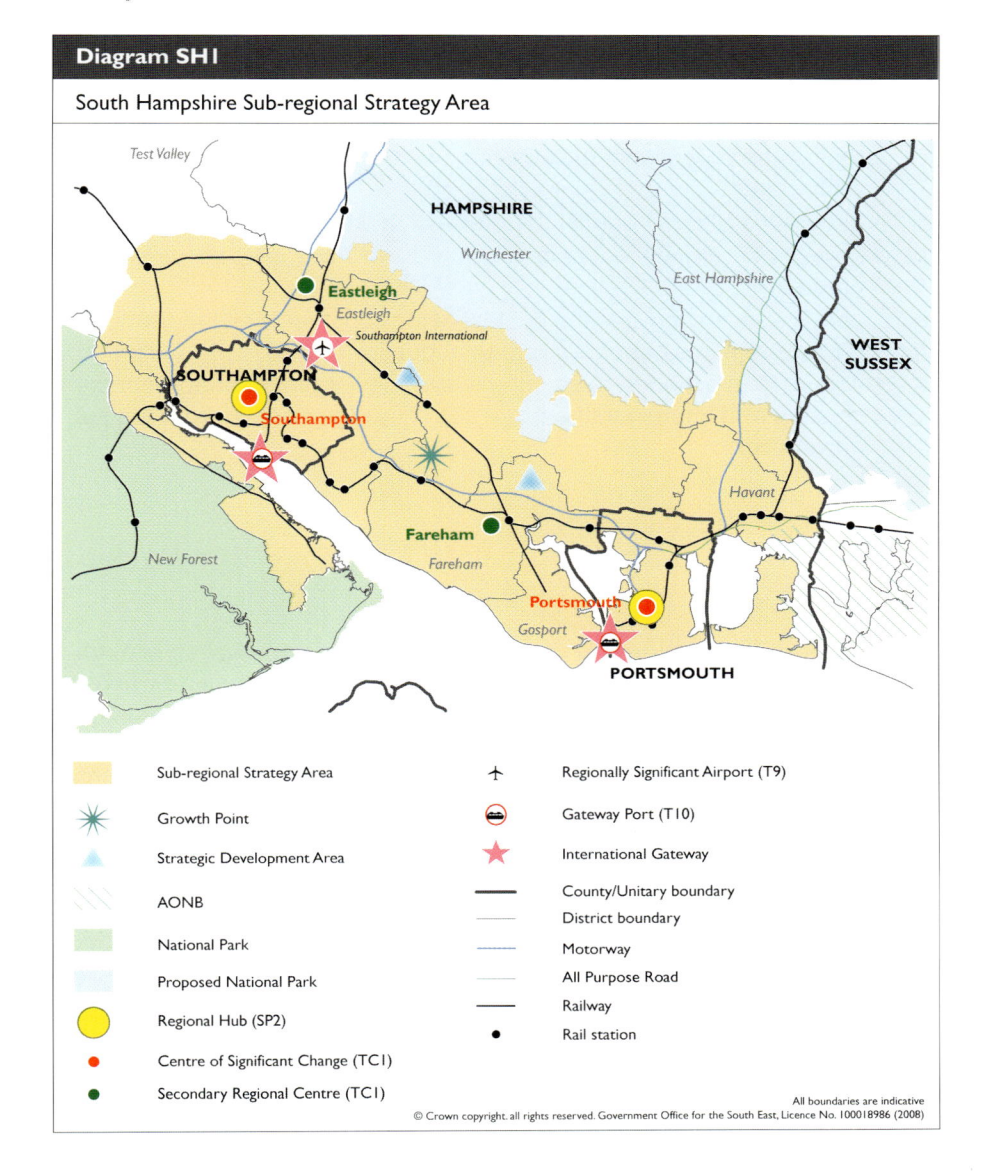

Legend:
- Sub-regional Strategy Area
- Growth Point
- Strategic Development Area
- AONB
- National Park
- Proposed National Park
- Regional Hub (SP2)
- Centre of Significant Change (TC1)
- Secondary Regional Centre (TC1)
- Regionally Significant Airport (T9)
- Gateway Port (T10)
- International Gateway
- County/Unitary boundary
- District boundary
- Motorway
- All Purpose Road
- Railway
- Rail station

All boundaries are indicative
© Crown copyright, all rights reserved. Government Office for the South East, Licence No. 100018986 (2008)

16.1 The South Hampshire sub-region covers the districts of Eastleigh, Fareham, Gosport, Havant, Portsmouth and Southampton, and parts of East Hampshire, New Forest, Test Valley and Winchester districts. The area is bounded to the north by the shortly to be confirmed South Downs National Park and to the west by the New Forest National Park. It forms an almost continuous spread of loose knit suburban development adjacent to the Solent coastline. Although it has many advantages, including significant potential for sustainable economic growth, a high quality environment, good communications and world class education institutions, the sub-region has recently suffered from a lower rate of economic growth compared with the regional average and has pockets of high unemployment and deprivation particularly in parts of Portsmouth and Southampton. Most of this sub-region was defined as a Priority Area for Economic Regeneration in RPG9. However, the sub-region now covers a wider area than that defined in RPG9 in recognition of the links between the coastal towns and cities and their immediate hinterland and the challenges faced. Diagram SH1 illustrates the extent of the South Hampshire sub-regional area.

16.2 The aim for this sub-region is to improve economic performance up to 2026, which will allow for the provision of 80,000 net additional dwellings in this same time frame, whilst at the same time seeking to address areas of social deprivation and protect and enhance its environmental quality. South Hampshire is supported by the Government's designation in October 2006 of this sub-regional strategy as a New Growth Point, with an accompanying phased allocation of funds for key projects.

16.3 The particular challenges faced by the sub-region are how to:

i. realise the potential of the sub-region to improve its sustainable economic performance
ii. ensure the above benefits the areas of economic and social deprivation
iii. deliver sufficient decent homes and provide a well integrated mix to meet the needs of the area
iv. achieve all the above in the context of the constraints on land supply and respecting the sub-region's high environmental quality
v. ensure joint action to raise skills levels, development of appropriate business clusters and improving the scale of knowledge transfer from the sub-region's universities.

Core Policy

POLICY SH1: CORE POLICY

Development in South Hampshire will be led by sustainable economic growth and urban regeneration. Portsmouth and Southampton will be dual focuses for investment and development as employment, retail, entertainment, higher education and cultural centres for the sub-region. The other towns will play a complementary role serving their more local areas. These urban areas will be enhanced so that they are increasingly locations where people wish to live, work and spend their leisure time. Investment and improvements in transport will reflect this, as will the location of sites for development. High density development will be encouraged in the city and town centres, around public transport hubs and at other sustainable locations.

Until around 2016, development will be concentrated on existing allocations and other sites within existing urban areas plus a number of urban extensions. Thereafter, development will be concentrated on sites within existing urban areas and in two Strategic Development Areas (see Policy SH2).

16.4 The strategy aims to improve its economic performance to at least match the regional average, with a target of achieving a gross value added (GVA) of 3.5% per annum by 2026. This will involve an increase in jobs as well as productivity, requiring land for business development and house building.

16.5 To facilitate this, the policy focuses development up to 2016 primarily on sites allocated in adopted development plans, on brownfield sites within existing urban areas, plus urban extensions. However, after 2016, while this focus will continue, the policy also provides for greenfield development concentrated in two 'strategic development areas' (SDAs). It is important that work commences prior to this date in order to deliver development on both SDAs from 2016 onwards. The urban extensions and SDAs will be located close to and with good transport links to Southampton and Portsmouth and other major employment centres. Their location will also help support improvements in public transport infrastructure and services across a wider area.

16.6 South Hampshire has a dense and complex settlement pattern, and accommodates a population of nearly one million people. Within the urbanised parts of the sub-region, there are substantial areas of undeveloped land. If local authorities in South Hampshire consider the inclusion of local gaps to be essential in terms of shaping the settlement pattern, this policy approach will need to be tested through development plan documents.

Strategic Development Areas

> **POLICY SH2: STRATEGIC DEVELOPMENT AREAS**
>
> Strategic development areas (SDAs) will be allocated in close proximity to the two cities in the following broad locations:
>
> i. within Fareham Borough to the north of the M27 motorway comprising 10,000 new dwellings
> ii. to the north and north-east of Hedge End comprising 6,000 new dwellings.
>
> In each SDA the housing will be of varying types/sizes including affordable housing. Provision will also be made for co-ordinated and integrated employment, transport and housing development, together with supporting health, community, social, shopping, education, recreation and leisure facilities, green space and other identified requirements.
>
> Particular attention will be paid to securing quality public transport links with neighbouring city and town centres, transport hubs and existing or planned major employment locations.
>
> Development at the SDAs should ensure that the national air quality standards are not breached.
>
> The precise form and location of SDAs will be established in development plan documents (DPDs). Their impact will be assessed in relation to their effect on surrounding districts and their sustainability, including their landscape impact.
>
> To prevent coalescence of the SDAs with neighbouring settlements and in order to protect the separate identities of individual settlements, areas of open land will be maintained between:
>
> i. the Fareham SDA and Wickham/Funtley/Knowle
> ii. the North/North East of Hedge End SDA and neighbouring settlements.
>
> The precise boundaries of these areas of land will be defined in DPDs to include land which has a predominantly open and/or rural appearance. The open land will be selected to respect the identity of the existing settlements while ensuring that opportunities for sustainable access to services and facilities in the SDA and the adjacent urban areas are not prejudiced. Only land necessary to achieve these long term objectives will be included. Within these areas, built development will not be allowed except for small scale buildings which cannot be located elsewhere and which are essential to maintain established uses within the areas of open land, or to enhance their recreational value.
>
> Local planning authorities should, where necessary work together, including in the preparation of joint DPDs where appropriate, to bring forward the SDAs. In addition, planning authorities in partnership with developers, will develop a masterplan for each SDA at an early stage in the development process. This should identify on and off-site infrastructure requirements and set out an implementation programme, including phasing. Core strategies, supported by area action plans or supplementary planning documents, will be prepared for the SDAs.

16.7 The need for these SDAs has already been referred to in paragraph 16.5 above. There are a number of critical success factors which are fundamental to their delivery:

> **At Hedge End:**
>
> i. attractive, high quality public transport connections to the main urban centres, in particular Southampton
> ii. maximise opportunities to improve services via Hedge End rail station

iii. maximise accessibility to the station from within the SDA
iv. careful balance between maintaining the identity of the existing settlements while ensuring that opportunities for sustainable access to services and facilities in the SDA and the adjacent urban areas is not prejudiced
v. protection and enhancement of landscape quality will be particularly important in the north/north eastern parts of the area
vi. close working, and possibly a joint area action plan, between Winchester City Council and Eastleigh Borough Council
vii. provision of green infrastructure.

At Fareham:

i. careful balance between maintaining settlement identity and maximising opportunities for sustainable movement between the SDA and the existing urban area
ii. Quality public transport connections with Portsmouth, including the development of an attractive bus based service linking Fareham and its associated SDA with Gosport and Portsmouth
iii. sensitive treatment of the relationship with Portsdown Hill to the east of the SDA location, and of the setting of the neighbouring settlements
iv. provision of green infrastructure.

16.8 The pace of housing development within the SDAs should be co-ordinated with progress on better transport demand and operational management, and with the rate of infrastructure provision (see Policy CC7). In addition, the proposed implementation agency (see Policy SH9) will have a role in monitoring and implementing strategic land allocations. Partnership working is essential for co-ordination of the overall delivery of both SDAs.

16.9 Whilst Area Action Plans may be the most appropriate delivery tool in some circumstances, local planning authorities may also wish to consider alternative means of delivery, such as a Core Strategy, supported by a supplementary planning document (see PPS12: *Local Spatial Planning*).

Economy and Employment

POLICY SH3 – SCALE, LOCATION AND TYPE OF EMPLOYMENT DEVELOPMENT

Land will be provided to accommodate two million square metres of new business floorspace as follows:

South West area:

B1 Offices - 680,000 m^2

B2 Manufacturing - 93,000 m^2

B8 Warehousing - 294,000 m^2

located on:

i. **previously developed land within the cities and towns - 677,000 m^2**
ii. **greenfield land in the North/North East of Hedge End Strategic Development Area - 74,000 m^2**
iii. **greenfield land in the larger urban extensions and other greenfield sites with high accessibility allocated for that purpose in development plan documents (DPDs) - 316,000m^2**

> Eastleigh Borough Council should, as a matter of priority, produce a Core Strategy or an Area Action Plan (either of these could be supported by a supplementary planning document) to bring forward a mixed use development including Classes B1(a), B1(b), B1(c), B2, B8 and other appropriate uses, together with necessary transport interventions at the South Hampshire Strategic Employment Area.
>
> South East area:
>
> Class B1 Offices - 535,000 m^2
>
> Class B2 Manufacturing - 123,000 m^2
>
> Class B8 Warehousing - 240,000 m^2
>
> located on:
>
> i. previously developed land within the cities and towns - 480,000 m^2
> ii. greenfield land in the Fareham Strategic Development Area - 121,000 m^2
> iii. greenfield land in the larger urban extensions and other greenfield sites with high accessibility allocated for that purpose in DPDs - 297,000m^2.
>
> Local planning authorities should audit their current employment allocations, taking into account Policy RE3: Employment and Land Provision, to ensure that they meet the needs of modern firms, especially those which will generate economic growth, and can be economically developed within the necessary timescale. They should ensure that sites confirmed through this review process as being suitable for employment development, are protected for that use in DPDs. Land already in use for employment should be safeguarded for that purpose.
>
> In phasing the release of sites priority should be given to sites which will contribute to achieving growth in Gross Value Added (GVA) and/or support urban renaissance whilst recognising the need to accommodate a full range of employment uses.
>
> Note : Office floorspace figures in this policy contain a 10% flexibility allowance.

16.10 Economic growth has varied widely across South Hampshire, with the two cities failing to match even national growth rates whilst the outermost parts of the strategy area have grown at rates above the regional average. The sub-region has a strong specialism in advanced manufacturing but it lags behind the South East region in the development of the high value added advanced business services. Rates of new business creation and self-employment are below South East and national averages. Its two cities, Southampton and Portsmouth are international gateways and sub-regional and locally significant employment areas respectively.

16.11 To address this poor performance and realise the sub-region's potential, the target economic growth rate of 3.5% per annum (gross value added) by 2026 is estimated to require around two million square metres of additional business floorspace (0.6 million square metres once extant permissions and allocations are subtracted) and will result in an employment increase of 59,000 between 2006 and 2026. Policy SH3 provides for this with about 60% of the floorspace required for knowledge based industries and industry services. The rest will be to provide new warehouse space for the predicted growth in distribution, transport and communications, and for the development of advanced manufacturing in which South Hampshire has a particular strength. The figures exclude floorspace for leisure and retail development which although forecast to grow significantly, will not require the type of space required by Policy SH3.

16.12 The policy refers to two sub-areas for land allocations, monitoring and management of delivery: the South West area centred on Southampton and including the whole of Eastleigh Borough, and those parts of New Forest District and Test Valley within the sub-region; and the South East area centred on Portsmouth and including the whole of Fareham, Gosport and Havant Boroughs, together with those parts of Winchester City and East Hampshire Districts which are within the sub-region.

16.13   Key strategic locations for accommodating significant amounts of the above floorspace are the city and town centres, the two SDAs and the site of around 130ha to the east of Eastleigh (the South Hampshire Strategic Employment Area), which is the largest employment area in South Hampshire and is capable of being developed for a wide range of uses. Particular attention needs to be given to the provision of new business floorspace in Gosport where job density at 0.57% is the lowest in the South East region and the volume of out-commuting seriously exceeds the transport capacity of the Gosport peninsula.

16.14   The selection of new sites for employment development will need to take account of the location of housing and other development to increase self containment of settlements and offer a greater mix of uses.

16.15   Whilst employment uses are set out in Policy SH3, land may also be required for port uses at Southampton Port. This includes land for infrastructure that maintains and enhances the role of the Port and the protection of waterfront land that may be required for port use. The safeguarding of sites important to the marine industry in and around Southampton and Portsmouth should also be noted (see Policies T10, T12 and RE3).

16.16   To take maximum advantage of the opportunities presented by this policy it is critical that smart growth is promoted in the context of Policy RE5 including through productivity improvements, making more efficient use of land through intensification and through improving the skills base. The latter should benefit from joint action to raise skills levels through development of appropriate business clusters, taking advantage of the knowledge base in the sub-region's universities in seeking high value added activity and programmes of up-skilling (see also Policy RE4).

POLICY SH4 – STRATEGY FOR MAIN TOWN CENTRES

Development Strategy for Main Centres

The strategy for the main centres of South Hampshire is to develop their individual character and complementary roles through: a proactive programme of high quality mixed-use development; improvements to the public realm and conservation initiatives within town centres; and improved access from central areas to parks, open spaces and waterfront destinations for business and leisure. Accessibility of the main centres will be improved through implementation of the sub-regional transport strategy in Policy SH7.

For each main centre, the relevant development plan document will define the future identity and growth of the centre, as follows:

i.   **in Southampton, expansion of retail, leisure, office employment and cultural facilities to enhance the city's role as a regional centre serving south west Hampshire and areas to the west and north of the sub-region by consolidating the existing primary shopping area, integrating redevelopment of the major city centre sites to the west of this in the medium term (to 2016), and possibly expanding towards the waterfront in the longer term (to 2026)**

ii. **in Portsmouth, expansion of the role of the city centre as a regional destination for shopping, leisure, office employment and culture serving south east Hampshire and areas to the north and east of South Hampshire and the city's national role as a leisure destination. There is potential for high density development at opportunity sites to reverse the recent trend of declining office employment in Portsmouth city centre. Any additional development at Gunwharf Quays would be subject to the policy set out in PPS6: *Planning for Town Centres* or its replacement**

iii. **in Fareham, limited expansion of the centre, with new mixed-use schemes in the enlarged town centre to improve retail, leisure and office employment provision and** support further development of the leisure and evening economy. Excellent access to the North of Fareham SDA is to be secured in advance of development, to ensure that Fareham town centre is the main sub-regional facility to serve the population of the SDA

iv. in Eastleigh, developing town centre capacity through redevelopment to provide high density, high quality retail, leisure and office employment schemes which address its growing potential market demand. A proactive approach is needed to deliver new strategic town centre opportunities. There is the potential to include a significant office component in the South Hampshire Strategic Employment Area in Policy SH3

v. in Havant and Gosport, developing opportunity sites to provide for appropriate retail and leisure growth and more substantial growth in office employment

vi. in other town centres, providing for the continued expansion of facilities to cater for their expanding population or to meet current local needs, as appropriate.

New Centres and Out of Centre Development

Over the period 2011- 2016, new district centres may be provided within the larger urban extensions.

Later in the Plan period (2016 onwards), two new centres will be required within the proposed SDAs. These will complement the roles of the established town centres within the sub-region and it is not envisaged that they will have full town centre status. In retailing and leisure terms, the new centres will serve as district centres. In terms of office employment, however, the new centres have the potential to serve a wider sub-regional role by providing new employment opportunities, with excellent accessibility and public transport provision, although any such development will need to satisfy the approach set out in PPS6 or its replacement.

Out of centre development for town centre uses will be limited to existing allocations up to 2016.

16.17 Large office, retail and leisure developments are well suited to city and town centres and other locations which have good public transport accessibility. Their presence within the heart of the urban area can also help create vitality and underpin regeneration. With significant pressure to develop these facilities outside existing centres, Policy SH4 will ensure that all development plan documents treat them in the same way. At the same time, the capacity of existing centres is limited. In order to compete effectively for potential investment by major retailers, corporations and international firms seeking a presence in the sub-region, a sub-regional strategy is required to address the full range of potential requirements.

16.18 The main centres in South Hampshire are the regional city centres of Southampton and Portsmouth (identified as Centres for Significant Change in Policy TC1), the sub-regional town centres of Fareham and Eastleigh (identified as Secondary Regional Centres in Policy TC1) and the network of local town centres, including Gosport and Havant.

16.19 The estimated need and capacity to cater for growth in town and city centre uses in South Hampshire is summarised below. The office figure in Policy SH3 differs, as the figures below do not include a 10% flexibility allowance.

16.20 These are robust mid-range estimates for long term, sub-regional planning purposes. More detailed appraisals should be carried out as part of the local development framework process. These forecasts, and the availability of appropriate opportunity sites within the main centres, will need to be updated at least every five years.

Net floorspace need, Thousand m²	Comparison Retail (High Street format)	Leisure – Food and Drink	Offices

		(Class A3, A4, A5)	
2005/06 - 2011	57 – 86	11 – 26	241 – 301
2005/06 - 2016	137 – 206	27 – 62	449 – 561
2005/06 - 2021	231 – 346	46 – 104	654 – 817
2005/06 - 2026	340 - 511	68 - 153	851 – 1,063

16.21 There are additional opportunities as set out below. Local planning authorities should work together taking into account the advice set out in PPS6: *Planning for Town Centres* or its replacement, in order to deliver these town centre uses through the local development framework process.

　　i. commercial leisure in the two city centres and within mixed use schemes in the town centres of Southsea, Eastleigh, Havant, Gosport and Fareham
　　ii. one or two major new strategic leisure destinations within South Hampshire over the next 15-20 years
　　iii. a major tourist attraction and events facility, to develop the attractiveness of the area for business and conference tourism
　　iv. hotel representation in the two cities, including upper tier/luxury hotels as part of a wider leisure and destination strategy.

16.22 Although much of the current development pipeline for business growth is out of town, the main centres have capacity and potential to accommodate most of the forecast growth requirements over the Plan period, and rebalance the provision of new floorspace back to South Hampshire's city and town centres.

Housing

POLICY SH5: SCALE AND LOCATION OF HOUSING DEVELOPMENT 2006-2026

Local planning authorities will allocate sufficient land and facilitate the delivery of 80,000 net additional dwellings in South Hampshire between 2006 and 2026.

In managing the supply of land for housing and in determining planning applications, local planning authorities should work collaboratively to facilitate the delivery of the following level of net additional dwellings in the sub-region:

DISTRICT	ANNUAL AVERAGE	TOTAL
East Hampshire (part)	60	1,200
Eastleigh	354	7,080
Fareham	186	3,720
Fareham SDA	500	10,000
Gosport	125	2,500
Havant	315	6,300
New Forest (part)	77	1,540
North East / North of Hedge End SDA	300	6,000
Portsmouth	735	14,700
Southampton	815	16,300
Test Valley (part)	196	3,920

Winchester (part)	337	6,740
Sub-Regional Total	4,000	80,000

The delivery of new housing will be monitored and managed separately within the south west and south east sub-areas of the sub-region. If that monitoring identifies a potential shortfall in the capacity of previously developed land to achieve the required provision of dwellings, the respective sub-area will bring forward measures to secure the delivery of housing within the plan period.

The distribution of development should be informed by strategic flood risk assessments. The results of these studies will need to be reflected in local development frameworks and future reviews of the RSS.

16.23 The provision in Policy SH5 both caters for demographic changes (e.g. more one and two-person households and longer life expectancy) and aims to provide sufficient new homes to help facilitate sustainable economic growth.

16.24 The housing distribution figures for individual districts in the policy broadly reflects the population distribution while taking account of environmental attributes. No new greenfield development (over and above existing commitments) is expected in Southampton, Portsmouth, Gosport, the part of New Forest district that lies within the sub-region, or in Fareham district outside the SDA to meet the above district distribution figures. Any decision on phasing and distribution may need to be taken in collaborative working. in order to find the most environmentally sustainable options under environmental legislation such as the Habitats Regulations and Water Framework Regulations. In addition, as set out in PPS25: *Development and Flood Risk* (Annex E) a Level 2 Strategic Flood Risk Assessment should be completed by the relevant PUSH authorities to further inform the sub-regional distribution of housing.

POLICY SH6: AFFORDABLE HOUSING

On average, 30-40% of housing on new development sites should be affordable housing.

A common policy framework will be developed by the South Hampshire authorities to ensure a consistent approach to the delivery of affordable housing. They will work together to establish the amount, types, sizes and tenure of affordable housing in South Hampshire, the site size thresholds above which the affordable housing policy will apply, and how such provision should be funded. Local development documents will set the percentage of housing on development sites which must be affordable in order to contribute towards the sub-regional targets.

16.25 It is a central priority for South Hampshire to ensure the affordable and key worker housing needs of the sub-region are met so as to support the economic development strategy as well as to deliver good quality public services. Overall, at least 30% of all new housing planned for 2006 – 2026 needs to be affordable in order to address a backlog of existing unmet need and to provide for newly arising needs. In order to achieve this target, Policy SH6 provides that 30-40% of housing on new development sites should be affordable housing. Research shows a need for affordable housing in South Hampshire to be about two thirds rented and one third shared ownership.

Transport

POLICY SH7: SUB-REGIONAL TRANSPORT STRATEGY

The transport and planning authorities will work together to:

> i. **reduce the need to travel through the development of smarter choices, such as travel planning and measures to discourage less sustainable journeys**
> ii. **manage the strategic transport network for longer distance journeys (especially from/to the ports of Southampton and Portsmouth and Southampton Airport) and the local network for shorter journeys**
> iii. **invest in new schemes to manage demand and provide additional public transport and highway capacity**
>
> **A delivery agency, based upon Transport for South Hampshire, will be developed for South Hampshire with the responsibility and necessary powers to manage and integrate public and private transport.**

16.26 Congestion is a major issue on several sections of the strategic transport network, particularly the M3, M27, A27, A3(M), A32 and A326. The traffic situation in the two city centres also suffers peak time congestion in a number of key corridors. By 2026, the natural and committed growth will exacerbate congestion, especially on the M3 and M27. Some links are predicted to have 70% over-capacity (all day average). There are constraints on rail capacity in both Southampton and Portsmouth and on the Fareham – Eastleigh east-west rail link. Without investment, the position is expected to get worse over the next 20 years irrespective of any additional development. In addition to the provision of new infrastructure, there will be a need for other measures and interventions to reduce the need to travel and offer alternatives to travel by single occupancy private car use. This is especially important for larger new developments, where new travel patterns and behaviours can be established from the outset.

16.27 The aim of Policy SH7 is to enhance the economic competitiveness of South Hampshire by securing improvements to the strategic network and accessibility to local services, facilities and places of work. It seeks to ensure that transport is provided to support growth and initiate a range of interventions and schemes necessary to deliver the economic growth strategy, provide access to the new development areas and tackle congestion.

16.28 The policy is set out within the Core Transport Policies of this Plan which seek:

   i. to tackle problems at source by implementing measures aimed at reducing the need to travel, e.g. by an area wide approach to changing travel behaviour and lifestyles, and through encouraging shorter journeys
   ii. to manage existing networks to make the best use of current road space and public transport
   iii. where neither of these approaches fully addresses the problems or issues, investment in new services and infrastructure will be proposed to help resolve them.

16.29 The 'hubs and spokes' concept will be developed to ensure that investment is concentrated along key corridors and nodes.

16.30 The schemes already committed for delivery to develop this sub-region are contained in Chapter 8, Appendix A: Strategic Transport Infrastructure Priorities. A separate Regional Implementation Plan will be produced and updated by the regional planning body (RPB) and will prioritise further strategic infrastructure requirements for the sub-region. Local requirements for infrastructure will be set out in LDDs and justified in accordance with national policy.

16.31 Key issues to be addressed are:

   i. the capacity and management performance of the M27, M271, M3 and A3(M)
   ii. sustainable access to major urban areas for trips originating by car
   iii. the role of high quality public transport routes with associated priority measures and multi-modal interchanges in providing high frequency and quality public transport links within the area

iv. the relief of traffic pressure on town centres and the need to improve access to regional hubs, particularly by improving local roads and bypasses
v. the capacity and need for reinstatement of passenger rail services and the need for additional freight facilities
vi. the adequacy of ferry services to/from Southampton and Portsmouth
vii. access to SDAs at North Fareham and Hedge End and the South Hampshire Strategic Employment Area and to open up other housing and employment areas
viii. the need to improve access to and transfer facilities at the ports of Southampton and Portsmouth and at Southampton Airport.

Environmental Sustainability

POLICY SH8: ENVIRONMENTAL SUSTAINABILITY

The South Hampshire authorities will:

i. **produce a common framework, for incorporation into development plan documents (DPDs), that establishes density ranges for development related to accessibility to services and public transport, that favours development around transport hubs and community infrastructure within a reasonable radius to encourage pedestrian and bicycle movement, and where possible joins development to the natural environment through linked and accessible open spaces that promote both recreational opportunities and high biodiversity**
ii. **jointly plan the infrastructure and approaches necessary to make sustainable management and use of natural resources an integral part of a growing economy in the sub-region**
iii. **co-operate on assessment of and planning for the delivery of effective coastal zone management to address the risk of sea level rise, and co-operate to minimise the risk of other forms of flooding and deliver opportunities for more sustainable flood risk management options**
iv. **achieve a decrease of between 8% and 20% in water use (compared to the national average in 2005) for all new development, help promote more efficient water use in existing developments and require implementation of sustainable urban drainage systems where feasible in all new developments**
v. **ensure that decisions on additional waste water treatment and water supply infrastructure will be taken on the basis of environmental sustainability as well as cost. Local authorities will work with the Environment Agency and water companies to ensure that water abstraction and discharges from waste water treatment into marine and fresh waters are in accordance with environmental legislation including European Directives.**

The authorities will develop common policies to achieve these aims in their DPDs.

16.32 The substantial development proposed in South Hampshire represents an important opportunity to build to high standards of sustainable design. Achieving sustainable and environmentally sensitive development will require joint working and the application of common standards across the sub-region.

16.33 The South Hampshire authorities will work together to implement the following principles and to find the most environmentally sustainable option to meet all legislative requirements:

i. net self-sufficiency in resource recycling and waste handling
ii. joint decision making on targets for resource usage and planning for resource management infrastructure
iii. the application of common environmental standards across the sub-region
iv. Infrastructure to reduce flood risk to be planned, funded and delivered based on adequate studies

v. concerted action and investment by relevant bodies to ensure adequate water supply within the sub-region

vi. further waste water studies to be fully integrated with the parallel supply/demand balance studies, which will influence the funding and/or phasing of proposed housing development. This will include ensuring that waste water treatment works that discharge to the River Itchen, and ultimately to the Solent European sites, incorporate necessary infrastructure improvements to comply with the Environment Agency's Review of Consents process and maintain sufficiently good water quality that adverse effects on these European sites do not occur. Where this is not possible by implementing BATNEEC (Best Available Technology Not Entailing Excessive Cost) plus better than BATNEEC (for nitrogen), alternative infrastructure provision (such as that which would avoid discharge to the River Itchen) must be considered

vii. the need to take account of green infrastructure (see Policy CC8)

viii. further consideration of the most environmentally sustainable options for wastewater disposal under current environmental legislation.

Implementation and Delivery

POLICY SH9: IMPLEMENTATION AGENCY

An implementation agency will be created for South Hampshire with the responsibility and necessary powers to implement this strategy.

16.34　Effective co-ordination of physical development and infrastructure provision to implement the strategy for South Hampshire will require a dedicated implementation agency and engagement with regional and local agencies. The Agency must provide for democratic leadership from the authorities that make up the Partnership for Urban South Hampshire.

16.35　Policy CC7: Infrastructure and Implementation sets out the general approach to implementation including the need to ensure that the pace of development is aligned to the provision of and management of infrastructure. Infrastructure investment priorities for South Hampshire will be set out in a separate Regional Implementation Plan which will be produced and updated by the RPB.

16.36　Data collected for annual monitoring reports for LDDs, will help inform reviews of this plan. It will be particularly important to monitor economic improvement and labour supply increases in parallel with housing completions. Regular reviews of the South East Plan will provide an opportunity to review economic growth, the rate of house building and the progress with the delivery of infrastructure and will enable corrective measures to be taken to ensure that the three remain in line.

17 Sussex Coast

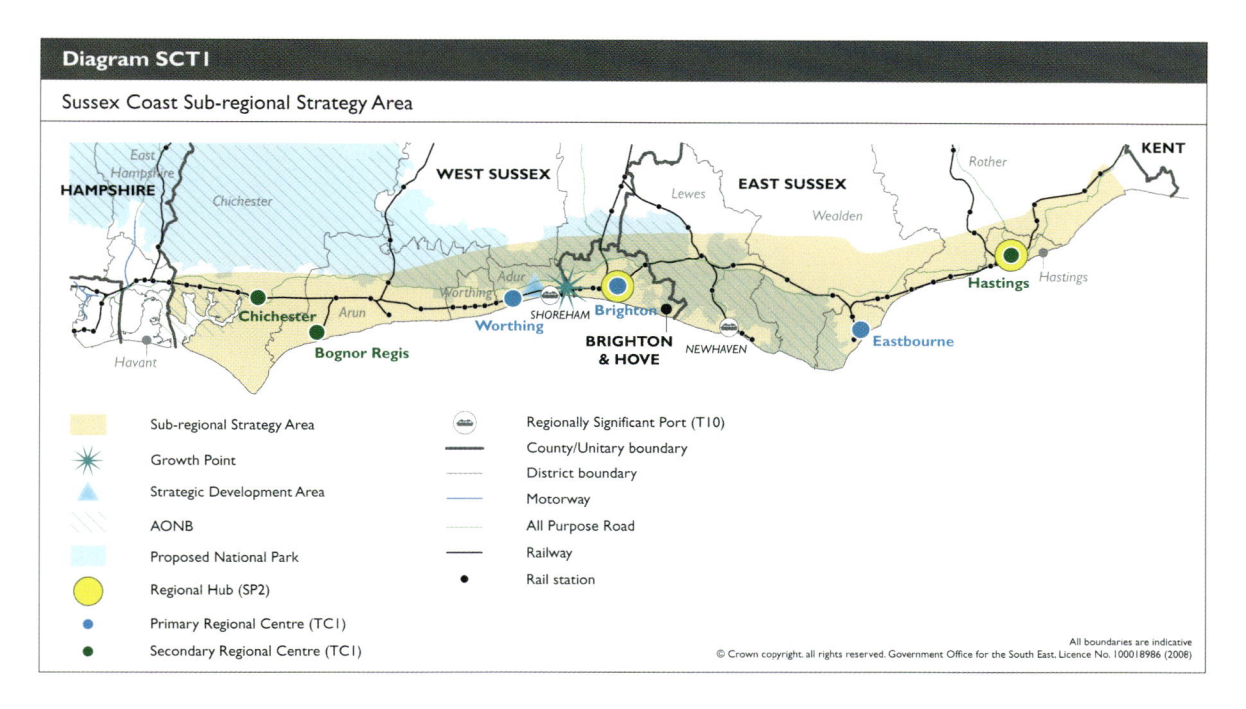

Diagram SCT1: Sussex Coast Sub-regional Strategy Area

17.1 The 'Sussex Coast and Towns' was a Priority Area for Economic Regeneration in RPG9 and was defined as extending from Shoreham Harbour to Hastings. The sub-regional strategy now extends from Chichester to Rye in recognition of the wider area of structural economic weakness, although there is significant variation in economic and social needs within the sub-region. Compared with South East averages there are higher levels of multiple deprivation, lower levels of GVA, lower earnings, higher levels of unemployment, lower rates of business formation, a poorer qualified workforce and an ageing population. As well as the coastal towns, the sub-region includes the immediate rural hinterland which extends into the Sussex Downs AONB (which is to be replaced by the South Downs National Park) and High Weald AONB, and includes protected coastal areas. It contains the two regional hubs of Brighton & Hove and Hastings. Diagram SCT1 sets out the extent of the sub-region.

17.2 The particular challenges faced by the sub-region are how to:

- improve economic performance and raise earnings
- deliver sufficient decent homes and provide a well integrated mix to meet the needs of the area
- create a better balance between jobs and homes, reduce the house price/local earnings 'affordability gap' and minimise the need for out-commuting
- reduce deprivation and social exclusion by spreading the benefits of sustainable new development as widely as possible across local communities
- improve the transport links to reduce peripherality and assist take up of strategic employment sites
- achieve all the above in the context of the constraints on land supply while respecting the sub-region's high environmental quality and nationally designated landscapes.

Core Strategy

POLICY SCT1: CORE STRATEGY

Local authorities and other agencies should, as a priority, pro-actively pursue and promote the sustainable economic growth and regeneration of the Sussex Coast that will:

> i. reduce intra-regional disparities and help bring the performance of the sub-regional economy up to the South East average
> ii. respond to the different needs, opportunities and characteristics of each town, or group of towns and all sections of their communities
> iii. provide for sustainable urban extensions in Arun, Chichester (at the city or, if this is not possible, in other suitable and deliverable locations in the district), Rother and Wealden Districts and for major regeneration opportunities through a strategic development area (SDA) and Growth Point at Shoreham Harbour, including mixed use developments
> iv. build upon and help deliver major improvements to the strategic transport infrastructure and services both to reduce its peripherality and to improve accessibility within the sub-region
> v. achieve a better balance between the provision of housing and the capability of both the local environment and economy to absorb this in a sustainable way whilst responding as far as possible to the needs of local people (including key workers) for decent homes at a price/cost that they can afford. In particular, care will be taken to optimise the use of previously developed land, particularly in Brighton & Hove, whilst ensuring sufficient green infrastructure is delivered alongside new development
> vi. protect and enhance the sub-region's high environmental quality and nationally designated landscapes(in both town and country), enhance its cultural and historic assets and promote excellence in the design of new developments in recognition of their importance to economic success and quality of life.

17.3 Policy SCT1 aims to address many of the challenges referred to above. In doing so the sub-region's high environmental quality is to be protected by optimising the use of previously developed land, making the most of existing infrastructure and services concentrated within the towns and promoting sustainable urban extensions with supporting infrastructure in the areas specified to meet housing requirements. The policy recognises that locally sensitive solutions will be necessary to respond to the different needs and opportunities in the sub-region. The interim estimate (excluding any further opportunities yet to be defined at Shoreham Harbour) is 30,000 net additional jobs between 2006 and 2016 which will be monitored.

Enabling Economic Regeneration

> **POLICY SCT2: ENABLING ECONOMIC REGENERATION**
>
> To help realise a step change in the sub-region's economic performance, national, regional and other relevant agencies and authorities should give increased priority to investment decisions and other direct support for the sub-region. Key measures should include:
>
> i. directing national and regional assistance and expenditure to promote the social and economic regeneration of areas in greatest need by:
>
> - continuing the support being given to Hastings/Bexhill and Shoreham in general, whilst
> - increasing the priority given to other parts of the Sussex Coast (from Shoreham to Rye, including Brighton and Hove and Hastings)
> - targeting other pockets of social and economic deprivation throughout the sub-region
>
> ii. delivering improvements to east-west transport links by road and rail to improve accessibility, facilitate strategic development opportunities and enable the better functioning of overlapping local labour and housing markets
> iii. maintaining and/or improving key north-south communication links that will also help to knit the coastal towns better into the rest of the South East and increase the sub-region's attractions as a business location.

17.4 Policy SCT2 will assist regeneration in the central and eastern parts of the sub-region where the most pressing economic and social needs exist. Better east-west transport links, especially the A27/A259, will improve complementary connections with other key sub-regions and accessibility within the sub-region. Improving north-south strategic transport links, especially to Gatwick and London, will help strengthen links with the rest of the region and key markets. For more information on these transport improvements see Policy T14:Transport Investment and Management Priorities and associated Appendix A: Strategic Transport Investment Priorities.

17.5 It is critical that smart growth is promoted in the context of Policy RE5: Smart Growth and in this sub-region it is particularly important that local skills are upgraded in line with Policy RE4: Human Resource Development. Policy SP4: Regeneration and Social Inclusion and Policy RE6: Competitiveness and Addressing Structural Economic Weakness are relevant also.

Management of Existing Employment Sites and Premises

POLICY SCT3: MANAGEMENT OF EXISTING EMPLOYMENT SITES AND PREMISES

To deliver sufficient appropriate sites and premises for business and other uses that will help to facilitate the regeneration of the local economy, local authorities should, in addition to Policy RE3:

i. **develop and co-ordinate with other agencies delivery mechanisms to unlock and implement existing allocated business parks, other important sites that have persistently remained undeveloped and other strategic sites with economic development potential. This includes:**

- large-scale, mixed-use development sites at Worthing and north of Bognor Regis
- Shoreham Harbour, Airport and Cement Works
- Newhaven Eastside and Port
- Eastbourne Park and Sovereign Harbour
- Polegate
- mixed-use development sites at North East Bexhill.

Development proposals identified in this list will need to comply with policy set out in NRM4, NRM5 and PPS25: *Development and Flood Risk* **(paying particular regard to the relative vulnerability of uses and the likely risks associated with development).**

ii. **in other areas be prepared to identify and bring forward mixed use sites on existing or allocated employment sites in circumstances where this would deliver necessary employment space at the right time on sites which would be unviable for an employment only scheme**

iii. **seek to improve and upgrade existing industrial estates and business areas to bring them up to modern standards required by business**

iv. **in rural areas, protect existing and allocated employment land from other uses where employment land reviews show them to be essential for the needs of small businesses.**

17.6 The majority of existing built stock is over 30 years old and not well suited to providing the range and quantity of sites and premises required to meet modern business needs and support the strategy. Policy RE3: Employment and Land Provision provides for employment land reviews to check that sites are suitable for business needs and Policy SCT3 will help ensure that sufficient appropriate sites are available to facilitate economic regeneration. Several key strategic employment sites and business park allocations have remained undeveloped, particularly in East Sussex, and drawing attention to them in Policy SCT3 will help unlock their potential by promoting effective delivery mechanisms. In exceptional circumstances, 'delivery mechanisms' for the identified strategic sites may include mixed use schemes in local development plans.

Employment Priority in New Land Allocations

> **POLICY SCT4: EMPLOYMENT PRIORITY IN NEW LAND ALLOCATIONS**
>
> In conjunction with the priorities set out in Policies RE3 and C3, in allocating land for development, Local Planning Authorities should give priority to delivering employment development in strategically accessible locations, particularly by rail, to ensure an appropriate mix of readily available sites and premises whilst also providing sufficient space to:
>
> - retain existing firms and enable their expansion or relocation (within the sub-region)
> - create attractive opportunities for inward investment and new uses
> - at least match anticipated increases in the resident workforce.
>
> New employment allocations should be included as appropriate within sustainable urban extensions in Arun, Chichester, Rother and Wealden districts.

17.7 Within the framework provided by national policy, Policy SCT4 gives priority to employment rather than other uses in those locations most conducive to business and industry to ensure delivery of employment is supported in this comparatively weak local economy.

Housing Distribution

> **POLICY SCT5: HOUSING DISTRIBUTION**
>
> Local planning authorities will allocate sufficient land and facilitate the delivery of 69,300 net additional dwellings in the the Sussex Coast between 2006 and 2026.
>
> In managing the supply of land for housing and in determining planning applications, local planning authorities should work collaboratively to facilitate the delivery of the following level of net additional dwellings in the sub-region:
>
> | DISTRICT | ANNUAL AVERAGE | TOTAL |
> |---|---|---|
> | Adur[1] | 105 | 2,100 |
> | Shoreham Harbour SDA[2] | 500 | 10,000 |
> | Arun | 565 | 11,300 |
> | Brighton & Hove[1] | 570 | 11,400 |
> | Chichester (part) | 355 | 7,100 |
> | Eastbourne | 240 | 4,800 |
> | Hastings | 210 | 4,200 |
> | Lewes (part) | 170 | 3,400 |
> | Rother (part) | 200 | 4,000 |
> | Wealden (part)[3] | 350 | 7,000 |

DISTRICT	ANNUAL AVERAGE	TOTAL
Worthing	200	4,000
Sub-regional Total	3,465	69,300

Footnotes

1. This figure excludes development at Shoreham Harbour.
2. This interim figure of 10,000 dwellings for Shoreham Harbour will be subject to detailed studies (including an SFRA) and assistance from the agencies as part of the strategic regeneration of the port.
3. This figure recognises that limitations at the Hailsham Waste Water Treatment Works may require the phasing of housing delivery to allow for the provision of new or improved waste water infrastructure.

Although the intention is for each authority to meet its contribution to the sub-regional total as shown, some flexibility will be allowed for those authorities not wholly within the sub-region to vary the relative amounts between the sub-region and the rest of county areas where this is necessary to meet the overall district provision, and achieve a more sustainable pattern of development without compromising the regeneration of the coastal towns.

Most of the development should be focused on existing towns by optimising the use of previously developed land and, where necessary, by making new land allocations as sustainable extensions of existing towns (including appropriate provision for employment uses, local services and facilities and open space).

17.8   Policy SCT5 provides for 69,300 net additional dwellings in the sub-region between 2006 and 2026, an average of 3,465 dwellings per annum. This requirement has regard to the level of economic and demographic needs in the area together with the extent and disposition of Natura 2000 and Ramsar sites and AONB.

17.9   The distribution of this housing requirement is informed by the estimated potential supply of housing land at 2006 and the scope for making further sustainable allocations as urban extensions in Arun, Chichester, Rother and Wealden districts in line with Policy SCT1.

17.10   Shoreham Harbour has scope to provide for a significant level of mixed use development to achieve significant social and economic objectives through regeneration, comprising employment, housing and other uses. It covers parts of Adur and Brighton & Hove. However, to reflect uncertainties pending completion of studies, the interim figure for Shoreham Harbour of 10,000 dwellings is shown separately from requirements for the rest of Adur and Brighton & Hove. To ensure the proposal achieves its full potential and secures the necessary infrastructure, development should not be reassigned to other areas outside the Shoreham Harbour Development Area (which will be defined through local development plans). For the remainder of the sub-region, further flexibility is provided for those districts that extend beyond the sub-region.

17.11   Policy H1: Regional Housing Provision 2006-2026 and Policy H2 on Managing the Delivery of the Regional Housing Provision are also particularly relevant.

Affordable Housing

> **POLICY SCT6: AFFORDABLE HOUSING**
>
> In line with Policy H3 and based on up to date assessments of housing need, local planning authorities will establish appropriate policies and local targets for the provision of affordable housing in their area. Such policies and targets should comply with the following principles:
>
> i. the appropriate proportion of affordable housing sought should be the maximum that the viability of particular developments can support, bearing in mind the likely contributions towards the provision of infrastructure required under Policy CC7 and the Implementation Plan
> ii. as a general guideline, 40% of new housing development should be affordable housing
> iii. this guideline should not restrain local authorities from seeking a higher or lower proportion of affordable housing provision where local circumstances clearly justify it
> iv. the type, size and nature of affordable housing sought should recognise the distinct needs of different sections of the community, including the elderly, other specialist groups in need of supported housing and key workers.

17.12   The Sussex Coast sub-region has a below average supply of affordable housing at 12.6% of total stock in 2001 compared to the national and regional averages of 19.3% and 14% respectively. Policy SCT6 seeks to redress this while acknowledging that, since development opportunities vary across the sub-region, authorities will need to set their own affordable housing thresholds to reflect local circumstances but consistent with achieving the overall guideline across the sub-region of 40% of new housing development being affordable.

Implementation and Delivery

> **POLICY SCT7: IMPLEMENTATION AND DELIVERY**
>
> Local authorities, regional agencies, government representatives and other key stakeholders should agree a long-term vision and together develop joint, multi-agency plans and frameworks as a focus for delivering economic and social regeneration for the following areas:
>
> i. **Hastings – Bexhill area** – to develop and extend the work already undertaken in the 'Five Point Plan' into the longer term and to capitalise on Hastings as a regional hub
> ii. **Eastbourne – Hailsham area** – to optimise the area's potential to provide employment space and associated housing in sustainable and strategically accessible locations along the A22 corridor
> iii. **Shoreham – Brighton & Hove and Adur** – to continue to strengthen the economy of Brighton & Hove and the adjoining area as a major centre and hub and at Shoreham to capitalise on strategic port and airport site opportunities
> iv. **Newhaven area** – to continue the regeneration of the town to strengthen its economic base, revitalise the port and improve the environment
> v. **coastal West Sussex from Selsey to Adur** – to continue to develop the co-ordinated approach fostered by the Area Investment Framework and other specific initiatives.
>
> Such multi-agency plans should focus on the provision of an appropriate balance of additional employment space, affordable housing and the necessary infrastructure, facilities and services required to support development, investigation of business clusters, skills development and promotion of the sub-region.

17.13 Consistent with Policy CC7: Infrastructure and Implementation, strong coordinated leadership and partnership working is critical to securing the sustainable development, regeneration and economic success sought by the strategy. Policy SCT7 provides an overarching vision for each area to support partnership working across administrative boundaries and communities of interest.

17.14 A separate Regional Implementation Plan will be produced and updated by the regional planning body and will further prioritise strategic infrastructure requirements for the sub-region (for example at Shoreham Harbour). Transport schemes already committed for delivery to develop this sub-region are contained in Chapter 8, Appendix A: *Strategic Transport Infrastructure Priorities.* Local requirements for infrastructure will be justified in accordance with national policy. Key issues to be addressed are:

   i. waste water treatment, particularly at Hailsham and Chichester to address Water Framework and Habitats Directives requirements
   ii. making better use of the rail network by relating as much new development as possible to the location of existing and possible new stations, given highway capacity issues on the A27/A259 at Arundel and Worthing and from Brighton through to Hastings
   iii. mitigation of tidal flood risk where the 'exceptions' clause in PPS25 justifies development in high risk areas
   iv. improving workforce skills across the board (adult qualifications are below the regional average at all levels).

17.15 See also Chapter 26 on implementation, monitoring and review.

18 East Kent and Ashford

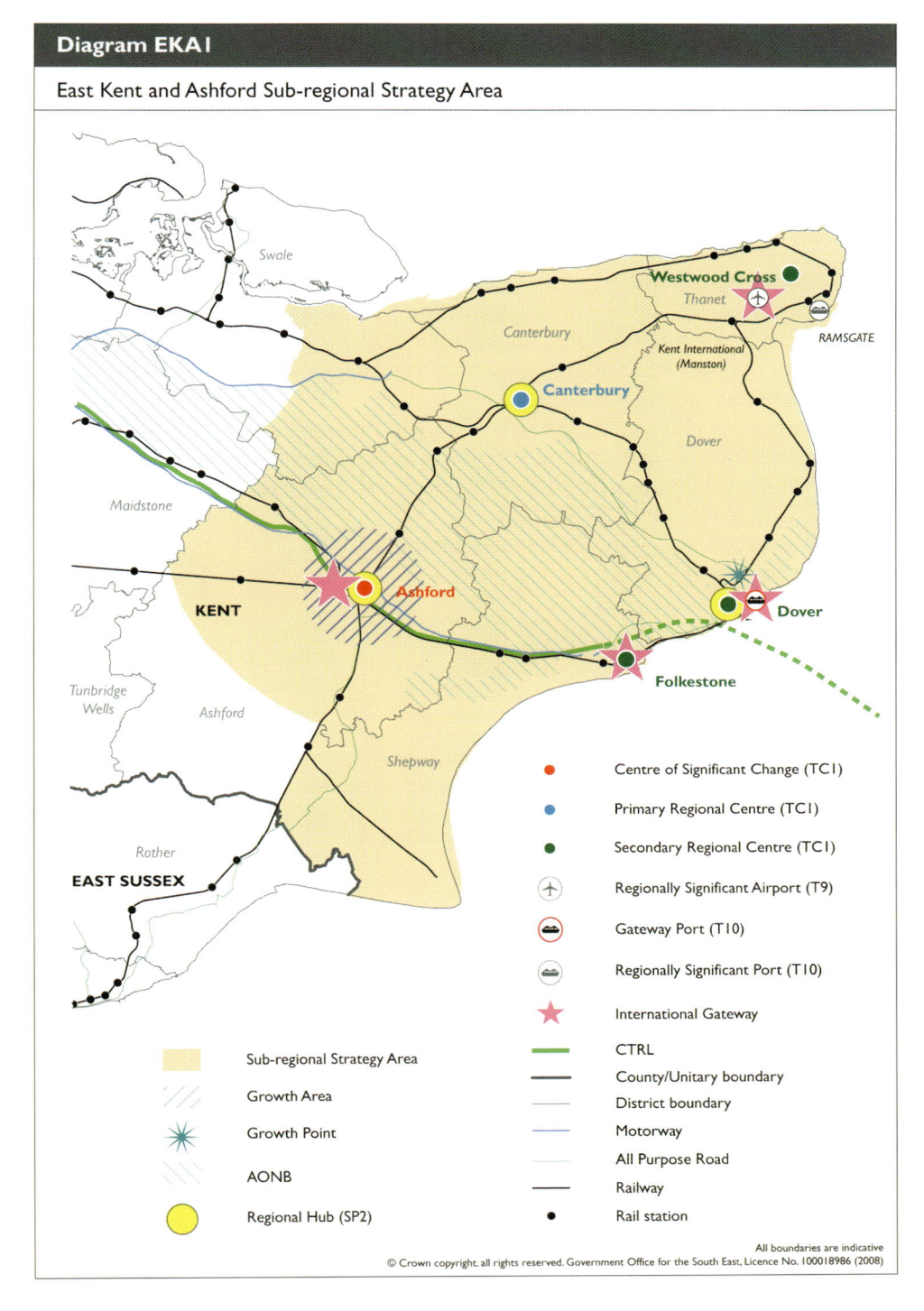

Diagram EKA1
East Kent and Ashford Sub-regional Strategy Area

Legend:
- Centre of Significant Change (TC1)
- Primary Regional Centre (TC1)
- Secondary Regional Centre (TC1)
- Regionally Significant Airport (T9)
- Gateway Port (T10)
- Regionally Significant Port (T10)
- International Gateway
- CTRL
- County/Unitary boundary
- District boundary
- Motorway
- All Purpose Road
- Railway
- Rail station
- Sub-regional Strategy Area
- Growth Area
- Growth Point
- AONB
- Regional Hub (SP2)

All boundaries are indicative
© Crown copyright. all rights reserved. Government Office for the South East, Licence No. 100018986 (2008)

18.1 East Kent and Ashford, previously considered as two separate sub-regions in RPG9, are now brought together as one sub-region in recognition of the advantages to be gained from improving connectivity, and the potential to share the benefits of major growth at Ashford across the wider area. The sub-region now comprises the districts of Canterbury, Thanet, Dover, Shepway, and parts of Swale and Ashford. The area encompasses the Growth Area of Ashford, the nine coastal towns from Whitstable to Hythe which have experienced the cumulative impact of the decline of traditional industries, and the former Kent coalfield. The sub-region plays a nationally significant role as a key gateway to mainland Europe, but is relatively remote from London and the remainder of the region and includes some of the least economically buoyant areas in the South East.

18.2 The introduction of new high-speed domestic rail services will be a key factor in supporting the growth of Ashford and stimulating the regeneration of the coastal towns, which will need to develop their own strengths and specialisms. This must be balanced against the need to manage and enhance an outstanding coastal landscape. The key challenges faced by this sub-region are how to:

- concentrate development and successfully spread the benefits of Ashford's growth across the wider sub-region
- ensure that each area makes a positive and distinctive contribution to the future success of the sub-region
- promote further growth at Dover
- develop Canterbury's role as an historic centre of learning and commerce with strong links between university research and business, and promote housing growth to provide balanced and sustainable mixed communities
- regenerate other urban areas and coastal towns whilst respecting important environmental constraints
- deliver a sufficient supply of housing to meet the needs of the future population and support its economic regeneration and growth
- maximise the benefits of international and domestic links provided by Channel Tunnel Rail Link (CTRL)
- protect and enhance the environment, heritage and quality of life across the sub-region.

Core Strategy

POLICY EKA1: CORE STRATEGY

The sub-region should exploit the potential for housing and business at locations served by the Channel Tunnel Rail Link (CTRL) domestic services, especially at Ashford.

It will build on the distinct economic roles of each area:

i. **Ashford, as a Growth Area, with high-speed rail links to London and Europe, should develop as an office, research and business node, providing market growth for the sub-region as a whole, and opportunity for large investments that need an expanding workforce**

ii. **the coastal towns, especially Dover as a Growth Point, should develop their international gateway roles and diversify and enlarge their research and manufacturing base**

iii. **Canterbury should develop links between university research and business, and continue as a commercial and cultural centre of international historic importance.**

New development will be primarily accommodated through the expansion of Ashford and at the other main settlements. The unique heritage and environment will be protected and promoted for its own sake, and to foster the economic success of the sub-region.

The accessibility to and within the sub-region should be improved to allow each area and its functions to more readily benefit the whole of the sub-region.

18.3 The Core Strategy promotes the provision of new housing at the main urban areas throughout East Kent, and the provision of infrastructure and services to support growth and a broad balance between jobs and housing. This applies particularly to Ashford where the strategy considerably increases the rate of house building. The scale of development proposed will be tested through local development documents.

18.4 Ashford is a major Growth Area and its future development should not be considered in isolation. It is important that the benefits of growth are shared across the whole of the sub-region and the wider population, whilst ensuring that all areas fulfil their own distinctive role in its future success.

18.5 All the urban areas of East Kent require regeneration to some degree, but Folkestone and Hythe are more constrained than Dover and Canterbury. Urban areas also require new employment and homes that are affordable and meet long term needs.

18.6 The Core Strategy recognises that locations served by CTRL domestic services will have increased attraction for commercial and residential development, particularly at Ashford. It also builds on the fact that the sub-region has a number of very important economic assets notably at Ashford, Dover and Canterbury, which have implications beyond their immediate sites for linkages with other businesses and institutions and for labour and service catchments. These are the economic engine of the sub-region and must be recognised in planning for the future pattern of development.

18.7 The spatial strategy is therefore for a dispersed pattern of growth which:

i. concentrates development and investment at Ashford Growth Area
ii. promotes further growth at Dover to support regeneration whilst respecting the important environmental constraints to development
iii. promotes further growth at Canterbury in order to support its development as a centre for learning and commerce
iv. responds to housing needs in the remaining urban areas, but on a scale that can be accommodated without major breach of constraints, and matches the employment pattern of the sub-region.

18.8 Employment growth at Ashford should not take place at the expense of the coastal regeneration areas. Equally, if there were to be delay in delivering new housing at Ashford this should not place pressure on other areas. Neither should housing provision at Ashford run ahead of the local economy for a prolonged period.

18.9 The town of Dover has an internationally important heritage but also has major sites and areas in need of regeneration. The economy relies on the ferry industry and there are areas of deprivation and poor quality housing. A new approach to regeneration and economic development is needed providing wider choice of new housing to support population growth and new services. In recognition of this, Dover District has been designated as a Growth Point. The local development framework needs to deliver high quality regeneration and acceptable development on greenfield land. The scale of growth needs to be supported by employment opportunities, infrastructure and services and managed within the constraints that apply to Dover. Within Dover District, the urban area of Dover has been selected for concentrating growth. However, the capacity of the urban area will not enable all the growth to be accommodated within existing built-up areas. There will therefore be a need for a substantial urban extension. The identified area of search for development lies outside the AONB and is set back from the immediate coast, in order to regenerate the urban area and to revitalise the economy.

18.10 The environment, heritage and quality of life in East Kent and Ashford will be protected and enhanced as they all contribute to the success of the sub-region. The opportunities for increased international linkages and the economic strengths of the sub-region should be exploited, provided they do not cause unacceptable harm to the environment.

18.11 In the past 20 years an additional 39,000 jobs have been generated in this area. However, a higher value is needed for the future that takes into account the impact of the strategic sites and other potential for growth arising from Ashford's Growth Area status and the objectives for the regeneration of the coastal towns.

18.12 The interim estimate for monitoring purposes is 50,000 net additional jobs between 2006 and 2026 distributed equally between the periods 2006-2016 and 2016-2026.

18.13 Smart economic growth should be encouraged and delivered through:

- upgrading skills
- improving economic activity rates
- improving business formation.

18.14 Policy RE5: Smart Growth and Policy EKA6: Employment Locations are also particularly relevant.

Spatial Framework for Ashford Growth Area

> **POLICY EKA2: SPATIAL FRAMEWORK FOR ASHFORD GROWTH AREA**
>
> New development in the Growth Area will be delivered through urban intensification and the development of new sustainable urban extensions integrated with the provision of new and enhanced bus-based public transport and interchanges. Major improvements will take place in parallel to the town centre and the public realm, linked to substantial additional provision of well-managed public open spaces. The urban fringe will be positively managed for recreation and biodiversity.
>
> Both quantitative and qualitative aspects of supply and demand for employment land should be kept under review in the local development document process, in order to meet forecast demand and encourage job growth to move forward in tandem with housing development.
>
> The growth envisaged at Ashford should deliver an enhanced quality of life following the principles of sustainable development. Particular sustainability aspects will include:
>
> i. more efficient use of resources, particularly energy, waste and water
> ii. water-related demand management measures in both the existing and new stock
> iii. strategic planning of surface water drainage management to minimise flood risk
> iv. the timely provision of additional infrastructure, local educational, health and community facilities
> v. a step-change in sustainable design, construction and innovation, including use of the SEEDA Sustainability Checklist
> vi. strategic planning of sewerage infrastructure and waste water treatment plants to ensure no deterioration in natural water quality.

18.15 The Ashford Growth Area is a key element to the Core Strategy for the sub-region. It is important to make full use of opportunities to consolidate the existing urban centre, and particularly to renew and reinforce the town centre. The scale of such opportunities, although significant, will not however be sufficient to cater for all needs, and additional greenfield land for development needs to be carefully phased through development plan documents so that it is part of a co-ordinated strategy for the regeneration of the existing town.

18.16 To improve the performance of the town centre and facilitate sustainable growth, it will be necessary to improve the physical fabric of the area, reduce the severance caused by the town centre road network and create a high quality public realm and network of open spaces.

18.17 Whilst the supply of employment land is considered adequate for envisaged needs until 2016, substantial additional office and service floorspace will be needed close to the town centre and international railway station. Strong and sustained job growth, together with a substantially enhanced economic development programme, will be essential to accompany housing development in order that Ashford develops into a sustainable community and does not become over-dependent on commuting.

18.18 As a regional Growth Area within the sub-region, Ashford has the potential to provide leadership on delivering sustainable development and construction with high quality design. Water related issues are of special importance given Ashford's location in an area of relative deficiency for water supply and the local river system's vulnerability to flood.

18.19　Additional education, health and community facilities will also be required to ensure that sufficient social infrastructure is provided and the development of new communities is sustainable.

Amount and Distribution of Housing

POLICY EKA3: AMOUNT AND DISTRIBUTION OF HOUSING

Local planning authorities will allocate sufficient land and facilitate the delivery of 56,700 net additional dwellings between 2006 and 2026.

In managing the supply of land for housing and in determining planning applications, local planning authorities should work collaboratively to facilitate the delivery of the following level of net additional dwellings in the sub-region:

DISTRICT	ANNUAL AVERAGE	TOTAL
Swale (part)	35	700
Shepway	290	5,800
Thanet	375	7,500
Dover	505	10,100
Canterbury	510	10,200
Ashford (part)	1,120	22,400
Sub-regional Total	2,835	56,700

Growth at each location will be supported by co-ordinated provision of infrastructure, employment, environmental improvement and community services. Active pre-planning is necessary to achieve capacity increases in strategic infrastructure and facilities, particularly at Ashford.

An indicative target for affordable housing of 30% of all new dwellings applies to East Kent and Ashford.

18.20　The number of new dwellings to be built from 2006 to 2026 in the East Kent and Ashford sub-region is to be 56,700. The Growth Area which, with much of rural Ashford, accounts for 22,400 (40%) of the housing proposed to 2026, is a prominent feature of the spatial strategy in this sub-region.

18.21　Policy EKA3 sets housing provision at a level that should enable the backlog of unmet need for affordable dwellings to be tackled within the first 10-year period of the Plan.

18.22　Housing markets in East Kent and Ashford are less buoyant than in most other parts of the South East and given the need to seek developer contributions for education, access and other services required by new developments, 30% affordable housing is the maximum practical in the sub-region. Even so, this would mean a substantial increase in the level of new affordable dwellings each year in the sub-region compared to recent average completion of about 250 per annum.

18.23　At Ashford the planned scale of new housing should accommodate the local need for affordable housing, key worker and shared equity housing. In the areas of high deprivation at the coast such as Thanet and Shepway, there is a particular need for improvement to the private rented stock, and the proportion of social rented accommodation may be above average. The delivery of affordable housing will depend on the scale of public funding, and in East Kent affordable housing programmes that do not depend entirely on the volume of market housing will be needed to meet the overall target. The proportions of affordable housing and their tenure in each district will be determined locally in this light.

18.24　Policies: H1 Regional Housing Provision 2006-2026 and H3: Affordable Housing are also particularly relevant.

Urban Renaissance of the Coastal Towns

> **POLICY EKA4: URBAN RENAISSANCE OF THE COASTAL TOWNS**
>
> Local authorities and development agencies will work together to encourage new economic impetus throughout the coastal towns including the following:
>
> i. regeneration measures will create high quality urban environments within the coastal towns
> ii. concentrations of employment in small businesses, education, culture and other services are encouraged, notably in central Folkestone, Margate and Dover
> iii. the economy of Thanet will be developed and diversified through provision of a full range of accessible local services, a regional role for Kent International Airport (Manston), expansion of Port Ramsgate as Kent's second Cross-Channel port and continued inward investment in manufacturing and transport, notably aviation and marine engineering
> iv. the Port of Dover and Eurotunnel have potential to generate freight handling and tourism
> v. further growth will be encouraged and supported at the large-scale pharmaceutical manufacturing and research plant at Sandwich
> vi. the regeneration of former colliery sites has attracted manufacturing and food processing and their transformation should be completed including mixed-use expansion of Aylesham
> vii. the smaller towns of Deal, Faversham, Herne Bay and Whitstable should develop stronger local service functions and mixed employment uses of a scale and character suitable to their size
> viii. new measures to increase local employment will be required in Shepway to coincide with the decommissioning of the nuclear power plant at Dungeness in the short term and around 2018.
>
> A broad balance between new housing and new jobs will be sought at each urban area at a level commensurate with the size and character of the town.

18.25 Improved education, skills and housing are essential to the urban renaissance of the coastal towns. Deprivation and exclusion must be tackled.

18.26 All the coastal areas require greater economic diversity and better access to London and beyond. Thanet is a major urban area that requires a much larger economic base. Dover, Folkestone and Hythe are major urban areas that require stronger business and community services. CTRL domestic services, and investment in the infrastructure through and beyond Kent, are vital to achieving this.

18.27 The smaller historic towns of Deal, Faversham, Herne Bay and Whitstable have strong urban character. They are attractive locations that need more local employment, but they will not achieve this unless public transport links and local services are maintained and improved.

18.28 Policy SP4: Regeneration and Social Inclusion is also particularly relevant.

The Gateway Role of the Sub-Region

> **EKA5: THE GATEWAY ROLE**
>
> The growth of the gateways will be supported as catalysts for economic development, including that associated with freight handling and tourism, and to encourage a choice of transport modes and adequate capacity on the cross- Channel routes:

> i. appropriate development of the Port of Dover will be supported to enable growth of freight and passenger traffic. Any such development outside the existing harbour will be subject to the reinstatement of the rail link to the Western Docks to enable a significant proportion of freight to reach the port by rail
> ii. at the Port of Ramsgate, proposals should assist the growth of port trade and not compromise its role as a major port.
>
> In the event of a second fixed cross-Channel link being proposed it will be considered on the basis of the economic, transport, social and environmental impacts. Such a proposal should be designed to increase the share of traffic carried by rail.
>
> The growth of Kent International Airport as a regional airport with up to six million passengers per annum is supported provided proposals satisfy policy criteria for the environment, transport and amenity.

18.29 The Kent ports and transport routes are of vital international importance and a choice of modes and adequate capacity should be maintained on the cross-Channel routes in order to foster economic development across the region. The flow of international traffic through Kent to the rest of the South East and the UK should be tapped for its tourist potential.

18.30 The key issue for Dover is to ensure that infrastructure supports further growth in port activity. Improving passenger and freight access to Dover is to be secured in association with the expansion of the harbour and town through a package of road and rail measures including a rail link and rail freight operation in the Western Docks. There will also be a need for inland facilities within East Kent to provide more port-related value-added services.

18.31 Kent International Airport with its long runway, has potential for growth with significant economic benefits for the sub-region. Environmental impacts will need to be addressed including noise and air quality. Large land reserves are available within and adjacent to the airport for ancillary uses and related activity.

18.32 Considerable investment will be required in surface access if the envisaged level of growth is to be realised.

Employment Locations

> **POLICY EKA6: EMPLOYMENT LOCATIONS**
>
> Local development documents should confirm the broad scale of new business and related developments already identified and give priority to completion of major employment sites at the following locations:
>
> i. Ashford
> ii. Canterbury City, linked to the University of Kent, and at Herne Bay/Whitstable
> iii. Dover, Richborough and the former coalfield
> iv. Folkestone-Hythe
> v. Thanet.
>
> New employment locations will be provided if required to keep employment and housing growth in balance at:
>
> i. Ashford
> ii. Dover.

> **High quality proposals for intensifying or expanding the technology, knowledge and scientific sectors will be supported at established and suitable new locations, unless there are overriding environmental impacts which cannot be adequately dealt with. These locations include:**
>
> i. **Canterbury - at a new site linked to the university**
> ii. **Dover - at the pharmaceuticals base at Sandwich and nearby at Richborough**
> iii. **Ashford - within the urban growth area.**
>
> **Town centres and inner urban areas will be given greater emphasis as locations for regeneration and employment growth in services and cultural activity.**
>
> **Expansion of higher and further education will be supported in Canterbury, and new investment in these sectors promoted at Ashford, Folkestone and Dover.**

18.33 The amount of employment land provided in East Kent should be generous where growth is concentrated and where the local economy is most urgently in need of regeneration.

18.34 Some major sites in East Kent and Ashford have been slow to develop. Much of the recent business investment has been by established firms and employment increase has been in activities that are not located on major business sites. There is therefore a need to consider not only land primarily for business use, but to provide more widely for new employment locations.

18.35 Concentrations of small businesses and workshops at the core of the urban areas, plus education and other services, can create important locations for new employment particularly at coastal environments. Town centres are important concentrations of retail, business services, finance and leisure and many have the capacity to increase the number of jobs on offer. Ashford and Canterbury provide services for wide catchments and each is identified as a regional hub. There is also potential in East Kent for a mixed rural economy close to the urban centres.

18.36 The existing strategic sites for new business uses provide a major opportunity for inward investment to the Ashford Growth Area and the coastal regeneration areas.

18.37 There is also a need to attract and retain higher 'added value' professional, technical and service jobs, and, in accordance with Policy EKA6, high quality proposals for intensifying or expanding the technology and knowledge sectors should be supported at established and suitable new locations if required at:

i. Ashford - in order to support sustainable growth and to ensure that Ashford does not depend on long distance commuting
ii. Dover - in order to support the new housing development
iii. Canterbury and Shepway - in order to deliver sufficient employment land for the whole Plan period.

18.38 In Thanet, the amount of existing employment land, the new Westwood centre, the potential growth in aviation, and the proximity of major employment at Sandwich mean that major new employment locations are not needed at present. Any major new investment proposals which may come forward should not, however, be ruled out.

18.39 At Faversham, planning policies are to diversify the town's economy through smaller scale projects for which some land has been identified.

18.40 Policy RE3: Employment Land Provision is also particularly relevant.

Integrated Coastal Management and Natural Park

> **POLICY EKA7: INTEGRATED COASTAL MANAGEMENT AND NATURAL PARK**
>
> The development, management and use of the coastal zone will be co-ordinated through a joint policy framework. This will include the conservation and enhancement of the most valuable habitats (including Natura 2000 and Ramsar sites) and environments (natural and built), the development and management of public access, recreation and tourism potential, and identification and management of development and commercial opportunities. This will be within the context of flood protection management and coastal defence measures contained in Catchment Management Plans, Shoreline Management Plans and Coastal Defence Strategies.
>
> A particular focus will be given to the catchment of the Lower Stour for the extension and creation of wetland and other habitats, and for improved access for visitors.

18.41   Policy EKA7 recognises that the coastal zone is exceptional for the variety of both its landscape and the potential pressures from industrial, transport and leisure activity. It has strong landscape and environmental elements which, taken together, need co-ordinated management and promotion. The lower catchment of the River Stour between Deal, Sandwich and south Ramsgate and parts of the former Wantsum Channel include protected wetland and other habitats that are fragmented. There is potential in this area to:

   i. create new natural habitats as alternatives to agriculture on marginal land
   ii. improve visitor facilities and access
   iii. create a tourist attraction.

Infrastructure, Implementation and Delivery

> **EKA8: EFFECTIVE DELIVERY**
>
> The structure of the Ashford Delivery Board, the local delivery vehicle, should be kept under review as growth progresses. The dedicated Delivery Team should be maintained, reporting to the Board. Delivery partners should investigate private and public sources of funding and work together to find a mechanism to forward fund strategic infrastructure.
>
> Further work is required to examine the linkages between infrastructure provision and development in other parts of East Kent, and these linkages need to be investigated to inform the identification of priorities and the timing and sequencing of growth. Joint working between the public and private sector and infrastructure providers should seek to find ways of unlocking infrastructure constraints.
>
> Existing partnership arrangements, including the East Kent partnership, have an important role in facilitating the timely delivery of the strategic infrastructure required to support growth across East Kent.

18.42   Investment in transport to improve access to the sub-region and enable the development of major sites is given a high priority. The schemes already committed for delivery to develop this sub-region are contained in Chapter 8, Appendix A: Strategic Transport Infrastructure Priorities. A separate Regional Implementation Plan will be produced and updated by the regional planning body and will prioritise further strategic infrastructure requirements for the sub-region. Local requirements for infrastructure will be set out in local development documents and justified in accordance with national policy.

18.43   Key issues to be addressed are:

   - new public transport and highway networks at Ashford to support the Growth Area

- improved access and management to Dover to allow management of international traffic, reduce congestion within the town, and support allocated sites to the north of the town
- improved access to Canterbury to assist the economic contribution of the city to be realised and reduce pressure.

18.44 Particular importance is attached to the improvement of skills and qualifications to underpin the competitiveness of the economy. Specific projects of sub-regional significance are the future expansion of higher education at Canterbury, the Thanet campus, a new arts campus at Folkestone, the Ashford Learning Campus and the expansion of further education colleges planned by the Learning and Skills Council. New academies will replace less successful secondary schools in Thanet and Folkestone. Policy RE4: Human Resource Development is also relevant.

18.45 The ability to transfer water across Kent means that water supply must be looked at in a wider context than East Kent and Ashford alone. Supply is likely to be tight by 2011 and early decisions are needed on how supply is to be increased in an environmentally acceptable manner if housing development levels are to be met. The water companies and the Environment Agency accept that in addition to the new strategic main from Bewl Water to Ashford, a further (preferably local) source of supply should be provided to meet long term needs. The Environment Agency believe that by supplementing this new supply source with rigorous water efficiency measures, there will be enough water resource available to meet the proposed level of growth at Ashford. Investment in new water supply in the rest of the sub-region must also be increased and the potential for a new reservoir at Broad Oak near Canterbury should be investigated.

18.46 The general district hospitals at Ashford, Canterbury and Thanet will not be able to provide all specialised services and will individually serve a wider catchment for some services. Consequently, in terms of access to health services there will be reducing importance in concentrating new development in the areas with large hospitals.

18.47 Policy CC7:Infrastructure and Implementation is relevant as it sets out the general approach to implementation, including the need to ensure that the pace of development is aligned to the provision and management of infrastructure. The general approach to monitoring and review is set out in Chapter 26 on implementation, monitoring and review.

19 Kent Thames Gateway

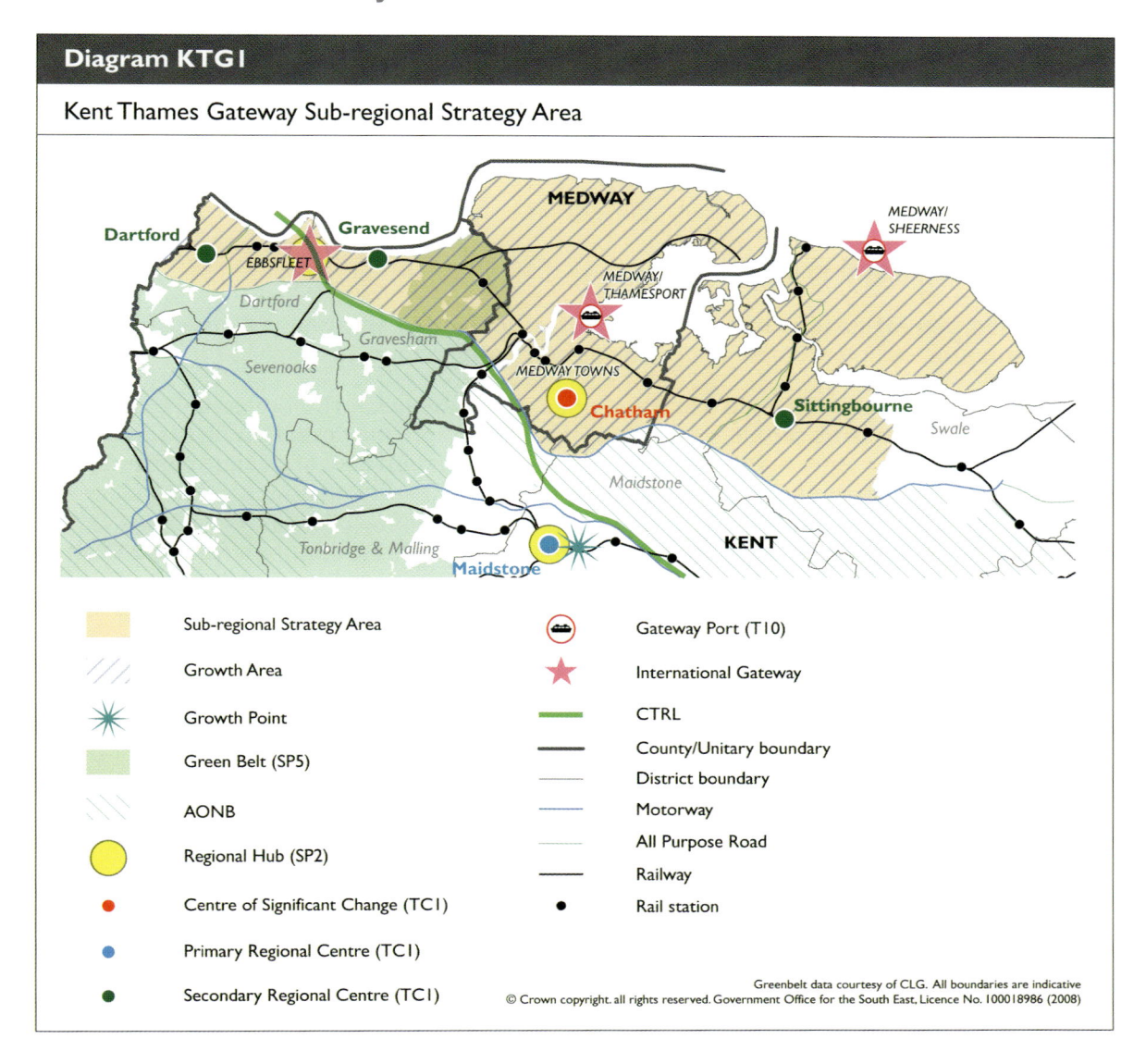

Diagram KTG1

Kent Thames Gateway Sub-regional Strategy Area

Legend:
- Sub-regional Strategy Area
- Growth Area
- Growth Point
- Green Belt (SP5)
- AONB
- Regional Hub (SP2)
- Centre of Significant Change (TC1)
- Primary Regional Centre (TC1)
- Secondary Regional Centre (TC1)
- Gateway Port (T10)
- International Gateway
- CTRL
- County/Unitary boundary
- District boundary
- Motorway
- All Purpose Road
- Railway
- Rail station

Greenbelt data courtesy of CLG. All boundaries are indicative
© Crown copyright. all rights reserved. Government Office for the South East, Licence No. 100018986 (2008)

19.1 The Thames Gateway was first recognised as a priority area for regeneration in the 1980s. Subsequently RPG9 and RPG9A (Thames Gateway Planning Framework) confirmed the area as a national and regional priority for regeneration and growth. From the outset the fundamental theme has been regeneration of large previously developed sites, improvement of poor urban environment and stimulus to the economy. The sub-region comprises the major urban areas of Dartford, Gravesham, Medway and Swale north of the A2/M2.

19.2 The Thames Gateway is identified as a major Growth Area and the particular challenges it faces are how to:

- expand the existing economic base and attract new office, manufacturing and service functions to create a flourishing local economy
- deliver sufficient decent homes and provide a well integrated mix to meet the needs of the future population of this major Growth Area and support its economic regeneration and growth
- create a safe and healthy environment with well designed public and green spaces and a 'sense of place'
- ensure development is of sufficient size, scale and density to support basic amenities
- provide adequate infrastructure and services to support sustainable growth. This includes good public and other transport both locally and linking to other centres and good quality education, training and health services

Kent Thames Gateway

- promote the right links with the wider regional, national and international community. In this, collaboration across the boundary with London will be particularly important
- upgrade the skills base of the local population to match economic needs
- encourage effective engagement and participation of local people
- ensure development supports the area's status as an Eco-Region through 'green initiatives'.

Core Strategy

> **POLICY KTG1: CORE STRATEGY**
>
> Local and central government, and all parties concerned with service provision and infrastructure, will co-ordinate their policies and programmes to:
>
> i. **as a first priority, make full use of previously developed land before greenfield sites, except where there are clear planning advantages from the development of an urban extension that improves the form, functioning and environment of existing settlements or a new community**
> ii. **locate major development in order to exploit the potential of the regional hubs at Ebbsfleet and the Medway Towns and locations served by the Channel Tunnel Rail Link, and locate housing, employment and community services where they are accessible by a choice of transport**
> iii. **ensure that the benefits of new services and employment are available to existing communities, and that new development is carefully integrated with them**
> iv. **raise the standards of education and skills in the workforce, including support for higher and further education, and achieve economic development and inward investment at an accelerated pace**
> v. **greatly increase the supply of new housing, and affordable housing in particular**
> vi. **set high standards for the design and sustainability of new communities, and for improvement of the existing urban areas, reflecting the riverside and historic character of the area**
> vii. **create higher density development in the main urban areas, linked by public transport to one another and to London**
> viii. **review local planning and transport policies to manage the forecast growth in car traffic related in particular to employment in the area and encourage greater use of sustainable modes**
> ix. **make progress in the transfer of freight from road to rail and by water, by improving the links between international gateways and the regions, including freight routes around London**
> x. **protect from development the Metropolitan Green Belt, the Area of Outstanding Natural Beauty and avoid coalescence with adjoining settlements to the south, east and west of the Medway urban area and to the west of Sittingbourne.**

19.3 The core strategy has the following objectives for sustainable regeneration and growth:

i. providing development that is necessary to meet the demographic, social and employment needs of the existing and future communities of Kent Thames Gateway and its role as a Growth Area
ii. transforming the scale and character of the economy, raising its growth rate above that of the region as a whole and strengthening its international competitiveness
iii. accommodating major new communities, and the community infrastructure required by the sub-region
iv. focusing development at the urban areas and protecting and enhancing the heritage and natural environment
v. creating a high quality environment in the Growth Area as a whole in order to foster the success of the area
vi. resolving problems related to access and congestion, the capacity of public transport, and use of the River Thames for freight.

Kent Thames Gateway

19.4 As a result of the core strategy and related policies, major development should be accessible by a choice of transport from a wide catchment, and employment and housing should be of a scale and location that minimises the necessity for long distance commuting. The relative importance of existing employment centres will change with the development of new sites, but access to town centres will remain important. Locations served by domestic services on the Channel Tunnel Rail Link (CTRL) will increase their attraction for commercial and residential development, particularly at Ebbsfleet.

19.5 The main locational effects of the core strategy and related policies will be:

i. concentrations of new dwellings, employment and services at major regeneration locations:
- at Thameside, notably at the strategic sites of Eastern Quarry, North Dartford, Ebbsfleet and the Thames riverside, and
- within the Medway urban area at riverside sites, and to the north on Ministry of Defence land at Chattenden.

Within the above, development will be particularly concentrated near the transport hubs of Ebbsfleet and the Medway Towns.

ii. new development to revitalise Sittingbourne/Sheppey in Swale, where some greenfield land has also been released.

The scale of reclamation and investment, the pace of new house building and creation of new jobs, and the provision of new infrastructure is challenging and will need continuous support.

Economic Growth and Employment

POLICY KTG2: ECONOMIC GROWTH AND EMPLOYMENT

The development of the economy in Kent Thames Gateway will be dynamic and widely based, to provide employment for the community as a whole. Provision will be made for the expansion of the existing economic functions of the area and for the introduction of new office, manufacturing and service functions on a large scale, with an emphasis on higher value activity including knowledge industries and research and development to address current under performance. The roles of the main economic locations will be promoted and developed as follows:

i. **Ebbsfleet will be developed as a major office centre of more than 20,000 jobs linked directly to central London and other European capitals, drawing its workforce from Thameside and beyond**
ii. **major sites in Thameside with access to the M25 motorway and the national rail network will continue to develop a mix of employment uses, including offices, regional distribution and manufacturing**
iii. **Medway will further develop the functions of a city centre within Thames Gateway, providing higher education, retail and other services**
iv. **major sites identified in Medway will be developed to their full potential, building on the existing high technology aerospace and automotive sectors and attracting new high value activity, or accommodating the expansion of transport, energy, distribution and manufacturing**
v. **in Sittingbourne the employment and occupation structure will be diversified though expansion of the service and science sectors. In Sheppey, provision has been made for the expansion of the distribution, transport and manufacturing sectors**
vi. **provision will be made for the continued presence and expansion of viable riverside employment uses, especially those using the river for transport.**

19.6 The development of new offices has taken place much more gradually than in other parts of the region, and the regeneration of waterside sites in Medway has succeeded only with public sector support. The economy of the Kent Thames Gateway differs from most other sub-regions in the South East in the relatively high proportions of jobs in manufacturing and distribution, and the presence of ports and power generation. These are essential functions for the region, London and the nation. Policy KTG1 will help ensure that provision is made for their future capacity and viable operation as well as new types of jobs to diversify the local economy. This will also help reduce over dependency on jobs outside the area although the sub-region will continue to need to take advantage of the jobs which London provides as a global city and financial centre. The interim estimate for monitoring purposes is 58,000 net additional jobs between 2006 and 2026.

19.7 It is critical that smart growth is encouraged and delivered in the context of Policy RE5 through:

- upgrading skills of existing residents as well as attracting skilled migrants
- improving economic activity rates
- encouraging business formation
- encouraging higher value activity
- reducing over reliance on jobs outside the sub-region.

19.8 Policies RE4: Human Resource Development and RE6: Competitiveness and Addressing Structural Economic Weakness are also particularly relevant.

Employment Locations

POLICY KTG3: EMPLOYMENT LOCATIONS

A range of readily available sites and premises will be provided to meet the needs of new business start ups, growing businesses and inward investors. Development plan documents (DPDs) should confirm the broad scale of new business and related development already identified and give priority to completion of major employment sites at the following locations:

i. **Dartford**
ii. **Ebbsfleet**
iii. **Medway**
iv. **Sittingbourne and the Isle of Sheppey.**

In addition, new employment locations should be provided at:

i. **Medway, in conjunction with new housing land**
ii. **Sittingbourne/Sheppey to expand and diversify the economy.**

High quality proposals for intensifying or expanding the technology and knowledge sectors will be supported at established and suitable new locations, unless there are overriding environmental impacts which cannot be dealt with adequately. These locations include:

i. **Medway - at Chatham Maritime and adjacent to Rochester Airfield**
ii. **Swale - at the Kent Science Park at Sittingbourne.**

Town centres and inner urban areas will be given greater emphasis as locations for regeneration and employment growth in services and cultural activity. Medway Towns and Ebbsfleet are identified as transport hubs. Chatham has a key role as a city of learning and culture.

> Medway is identified as a major location for the expansion of higher and further education, and Dartford-Ebbsfleet and Sittingbourne as locations for new investment in higher and/or further education.
>
> In Medway and Swale, if existing employment sites fail to provide readily and immediately available land for a variety of business types, the use of the land should be reviewed and alternative sites allocated, taking into account Policy RE3: Employment and Land Provision.
>
> The provision of employment locations by DPDs in the sub-region should be as set out above.

19.9 An important intention of Policy KTG3 is that the amount of employment land provided in the sub-region should be generous to match housing and labour supply and help widen and revitalise the local economy.

19.10 Some major sites in the sub-region have been slow to develop, and much of the recent employment increase has been in activities that are not located on major business sites. Policy KTG3 not only provides for major employment sites but also provides more widely for new employment locations. Concentrations of small businesses and workshops at the core of the urban areas, plus education and other services, can create important locations for new employment particularly at coastal towns with low costs and high quality environments. Town centres are important concentrations of retail, business services, finance and leisure and have the capacity to increase the number of jobs on offer.

19.11 The policy also aims to attract and retain higher 'added value' professional, technical and service jobs. It also seeks to support high quality proposals for intensifying or expanding the technology and knowledge sectors together with creative industries, which are important in the Medway towns, at established and suitable new locations. The policy reflects the following assessment:

   i. in Dartford and Gravesham the scale of new employment planned at Ebbsfleet and other sites is sufficient. If fully developed it will reduce out-commuting from the area and draw its workforce from a wider catchment, accepting that out-commuting will continue to be necessary to the jobs which London provides as a global city and financial centre
   ii. in Medway, the high level of commuting to London calls for new employment provision in conjunction with new housing
   iii. in Sittingbourne/Sheppey there is enough existing land for employment uses to meet the growing workforce but only if used more intensively than in the past. There is, however, a high level of out-commuting and a need to provide a different quality of land to diversify the economy into activities such as business and 'knowledge' sectors. Out-commuting will continue to be necessary for the reasons referred to at i above. Over the Plan period new land will be needed for this diversification and for the growth of the established transport, distribution and manufacturing sectors.

Amount, Distribution and Affordability of Housing Development

> **POLICY KTG4: AMOUNT AND DISTRIBUTION OF HOUSING DEVELOPMENT**
>
> Local planning authorities will allocate sufficient land and facilitate the delivery of 52,140 net additional dwellings in Thames Gateway between 2006 and 2026.
>
> In managing the supply of land for housing and in determining planning applications, local planning authorities should work collaboratively to facilitate the delivery of the following level of net additional dwellings in the sub-region:
>
> | DISTRICT | ANNUAL AVERAGE | TOTAL |
> | --- | --- | --- |
> | Swale (part) | 505 | 10,100 |

Dartford (part)	857	17,140
Gravesham (part)	460	9,200
Medway (part)	785	15,700
Sub-Regional Total	2,607	52,140

Growth at each location will be supported by co-ordinated provision of infrastructure, employment, environmental improvement and community services. Active pre-planning will be required to achieve necessary capacity increases.

An indicative target for affordable housing of 30% of all new dwellings applies to Kent Thames Gateway.

19.12 The above level of housing provision should enable the backlog of unmet need for affordable dwellings to be tackled within the first 10-year period of the Plan.

19.13 Average house prices in the sub-region are generally below the average price for the South East. However, the proximity of Kent Thames Gateway to London adds to demand. The major regeneration sites in the area have high reclamation costs and require substantial developer contributions for education, access and other services. Some sites may not be viable with high proportions of affordable dwellings, and 30% affordable housing is the maximum judged practical in the sub-region. This respects the need to ensure mixed communities and that there may be scope for meeting some of the needs for social rented accommodation in neighbouring districts.

19.14 Requirements for the provision of affordable housing in individual districts will be set out in local development documents, taking account of the results of strategic housing market assessments, the funding for affordable housing and the circumstances of the major development sites. Where justified, the tenure of housing being sought will also be specified.

19.15 Policies H1: Regional Housing Provision 2006-2026 and H3: Affordable Housing Provision are also particularly relevant.

The Role of the Retail Centres

POLICY KTG5: THE ROLE OF THE RETAIL CENTRES

A network of retail and service centres will be developed in which:

i. **Bluewater will continue to maintain its specialist regional role as an out of centre regional shopping centre for comparison goods shopping. Any proposals for additional floorspace at the centre that would maintain this role will be considered through a review of the RSS. Any such proposals should provide for improved access to the centre by non-car modes**

ii. **the town centres of Dartford, Gravesend, Sittingbourne and, on a larger scale, Chatham, will be further developed as the major town centres at which new mixed retail, leisure and service uses will be concentrated**

iii. **at Ebbsfleet, ancillary retail and service space will be provided at a scale and character to serve the resident and daytime population**

iv. **local development documents will make provision for local and district facilities in appropriate town centres in conjunction with the development of major new neighbourhoods.**

19.16 The owners of Bluewater shopping centre have indicated that they wish to evolve Bluewater from an isolated out-of-town shopping centre to a sustainable mixed use development, linked into the wider growth area. The Government takes the view that further development at Bluewater could affect a wide area, given the catchment that it serves within and outside the region. Any such proposals must be considered as part of

19.17   Any proposals for the expansion of Bluewater should be accompanied by an assessment of how access by public transport, walking and cycling might be improved. The improvement of access other than by car is an important consideration in order that any necessary growth is delivered in a sustainable manner. Developers are encouraged to work with the relevant local authorities and other key stakeholders on these proposals.

19.18   Policy KTG5 acknowledges that due to large-scale regeneration and residential development, additional development will be appropriate in the town centres listed in order that they remain competitive, provide an appropriate range of uses, and fulfil their distinctive role within the network of centres. At Ebbsfleet, the policy allows ancillary retail and service space to be provided to support its role as a regional hub. Policy TC2: New Development and Redevelopment in Town Centres is also particularly relevant.

POLICY KTG6: FLOOD RISK

In order to accommodate the growth levels proposed in this strategy it will be necessary to implement co-ordinated measures for flood protection and surface water drainage associated with the Rivers Thames, Medway and Swale.

Strategic flood risk assessments will be kept up to date having regard to the latest intelligence on flood levels, and local assessments will be undertaken for major sites at risk, in the light of the Environment Agency's long term plans for flood risk management. Development will be planned to avoid the risk of flooding and will not be permitted if it would:

i.   **be subject to an unacceptable risk of flooding or significantly increase the risk elsewhere**
ii. **prejudice the capacity or integrity of flood plains or flood protection measures**

Development plan documents will include policies to:

i.   **adopt a risk based approach to guiding categories of development away from flood risk areas**
ii. **ensure that development proposals are accompanied by flood risk assessments**
iii. **identify opportunities for flood storage areas to contribute to green infrastructure networks.**

19.19   Many of the major development sites in the sub-region are in whole or in part within the coastal and fluvial flood zones defined by the Environment Agency.

19.20   Thames Estuary 2100 (TE2100) is an Environment Agency project to develop a tidal flood risk management plan for the Thames estuary through to the end of the century. The final plan will be published in 2010. The plan will recommend what flood risk management measures will be required in the estuary, where they will be needed, and when over the coming century, based upon climate change and projected sea level rises.

19.21   The 'Green Grid' (see below) and green space outside urban areas may provide opportunities for flood storage as part of the Thames Estuary 2100 solutions. Policy NRM4: Sustainable Flood Risk Management is also particularly relevant.

19.22   The Thames Gateway Parklands Initiative will support the aspiration for the Thames Gateway to be the UK's first Eco-Region, which addresses: climate change (adaptation and mitigation); landscape and biodiversity; flood risk; water quality; water supply and treatment; air quality; sustainable waste management and treatment; energy efficiency; decentralised and renewable energy; sustainable construction; sustainable transport and community involvement.

Green Initiatives

> **POLICY KTG7: GREEN INITIATIVES**
>
> In order to take forward the Thames Gateway Parklands aim of transforming the environment and image of the Gateway:
>
> The development, management and use of the countryside, urban green spaces and areas requiring flood management will be co-ordinated by the responsible organisations. Provision should be made for green grid networks, recreation and public access, and enhancement of landscapes, habitats, heritage and the environment.
>
> Countryside initiatives should complement the areas for growth, and recognise that it is a predominantly working landscape. They should define the important points of separation between settlements and the urban edges to be actively managed, and identify the connections between the urban 'green grid' and the rural area.
>
> Development should be of the highest standards of design, and adopt best practice in the use of sustainable techniques.

19.23 The successful regeneration of the sub-region requires investment in the environment, emphasis on the setting of urban areas and provision of 'green space' for existing and new communities. This will increase the attraction of the area to new investment. 'Greening the Gateway' (Defra/ODPM, January 2004) called for a network of green spaces both serving and linking urban and rural areas. It recognised the importance of the riverside location and the need to manage flood risk in a sustainable way. In November 2006 DCLG took this further in the Thames Gateway Interim Plan Policy Framework which created a new identity for the area, 'the Thames Gateway Parklands'. Policy KTG7 sets out measures to help deliver the environmental aim of this new initiative. Policy CC8: Green Infrastructure is also particularly relevant.

Implementation and Delivery

19.24 The efficient functioning of the Kent Thames Gateway depends on reliable east-west road and public transport routes, and the growth already planned depends entirely on their timely improvement. Efficient north-south movement by public transport and by road will be of increasing importance even with the existing level of planned growth. Regional and international traffic will be affected by congestion on the transport networks serving development in the Growth Area. Therefore, there are regional and national reasons to improve transport capacity.

19.25 While a Lower Thames Crossing would form an inter-regional route, it would have important implications for the local economy of the sub-region and would support the planned growth in north Kent.

19.26 It is important that the infrastructure required to support development proposals is identified sufficiently early in the planning process so that its provision can be phased in relation to that development.

19.27 A separate Regional Implementation Plan will be produced and updated by the regional planning body and will prioritise further strategic infrastructure requirements for the sub-region. Local requirements for infrastructure will be set out in local development documents and justified in accordance with national policy.

19.28 The following are of particular significance for the sub-region:

   i. the creation of a skilled and qualified workforce able to support a newly developed economic base and to exploit new opportunities in technology and the knowledge economy

ii. the provision of environmental infrastructure, including flood defence, coastal flood protection, water resources, waste water treatment and water quality, together with measures to improve water efficiency are essential for the delivery of growth. The current necessity to transfer water across Kent and from neighbouring areas means that new water supplies will be needed. It is likely that water supply and treatment can respond to increased growth but there will be a need for accelerated and increased investment

iii. the scales of growth envisaged may mean that the capacity for acute health services has to be increased. The implications of full teaching status for existing acute hospitals would need careful appraisal

iv. improving the quality and quantity of social infrastructure including higher education at Chatham and Ebbsfleet.

19.29 The transport schemes already committed for delivery to develop this sub-region are contained in Chapter 8, Appendix A: Strategic Transport Investment Priorities. Key transport themes for the sub-region are:

- A2/A282/M2 corridor schemes to improve connectivity through the area and with London and access from east-west routes to open up development sites
- study of Thames Crossing options
- Crossrail and CTRL related rail improvements and additional capacity to support growth in passenger and freight demand
- Fastrack and other public transport, walking and cycling schemes to promote modal shift as part of integrated local packages.

19.30 The rate of growth in new houses and jobs will be monitored to assess changes in the sub-regional economy and ensure that the relationship between them and increased capacity in strategic infrastructure is managed and kept under review. These and other monitoring indicators will inform reviews of this sub-regional strategy (see also Chapter 26 on implementation, monitoring and review).

Kent Thames Gateway

19

20 London Fringe

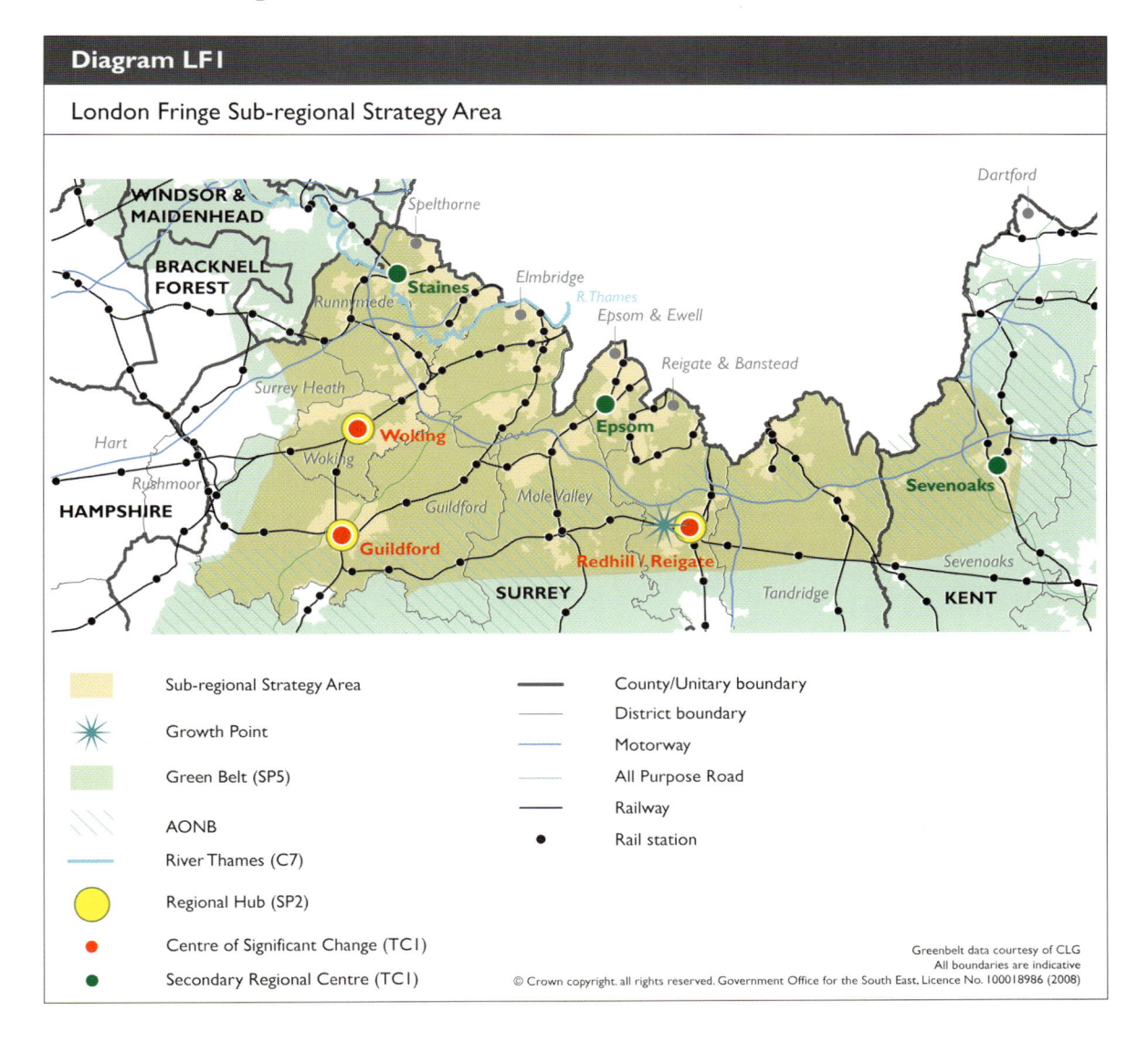

Diagram LF1

London Fringe Sub-regional Strategy Area

Legend:
- Sub-regional Strategy Area
- Growth Point
- Green Belt (SP5)
- AONB
- River Thames (C7)
- Regional Hub (SP2)
- Centre of Significant Change (TC1)
- Secondary Regional Centre (TC1)
- County/Unitary boundary
- District boundary
- Motorway
- All Purpose Road
- Railway
- Rail station

Greenbelt data courtesy of CLG
All boundaries are indicative
© Crown copyright. all rights reserved. Government Office for the South East. Licence No. 100018986 (2008)

20.1 The London Fringe, although covered by much of the Western Policy Area, was not defined as a separate sub-region in RPG9. However, it is defined as a sub-region in this Plan in recognition of the common contextual issues and challenges now facing the area. The sub-regional strategy covers a large proportion of Surrey from the Greater London boundary to beyond the towns of Guildford, Woking and Redhill. It also covers a very small part of west Kent including the town of Sevenoaks. Specifically, it includes the whole of the Surrey districts of Spelthorne, Runnymede, Woking, Elmbridge and Epsom & Ewell, and partially the districts of Surrey Heath, Guildford, Mole Valley, Reigate and Banstead and Tandridge and, in Kent, part of the district of Sevenoaks.

20.2 The overarching challenge facing this sub-region is how to balance development pressures in this area of buoyant economic growth close to London, Heathrow and Gatwick without compromising the quality of life of its residents. The particular challenges are how to:

- support sustainable economic growth having regard to its role in the regional economy, the labour supply and infrastructure problems facing the area, and environmental constraints such as landfill/waste management needs, water resources, water quality and flood risk
- deliver sufficient decent homes and provide a well integrated mix to meet the needs of the area, including affordable housing for which there is a very high need in this sub-region

- maintain the regional role of the Metropolitan Green Belt in containing London and retaining the identity of existing towns in this densely settled area while allowing for necessary urban extensions
- realise the potential of existing urban areas to deliver future development in a sustainable way which enhances the quality of life, whilst simultaneously addressing the associated infrastructure and environmental consequences
- support the role of three regional hubs which play an important part in the regional economy – Guildford, Redhill and Reigate, and Woking – and the hierarchy of smaller centres
- respect and develop the character and identity of the towns and the natural and cultural resources of the countryside, including the high quality landscapes, which are also an asset in economic terms and a resource for informal recreation for residents and visitors.

Core Strategy

> **POLICY LF1: CORE STRATEGY**
>
> **Provision will be made for development and infrastructure to support the sustainable economic growth of the sub-region, recognising its importance to the wider region and London, while conserving and enhancing its environmental assets. This will be achieved by:**
>
> i. **meeting development requirements predominantly within urban areas and protecting the broad extent of the Metropolitan Green Belt across the sub-region**
> ii. **meeting housing needs mainly within urban areas but, where this is not possible, by urban extensions involving selective or small-scale reviews of the boundary of the Metropolitan Green Belt and by redevelopment of a major developed site at Chertsey**
> iii. **sustaining growth in the economy, supported by comprehensive monitoring of labour supply and demand, and movement patterns across the sub-region and in adjoining areas including London**
> iv. **generally focusing employment-related development to take place on land already in employment use or available for such use**
> v. **encouraging a broad base of economic activity which utilises existing skills in the workforce and supporting retraining and re-skilling of the workforce**
> vi. **seeking increased provision of affordable housing to underpin the economy**
> vii. **improving travel choice by investment in alternatives to single-occupancy car use**
> viii. **conserving and enhancing biodiversity, the quality of the built environment and the character of natural and cultural resources in the sub-region.**

20.3 The core strategy set out in Policy LF1 recognises the economic importance of the sub-region to the regional economy and beyond, the housing needs of the area and the importance of retaining the overall quality of life. The economy, while buoyant with high participation rates, strong representation of ICT and other growth sectors and a skilled workforce, is likely to face labour supply shortages unless action is taken. The risk is that otherwise economic growth would be constrained and/or unsustainable commuting pressures imposed on the transport network which is already at or beyond capacity in the peak hours. Providing sufficient housing to meet needs, in particular for affordable housing, is also critical.

20.4 The strategy focuses on sustainable development within existing urban areas respecting the high quality of the surrounding countryside, which provides an important recreation resource, and the need to retain the identity of towns. Where necessary the policy allows for urban extensions with the safeguards of sustainable development and good design provided by the other policies in this Plan: these include Policies LF5: Urban Areas and Regional Hubs, SP3: Urban Focus and Urban Renaissance and CC6: Sustainable Communities and Character of the Environment. Policy LF1 provides that in planning these extensions the broad extent of the Green Belt will be protected as will its fundamental purposes. Important to the success of this strategy in reducing the scale of development otherwise required is smart economic growth (see paragraph 20.6 below).

Economic Development

> **POLICY LF2: ECONOMIC DEVELOPMENT**
>
> Employment-related development will take place primarily on land already in employment use or available for such use. In judging whether such land is sufficient to meet employment land needs, local authorities will work jointly with neighbouring authorities as appropriate, having regard to:
>
> i. the evidence of local and strategic demand for employment floorspace
> ii. the broad balance between labour supply and demand within that part of the sub-region
> iii. the suitability of existing employment land to continue in that use;
> iv. the availability of land for housing, relative to local needs, and the scope for any shortfalls to be met through the release of employment land suitable for residential use
> v. any other considerations relevant to the maintenance of an appropriate balance of land uses.
>
> If the existing stock of land is judged to be insufficient, new areas of employment land may be allocated in development plan documents as part of the sustainable urban extensions identified in accordance with Policy LF5 and on the former DERA site at Chertsey (Policy LF6).
>
> Development plan documents will identify strategic employment land which will be safeguarded for employment purposes.
>
> Mixed-use development will be encouraged in and around town centres and other areas of good public transport accessibility. Residential or mixed-use development may be allowed on employment land that is not identified as being strategically important, particularly if amenity and environmental gains are achieved and more sustainable forms of development result.

20.5 The economy of this sub-region cannot be divorced from that of the adjoining areas in south and west London, and adjoining parts of the South East. Therefore, Policy LF2 requires joint working on employment land reviews between neighbouring authorities taking into account strategic as well as local demands as well as the other factors listed in the policy. It is particularly important that this happens in the inter-related economies of Surrey, South/South West London and parts of the Western Corridor and Blackwater Valley sub-region. These reviews also need to have regard to Policy RE3: Employment and Land Provision. The policy gives priority towards the recycling of existing employment land for continuing employment use, as has been the pattern in the past. If new employment land is necessary, the policy provides that this should be part of the development allowed for in Policies LF5 and LF6 below. It will also need to be in accordance with the principles of sustainable development and good design referred to in the Core Regional Policies.

20.6 The interim estimate is 39,500 net additional jobs between 2006 and 2016 which will be monitored/reviewed. This may be below the trend employment growth and assumes the application of Policy RE5: Smart Growth. Achieving smart economic growth in this sub-region requires the attraction of high value, low impact sectors with an emphasis on knowledge-based enterprises. Policy RE6: Competitiveness and Addressing Structural Economic Weakness is particularly relevant to achieving this. Smart growth also requires additional productivity improvements and raising economic activity together with changes in commuting patterns as a labour market adjustment.

London Fringe

Broad Amount and Distribution of Future Housing Development

POLICY LF3: BROAD AMOUNT AND DISTRIBUTION OF FUTURE HOUSING DEVELOPMENT

Local planning authorities will allocate sufficient land and facilitate the delivery of 47,880 net additional dwellings in the London Fringe between 2006 and 2026.

In managing the supply of land for housing and in determining planning applications, local planning authorities should work collaboratively to facilitate the delivery of the following level of net additional dwellings in the sub-region:

DISTRICT	ANNUAL AVERAGE	TOTAL
Elmbridge [1]	281	5,620
Epsom & Ewell [1]	199	3,980
Guildford (part)[2]	397	7,940
Mole Valley (part)[2]	188	3,760
Reigate & Banstead (part)[3]	375	7,500
Runnymede [4]	286	5,720
Sevenoaks (part)	85	1,700
Spelthorne	166	3,320
Tandridge (part)[2]	125	2,500
Woking	292	5,840
Sub-Regional Total	2,394	47,880

In the primarily rural parts of Surrey Heath which lie in the London Fringe sub-region, only limited housing supply is expected and this is included in the Western Corridor and Blackwater Valley sub-region figures.

Local authorities should consider the phasing of housing delivery within the vicinity of the Thames Basin Heaths Special Protection Area in order to ensure that appropriate avoidance and mitigation measures are secured in advance of development being occupied and should work with the regional planning body and Natural England to monitor housing delivery in their area against the provision of avoidance and mitigation measures (see Policy NRM6: Thames Basin Heaths).

The selective reviews of the Metropolitan Green Belt to accommodate sustainable urban extensions at Guildford and possibly at Woking will need to be informed by flood risk assessments.

Footnotes

1. The River Hogsmill is currently failing to meet good ecological status as a result of phosphorous concentrations and the capacity of the Hogsmill Sewage Treatment Works (STW) to accept further effluent is severely constrained as a result. This may have implications for housing delivery in the catchment area of the Hogsmill STW in Epsom & Ewell and Elmbridge. The satisfactory resolution of this problem will require further work, which will need to be reflected in local development frameworks and future reviews of the RSS.

> 2. In the primarily rural parts of Mole Valley and Tandridge which lie outside the sub-region, and in the rural part of Guildford outside both this and the Western Corridor and Blackwater Valley sub-regions, only limited housing supply is expected and this is included in the London Fringe sub-region figures.
>
> 3. Flexibility will be allowed for Reigate and Banstead to vary the provision levels between London Fringe and Gatwick subject to maximising the capacity of the Redhill and Reigate hub for sustainable development.
>
> 4. The figure for Runnymede includes 2,500 homes for the reuse of the former DERA site at Chertsey to be provided in Runnymede. The precise housing contribution from this site will be tested in accordance with Policy LF6. This allocation will be delivered in the period between 2016-2026. Between 2006-2015 the annual requirement will be 161 dwellings per annum. In the event that the site cannot be released for housing, there is no expectation that the shortfall should be provided elsewhere within Runnymede.

20.7 Consistent with Policy H1: Regional Housing Provision 2006-2026, the level of housing provision in Policy LF3 takes account of housing needs, including the need to address the wide and growing gap that would otherwise occur between labour supply and demand even with smart growth. There would be serious economic, environmental and social costs to the sub-region and the wider region beyond if this approach were not taken. Housing development will be carried out in a sustainable way consistent with the other policies in this chapter, the Core Regional Policies and Policy H4:Type and Size of New Housing.

20.8 The housing distribution in Policy LF3 is strongly influenced by the development pattern currently in the sub-region given the urban focus of the strategy, but it also reflects the opportunities provided by the proposed urban extensions and reuse of the former DERA site at Chertsey. Local authorities will adopt a plan, monitor and manage approach to housing, to deliver a sufficient and suitable land supply throughout the Plan period in accordance with the levels of provision set out in Policy LF3 (see also Chapter 27, Implementation, Monitoring and Review).

20.9 It will be critical to promote water efficiency along with resource development and integration of supply infrastructure to ensure that the water supply/demand balance can be maintained within this sub-region. In accordance with Policy NRM1: Sustainable Water Resources and Groundwater Quality, all relevant local development documents will need to contain policies and measures that account for and promote the twin-track approach of demand management and water resource development.

20.10 Policy on flooding is contained in Policy NRM4: Sustainable Flood Risk Management. Local authorities should prepare strategic flood risk assessments to inform their local development frameworks. They should have regard to the Environment Agency's Catchment Flood Management Plan(s) and recognise that the natural flood plain is generally the most important asset in managing flood risk. The location, layout and design of developments are the most vital factors in managing future flood risk.

Affordable Housing

> **POLICY LF4: AFFORDABLE HOUSING**
>
> **40% of all new housing in the sub-region should be affordable, with the precise level and the split between social rented and other forms of tenure being determined locally having regard to local housing assessments.**

> Local development documents should seek provision of affordable housing on all sites where it can be justified by local housing assessments and the economics of provision. In cases where on-site provision of affordable housing is not feasible, commuted payments will be required. Non-residential development which generates needs for additional housing will also make an appropriate contribution to affordable provision.

20.11 In Surrey generally, and within the sub-region, affordable housing needs are high, reflecting the high market price of housing in the area and the high proportion of owner-occupied stock. Evidence suggests that 40% of the housing requirement should be in the form of affordable housing, although local need assessments may justify variations from this figure in individual boroughs and districts.

20.12 Future land supply in the sub-region will come predominantly from relatively small previously developed sites within established urban areas. This pattern of supply means that contributions towards affordable housing should be sought from all new residential development, either on-site or through a financial contribution to provision elsewhere. Non-residential development which would generate a need for additional housing should be expected to make a contribution towards its provision where market pressures are especially strong and the need for affordable housing is acute.

Urban Areas and Regional Hubs

> **POLICY LF5: URBAN AREAS AND REGIONAL HUBS**
>
> The focus for development will be within existing built-up areas. Local authorities through their local development documents (LDDs) and through integrated approaches developed with other service providers, the development industry and local communities, will ensure development contributes towards the delivery of necessary physical and social infrastructure.
>
> Improvements to the physical environment will be achieved by setting high design standards for new development and its relationship to existing buildings and spaces. This focus requires that existing urban open land will be safeguarded.
>
> Development at the regional hubs of Guildford, Redhill/Reigate and Woking should take place as far as possible within the existing urban areas and, to maintain their role as key centres within the sub-region, must be accompanied by commensurate investment in infrastructure and be planned to be accessible through measures which reduce demand and improve transport management.
>
> Notwithstanding this imperative, at Guildford, a sustainable urban extension of 2000 dwellings is likely to be required to meet the housing allocation. This should be located to the north-east of the town and be brought forward in accordance with Policy SP5: Green Belts.
>
> Some expansion into the Metropolitan Green Belt may also be required at Woking in order to meet the housing allocation. The scale of boundary review that may be necessary should be tested through the LDD process and guided by Policy SP5: Green Belts but, if more than minor boundary adjustments are required, it should focus on the area to the south of the town.
>
> A smaller-scale local review of the Metropolitan Green Belt boundary should be undertaken as required at Redhill/Reigate, in accordance with Policy SP5: Green Belts.

20.13 Policy LF5 focuses development within existing urban areas while identifying that urban extensions may be required as outlined below to accommodate necessary development. Consistent with Policy BE1: Management for an Urban Renaissance, the policy seeks to take advantage of the opportunities associated with new development to contribute

20.14 In line with Policy SP2: Regional Hubs, the policy supports the regional hubs of Guildford, Redhill and Reigate and Woking. An urban extension of Guildford is likely to be required in keeping with its increasing economic importance, the continuing expansion of the university and its major retail role and transport connectivity. A smaller scale extension in Woking may also be required which could complement the expansion of Guildford, given the scope to improve inter-connectivity between the two towns while maintaining their separate identity. It is important that the local authorities for Guildford and Woking work with partners to ensure that these towns retain their role in the spatial structure of the area, develop their role as transport hubs, support their economies by encouraging urban development and renewal which is sympathetic to their character and promote their interconnectivity. Any urban extension needs to be consistent with the principles of sustainable development and good design already referred to. A smaller-scale local review of the Green Belt may also be necessary at Redhill/Reigate.

Former DERA Site, Chertsey

POLICY LF6: DEVELOPMENT AT FORMER DERA SITE, CHERTSEY

Large-scale mixed-use development on the former DERA site at Chertsey, which lies in Runnymede and Surrey Heath districts, will be brought forward during the Plan period to meet wider regional needs. The precise scale of development, mix of uses, provision of avoidance and mitigation measures to protect the Thames Basin Heaths Special Protection Area and other relevant European sites such as the Thursley, Ash, Pirbright & Chobham Special Area of Conservation, and the review of the boundary of the Metropolitan Green Belt will be tested through local development documents (LDDs), including jointly prepared LDDs where appropriate.

The review of the Green Belt boundary should be carried out in accordance with Policy SP5: Green Belts. Development at Chertsey should ensure that national and European air quality standards are not breached.

20.15 In accordance with Policy H1: Regional Housing Provision 2006-2026, the former DERA site near Chertsey, which lies mostly in Runnymede but straddles the boundary with Surrey Heath, is identified as a mixed-use site. The site has the potential to serve wider than local needs and should be brought forward in a phased programme. The Metropolitan Green Belt status of the site will require a review in accordance with Policy SP5: Green Belts. The precise scale of the development and the mix of uses that would be appropriate, the relationship of the site to the adjacent Special Protection Area, and the impact on the purposes served by the Green Belt in this location are amongst the matters that will require detailed examination through joint working between the local authorities and other stakeholders.

Town Centres

POLICY LF7: TOWN CENTRES

The polycentric pattern of the settlement structure will be maintained with town and district centres being the focus for retailing, employment, built leisure and community facilities. Mixed-use development offering both jobs and housing will be encouraged to offer opportunity to access jobs, services and facilities, and reduce the need for longer distance travel. Local centres will be identified which can be upgraded by mixed-use development.

> Investment in development, infrastructure and services will be directed particularly to Guildford, Redhill and Woking and, on a scale consistent with the capacity of each centre, to Epsom, Sevenoaks and Staines, to maintain their roles in the strategic town centre network.
>
> Significant improvements to the arrangements for interchange between bus and rail, particularly in the quality of facilities, integration and frequency of services, should be linked to restraint-based town centre parking strategies.
>
> In all centres, the design and form of development should improve the streetscape and produce high quality, accessible and coherent pedestrian environments.

20.16 The existing polycentric pattern of the settlement structure provides people with the benefit of greater opportunity to access services and facilities. Policy LF7 maintains this, with town centres being a focus for mixed-use development which can further reduce the need for longer distance travel. Centres in south London, particularly the metropolitan centres of Croydon, Kingston, Sutton and Bromley, also contribute to the range of facilities and services available to people living in the sub-region.

20.17 In principle, investment in the modernisation of facilities in all town centres will benefit local communities. Major development will be encouraged to locate in the centres identified in Policy TC1: Strategic Network of Town Centres, focusing in particular on the Primary Regional Centres, guided by comprehensive proposals within local development documents which are consistent with the capacity of each centre.

Sub-Regional Transport Hubs and Spokes

> **POLICY LF8: SUB-REGIONAL TRANSPORT HUBS AND SPOKES**
>
> Local transport authorities should give consideration to the identification and inclusion of sub-regional hubs and spokes or corridors in local transport plans to support local service provision and interchange with inter-urban public transport. These should be developed in co-ordination with local authorities in preparing spatial strategies for urban areas in local development documents.

20.18 Policy LF8 encourages local transport authorities to develop an appropriate network of sub-regional spokes that link the sub-regional hubs to each other. This will also mean linking these centres to the regional hubs and to adjoining centres in south London where relevant.

Green Belt Management

> **POLICY LF9: GREEN BELT MANAGEMENT**
>
> Local development documents will promote improved management to increase opportunities for access to the open countryside, the retention of attractive landscapes and enhancement of damaged ones, and conservation in areas of the rural-urban fringe easily accessible to people within the sub-region and beyond. The Green Arc (South West) initiative to manage and enhance Metropolitan Green Belt countryside as a multi-functional resource, integrated with greenspace strategies in urban areas, will be promoted and the management plans for the Surrey Hills, Kent Downs and High Weald Areas of Outstanding Natural Beauty supported.

20.19 Policy LF9 promotes specific initiatives to manage Green Belt countryside as a multi-functional resource. This will support a more positive role for the Green Belt as well as secure improvements to countryside easily accessible to people within the sub-region and beyond, in line with the advice on urban rural fringe land management in Policy C5: Managing the Rural-Urban Fringe. The management plan for the Surrey Hills Area of Outstanding Natural Beauty (AONB) provides a mechanism for achieving these objectives within that part of the Green Belt. The Green Arc (South West) initiative applies to the area of the sub-region to the north of the Surrey Hills AONB and is a partnership designed to secure greater investment in landscape enhancement, improved access and conservation across a crucial part of the Metropolitan Green Belt.

Infrastructure, Implementation and Delivery

> **POLICY LF10: SMALL SCALE SITE TARIFF**
>
> **Local planning authorities will work jointly with infrastructure and service providers and developers to establish a programme for the provision of infrastructure within the sub-region which takes into account the cumulative impact of small scale development.**
>
> **Contributions from new development, based on a co-ordinated and consistent approach, will be secured to support delivery of the infrastructure and services required to mitigate the impact of cumulative development and to maintain quality of life in the area.**

20.20   Development in the sub-region is characterised by the re-use and redevelopment of relatively small sites within established urban areas. The cumulative impact of this development on infrastructure and service requirements is as significant as it is for more concentrated greenfield development, but more difficult to capture in specific infrastructure packages. This underlines the need for the joint approach to provision identified in Policy CC7: Infrastructure and Implementation. The small site tariff approach to developer contributions towards infrastructure and service provision introduced by Policy LF10 will help address this cumulative impact issue and assist delivery. To work effectively the policy will depend on the early identification of the necessary infrastructure and services, in order to assist the latter's timely delivery in relation to development.

20.21   The transport schemes already committed for delivery to develop this sub-region are contained in Chapter 8, Appendix A: Strategic Transport Infrastructure Priorities, with further transport improvements identified in the supporting text to Policy T14: Transport Investment and Management Priorities. A separate Regional Implementation Plan will be produced and updated by the regional planning body and will prioritise further strategic infrastructure requirements for the sub-region. Local requirements for infrastructure will be set out in local development documents and justified in accordance with national policy.

20.22   The road network suffers from congested and unreliable journeys in the peak periods and rail journeys to and from London are also highly congested during peak hours. During peak hours, transport demand as a whole exceeds supply and as a result efforts should be focused on reducing demand, making best use of existing infrastructure, and investing in public transport alongside bottleneck improvements to the road network.

20.23   Policy CC7: Infrastructure and implementation sets out the general approach to implementation, including the need to ensure that the pace of development is aligned to the provision and management of infrastructure. In this sub-region infrastructure and service requirements need to be related not just to the scale and pace of growth in the area but also in adjoining areas where cross-boundary movements are significant. The general approach to monitoring and review is set out in Chapter 26 on implementation, monitoring and review.

London Fringe

Western Corridor and Blackwater Valley

21 Western Corridor and Blackwater Valley

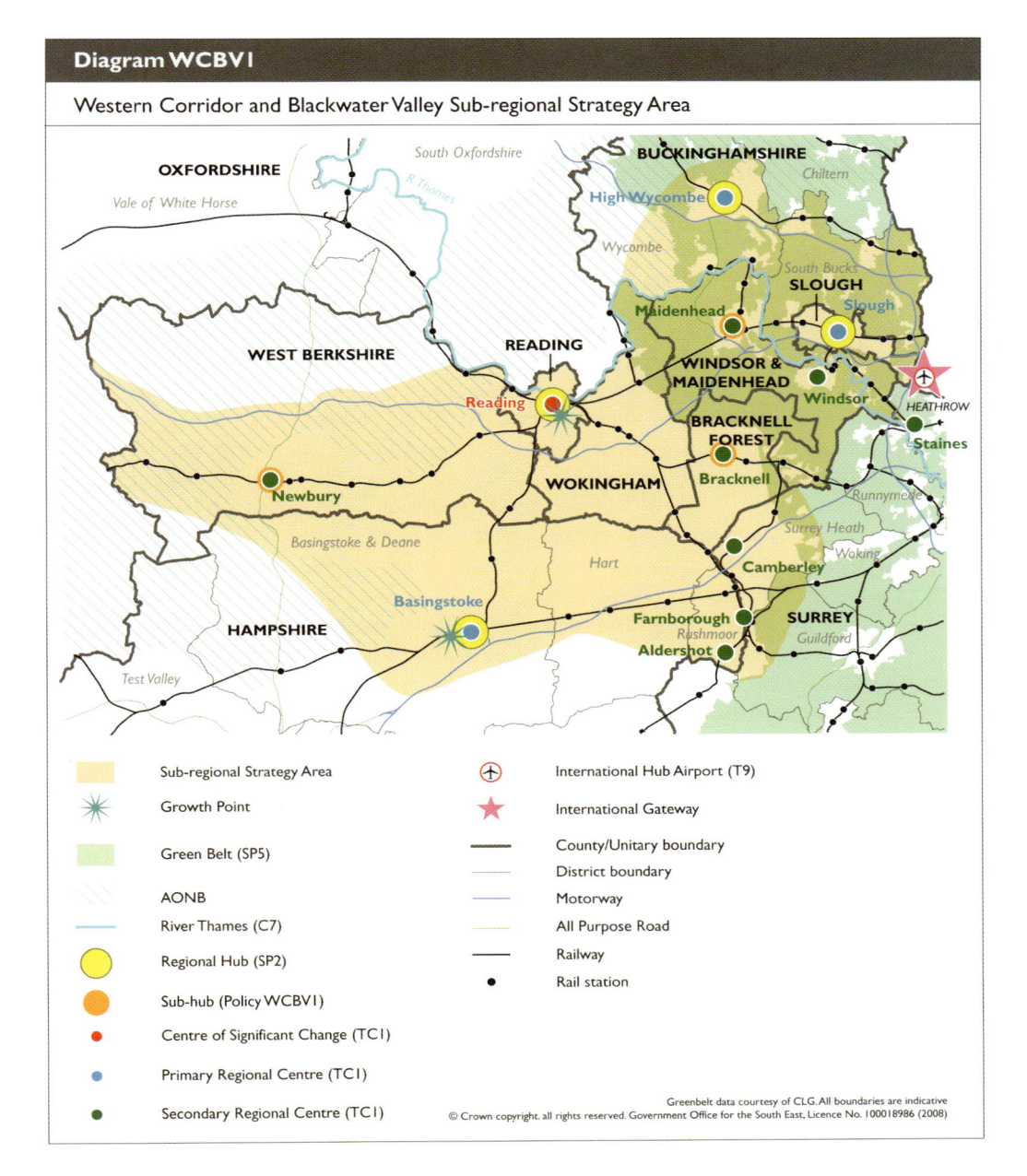

Diagram WCBV1
Western Corridor and Blackwater Valley Sub-regional Strategy Area

Legend:
- Sub-regional Strategy Area
- Growth Point
- Green Belt (SP5)
- AONB
- River Thames (C7)
- Regional Hub (SP2)
- Sub-hub (Policy WCBV1)
- Centre of Significant Change (TC1)
- Primary Regional Centre (TC1)
- Secondary Regional Centre (TC1)
- International Hub Airport (T9)
- International Gateway
- County/Unitary boundary
- District boundary
- Motorway
- All Purpose Road
- Railway
- Rail station

Greenbelt data courtesy of CLG. All boundaries are indicative
© Crown copyright, all rights reserved. Government Office for the South East, Licence No. 100018986 (2008)

21.1   The Western Corridor and Blackwater Valley (WCBV) sub-region extends from the western edge of London to the boundary of the South West region in the Swindon area (See Diagram WCBV1). It adjoins the London Fringe, and lies close to the Central Oxfordshire and Milton Keynes & Aylesbury Vale sub-regions. The WCBV sub-region includes all or part of the administrative areas of the following local authorities: West Berkshire, Reading, Wokingham, Bracknell Forest, Windsor and Maidenhead, Slough, South Bucks, Wycombe, Surrey Heath, Guildford, Hart, Rushmoor and Basingstoke and Deane.

21.2   The sub-region has its planning origins in the proposals in the 1960s for sub–regional growth linking Reading and Wokingham in the north with Basingstoke to the south-west. Much of the sub-region was covered by parts of the Thames Valley and Blackwater Valley sub-regions in RPG9. The sub-region as defined in this Plan recognises the common economic geography, functional linkages, environmental designations and strategic planning challenges facing the area. In particular the sub-region:

- exhibits high economic and other growth potential related in part to its historic proximity to London and Heathrow but increasingly being self-generated

Western Corridor and Blackwater Valley

- contains a complex pattern of settlements, administrative structures and environmental designations as well as high pressure for, and on, infrastructure that all require careful co-ordination and management
- has a long history of sub-regional planning as a means to deliver growth and development that needs to evolve to meet modern requirements and challenges.

21.3 The proposed boundary of the sub-region reflects current and future planning needs. However, collaborative working and action in connection with settlements just beyond the boundary, for example Farnham, and other nearby areas or sub-regions will also need to take place.

21.4 The particular challenges faced by the sub-region are how to:

- realise the economic potential of the area, without compromising the quality of life of its residents, and spread the benefits to all places and sections of the community given that the sub-region contains some of the most deprived wards in the region (initial interim estimate is a minimum 79,300 additional jobs created by 2016)
- deliver sufficient decent homes and provide a well integrated mix to meet the needs of the area, including affordable housing for which there is a very high need in this sub-region (102,100 net additional dwellings to be delivered by 2026)
- achieve a better balance between the location and growth of jobs and homes while protecting the area's environmental assets, including the Thames Basin Heaths Special Protection Area
- manage demand on the area's transport networks so as to maintain accessibility, and ensure access to London and Heathrow, particularly by public transport
- deliver the requirements for physical, social and environmental infrastructure needed to support existing and future economic and housing growth
- take proper account of the implications flowing from major planned growth within and beyond the sub-region: for example at Aylesbury Vale/ Milton Keynes, Basingstoke, Greater Reading, Heathrow, Oxford and Swindon
- deliver in a timely fashion the individually and/or collaboratively produced development plan documents that will implement the South East Plan locally.

Core Strategy

> **POLICY WCBV1: CORE STRATEGY**
>
> **Provision for development and infrastructure will be made to sustain the economic growth of the sub-region.**
>
> **Regional and sub-regional hubs will be the main focus for transport investment and development in the sub-region.**
>
> **The following settlements are identified as regional hubs:**
>
> **Basingstoke**
>
> **High Wycombe**
>
> **Reading**
>
> **Slough**
>
> **A second tier of sub-regional hubs comprises:**
>
> **Bracknell**
>
> **Maidenhead**
>
> **Newbury**

Western Corridor and Blackwater Valley

> To the extent that development cannot be satisfactorily accommodated in the existing built-up areas, sustainable urban extensions will be promoted at selected settlements. Sustainable greenfield allocations should be mainly focused on the periphery of those hubs where other constraints do not prevent this – Basingstoke, Reading, Bracknell and Newbury – but smaller allocations may be brought forward at other settlements, subject to their meeting the same sustainability considerations. These urban extensions should minimise incursions into Green Belt or areas protected (or proposed for protection in local development documents) as Areas of Outstanding Natural Beauty or by other policies of regional, national and international importance.

21.5 The strategy respects the multi-centred settlement pattern, subject to a refocusing of economic and housing growth on the identified regional and sub-regional hubs and other sustainable locations. The amount and location of growth will reflect the various national to local roles to be played by individual or groups of settlements and will be given clear expression in, and delivered via, the relevant local development documents (LDDs). It will also reflect the need to provide a better balance of jobs, housing and transport at both the sub-regional and individual settlement level. As necessary, local authorities will therefore review current planning and other designations in order that the future roles of their settlements can be fulfilled, including via urban extensions or other forms of development serving the same purpose, while protecting appropriately their environmental assets.

21.6 While Green Belt policy remains central to the core strategy, its current boundaries should not be considered inviolate if the economy is to be supported and a step change in housing achieved. There are areas within the sub-region, for example Maidenhead, where a thorough assessment of options has or will most likely show that alterations to the Green Belt will be the most sustainable option for locating employment and housing as part of mixed use schemes. Therefore, in accordance with PPG2: *Green Belts*, all authorities will need to demonstrate via their core strategies that all necessary development can be accommodated up to and beyond the Plan period without the need to revise their Green Belt boundaries. Where this is not the case they will need to consider small scale reviews or other revisions that may also include the use of existing, or designation of new, safeguarded land.

21.7 In accordance with the general policies, for example SP3: Urban Focus and Urban Renaissance and CC6: Sustainable Communities and Character of the Environment, the aim is to create and maintain a network of sustainable communities. Consequently, factors such as deliverability, meeting needs where they arise and the timing of infrastructure delivery will be taken into account. Thus, while the use of previously developed land and/or urban regeneration will be priorities, minimising the take-up of greenfield land will not be a factor that overrides all others.

21.8 Greater Reading comprises the existing and planned future built-up area of the town and those areas nearby functionally reliant on the town. Within the sub-region, it includes areas administered by Reading, West Berkshire and Wokingham Councils. While the boundaries are not necessarily contiguous, Greater Reading's importance as a regionally important centre for employment, transport, retailing and leisure activity is reflected in the designation of the area as an economic Diamond for Growth in the Regional Economic Strategy while Reading Borough is a New Growth Point.

Settlement Shaping

21.9 A range of other factors (listed below in alphabetical order) will also influence the distribution of development within the sub-region over the Plan period. While national policy and the general policies in this Plan provide the policy framework, there are some local implementation considerations to be taken into account:

- **Flood Risk Management** – the policy is contained in PPS25: *Development and Flood Risk and* NRM4: Sustainable Flood Risk Management. In accordance with that policy, given the location, level and forms of development proposed, and the identified flood risks within parts of the sub-region, it is especially important that all authorities, singularly or together, work closely with the Environment Agency to prepare adequate strategic flood risk assessments (SFRAs). Local development documents should be informed by the results of SFRAs and contain clear local implementation guidance to facilitate the delivery of required development that also delivers appropriate on or off-site flood risk management and/or measures.

- **Gaps** – the policy is contained in PPS7: *Sustainable Development in Rural Areas*. In implementing it, those Berkshire authorities operating gap policies will need to review them carefully to ensure that they have a continuing justification that accords with the purposes and requirements set out in PPS7, do not unnecessarily duplicate other protection policies such as Green Belt and have regard to the other policies of this Plan.
- **Green Belt** – the policy is contained in SP5: Green Belts. The points made in paragraph 21.6 above are also relevant.
- **Thames Basin Heaths Special Protection Area** – the policy is contained in NRM6: Thames Basin Heaths Special Protection Area. In accordance with that policy, given the significance of the SPA for the sub-region, all local authorities will need to collaborate as necessary to ensure that the best and most efficient use of land and resources is made and their obligations in terms of protection, management and mitigation are met.
- **Transport** – the policy is contained in SP2: Regional Hubs and in the general transport policies including T1: Manage and Invest, T2: Mobility Management and T14: Transport Investment and Management Priorities (specific transport priorities are referred to in paragraphs 21.21 & 21.22 below). The WCBV core strategy is to a significant degree transport led. This is in recognition of the paradox that while a key advantage of the sub-region is its location and accessibility to international and regional transport hubs, congestion and other pressures on transport may put at risk future economic, social and environmental progress. Therefore, the local and county highways authorities, Highways Agency, Network Rail and others as appropriate will need to work together to provide a co-ordinated approach to manage transport demand, network management and investment and thus facilitate the delivery of required development (see the reference to a WCBV Transport Group in paragraph 21.25 below). In particular, and in accordance with those policies, local authorities will need to promote locations and forms of development and manage mobility to: (a) reduce the need to travel; (b) reduce average journey distances; (c) make it possible for a greater proportion of trips to be made by alternatives to single occupancy private car use and (d) aid intra-urban accessibility and/or network efficiency.
- **Waste Water Treatment** – the policy is contained in NRM2: Water Quality. Plans and development at Basingstoke (as noted in Policy WCBV3) or any other location in the sub-region where water quality or treatment is an issue will be informed by water cycle studies and all other material considerations.
- **Water Supply** – the policy is contained in NRM1: Sustainable Water Resources and Groundwater. While no insurmountable water supply problems have been identified in WCBV, there can be no room for complacency. Therefore, in accordance with the policy, all relevant local development documents will need to contain measures that will maintain, and enhance the recycling of, water resources.
- **Groundwater Quality** - the policy is contained in NRM1: Sustainable Water Resources and Groundwater Quality. Local development frameworks (LDFs) should contain, as appropriate, policies and measures to protect groundwater quality from inappropriate development and land contamination.

Economy

> **POLICY WCBV2: EMPLOYMENT LAND**
>
> The need for additional new employment floorspace will, to the extent possible, be met through the more efficient use of employment land in town centres and established employment areas. Local development documents will therefore give priority to the retention of existing employment land in employment use.
>
> In judging whether such land is sufficient to meet employment land needs, local authorities will work jointly with neighbouring authorities as appropriate, having regard to:
>
> i. the evidence of local and strategic demand for employment floorspace
> ii. the broad balance between labour supply and demand within that part of the sub-region
> iii. the suitability of existing employment land to continue in that use
> iv. the availability of land for housing, and the scope for any shortfalls to be met through the release of employment land, suitable for residential use
> v. any other considerations relevant to the maintenance of an appropriate balance of land uses.
>
> If existing land is judged to be insufficient, new areas of employment land will be identified in development plan documents in line with the sustainable urban extensions identified in the core strategy.

21.10 Sufficient existing and allocated employment land may be available to meet the short-term needs of the sub-region, i.e. to accommodate the minimum 79,300 net additional new jobs which, as an interim estimate for monitoring purposes, need to be created within the sub-region by 2016. Local authorities not only need to check this is the case but also look beyond 2016 to the plan period to be covered by the relevant LDDs. Therefore, consistent with Policies RE3: Employment and Land Provision and RE6: Competitiveness and Addressing Structural Economic Weakness, Policy WCBV2 requires individual or appropriate groups of authorities to work together to review the suitability of existing employment land to meet local and long-term strategic needs, protect it as necessary and identify new sustainable locations and sites accordingly. Local authorities will need to act quickly if there is a risk of the economy faltering due to a lack of suitable employment land. In carrying out these reviews, authorities will need to take account of the importance of the sub-region to the South East and UK economies, the designation of Basingstoke and Reading as both Regional Diamonds for Investment and Growth in the Regional Economic Strategy and New Growth Points, and the challenges posed by issues such as congestion, labour shortages and a globalised economy. Given the complex inter-relationship between WCBV and London/ the London Fringe, it will also be important for there to be compatible cross-boundary monitoring of land and labour demand and supply.

21.11 While achieving a better balance between the location and growth of jobs and homes may be an important aim at the local level, this aim should not override the greater need for the sub-region to continue to contribute in due part to regional and/or national economic prosperity.

21.12 As part of the achievement of economic prosperity, it will also be important to ensure that opportunities for smart growth (see Policy RE5 for further details) are maximised in this sub-region through:

- using existing employment land as efficiently as possible
- taking account of any potential for clustering and of opportunities to promote key innovative, higher value or knowledge based sectors with low environmental impact
- driving up skill levels in accordance with Policy RE4: Human Resource Development

- improving productivity
- increasing mobility and accessibility by a range of sustainable means.

21.13 However, further smart growth by itself will be unable to realise the economic potential of the sub-region. Similarly, given the continuing primacy of London, the already complex patterns of travel to work and the increasing opportunities to work outside the sub-region, seeking significant additional in-commuting is also unrealistic as a means of addressing any significant jobs-housing mismatch. Therefore, as part of the response, appropriate new allocations or reuse of existing employment land are likely to be necessary. For example, a need for new employment land has been identified in north Hampshire (initially estimated at 40-60 hectares, the final figure will be based on the type of joint working described in para 21.10) that may be substantially met within Basingstoke. Similarly, subject to the detailed case being proven, the Greater Reading authorities are encouraged to work together to facilitate the expansion and diversification of Reading University as (a) a higher education establishment and (b) as a promoter of research and development in collaboration with the commercial sector via the development of a research-based science park within the Greater Reading area that may require release of greenfield land.

Scale and Distribution of Housing Development

POLICY WCBV3: SCALE AND DISTRIBUTION OF HOUSING DEVELOPMENT

Local planning authorities will allocate sufficient land and facilitate the delivery of 102,100 net additional dwellings in the the Western Corridor and Blackwater Valley sub-region between 2006 and 2026.

In managing the supply of land for housing and in determining planning applications, local planning authorities should work collaboratively to facilitate the delivery of the level of net additional dwellings in the sub-region as set out below.

Local authorities should consider the phasing of housing delivery within the vicinity of the Thames Basin Heaths SPA in order to ensure that appropriate avoidance and mitigation measures are secured in advance of development being occupied and should work with the regional planning body and Natural England to monitor housing delivery in their area against the provision of avoidance and mitigation measures.

DISTRICT	ANNUAL AVERAGE	TOTAL
Basingstoke & Deane (part)[1]	915	18,300
Bracknell Forest	639	12,780
Guildford (part)	25	500
Hart (part)	215	4,300
Reading	611	12,220
Rushmoor[2]	310	6,200
Slough[3]	315	6,300
South Bucks[3]	94	1,880
Surrey Heath	187	3,740
West Berkshire	475	9,500
Windsor & Maidenhead	346	6,920
Wokingham[4]	623	12,460

Western Corridor and Blackwater Valley

DISTRICT	ANNUAL AVERAGE	TOTAL
Wycombe (part)	350	7,000
Sub-Regional Total	5,105	102,100

Footnotes

1. Provision levels at Basingstoke, for locations within the catchment of Blackwater Sewage Treatment Works and any other locations where potential water quality, supply or treatment issues are identified will need to be informed by a water cycle study. Similarly, the distribution of development should be informed by strategic flood risk assessments. The results of these studies will need to be reflected in local development frameworks and future reviews of the RSS.

2. In the event that the Aldershot Urban Extension in Rushmoor cannot be released for the delivery of 4,500 dwellings, there is no expectation that equivalent land in the Borough or elsewhere will be allocated to meet the overall district figure set out in Policy H1.

3. If the level for Slough necessitates an urban extension within the Borough, cross-boundary working with South Bucks DC with regards to their own intended housing distribution should help determine the best location for it.

4. The figure for Wokingham also includes some 2,500 dwellings that will contribute to the delivery of housing to serve the needs of Greater Reading and a further 3,500 dwellings at Arborfield Garrison, where there is also potential for continuing development during and/or beyond the Plan period.

Housing provision figures for those parts of each authority not within the sub-region may be found in the Areas Outside the Sub-Regions Chapter.

21.14   Consistent with Policy H1: Regional Housing Provision 2006-2026, the provision in Policy WCBV3 of 102,100 net additional dwellings between 2006 and 2026 recognises regional, economic, demographic and other more local imperatives, the ability of the sub-region to accommodate at least the numbers proposed, the implications of the Thames Basin Heaths SPA and other environmental constraints and the existing pattern and/or future delivery of infrastructure. There are likely to be serious economic, environmental and social costs to the sub-region and the wider region beyond if this approach is not followed given the imbalance between jobs and housing that will otherwise occur.

21.15   While contributing to the regional reuse of previously developed land target of 60%, some greenfield development will be required. In accordance with Policy WCBV1 some of this may need to be on land currently designated as Green Belt land if the new housing is to be provided in the most sustainable locations. Housing development will be carried out in a sustainable way consistent with the general policies, including SP3: Urban Focus and Urban Renaissance, CC6: Sustainable Communities and Character of the Environment , H5: Housing Design and Density, NRM1, 2 & 4 regarding water and flooding and NRM6: Thames Basin Heaths Special Protection Area.

21.16   Housing figures for Wokingham district include the development of at least 2,500 dwellings in Wokingham Borough south of the M4 to, inter alia, serve the needs of Greater Reading. The location and timing of this housing, if developed in the Shinfield/Spencers Wood/Three Mile Cross area, will need to have regard to the potential development of a Reading University Science Park in the vicinity.

21.17   In order to help achieve the housing step change elsewhere and support the WCBV economy, authorities should not unnecessarily constrain smaller towns and larger villages from growing to a degree commensurate with their location, accessibility and future roles. Equally, authorities must carefully consider whether large brownfield sites outside settlement boundaries could make a contribution towards the creation of a network of sustainable communities. For example, various defence sites may become available for redevelopment before 2026.

> **POLICY WCBV4: THE BLACKWATER VALLEY**
>
> **The Blackwater Valley authorities will work together and with other agencies in order to plan and implement in an integrated way:**
>
> i. **a shared vision for the area taking into account social, environmental and economic needs**
> ii. **the means by which to facilitate and co-ordinate the delivery of development while complying with the Habitats Regulations in connection with designated European sites such as the Thames Basin Heaths SPA**
> iii. **improvements to the quality of the built and natural environments, including the provision of green infrastructure networks**
> iv. **improvements to the quality, and the increased integration, of the local transport network.**

21.18 The Blackwater Valley straddles a large number of local authority boundaries and as a consequence the planning of the area has not always been fully integrated. A Blackwater Valley Study was jointly undertaken by the local authorities in 2002/3. Policy WCBV4 recognises the need to build on this through the development of a shared vision for the area's future which reconciles the pressures for economic and residential growth and the aspirations of individual landowners, with the constraints represented by local labour supply, the area's limitations in transport terms and the extent of Green Belt and other designations such as the Thames Basin Heaths SPA.

> **POLICY WCBV5: THE COLNE VALLEY PARK**
>
> **The local authorities will work together and with other agencies in pursuance of the agreed aims of the Colne Valley Park:**
>
> i. **to maintain and enhance the landscape (including settlements) and waterscape of the Park, in terms of their scenic and conservation value and their overall amenity**
> ii. **to resist urbanisation of the Colne Valley Park and to safeguard existing areas of countryside from inappropriate development**
> iii. **to conserve the nature conservation resources of the Park through the provision of green infrastructure networks and protection and management of its diverse plant and animal species, habitats and geological features**
> iv. **to provide accessible facilities and opportunities for countryside recreation where this does not compromise i, ii or iii.**

21.19 The Colne Valley Park comprises some 17 hectares encompassing parts of the WCBV, the London Borough of Hillingdon and Three Rivers District in Hertfordshire. It provides the first significant area of countryside to the west of London. It has varied scenery, ranging from fragmented urban fringe land which has suffered from a range of urban developments and other uses not complementary to its character, to areas of unspoilt countryside. Large parts of the Park are in the Metropolitan Green Belt; the only parts not so designated are the existing settlements. Policy WCBV5 reflects the agreed main aims for the Park.

Infrastructure, Implementation and Delivery

21.20　Policy CC7: Infrastructure and Implementation sets out the general approach to implementation, including the need to ensure that the pace of development and the provision of and management of infrastructure are suitably aligned. The Implementation Plan will set out specific strategic infrastructure requirements for the sub-region.

21.21　Policy T14: Transport Investment and Management Priorities and the associated Appendix A: Strategic Transport Investment Priorities are relevant to the transport improvements. Two major schemes listed in that appendix which are important for this sub-region as well as having much wider regional significance are:

- **Crossrail:** which will increase station capacities at least as far west as Maidenhead, with all parties also needing to consider its extension and/or connectivity into the wider network, and
- **Airtrack:** which, if it or a similar scheme goes ahead, will provide enhanced accessibility to Heathrow.

21.22　The supporting text to Policy T14 mentions work being required on two other regionally significant schemes of particular importance to this sub-region:

- **Reading Station** improvements which will help deliver improved inter and intra regional accessibility and growth at Reading, and
- **M4:** the Highways Agency will re-examine in conjunction with appropriate other parties the options for increasing and managing the capacity of the M4 motorway within the sub-region, particularly taking account of planned growth in Greater Reading.

21.23　In early 2009 the Government announced there may be a case for developing a new western rail connection between Heathrow Airport and the Great Western Main Line, allowing direct access by rail services to and from the west. DfT will work together with the airport operator, Network Rail and regional partners to consider feasibility options and undertake further study work.

21.24　Other transport improvements of sub-regional significance to be prioritised include:

- improvements in access to and interchanges within hubs as part of demand management packages for all hub towns
- sub-regional mobility management measures including park and ride, local bus, travel planning and other modal shift initiatives
- additional rail capacity particularly at stations as required in the future to support growth in passenger and freight demand.

21.25　Other necessary infrastructure of particular relevance to this sub-region includes:

- the delivery of sufficient waste water treatment infrastructure in locations where upgraded need is demonstrated via robust evidence, and
- the delivery of open space and other mitigation measures required as a result of the Thames Basin Heaths SPA.

21.26　The success of the sub-regional strategy will ultimately depend upon the commitment of national, regional and local agencies, in conjunction with the public, private and voluntary sectors, to its implementation. For example, the Environment Agency will work with individual or groups of authorities in order to ensure the preparation and implementation of LDFs in accordance with agreed local development scheme timetables. The strategic policies need to be translated into more detailed policies, action plans and, crucially, investment and implementation programmes. Examples of the range of formal and other partnerships needed to deliver the strategy include:

- **The Berkshire Economic Strategy Board** - this newly formed partnership comprising local authority, business and other representatives will have various roles, including responding to regional /sub-regional issues, and overseeing economic development strategy within the county and the work of the Berkshire Strategic Transport Forum.

- **The Berkshire Strategic Transport Forum** - which should embrace all WCBV highway authorities, business partners and transport operators in developing and delivering the sub-regional strategy.
- **Cross Boundary Working** - local authorities will need to work together as necessary to deliver development that will straddle or have influence across administrative boundaries. In particular, authorities in the vicinity of Greater Reading will need to work together, as appropriate, to deliver the development and change needed to enable the area to fully carry out its local, sub-regional and wider roles.

21.27 The general approach to monitoring and review is set out in Chapter 26 on implementation, monitoring and review.

22 Central Oxfordshire

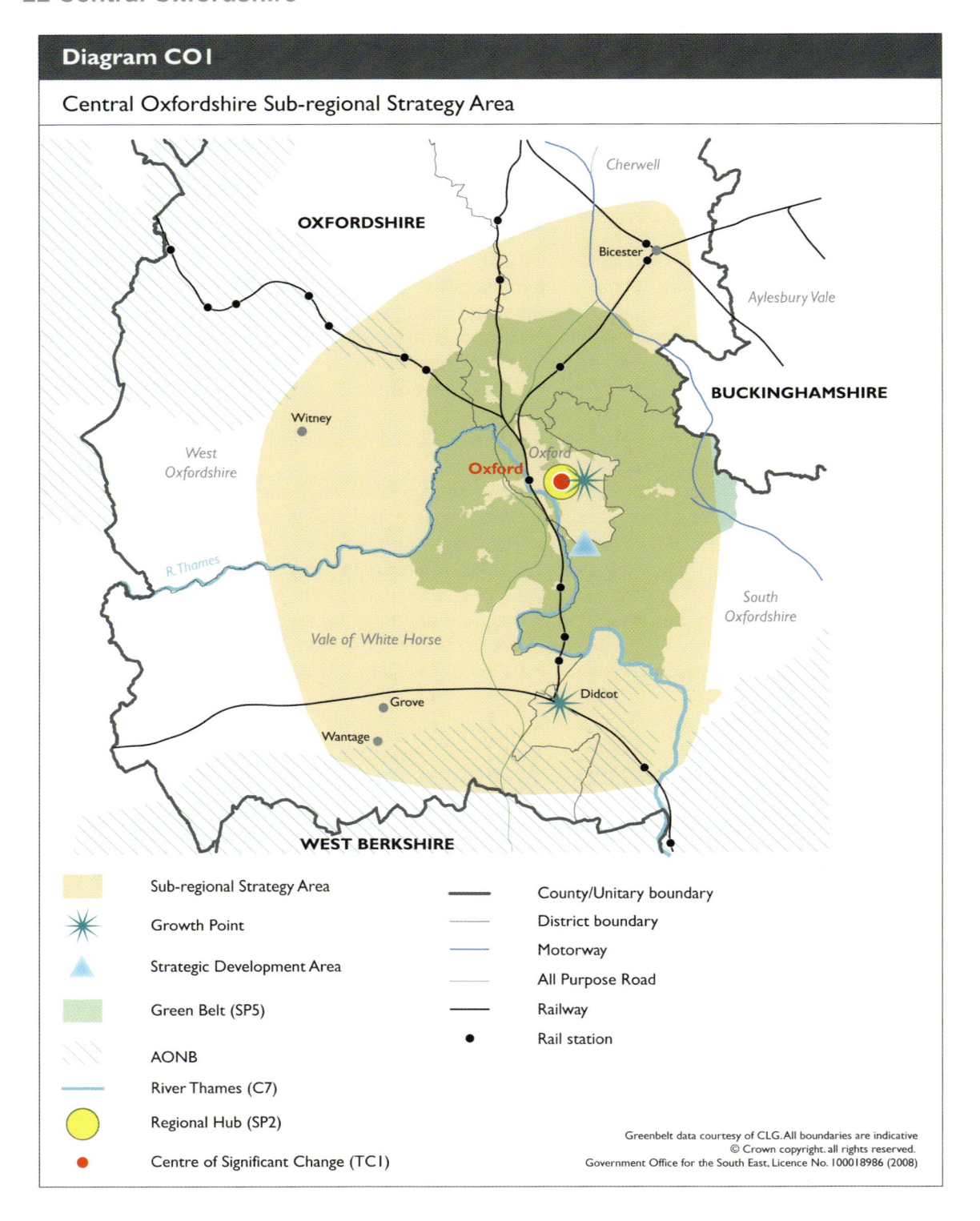

Diagram CO1

Central Oxfordshire Sub-regional Strategy Area

Legend:
- Sub-regional Strategy Area
- Growth Point
- Strategic Development Area
- Green Belt (SP5)
- AONB
- River Thames (C7)
- Regional Hub (SP2)
- Centre of Significant Change (TC1)
- County/Unitary boundary
- District boundary
- Motorway
- All Purpose Road
- Railway
- Rail station

Greenbelt data courtesy of CLG. All boundaries are indicative
© Crown copyright. all rights reserved.
Government Office for the South East, Licence No. 100018986 (2008)

22.1 The extent of the Central Oxfordshire sub-region is shown on Diagram COX1. It adjoins, or in is proximity to, the Milton Keynes & Aylesbury Vale and Western Corridor and Blackwater Valley sub-regions in the South East and the Swindon sub-region in the South West. It includes all or part of the following administrative areas: Oxfordshire County Council, Oxford City, and Cherwell, South Oxfordshire, Vale of White Horse and West Oxfordshire districts.

22.2 This sub-region has been established for the following reasons. It:

Central Oxfordshire

- corresponds to a city region with Oxford providing higher order services (retail, health, education etc) for the surrounding area
- exhibits a high degree of coherence representing a relatively self-contained labour market area and a single Housing Market Area
- faces a number of challenges, including New Growth Points initiatives, that will require joint working across local authority boundaries
- will facilitate the implementation of key regional policies by local authorities and other stakeholders.

22.3 The particular challenges faced by Central Oxfordshire are how to:

- harness the unique potential of the dynamic, innovative economy of the sub-region (initial interim estimate is a minimum 18,000 additional jobs created by 2016)
- deliver sufficient decent homes and provide a well integrated mix to meet the needs of the area, including affordable housing for which there is a very high need in this sub-region (40,680 net additional dwellings to be delivered by 2026)
- nurture the future success of Oxford while protecting and, where appropriate, enhancing its historic and environmental character and setting
- strengthen the public transport network, promote alternatives to car and lorry traffic and tackle congestion
- deliver the requirements for physical, social and economic infrastructure needed to support existing and future economic and housing growth
- deliver in a timely fashion the individually and/or jointly produced development plan documents that will implement the South East Plan locally
- create and maintain a network of sustainable communities that meet future social and economic need and protect and enhance the environment. This will require sustainable urban extensions to a number of settlements including Oxford, Didcot and Grove and a selective review of the Oxford Green Belt.

Core Strategy

> **POLICY CO1: CORE STRATEGY**
>
> The strategy for Central Oxfordshire is to strive to be a world leader in education, science and technology by building on the sub-region's economic strengths in ways which will:
>
> i. **ensure the provision of infrastructure which is essential to the proper functioning and future development of the area**
> ii. **protect and enhance the environment and quality of life of the sub-region**
> iii. **protect the setting and character of Oxford**
> iv. **make best use of previously developed land within urban areas to reduce the need for greenfield development**
> v. **concentrate development where the need to travel, particularly by single occupancy car use, can be reduced.**
>
> The main locations for development will be Bicester, Didcot, and Wantage and Grove to improve their self-containment, and within and immediately adjacent to the built-up area of Oxford.
>
> Elsewhere limited development will be permitted to support the social and economic well-being of local communities.

22.4 Policy CO1 will enable Central Oxfordshire to make the most of the opportunities provided by its location and relationships with other sub-regions. Potential opportunities that could be pursued are the Oxford to Cambridge Arc initiative[1], East-West rail link reinstatement and existing or new employment clusters based upon university spin-off or other innovative industries (see also Policy RE2: Supporting Nationally and Regionally Important Sectors

---

[1] www.oxford2cambridge.net

and Clusters). A range of other factors will also influence the distribution of development within the sub-region over the Plan period. Plan users should ensure they are acquainted with national policy and the general policies of this Plan (for example CC1-4, 6-8 and NRM1-5 & 11) when making use of this chapter.

22.5 The settlement pattern of the sub-region will change over the Plan period. Oxford itself will be allowed to grow physically and economically in order to accommodate its own needs, contribute to those in the wider region and help maintain its world-class status. Greater emphasis will be given to increasing social and economic self-containment at Bicester, Didcot, Wantage/Grove, to a lesser extent Witney and, outside the sub-region, Banbury. Bicester should seek to maximise the benefits accruing from its location, for example, on the evolving Oxford to Cambridge Arc and railway network. At the southern end of the sub-region, a development corridor encompassing Didcot and Wantage/Grove (known as Science Vale UK), utilising its economic strengths and delivering improved transport links between homes and jobs, is being pursued by the local authorities and others.

Economy

POLICY CO2: ECONOMY

Development for employment purposes will provide for the requirements of activities which contribute to regional and local priorities for economic development. This includes providing a range of accommodation for small businesses and innovation, skills development, business infrastructure and linkages within the knowledge-based economy.

Priority should be given to development which supports educational, scientific and technological sectors and responds to the needs of established and emerging clusters within the county.

Additional land for employment will be provided where justified at Bicester and Didcot, for the expansion and relocation of existing local firms to foster knowledge-based industry.

In Oxford, development for employment uses will be expected to take place primarily on previously developed land and former safeguarded land or in conjunction with development schemes for mixed uses incorporating housing, town centre or other facilities. In the city centre, development which maintains and enhances the sub-regional role and diversity of the centre will be permitted, provided it is consistent with the protection of Oxford's architectural and historic heritage.

22.6 Central Oxfordshire possesses a world-class economy, with the education, health, knowledge intensive and high technology businesses, motorsport, car manufacture, publishing, retail and tourism sectors of particular importance. It also has potential to grow (it is a Regional Economic Strategy Diamond for Investment & Growth). Policy CO2 will enable the sub-region to capitalise on its dynamism and build on its economic strengths.

22.7 The number, location and types of jobs generated over the Plan period are difficult to predict but for monitoring purposes and pending any updated evidence or guidance, a guide figure of a minimum 18,000 net additional new jobs will be created within the sub-region from 2006 to 2016. Over the whole Plan period to 2026 there is a need to ensure that the balance of jobs and houses at both the sub-regional and main settlement level does not worsen and preferably improves.

22.8 Part of the future success of Central Oxfordshire will rely on maximising the opportunities afforded by 'Smart Growth'. Policy RE5 provides the basic guidance on the matter, augmented by Policy RE4: Human Resource Development. Within this sub-region this will particularly mean:

- using existing employment land as efficiently as possible

Central Oxfordshire

- promoting the commercialisation of R&D outputs
- upgrading the skills of those least qualified, including basic literacy and numeracy
- focusing training and development activities in those areas and sectors experiencing greatest recruitment and retention difficulties
- increasing economic activity rates, particularly in Oxford City.

22.9 Spatially, economic growth will need to be delivered alongside other housing, social and environmental development throughout the sub-region. In particular, regard will be had to the following considerations. Within Oxford the overall aim will be to achieve a broad balance between housing and jobs by protecting, as appropriate, existing sites and allocating new land suited to providing for a range of opportunities in accordance with Policy RE3. Options regarding the location, level and form of employment or other development, including the possible use of land at and in the immediate vicinity of the currently safeguarded land at Peartree, will be a matter for local determination. Land should not be released for employment to the north of Oxford that could adversely affect the future economic buoyancy of Bicester, Kidlington or Witney or undermine opportunities to integrate the south of Oxford urban extension into the wider southern urban area. Opportunities should be taken for new mixed-use development delivered through redevelopment and intensification of the west end of the city following redevelopment of the Westgate shopping centre and conversion of the prison and castle mound for hotel and cultural activity.

22.10 At Bicester every opportunity should be taken to promote the town, *inter alia*, as a new location for higher value and knowledge-based business, separately or in association with the Oxford to Cambridge Arc initiative.

22.11 The southern part of the county encompassing Didcot, Wantage/Grove area should similarly be promoted, *inter alia*, based upon the designation of Didcot as a New Growth Point, the potential the established research and business parks have for further growth and/or intensification, and/or in association with the local Science Vale UK initiative.

HOUSING: SCALE & DISTRIBUTION

POLICY CO3: SCALE AND DISTRIBUTION OF HOUSING

Local planning authorities will allocate sufficient land and facilitate the delivery of 40,680 net additional dwellings in Central Oxfordshire between 2006 and 2026.

In managing the supply of land for housing and in determining planning applications, local planning authorities should work collaboratively to facilitate the delivery of the following level of net additional dwellings in the sub-region:

DISTRICT	ANNUAL AVERAGE	TOTAL
Cherwell (part)	320	6,400
Oxford	400	8,000
South of Oxford SDA [1]	200	4,000
South Oxfordshire[2] (part)	412	8,240
Vale of White Horse[3] (part)	512	10,240
West Oxfordshire (part)	190	3,800
Sub-Regional Total	2,034	40,680

At least 40% of all new housing in the sub-region should be affordable, including housing for key workers.

Central Oxfordshire

> Development at Cherwell, Oxford and South Oxfordshire should ensure that the national air and water quality standards are not breached.
>
> **Footnotes**
>
> Housing provision figures and distributions within districts will be informed by strategic flood risk assessments, water cycle studies and all other material considerations as appropriate. The results of these studies will need to be reflected in local development frameworks and future reviews of the RSS.
>
> 1. This represents an allocation for a southern extension to Oxford for the period to 2026. The apportionment between South Oxfordshire and Oxford City will be determined through subsequent studies.
>
> 2. The figure for South Oxfordshire includes some 6,000 to be located at Didcot.
>
> 3. The figure for Vale of White Horse includes 2,750 to be located at Didcot.
>
> Housing provision figures for those parts of each authority not within the sub-region may be found in the areas outside sub-regions chapter.

22.12   In accordance with Policy CO3, the Central Oxfordshire sub-region will make provision for 40,680 net additional dwellings between 2006 and 2026; an average of 2,034 dwellings per annum. These figures recognise and reflect regional, economic, demographic and other local imperatives, the ability of the sub-region to accommodate at least the numbers proposed, the heritage importance of Oxford, the extent of the Wessex Downs and Cotswolds Areas of Outstanding Natural Beauty and the existing pattern/ future delivery of infrastructure. While contributing in due part to the regional reuse of previously developed land target of 60%, some greenfield development that includes housing, will be necessary. A selective review of the Oxford Green Belt will be carried out in accordance with Policy CO4.

22.13   Housing will be distributed as set out in Policy CO3. It is assumed that about 4,900 will be built at Bicester, about 8,750 at Didcot and about 3,400 at Wantage/Grove. The Vale of White Horse and South Oxfordshire, via their local development documents (LDDs) or by other means, will ensure that Didcot's growth is achieved in a phased and timely manner within the Plan period. This may include the pooling of resources and/or development contributions to help deliver any needed transport improvements that support growth in the wider area or help reduce pressure on the A34.

22.14   . An allocation of 4,000 dwellings for the period up to 2026 is included as part of the mixed use South of Oxford SDA. The exact location and apportionment will be determined following more detailed work by South Oxfordshire and Oxford City.

22.15   It will be a matter for the relevant LDDs to respond the figures in Policy CO3. While a degree of flexibility is associated with these figures, local authorities must in the first instance seek to deliver their sub-regional allocations within their part of Central Oxfordshire. Each relevant core strategy development plan document (DPD) within the sub-region must, therefore, set out a clear distribution, setting out where, when, how and in what numbers the housing will be developed and, in turn, how this will help deliver this sub-regional strategy as well as any local vision and strategy. Since the Examination in Public, the Government has announced that land at Weston Otmoor (Cherwell District) has been short-listed as a potential eco-town. Policy H2 states that local planning authorities will need to take account of any proposals for eco-towns arising from the Government's eco-towns initiative.

22.16   An affordable housing target above the regional average is justified for Central Oxfordshire. Housing affordability ratios are among the worst in the region; housing needs surveys indicate affordable housing need exceeds the total amount of new development proposed; overcrowding and unfit homes are prevalent, particularly within Oxford, and higher targets already exist in adopted local plans. The indicative target should therefore be used to guide DPD preparation and development control, and provides a monitoring benchmark. However, it must be applied with genuine realism, based on robust evidence such as the results of up-to-date housing market assessments and other viability work. It must also be applied such that the sub-region contributes in due part to the delivery of Policy H3. Local development frameworks should also consider how best to secure suitable accommodation for key workers as part of the achievement of this target.

GREEN BELT

> **POLICY CO4: GREEN BELT**
>
> **A Green Belt will be maintained around Oxford to:**
>
> i. **preserve the special character and landscape setting of Oxford**
> ii. **check the growth of Oxford and prevent ribbon development and urban sprawl**
> iii. **prevent the coalescence of settlements**
> iv. **assist in safeguarding the countryside from encroachment**
> v. **assist in urban regeneration, by encouraging the recycling of derelict and other urban land.**
>
> **A selective review of Green Belt boundaries will take place on the southern edge of Oxford through one or more co-ordinated development plan documents. It will identify land to be removed from the Green Belt to facilitate a sustainable urban extension to Oxford with minimal impact on village identity and the landscape setting of the city.**
>
> **Development in the Green Belt will only be permitted if it maintains its openness and does not conflict with the purpose of the Green Belt or harm its visual amenities.**

22.17   The Green Belt was conceived in the 1950s and its general extent was set at that time. The special character of Oxford and its landscape setting means not just the university and the views of the dreaming spires, but a broader concept including the countryside around the city, the Cherwell and Thames floodplains, and the relationship of nearby settlements to Oxford.

22.18   The Green Belt has served Oxford well but exceptional circumstances now exist that justify a review taking place. They are:

- the regional imperative to deliver higher housing numbers and economic growth
- persisting jobs-housing imbalances
- poor housing affordability and a backlog of need
- worsening congestion and staff recruitment and retention problems
- a lack of realistic alternatives to focusing growth at Oxford, combined with a lack of capacity within Oxford.

22.19   A strategic review appears to be unnecessary. Rather, the evidence indicates that the review should focus on the southern edge of the city since this would:

- reduce the risk of coalescence with surrounding settlements present elsewhere
- facilitate better integration with existing public transport systems and sources of employment
- reduce the competition for employment growth faced by Bicester and Witney
- utilise the existing evidence base.

22.20   In accordance with Policy CO4, the approximate area of search for the review is indicated on Diagram COX1. The review and any subsequent plan-making will be carried out collaboratively by South Oxfordshire District Council and Oxford City Council to a timetable and in a form to be agreed by the Government Office for the South East. The agreement will also cover evidence base compilation, including a transport assessment. Consultation will take place in accordance with, or to standard exceeding, adopted statements of community involvement. The lead Councils will involve other relevant parties in the process as appropriate. The boundaries of the revised Green Belt, Strategic Development Area, and any additional safeguarded land necessary to ensure the new boundaries endure over the long term, will be shown in the relevant parts of the South Oxfordshire and Oxford City LDFs. They will contain such detail as is necessary to show where, how and when the component parts of the SDA, including the housing, will be delivered. The relevant plans will also take account of the opportunities the urban extension may present as a catalyst for regeneration in The Leys area, and how best to integrate the new development into the wider city. If overwhelming evidence demonstrates the unsuitability of the initial area of search, the Central Oxfordshire authorities will ensure that a wider review (the form and extent of which will be agreed with GOSE) takes place in order to identify and deliver one or more alternative suitable locations by 2026.

Transport

POLICY CO5: TRANSPORT

Oxfordshire County Council, working with the Highways Agency, Network Rail and others as appropriate, will provide a co-ordinated approach to the effective management and development of transport networks in Central Oxfordshire. This will be done in order to meet both strategic and local access requirements while reducing the need to travel, and encouraging the use of more sustainable modes where there is a need to travel. Access to Oxford from major towns in the sub-region and from neighbouring sub-regions will be a priority. Priority schemes to aid the delivery of the Central Oxfordshire sub-regional strategy will be set out in the Implementation Plan and in local transport plans.

22.21   An efficient and effective transport system has a crucial role to play in delivering housing, economic growth and environmental protection in Central Oxfordshire, the rest of Oxfordshire and in the wider South East. The County Council, in conjunction with the Highways Agency, Network Rail and others will work together to provide this system.

22.22   At the regional/sub-regional level, the County, Highways Agency and relevant local authorities will work together to bring forward local solutions to enable the A34, and the network in its vicinity, to fulfil its various local to international roles. This may involve measures or concepts such as active traffic management, intelligent transport systems, real-time information and access management. Similarly the County, Network Rail and others within and beyond Central Oxfordshire will work together, as appropriate, to protect and promote existing and potential new rail routes and/or multi-modal interchanges; for example, with regard to the potential East-West rail link and the South Hampshire-West Midlands freight capability upgrade (see Policy T13). The County and local authorities, in conjunction with service providers, will also investigate and bring forward, as necessary, proposals that will enable the sub-region to play its due part in the national and regional bus and park and ride network.

22.23   Within the sub-region, all relevant parties will collaborate to promote and/or deliver a range of measures and initiatives aimed at improving transport links between the main settlements by sustainable means. Examples could include frequent, high quality premium bus routes supported by bus priority measures and local park and ride facilities, exploring the potential to improve rail services in the vicinity of the A34 corridor and improving the homes to jobs transport links for all modes within the emerging Didcot-Wantage/Grove growth corridor.

22.24   At the more local level, the City of Oxford's function as a regional transport hub will be enhanced. The County, City and other authorities, in conjunction with service providers, will improve access by public transport and introduce measures to manage congestion along key corridors. This may involve junction improvements where radial roads meet the Oxford Ring Road. It is also likely to involve the creation of additional capacity at Oxford Station to cope with growth in passenger and freight traffic and assist in reducing pressure on the A34.

22.25 Elsewhere within the sub-region, local road and junction improvements will be required in the country towns to cater for recent and ongoing housing and economic growth, including at Didcot, Wantage and Grove, Witney and Bicester. For example, improvements to the A415, particularly the Marcham bypass, would provide an improved alternative to the A34 and A40 radial routes.

22.26 The County, local authorities and others as appropriate will ensure that transport initiatives, projects and management within the sub-region, the rest of Oxfordshire and adjoining areas are suitably co-ordinated and delivered in a timely and effective manner.

Infrastructure, Implementation and Delivery

22.27 Policy CC7: Infrastructure and Implementation sets out the general approach to implementation, including the need to ensure that the pace of development and the provision and management of infrastructure are suitably aligned. The Implementation Plan will set out specific strategic infrastructure requirements for the sub-region (see Chapter 26).

22.28 Central Oxfordshire will play its part in hosting regionally significant infrastructure. For example, it contains Didcot Power Station and, if the case is proven, will need to accommodate an Upper Thames Reservoir (see Policy NRM3). Infrastructure and other projects of sub-regional or wider significance are identified in the Regional Implementation Plan.

22.29 At the more local level, LDFs, in conjunction with sustainable communities strategies and local area agreements (LAAs) will set out the main locations or forms of infrastructure to be provided over the Plan period and the means by which it will be delivered. Examples include the current and emerging proposals to improve the attractions and town centre facilities for Bicester and Didcot to enable them to fulfil their future roles within the sub-region.

Implementation

22.30 The success of the sub-regional strategy will ultimately depend upon the commitment of national, regional and local agencies, in conjunction with the public, private and voluntary sectors, to its implementation. For example, the Environment Agency will work with individual or groups of authorities in order to ensure the preparation and implementation of LDFs in accordance with agreed local development scheme (LDS) timetables. The strategic policies need to be translated into more detailed policies, action plans and, crucially, investment programmes. Examples of the range of formal and other partnerships that will be needed to deliver the strategy include the:

- Didcot New Growth Point partnership between central, regional and local government
- recently formed County/Highways Agency Management Board
- Science Vale UK initiative linking Didcot and Wantage/Grove
- Oxford West End regeneration partnership
- Bicester business-led group.

22.31 In particular, all local authorities will work together as necessary and appropriate in order to deliver development that will straddle or influence across administrative boundaries. For example, South Oxfordshire and Vale of White Horse will continue to work together to deliver growth at Didcot while South Oxfordshire, Oxford City and any other affected authority will work together to deliver the South of Oxford urban extension. In any joint working, the council administering the largest area to be planned for would normally be expected to act as lead authority. The more detailed mechanisms and arrangements, focused on delivering the required outcomes, will be set out in LDSs, sustainable community strategies and/or LAAs. By these and other means the Plan, Implement, Monitor, Manage regime will be proactively pursued within Central Oxfordshire and hence the aims and objectives of national, regional and sub-regional policy achieved.

Central Oxfordshire

22

Milton Keynes and Aylesbury Vale

23 Milton Keynes and Aylesbury Vale

Diagram MKAV1
Milton Keynes and Aylesbury Vale Sub-regional Strategy Area

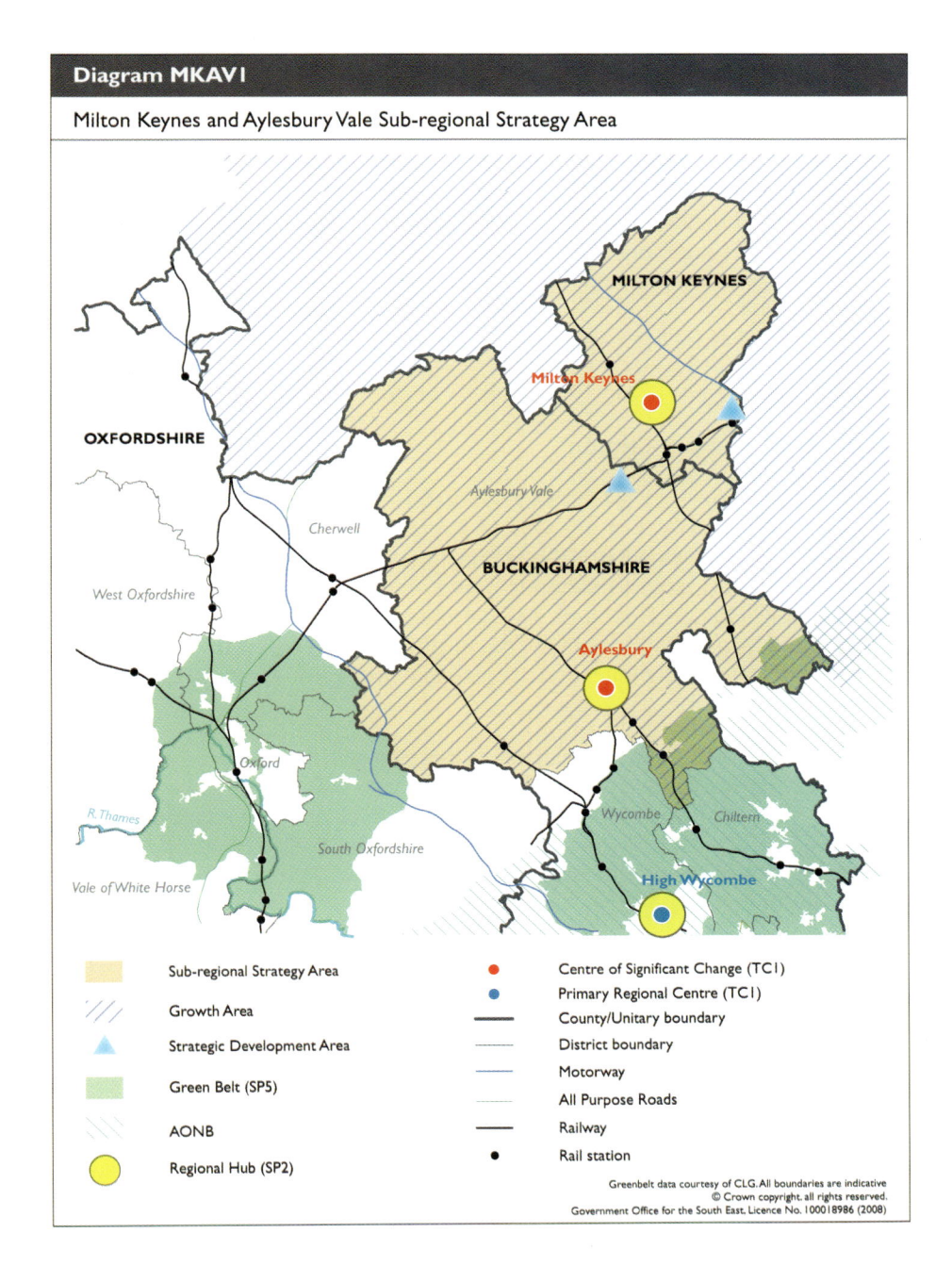

Legend:
- Sub-regional Strategy Area
- Growth Area
- Strategic Development Area
- Green Belt (SP5)
- AONB
- Regional Hub (SP2)
- Centre of Significant Change (TC1)
- Primary Regional Centre (TC1)
- County/Unitary boundary
- District boundary
- Motorway
- All Purpose Roads
- Railway
- Rail station

Greenbelt data courtesy of CLG. All boundaries are indicative
© Crown copyright, all rights reserved.
Government Office for the South East. Licence No. 100018986 (2008)

23.1 RPG9 recognised Milton Keynes and adjoining parts of Buckinghamshire, Bedfordshire and Northamptonshire as having considerable growth potential and recommended an interregional study to consider this. The subsequent study informed the sub-regional strategy for Milton Keynes South Midlands (MKSM), published in March 2005 as a partial revision to the Regional Spatial Strategies for the East of England, East Midlands and South East England. That strategy comprised a Part A Statement, which provides overarching objectives and strategic policies for the MKSM area as a whole, and three separate Part B Statements with more specific guidance in relation to the individual areas covered by the three separate Regional Spatial Strategies. The Part B statement for the Milton Keynes Unitary Authority and Aylesbury Vale district area (MKAV), for 2001-2021, has been superseded by the strategy set out in this sub-regional chapter for 2006-2026. However, the Part A Statement continues to apply in so far as it has been taken forward by the policies in this chapter, the Core Regional Policies and the Implementation Plan.

Milton Keynes and Aylesbury Vale

23.2 Key challenges facing this sub-region are how to:

  i. continue to assimilate high levels of new growth
  ii. improve connectivity between Aylesbury and Milton Keynes as well as between Aylesbury and the more buoyant economies in adjoining sub-regions
  iii. strengthen the economic and employment role of Aylesbury town, attract knowledge–based industries and reduce its dependence on out-commuting
  iv. improve skills levels and educational attainments
  v. deliver the requirements for physical, social and environmental infrastructure needed to support existing and future economic and housing growth
  vi. ensure development is planned with regard to protecting strategic environmental assets and seeking opportunities for their enhancement.

23.3 Although specific policies relating to MKAV are set out below it is important to take account of the Core Regional Policies in this Plan, including those which are referred to in this chapter.

Strategic Framework for the Sub-Region

23.4 The strategic framework for the sub-region takes as its starting point the strategy set out in the Part A Statement of the MKSM strategy, and in particular the spatial vision for Milton Keynes and Aylesbury as reflected in Policies MKAV2 and MKAV3 below. In taking this vision forward, smart economic growth needs to be promoted, as provided for by Policies RE4: Human Resource Development and RE5: Smart Growth, exploiting the opportunities presented by MKAV being part of the Oxford to Cambridge Arc. Policy RE2: Supporting Nationally and Regionally Important Sectors and Clusters is also particularly relevant.

23.5 The Oxford to Cambridge Arc links this sub-region with the Central Oxfordshire sub-region in this Plan and with the Bedford growth area and Cambridge sub-region in the East of England RSS. In taking advantage of this arc of economic potential, the two local authorities in the sub-region intend to build on their strengths and foster closer interrelationships with each other and the wider Arc. The opportunities include:

  i. at the centre of this Arc, Milton Keynes, the largest of the two main centres in the MKSM sub-region, has a modern growing economy and is developing a city-region role extending into neighbouring regions. It could become a location for knowledge-based businesses and a networking hub, especially if orbital and east-west communications can be improved
  ii. improved connectivity between Aylesbury and Milton Keynes along with other towns and cities along the Oxford to Cambridge Arc might help strengthen the economic role of Aylesbury town provided it did not result in increased out-commuting
  iii. improved networking into the Oxford and Cambridge business communities helping to secure an increase in high-technology activity in Aylesbury, as being taken forward by the Aylesbury Vale Economic Development Strategy
  iv. in addition, MKAV sub-region sits at the outer end of the M1 corridor growth area identified in the London Plan. This may present opportunities for reverse commuting away from London.

23.6 In realising these opportunities, educational attainment and skills levels at Milton Keynes and Aylesbury need to be improved in order to support economic growth, enable local people to participate fully in it and help bring the long-term unemployed back into the labour market. Policy RE4: Human Resource Development provides the framework for this. Although educational attainment is high in Aylesbury, the less skilled sections of the working population will benefit from improved access to higher education in Aylesbury to enhance their skills. Milton Keynes is home to the Open University and has close proximity to Cranfield and Buckingham Universities, while the 'Unis4MK' collaboration between higher education providers in the area provides co-ordinated and targeted high-quality higher education provision to meet local needs. By taking advantage of these

Milton Keynes and Aylesbury Vale

23.7 The intention is to seek an approximate 1:1 ratio between new jobs and dwellings proposed for the two growth areas within the sub-region in order to secure no net change in overall net out-commuting in line with the objectives of the MKSM strategy. It is not a development control tool to constrain development. Housing provision and job targets are covered in Policies MKAV1, MKAV2 and MKAV3 below. The new jobs figures in Policies MKAV2 and MKAV3 are significantly above the employment growth trend and are a reference point for monitoring. They are subject to review and are not intended to constrain economic development.

Housing Distribution By District 2006 - 2026

POLICY MKAV1: HOUSING DISTRIBUTION BY DISTRICT 2006-2026

Within Milton Keynes Unitary Authority, provision will be made for 41,360 dwellings between 2006 and 2026 from the following sources:

i. **34,160 dwellings in and around the Milton Keynes urban area including sites identified in the adopted local plan and additional sites to be found through strategic housing land availability assessments**
ii. **4,800 dwellings as part of a development of 10,400 dwellings to the south-east of Milton Keynes (leaving a balance of 5,600 dwellings to be found in Bedfordshire subject to assessment through the East of England RSS review)**
iii. **2,400 dwellings in the rural area/rest of Milton Keynes.**

Within Aylesbury Vale District, provision will be made for at least 26,890 dwellings between 2006 and 2026 from the following sources:

i. **5,390 dwellings as an urban extension to the south-west of Milton Keynes**
ii. **16,800 dwellings in and around the Aylesbury urban area, including urban extensions**
iii. **4,700 dwellings in the rural area/rest of Aylesbury Vale.**

23.8 The levels and distribution of housing provision in Policy MKAV1 will help deliver the spatial vision for Milton Keynes and Aylesbury Vale set out in Policies MKAV2 and MKAV3 below. The policy clarifies the housing provision split between the local authority areas in advance of Policy MKV2 which relates to the larger growth area rather than the smaller administrative area of Milton Keynes.

23.9 Of the 34,160 dwellings provided for in this policy from within and around the Milton Keynes urban area, it is anticipated that some 23,750 will be provided within expansion areas and other greenfield sites identified in the adopted local plan with the remaining 10,410 expected to come from within the urban area. In addition, under this policy, the remaining areas of Milton Keynes outside the city will continue to meet local needs and provide for 2,400 dwellings.

23.10 In the longer term it is possible that some future growth of Milton Keynes may need to be accommodated east of the M1 motorway, but no allowance is made at this stage in housing figures for Milton Keynes pending future review of the South East Plan and the local development plan. Further testing of this (including a detailed SFRA) and other alternatives for additional strategic development areas and urban extensions should be undertaken with stakeholders to inform a future review of the RSS and local development plan. Also, in the longer term it is possible that some of the growth of Leighton-Linslade or associated facilities may need to be accommodated in Aylesbury Vale District but no allowance is made at this stage in the housing figures for Aylesbury Vale pending future review of the South East Plan.

Milton Keynes and Aylesbury Vale

The Spatial Framework for Milton Keynes Growth Area

> **POLICY MKAV2: SPATIAL FRAMEWORK FOR MILTON KEYNES GROWTH AREA**
>
> Within the South East Region, Milton Keynes will accommodate an additional 44,350 dwellings over the period 2006-2026, at an average rate of 2,218 dwellings per annum, of which 30% should be affordable. The figure:
>
> i. includes 5,390 dwellings to be located in Aylesbury Vale District
> ii. excludes 5,600 dwellings to be located in Mid Bedfordshire subject to a review of the East of England RSS
> iii. excludes housing in Milton Keynes District outside the Milton Keynes growth area.
>
> New development will be delivered through a combination of urban intensification, locations established through the Milton Keynes Local Plan, and two strategic development areas (SDAs) as new sustainable urban extensions, integrated with the provision of new and enhanced public transport systems and interchanges. One SDA will be to the south-east of Milton Keynes and the second to the south-west of Milton Keynes.
>
> The distribution of development should be informed by strategic flood risk assessments and water cycle studies. The results of these studies will need to be reflected in local development frameworks and future reviews of the RSS.
>
> Sustainable urban extensions should be carefully programmed so as to complement and not undermine the contribution of development and regeneration within the urban area. Both urban intensification and sustainable urban extensions will be planned in such a way as to maintain, extend and enhance green infrastructure, and to ensure that issues of impact on landscape character and coalescence of settlements are addressed.
>
> The levels of development proposed will be monitored against an increase in employment of 44,350 jobs in the period 2006 to 2026. Key locations for employment-related development will be Central Milton Keynes, Bletchley, Wolverton and Newport Pagnell and some locations within new urban extensions at focal points on the public transport system. At present there is sufficient planned employment land supply in Milton Keynes to meet forecast demand to 2016. Both quantitative and qualitative aspects of supply and demand for employment land will be kept under review, to ensure provision of a range of types and sizes of premises to meet the needs of the economy, and that any land no longer required for employment purposes is considered for other use.
>
> Local transport infrastructure and water services infrastructure will require early development and continued enhancement and upgrades to facilitate the delivery of sustainable growth throughout the period 2006-2026 and beyond. Key elements are:
>
> i. core bus network upgrade across the whole of Milton Keynes
> ii. high quality public transport serving East-West and North-South Corridors
> iii. park and ride accompanied by appropriate traffic management measures
> iv. measures to resolve east-west traffic problems across the southern half of Milton Keynes
> v. water services infrastructure to be planned in accordance with a strategic approach to ensure timely, phased delivery of sustainable solutions that minimise disturbance to existing communities.
>
> New and upgraded strategic transport links will be vital in underpinning the growth of Milton Keynes, including enhanced east-west public transport and possible new parkway stations.
>
> Measures are needed to address traffic problems on the existing A421, to improve access to the M1 and to make space available for enhanced public transport.

Milton Keynes and Aylesbury Vale

23.11 Consistent with the spatial vision for Milton Keynes in the Part A Statement of the MKSM strategy, Policy MKV2 will enable Milton Keynes to embrace its growth potential to mature as a major regional centre, particularly through the substantial development of its central area, supported by a significantly enhanced public transport system to facilitate and support growth in major development areas.

23.12 The policy provides for some 44,350 dwellings to be added to the urban area between 2006 and 2026, consistent with the overall aspiration for 68,600 additional homes between 2001 and 2031 set out in the MKSM strategy. In addition to the 34,160 dwellings to be found from within and around the Milton Keynes urban area, two urban extensions will be provided as strategic development areas (SDAs) with comprehensive master-planning including provision of employment land, retail, leisure, education and other facilities required to create sustainable communities. These extensions cross administrative boundaries and joint working between authorities and/or local delivery vehicles will facilitate delivery. The two areas, as provided by Policies MKV1 and MKV2, are:

  i. 4,800 dwellings within the authority's area as part of a SDA area to the south-east of Milton Keynes. A further 5,600 dwellings may be found in the Mid Bedfordshire part of this SDA subject to a review of the East of England RSS, and
  ii. 5,390 dwellings as a SDA to the south-west of Milton Keynes within Aylesbury Vale district.

23.13 In order to accommodate the additional jobs, in the longer term it is assumed that additional employment land will need to be provided as part of the proposed sustainable urban extensions.

23.14 The transport improvements set out in the policy are essential for enhancing accessibility for all and achieving more sustainable travel patterns within the urban area.

23.15 Milton Keynes urban area benefits from a well-managed strategic open space resource which new development needs to complement. In accordance with Strategic Policy 3 of the MKSM Part A Statement and Policy S5: Cultural and Sporting Activity in this Plan, the provision of formal recreation and sporting facilities will also need further enhancement as the population and workforce increases.

23.16 Policies H1: Regional Housing Provision 2006-2026, H3: Affordable Housing Provision, RE3: Employment Land Provision and RE6: Competitiveness and Addressing Structural Economic Weakness are also relevant.

Spatial Framework for Aylesbury Growth Area

POLICY MKAV3: SPATIAL FRAMEWORK FOR AYLESBURY GROWTH AREA

An expanded Aylesbury Town will accommodate a total of 16,800 new dwellings over the period 2006-2026 at an average rate of 840 dwellings per annum. Other parts of Aylesbury Vale District should provide for a further 4,700 new dwellings over the same period, at an average rate of 235 dwellings per annum to meet the local needs of its settlements and rural areas. Additional growth related to a sustainable urban extension to the south-west of Milton Keynes is identified in Policy MKAV1.

Development at Aylesbury should be delivered through maximising the use and re-use of land within the urban area and through the development of new sustainable urban extensions integrated with the provision of new and enhanced public transport systems and interchanges.

The distribution of development should be informed by strategic flood risk assessments. The results of these studies will need to be reflected in local development frameworks and future reviews of the RSS.

> **Sustainable urban extensions to the north of the town at Berryfields and Weedon Hill have already been identified through the Aylesbury Vale District Local Plan. While every effort should be made to maximise the use of urban land, further extensions will also be identified.**
>
> **A strategic long-term framework should be provided for the development of the town focusing on:**
>
> i. **identifying land for new housing as above**
> ii. **identifying and ensuring the availability of appropriate strategic high quality employment sites**
> iii. **identifying and implementing measures to achieve an urban renaissance of the town centre, strengthening its traditional role and heritage as a county town**
> iv. **providing for a sustainable transport system for the expanded town, including strategic bus corridors with bus priority measures and good links to the strategic rail network**
> v. **the levels of development proposed will be monitored against an increase in employment of 21,500 jobs in Aylesbury Vale district in the period to 2006-2026, the majority of which should be focused on the urban area of Aylesbury.**
>
> **In and around Aylesbury, there is a strong amenity need for informal recreational facilities of a much larger scale than has been provided in the past. An allowance for this should be made in the master-planning and design processes.**

23.17　Consistent with the spatial vision for Aylesbury in the Part A Statement of the MKSM strategy, Policy MKV3 will enable Aylesbury to grow through strengthening and extending its traditional role as a county and market town, including urban renaissance of the centre, that will allow it to meet the demands of a larger population. In parallel, Aylesbury will be able to provide high added value employment opportunities to complement its growing population.

23.18　The policy provides for 16,800 dwellings (the majority of growth) to be focused on Aylesbury with the rural areas taking a further 4,700 dwellings to meet local needs. A further 5,390 dwellings are to be provided to the south-west of Milton Keynes as part of the major expansion of the city as provided for in Policies MKAV1 and MKAV2. Although no policy target for has been fixed for the area, the expectation is that an average proportion of 35% affordable housing will be sought in line with the regional target in Policy H3.

23.19　The policy requires further sustainable urban extensions around Aylesbury town. In accordance with Strategic Policy 3 of the MKSM Part A Statement and the Core Regional Policies in this Plan, the emphasis will be on locations able to provide enhanced public transport corridors and nodes and opportunities sought to promote urban intensification of existing residential areas and redevelopment of redundant employment land. In line with national policy, a rigorous assessment of proposals to release employment land for other uses needs to be undertaken, particularly on sites close to Aylesbury town centre.

23.20　The Economic Development Strategy for Aylesbury Vale recognises that quality office space is needed in Aylesbury town to attract high value businesses in the business and financial services sector. Some additional employment land, for example in association with the future urban extensions, may be needed to achieve this and also attract firms within the ICT and R&D sectors.

23.21　In accordance with Strategic Policy 3 of the MKSM Part A Statement and Policy S5: Cultural and Sporting Activity in this Plan, the provision of formal recreation and sporting facilities will also need further enhancement as the population and workforce increases. In implementing Strategic Policy 3 and Policy CC8: Green Infrastructure, the local planning authority will ensure that, where necessary, steps are taken to ensure that strategic green infrastructure is managed to accommodate increased visitor pressure arising from growth. In rural areas, development needs to support the vitality of the district's small market towns and villages and respect their inherent character and distinctiveness in accordance with Policy SP3: Urban Focus and Urban Renaissance and Policies BE4: The Role of Small Rural Towns and BE5: Village Management.

23.22 Policies H1: Regional Housing Provision 2006-2026, H3:Affordable Housing Provision, RE3: Employment Land Provision and RE6: Competitiveness and Addressing Structural Economic Weakness are also particularly relevant.

Effective Delivery

> **POLICY MKAV4: EFFECTIVE DELIVERY**
>
> **Delivery of the sub-regional strategy will be secured through:**
>
> i. **the Inter-Regional Board**
> ii. **the two Local Delivery Vehicles (LDVs) to help drive the sustainable growth of the sub-region and a possible extension of powers of Milton Keynes Partnership or establishment of new delivery arrangements to cover the sustainable urban extensions south-west and south-east of Milton Keynes**
> iii. **preparation and updating of Business Plans by each LDV**
> iv. **early preparation of priority local development documents (LDDs) to guide development in areas of change in accordance with local development schemes.**
>
> **Progress in achieving resources for the sub-region and in implementing the sub-regional framework will be monitored regularly and reported as part of the annual monitoring reports (AMRs) prepared for this region and also for the wider MKSM area.**
>
> **The scale of growth envisaged in Milton Keynes and Aylesbury must be harnessed to deliver an enhanced quality of life following the principles of sustainable development. This will necessitate the programmed provision of high quality community, economic, environmental and social infrastructure and services.**

23.23 In addition to the institutional arrangement required by Policy MKV4, joint LDDs may be considered if they will bring forward sustainable cross-boundary development and support infrastructure in a timely way that supports the programming in Policy MKAV2.

23.24 Policy CC7: Infrastructure and Implementation sets out the general approach to implementation. A separate Regional Implementation Plan will be produced and updated by the regional planning body and will prioritise further strategic infrastructure requirements for the sub-region. Local requirements for infrastructure will be set out in LDDs and justified in accordance with national policy.

23.25 The transport schemes already committed for delivery to develop this sub-region are contained in Chapter 8, Appendix A: Strategic Transport Infrastructure Priorities. Key themes that should be addressed include:

   i. a high quality east-west public transport offer, including bus and coach networks
   ii. rail improvements and additional capacity to support growth in passenger demand
   iii. other public transport and demand management schemes including integrated inter-modal hubs
   iv. M1 capacity and management improvements
   v. local roads and bypasses, to relieve pressure on town centres and improve access to regional hubs
   vi. higher and further education facilities including new university
   vii. upgrades at Cotton Mill and Aylesbury Waste Water Treatment Works to support planned development (including any requirements to meet water quality standards in the River Thame)
   viii. major development and other urban extensions will require significant upgrades in electricity supply for both Milton Keynes and Aylesbury from 2011.

23.26 The Milton Keynes 'tariff' is proving an effective way to secure funding for the strategic infrastructure projects associated with development. This approach will be rolled forward with partners in future evidence-based LDDs and operated by development control authorities on the basis of development plan policy.

23.27 The approximate 1:1 ratio between new jobs and dwellings will assist monitoring both at the district level through AMRs and as part of the wider MKSM strategy:

i. future cross-boundary urban extensions to Milton Keynes should be treated as part of Milton Keynes City for the purposes of this monitoring
ii. a period of about 5 years is necessary for the reliable interpretation of this monitoring. This takes account of time-lags in employment data and of employment delivery that (unlike housing) is not in regularly sized units
iii. monitoring this ratio will not be used as a development control tool to limit housing growth in any way, including release of any additional opportunities that may come forward. Instead, any revision to baseline housing figures will be made through a future review of the South East Plan, taking account of the need for a step-change in housing delivery, the relationship between jobs and homes, changing commuting patterns and any skills shortages within the wider MKSM area.

23.28 These and other monitoring indicators will inform reviews of this sub-regional strategy (see also Chapter 26 on implementation, monitoring and review).

24 Gatwick

Diagram GAT1 — Gatwick Sub-regional Strategy Area

Legend:
- Sub-regional Strategy Area
- Green Belt (SP5)
- AONB
- Proposed National Park
- Regional Hub (SP2)
- Centre of Significant Change (TC1)
- Secondary Regional Centre (TC1)
- Nationally Significant Airport (T9)
- International Gateway
- County/Unitary boundary
- District boundary
- Motorway
- All Purpose Road
- Railway
- Rail station

All boundaries are indicative
© Crown copyright, all rights reserved. Government Office for the South East, Licence No. 100018986 (2008)

24.1 Gatwick was part of the "Western Policy Area" in RPG9 and extends north to the edge of Redhill, east to East Grinstead, south to Burgess Hill and Haywards Heath, and west to Horsham with strong functional links with Redhill and Reigate to the north and Southwater to the west. Gatwick Airport is the single most important element of the area's economy and is of significant economic importance to the Region as a whole. The airport has helped to foster clusters of employment in the chemicals and pharmaceutical industries, in financial services and there are a number of aviation-related industries in Crawley.

24.2 The particular challenges faced by the sub-region are how to:

i. capitalise on its location in relation to Gatwick Airport, London and Brighton, maximise the value added by the sub-region's economy and diversify the economy to reduce direct reliance on the airport

ii. reconcile the competing demands for economic growth with providing adequate new housing and other development, including affordable housing in well-served sustainable locations
iii. ensure transportation systems can continue to meet the demands of the economy
iv. maintain the High Weald and Sussex Downs Areas of Outstanding Natural Beauty (AONBs), natural habitats (particularly the Ashdown Forest) and distinctive towns and villages.

24.3 Although specific policies relating to the Gatwick area are set out below, it is important to take account of the Core Regional Policies in this Plan, including those which are referred to in this chapter.

Core Strategy

POLICY GAT1: CORE STRATEGY

The strategy is based on maximising the potential for sustainable economic growth in the sub-region while maintaining and enhancing its character, distinctiveness, sense of place and important features. This will be achieved by:

i. **sustaining and enhancing the pivotal role played by Crawley-Gatwick in the sub-regional and wider economy**
ii. **recognising and sustaining the sub-region's interrelationships with London and the South Coast and the international gateway role of Gatwick Airport**
iii. **protecting and enhancing the sub-region's distinctive environmental assets, in particular the High Weald and Sussex Downs Areas of Outstanding Natural Beauty**
iv. **maintaining the broad extent of the Metropolitan Green Belt within the sub-region.**

24.4 The spatial strategy for the sub-region is set out in Policy GAT1. The spatial strategy aims to maximise opportunities arising from the Gatwick-Crawley area, recognising the need to maintain the importance of Gatwick Airport as an international gateway and the links between the sub-region and London and the South Coast. The strategy recognises the need to balance growth opportunities in an area containing significant environmental assets including the High Weald and South Downs AONBs.

Economic Development

POLICY GAT2: ECONOMIC DEVELOPMENT

High value-added economic growth, and development that seeks to maximise the value added by the sub-region's economy will be encouraged, as will development that contributes to the improvement in the skills and flexibility of the local workforce. This includes:

i. **provision for enhanced learning opportunities, including a university campus at Crawley and other improvements to tertiary education**
ii. **re-generation of the town centres to provide first choice, highly attractive locations for inward investment**
iii. **providing employment floorspace in association with the major developments and strategic locations identified under Policy GAT3**
iv. **provision of high quality sites for start-up and micro-businesses, to support the growth of existing local businesses and the attraction of high value-added inward investment**
v. **retention of existing businesses**
vi. **the continued functioning of Gatwick Airport to serve the needs of the business community, recognising its major employment role and attractiveness for world class business investment in the sub-region.**

24.5 The sub-region lies at the heart of the 'Gatwick Diamond' – a business led, joint venture by the Surrey and West Sussex Economic Partnerships to stimulate and maintain strong economic growth. Policy GAT2 seeks to reflect and help to implement some of the key elements in the economic strategy for the Gatwick Diamond.

24.6 In order to support the expanding economic role of Gatwick Airport and at the same time take advantage of the opportunities that arise, Policy GAT2 aims to promote economic growth and regeneration through 'smart growth' alongside the provision of new sites and premises in appropriate locations. An interim estimate indicates that a net increase of 17,400 jobs will be needed during the first part of the Plan period between 2006 and 2016. For the period after 2016, further monitoring and analysis will be required at the local level. It is critical that the opportunities for smart growth are maximised in this sub-region in the context of Policy RE5: Smart Growth by using existing employment land as efficiently as possible, continuing to attract high-value business and driving up skill levels in accordance with Policy RE4: Human Resource Development. Policies RE6: Competitiveness and Addressing Structural Economic Weakness and RE3: Employment Land Provision are also relevant to this policy.

Housing Distribution

POLICY GAT3: HOUSING DISTRIBUTION

Local planning authorities will allocate sufficient land and facilitate the delivery of 36,000 net additional dwellings in the the Gatwick sub-region between 2006 and 2026.

In managing the supply of land for housing and in determining planning applications, local planning authorities should work collaboratively to facilitate the delivery of the following level of net additional dwellings in the sub-region:

DISTRICT	ANNUAL AVERAGE	TOTAL
Crawley[1]	375	7,500
Horsham (part)	460	9,200
Mid Sussex (part)	840	16,800
Reigate & Banstead (part)	125	2,500
Sub-Regional Total	1,800	36,000

Footnote

1. Provision levels at Crawley will need to be informed by the findings of a water cycle study. The results of this study will need to be reflected in local development frameworks and future reviews of the RSS.

In accordance with the development strategy for the region, and more particularly the sub-region:

i. the majority of future development should be in the form of major developments at or adjoining Crawley (supporting its role as a transport hub and regional centre) and the other main towns within the main north/south and east/west transport corridors
ii. smaller-scale, gradual growth of other settlements to meet local needs and support the rural economy should be facilitated
iii. new homes and employment should be developed in tandem with the infrastructure and services needed to support them
iv. a target of achieving 40% affordable housing should be aimed for, to be delivered through a variety of mechanisms and tenures, including Government funding through the Homes and Communities Agency's affordable housing programme.

Gatwick

24.7   Policy GAT3 provides for 36,000 new homes between 2006 and 2026 at an average of 1,800 dwellings per annum. This requirement has regard to the level of economic performance in the area together with the extent and disposition of Natura 2000 and Ramsar Sites and AONBs. Local planning authorities will provide for the level of housing development within this sub-region in accordance with the distribution in this policy. In exceptional circumstances, will provide for the balance of their sub-regional requirement in the remainder of their area provided the objectives of the sub-regional strategy can be met. Policies CC7: Infrastructure and Implementation, H1: Regional Housing Provision 2006-2026 and H3: Affordable Housing Provision are also relevant.

24.8   The following locations have previously been identified for some development in adopted development plans. Where possible, development should be brought forward as follows:

   i. westward expansion of Crawley for 2,500 homes after 2006
   ii. westward expansion of Horsham for 2,000 homes after 2006
   iii. west and south-west of East Grinstead for 2,500 homes after 2006
   iv. south-east and south-west of Haywards Heath for the residue of at least 1,400 homes not already completed by April 2006
   v. north-west and north-east of Horley for the residue of 2,600 dwellings not already completed by April 2006
   vi. North East Sector, Crawley for up to 2,700 dwellings.

24.9   If the above developments cannot be delivered, it will be for the relevant local planning authority to plan for alternative locations and strategies to deliver the scale of development required by Policy GAT3.

24.10   In Mid Sussex District, there may be potential for future strategic growth at Burgess Hill given its position on the London-Brighton rail line, a commitment to increase capacity on the Thameslink line, two rail stations and aspirations to regenerate the town centre. In Reigate and Banstead small scale local reviews of the Metropolitan Green Belt may be required to provide for the Borough's overall housing requirement. Where development is planned close to administrative boundaries, for example at East Grinstead, neighbouring authorities will take the necessary steps to ensure that essential infrastructure is put in place to support development.

Infrastructure Implementation and Delivery

24.11   The general approach to implementation is set out in Policy CC7: Infrastructure and Implementation. This includes the need to ensure that the pace of development is aligned to the provision and management of infrastructure.

24.12   A separate Regional Implementation Plan will be produced and updated by the regional planning body and will prioritise strategic infrastructure requirements for the sub-region. Local requirements for infrastructure will be set out in local development documents (LDDs) and justified in accordance with national policy.

24.13   The transport schemes already committed for delivery to develop this sub-region, including Thameslink, are contained in Chapter 8, Appendix A: Strategic Transport Infrastructure Priorities. Future key transport areas that need to be addressed include:

   i. improving north-south public transport and road connections
   ii. rail improvements and additional passenger rail capacity to support growth in demand.

24.14   Other schemes and issues include:

   i. waste water treatment, particularly at Crawley and Horsham to address environmental legislation including the Habitats Directive and the Water Framework Directive

    ii.   Clay Hill reservoir (which would be located in Lewes district outside this sub-region), to increase water supply in the region plus additional water resource infrastructure in North West Sussex
    iii.   university campus at Crawley
    iv.   management of flood risk in areas likely to be at risk from flooding or where development elsewhere could exacerbate risks.

24.15 Consistent with Policy CC7: Infrastructure and Implementation, strong co-ordinated leadership and partnership working by authorities, service and infrastructure providers plus stakeholders is critical to securing the sustainable development, regeneration and economic success sought by the strategy including working with:

    i.   the Gatwick Diamond agencies to help implement the economic development strategy
    ii.   neighbouring planning and transportation authorities where cross-boundary issues exist (for example at East Grinstead) to bring forward strategic developments and associated infrastructure, including through joint working on LDDs.

24.16 See also Chapter 26 on implementation, monitoring and review.

24 Gatwick

25 Isle of Wight and Areas Outside Sub-Regions

Isle of Wight and Areas Outside Sub-regions

25.1 This chapter sets out specific policies and guidance for areas of the South East not covered by the nine identified sub-regions, together with the Isle of Wight. It only covers topics on which the relevant regional policies need to be supplemented, and mainly covers housing figures for districts (or parts of districts) which lie outside identified sub-regions. It also contains specific policies on the strategic development area at Whitehill/Bordon and for the two regional hubs lying in the 'Rest of Kent' area.

> Six spatial planning principles for areas lying outside sub-regions are identified:
>
> i. the quality and character of the rural environment must be maintained and enhanced
> ii. natural resources and biodiversity must be protected and improved
> iii. local communities must be sustained through sensitive development of market and affordable housing to help maintain rural vitality and improve access to local services and employment
> iv. opportunities to support, improve and diversify local economies must be identified and developed
> v. accessibility and rural public and community based transport must be improved
> vi. the importance of the countryside as a resource to attract visitors and provide a healthy recreational environment must be recognised and strengthened.

Isle of Wight and Areas Outside Sub-Regions

The Isle of Wight

Isle of Wight

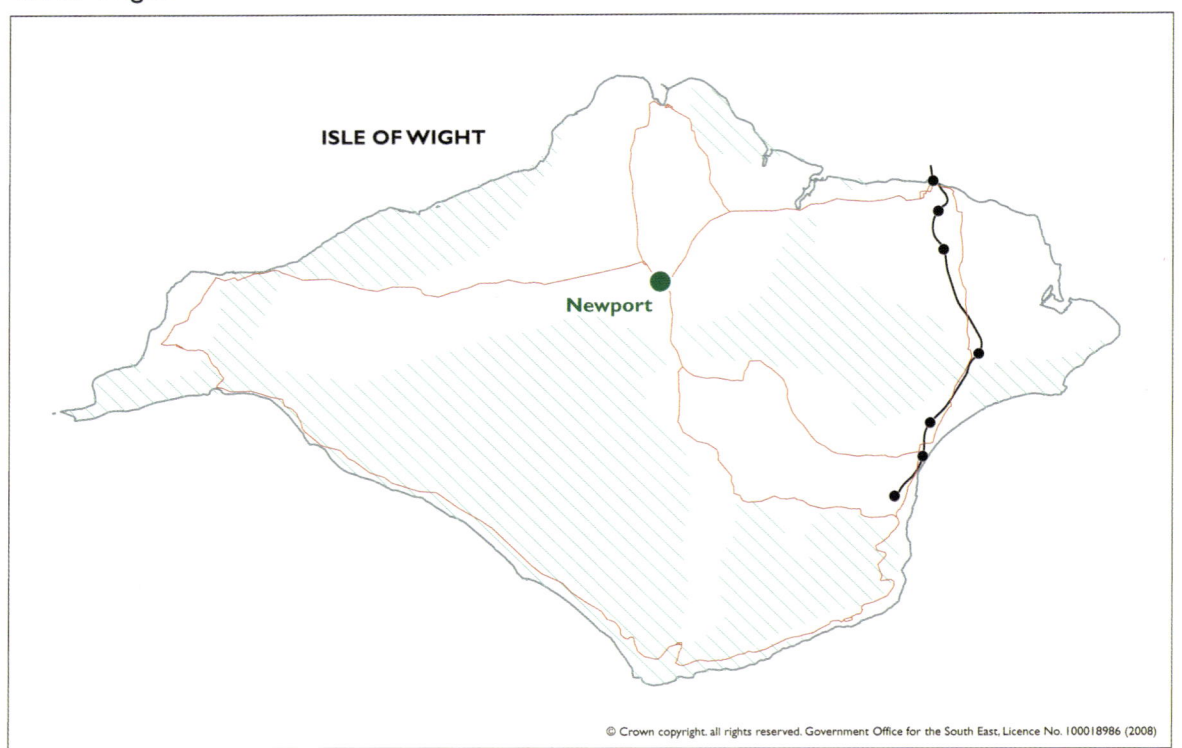

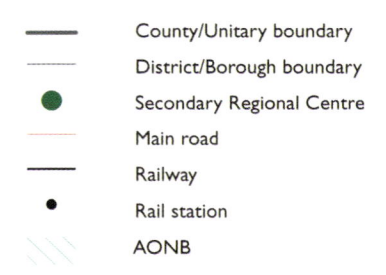

Map of the Isle of Wight showing Newport as Secondary Regional Centre, main roads, railway along the east coast with rail stations, and AONB areas.

© Crown copyright, all rights reserved. Government Office for the South East, Licence No. 100018986 (2008)

- County/Unitary boundary
- District/Borough boundary
- ● Secondary Regional Centre
- Main road
- Railway
- ● Rail station
- AONB

25.2 The Isle of Wight has unique characteristics, the result of its attractiveness and its island economy. The high environmental quality of the island is an important element in its character and acts as a major asset and selling point. A substantial area of the island is designated as an Area of Outstanding Natural Beauty, while much of its coastline is designated Heritage Coast. Areas of land and stretches of coastline are also designated for their international and national importance for wildlife.

25.3 Set against this, the island has particular challenges:

i. localised labour markets, with small and medium sized enterprises forming a large proportion of the businesses on the island. Though there are transport links between the mainland and the island, the island's relative inaccessibility is a factor in terms of providing access to employment opportunities and other services

ii. above average unemployment, particularly amongst the young. The once dominant agricultural sector has shed workers and, given the major role that tourism plays in the island economy, there is a heavy reliance on seasonal and part time work

iii. a deficit between the skills available locally and those needed to meet the requirements of recent growth sectors

iv. a changing tourism sector. Whilst still valuable to the island's economy, visitors to the island bring with them additional pressure on local infrastructure and do not generate sufficient economic return in terms of investment and job opportunities.

Hotels and catering now account for a smaller proportion of the economy than they did in the late 1990s, and the quality and range of accommodation is no longer sustainable if the island is to prosper

v. access to affordable housing. This is a key issue which is exacerbated by a high proportion of second homes

vi. a need to plan positively to overcome water shortages and avoid adverse environmental effects from over abstraction.

25.4 The strategy for the Isle of Wight is based on managed economic growth and regeneration to provide for the island's particular characteristics and needs. Future development is expected to create wealth and a sustainable economy, to address skills deficits and housing need, to provide for improved public transport infrastructure and to respect the environment, safeguarding biodiversity and areas of landscape and ecological importance.

Enabling Economic Regeneration

POLICY IW1: ENABLING ECONOMIC REGENERATION

National, regional and other relevant agencies and authorities will give increased priority to investment decisions and other direct support for the island to help realise a step-change in the Isle of Wight's economic performance, to actively support economic regeneration and renewal, an improved quality tourism product and inward investment. Key measures should include:

i. **the development of infrastructure and inward investment opportunities in the Medina Valley**

ii. **support for the development of centres of vocational excellence in the sectors of composites, marine and aeronautical skills and construction related industries including any associated academic establishments**

iii. **support for inward investment and development to regenerate key areas identified in Ryde, Sandown Bay, Ventnor and West Wight, subject to minimal environmental impact**

iv. **support for urban renewal and intensification particularly where this can secure contributions for improvements in the public realm**

v. **the need to improve the tourism offer to one that focuses on a higher quality, higher value product.**

25.5 As an island economy, tailored solutions will be required to tackle the problems of unemployment and deprivation. A consequence of recent growth patterns is a change in the industrial composition of the island's economy. Business services and retailing have increased the share of the economy, whilst there has been a decline in employment in agriculture and related industries.

25.6 As a result of the island's economic activity in recent years, a smart growth approach is the most appropriate way forward. The main elements of smart growth relevant on the island until 2026 are as follows:

i. continuing to attract high value-added businesses

ii. upgrading skills, including the need to reverse out-migration of young people with good academic qualifications

iii. increasing economic activity, to counter the effects of an ageing population, bearing in mind that economic activity rates (at 75%) are lower than the regional average

iv. seeking to attract higher value tourism.

25.7 In addition, the development of infrastructure on the island is important as a means of enabling future economic regeneration, in particular improving transport links between Newport and Cowes to support the regeneration of the Medina Valley area.

25.8 The development of tailored tourism development strategies will particularly need to address:

i. support for high quality hotel development and conferences facilities
ii. support for appropriate tourism related retail facilities
iii. support for tourism related centres of vocational excellence including any associated academic establishment
iv. exit strategies for redundant tourism accommodation coupled with contributions to improved tourism related infrastructure.

25.9 In terms of retail provision on the island, Newport is included in Policy TC1: Strategic Network of Town Centres. Newport is listed as a secondary regional centre and advice on new development and redevelopment is set out in Policy TC2.

25.10 It is expected that an increase of 7,000 new jobs will be created between 2006-2016, which is the interim figure for monitoring purposes. This will help to assess changes in the local economy, and to inform future policy development.

Housing Development

POLICY IW2: HOUSING DEVELOPMENT

The local planning authority will allocate sufficient land and facilitate the delivery of 10,400 net additional dwellings in the Isle of Wight between 2006 and 2026.

DISTRICT	ANNUAL AVERAGE	TOTAL
Isle of Wight	520	10,400

25.11 Provision will be made for an average of 520 dwellings (including homes of all types created by conversion and/or new build) per annum. This is proposed to provide for:

i. housing to meet needs of economic growth
ii. housing to meet local affordable needs
iii. an element of market housing

25.12 Higher levels of housing provision will only be expected to be provided once the economic drivers are in place and being implemented, and are likely to come into play during later stages of the Plan period.

25.13 Housing linked to employment will be concentrated in the main urban areas of Cowes, Newport, Ryde, Sandown and Shanklin. The overall regional affordability target set out in Policy H4 of the Plan will be applied.

Rural Areas

POLICY IW3: RURAL AREAS

The quality and character of the rural environment and its biodiversity will be maintained and enhanced for its own sake, and to foster the economic success of the island. Necessary change to meet economic and social needs, including rural diversification and the delivery of small scale local affordable housing, should be accommodated.

25.14 The island's rural areas are less accessible and, with fewer job opportunities, suffer from problems of isolation and lower incomes. Redressing this will include focusing on people as well as places, and maintaining and enhancing the environment while encouraging the development of diverse and sustainable communities.

Isle of Wight and Areas Outside Sub-Regions

Transport and Infrastructure

POLICY IW4: STRATEGIC TRANSPORT LINKS

The Isle of Wight is reliant upon efficient and well managed links to the mainland. The strategic cross-Solent links should be maintained and improved to provide a service which fits with this role, and should form part of an integrated transport approach developed at the local level.

25.15 The importance of maintaining and improving cross-Solent links is an important element in the Island's sustainable transport strategy. The development of a new transport interchange at Ryde will contribute to improved mainland access and consideration should be give to the potential to provide a second local transport hub to support regeneration initiatives.

POLICY IW5: INFRASTRUCTURE

The key regeneration objectives for the island will only be achieved through the provision of necessary, appropriate and timely infrastructure over the Plan period. The schemes, projects and longer term issues identified in the Regional Implementation Plan will need to be considered as part of the Isle of Wight's Core Strategy Development Plan Document.

25.16 The provision of infrastructure is vital to the delivery of development. An important issue for the island is the promotion of water efficiency. However, increasing efficiency alone is unlikely to be sufficient to meet future demands. It is therefore essential that additional water resources are developed in parallel with improvements to water efficiency that can be achieved over and above current levels and in parallel with infrastructure enhancements.

Area Based Policies and Principles

Rest of Buckinghamshire, Oxfordshire and Berkshire

POLICY AOSR1: SCALE AND LOCATION OF HOUSING DEVELOPMENT 2006-2026

Provision will be made for 19,220 net additional dwellings between 2006 and 2026 distributed as follows:

DISTRICT/PART OF DISTRICT	ANNUAL AVERAGE	TOTAL
Chiltern	145	2,900
Wycombe	40	800
Cherwell	350	7,000
South Oxfordshire	135	2,700
West Oxfordshire	175	3,500
Vale of White Horse	66	1,320
West Berkshire	50	1,000
Total	961	19,220

Chiltern District

25.17 Strong protection for existing employment land in Chiltern district should be maintained unless new land is substituted.

Isle of Wight and Areas Outside Sub-Regions

Cherwell District

25.18 The town of Banbury will continue to play an important role as a small market town in supporting its wider hinterland. Given its accessibility by rail and road and its lack of serious environmental constraints, it is expected that the town will help meet wider housing needs through the provision of new housing.

25.19 Flood alleviation works at Banbury are a priority for investment.

Rest of Hampshire

POLICY AOSR2: SCALE AND LOCATION OF HOUSING DEVELOPMENT 2006-2026

Provision will be made for 18,900 net additional dwellings between 2006 and 2026 distributed as follows:

DISTRICT/PART OF DISTRICT	ANNUAL AVERAGE	TOTAL
New Forest	119	2,380
New Forest National Park	11	220
Test Valley	305	6,100
Winchester	275	5,500
East Hampshire[1]	200	4,000
Basingstoke & Deane	30	600
Hart	5	100
Total	945	18,900

Footnote

1. The figure for East Hampshire does not include any specific provision for Whitehill/Bordon.

25.20 The interim job growth estimate for monitoring is 14,500 for the 2006-2016 period.

East Hampshire - The Whitehill/Bordon Opportunity

POLICY AOSR3: THE WHITEHILL/BORDON OPPORTUNITY

Local development documents for East Hampshire District will allocate land and set out planning objectives for a new strategic development area at Whitehill/Bordon. This will include provision for the delivery of 5,500 dwellings (net), in accordance with Policy H1. Objectives should include:

i.   **a mix of housing types and tenures should be provided to help promote a balanced and sustainable community**
ii. **new employment opportunities should be provided to support the local community**
iii. **new green infrastructure to support local biodiversity and promote recreational opportunities**
iv. **new development should contribute to improved town centre facilities and services**
v.   **improved access to town centre facilities, including increased modal shift from private cars to other forms of transport.**

> The housing provision figure for this site is based on ongoing work including a water cycle study to assess and manage the integrated water environment and Habitats Regulation Assessment work, and should be regarded as an indicative figure. Should additional constraints or opportunities become apparent then a different scale of development should be identified and pursued through the local development framework.
>
> In the event that the site cannot be released for the delivery of 5,500 dwellings, there is no expectation that equivalent land elsewhere in East Hampshire District will be allocated to meet the overall district figure set out in Policy H1.

25.21 Around 300 hectares of land around Whitehill/Bordon in East Hampshire is currently in the ownership of the Ministry of Defence (MOD). As the result of the ongoing Defence Training Review, parts of this estate are likely to be available for development over the lifetime of this Plan. Ongoing master planning work by East Hampshire District Council and its partners has identified that the area may be able to accommodate around 5,500 dwellings, alongside new employment, retail and service uses. There will be a need to appropriately assess this development and adequate mitigation is also required. Housing provision for this MOD site remains separate from the rest of East Hampshire District and is separated out in Policy H1.

Test Valley District

25.22 Any waste water constraints that may impede identified levels of development in the parts of Test Valley that lie within the 'Areas Outside Sub-Regions' area should be identified, with partnership action working to remove constraints or identify their implications for housing delivery. There is limited remaining capacity at the Chickenhall Waste Water Treatment Works that is unlikely to be increased due to concerns about water quality in the River Itchen (which is designated as a European site under the Habitats Directive). However, wise use of the remaining capacity within the discharge consent will negate the need to consider alternative discharge locations for new development.

Winchester District

25.23 The town of Winchester will continue to play an important role in supporting its wider hinterland in accordance with its secondary regional centre status (Policy TC1). Given its accessibility by rail and road, it is expected that the town will help meet wider housing needs through the provision of new housing. Although in general the town has few serious environmental constraints, there are issues over local sewerage infrastructure capacity for new development which will require careful evaluation, particularly in relation to potential effects on European wildlife sites.

Hart District

25.24 Some rural parts of Hart district are within 5km of the Thames Basin Heaths Special Protection Area, for which Policy NRM6 applies.

Rest of Surrey

POLICY AOSR4: SCALE AND LOCATION OF HOUSING DEVELOPMENT 2006-2026

Provision will be made for 5,000 net additional dwellings between 2006 and 2026 distributed as follows:

DISTRICT/PARTS OF DISTRICT	ANNUAL AVERAGE	TOTAL
Waverley	250	5,000

Guildford[1]	0	0
Mole Valley[1]	0	0
Tandridge[1]	0	0
Total	250	5,000

Footnote

1. See Policy LF3 regarding the distribution of housing in the rural parts of named authority areas

25.25 The indicative job growth figure for monitoring purposes is 2,300 for that part of Surrey outside sub-regional areas.

25.26 Part of Waverley district is within 5km of the Thames Basin Heaths Special Protection Area, for which Policy NRM6 applies.

Rest of East and West Sussex

POLICY AOSR5: SCALE AND LOCATION OF HOUSING DEVELOPMENT 2006-2026

Provision will be made for 13,200 net additional dwellings between 2006 and 2026 distributed as follows:

DISTRICT/PART OF DISTRICT	ANNUAL AVERAGE	TOTAL
Chichester	125	2,500
Lewes	50	1,000
Wealden	200	4,000
Rother	80	1,600
Horsham	190	3,800
Mid Sussex	15	300
Total	660	13,200

Wealden District

25.27 The town of Uckfield will continue to play an important role as a small market town in supporting its wider hinterland. Given its accessibility by rail and road and its potential to address constraints, it is expected that the town will help meet wider housing needs through provision of new housing.

25.28 A 'balanced dispersal' strategy should be used in making local development framework site allocations taking account of the role and accessibility of each rural settlement moderated by environmental designations.

Rest of Kent

POLICY AOSR6: SCALE AND LOCATION OF HOUSING DEVELOPMENT 2006-2026

Provision will be made for 28,880 net additional dwellings between 2006 and 2026 distributed as follows:

DISTRICT	ANNUAL AVERAGE	TOTAL
Maidstone	554	11,080
Tonbridge and Malling	450	9,000

Tunbridge Wells	300	6,000
Sevenoaks	80	1,600
Dartford	10	200
Gravesham	5	100
Medway	30	600
Ashford	15	300
Total	1,444	28,880

25.29 The indicative job growth figure for monitoring purposes should be 15,000 for that part of Kent outside sub-regional areas.

25.30 Two regional hubs - Maidstone and Tonbridge-Tunbridge Wells - are identified as accessible settlements of regional significance with Maidstone identified as having the potential to accommodate significantly higher levels of development during the Plan period than other urban settlements located outside the sub-regional strategy areas. The following policies set out the spatial strategy for these hubs.

The Borough of Maidstone

POLICY AOSR7: MAIDSTONE HUB

The local development framework at Maidstone will:

i. **make new provision for housing consistent with its growth role, including associated transport infrastructure**
ii. **make new provision for employment of sub-regional significance, with an emphasis on higher quality jobs to enhance its role as the county town and a centre for business. The concentration of retail, leisure and service uses at the centre will allow close integration between employment, housing and public transport**
iii. **confirm the broad scale of new business and related development already identified and give priority to completion of the major employment sites in the town**
iv. **make Maidstone the focus for expansion and investment in new further or higher education facilities**
v. **support high quality proposals for intensifying or expanding the technology and knowledge sectors at established and suitable new locations**
vi. **ensure that development at Maidstone complements rather than competes with the Kent Thames Gateway towns and does not add to travel pressures between them**
vii. **avoid coalescence between Maidstone and the Medway towns conurbation.**

25.31 Maidstone is the county town of Kent and serves as the focus for administrative, commercial and retail activities. It is designated as a hub under Policy SP2 of this Plan as it is well related to strategic rail and road networks and serves as an interchange point between intra and local rail services. It also offers opportunities for some new housing development. An indicative 90% of new housing at Maidstone should be in or adjacent to the town. Associated infrastructure to support growth should include the South East Maidstone Relief Route and Maidstone Hub package.

The Boroughs of Tonbridge & Malling and Tunbridge Wells

POLICY AOSR8: TONBRIDGE/TUNBRIDGE WELLS HUB

The local development frameworks for Tonbridge and Tunbridge Wells will:

i. **provide for full and effective use of development capacity within the regional hub of Tonbridge/Tunbridge Wells. This will aim for a balance of business, commercial and residential development paying particular attention to meeting locally based needs**

> for housing and business premises, and improving the links between the two urban areas
>
> ii. at Tunbridge Wells give priority to conservation of the urban and natural environment, and the setting of the town. At Tonbridge concentrate development on substantial regeneration sites in and near to the town centre
>
> iii. make Tonbridge the focus for expansion and investment in new further or higher education facilities
>
> iv. support high quality proposals for intensifying or expanding the technology and knowledge sectors at established and suitable new locations.

25.32   The Tonbridge/Tunbridge Wells hub has been identified in Policy SP2 as it reflects not only the proximity of the two centres, but also their complementary roles: Tunbridge Wells as significant economic and service centre and Tonbridge as a major transport interchange.

25.33   To support its role as a hub, new infrastructure investment should include improvements to links with East Sussex and Crawley/Gatwick and Maidstone, as well as sustainable transport links between the two hub towns.

25.34   If any greenfield releases are necessary to meet the housing provision for Tonbridge and Malling, these should be within the second half of the Plan period in order to avoid diverting investor interest in its major brownfield opportunity sites. There may be a need for a small scale Green Belt review at Tunbridge Wells in accordance with Policy SP5.

25.35   A higher proportion of key worker and shared equity housing is appropriate in the West Kent area to meet high aspirations for owner occupation.

25.36   High-quality proposals for intensifying or expanding technology and knowledge-based activities will be supported at established and suitable new locations unless there are overriding environmental impacts which cannot be adequately dealt with, including at Kings Hill in Tonbridge and Malling and for development related agriculture at East Malling Research suitable to its rural location in Tonbridge and Malling.

26 Implementation, Monitoring and Review

Implementation

The policies within this RSS provide the spatial direction for the region. Their delivery needs to be integrated and co-ordinated with national, regional, sub-regional and local plans and programmes that are likely to have a significant bearing on land use or are affected by spatial planning policies within this RSS.

Effective implementation of the RSS is therefore crucial and central; and achieving the implementation of this RSS at the required pace and in a sustainable way is a major task for the region. The delivery of this RSS will be a primary function of many public and other organisations as well as for local authorities via their local development frameworks (LDFs) and local transport plans (LTPs).

A non-statutory Regional Implementation Plan has been prepared by the regional planning body (RPB) and is intended to support the realisation of this spatial strategy, articulating the infrastructure and other interventions which should be delivered in connection with new spatial development.

The successful implementation of the South East Plan will rely, *inter alia*, on five elements. They are:

Delivery Mechanisms

There are four main delivery mechanisms requiring attention. First, behavioural change will be critical to the achievement of the objectives of the Plan, particularly in relation to transport, water, waste and energy. The second and third mechanisms, namely, fiscal incentives and regulatory changes will need to be, and are being, initiated by central government to bring about the necessary changes in behaviour.

The challenges of delivering major infrastructure when regulatory review cycles are short in comparison with infrastructure delivery timescales need further consideration. They should be taken into account in reviewing regulatory regimes and mitigated through close working between spatial planning authorities and delivery bodies.

Lastly, in addition to behavioural change and regulatory action, there should be a focus on effective management of existing assets along with investment in additional infrastructure capacity.

Funding Arrangements

No single funding mechanism will provide an adequate answer to address the level and timing of investment required. Rather the mix of mechanisms is likely to include:

- commitments by central and local government to sustained public sector funding at a level appropriate to the scale of growth for which provision is being made
- the enhancement of current arrangements for capturing increases in land value through the local tariff approach pioneered in the growth areas and/or a national system, such as the Communities Infrastructure Levy
- the creation of a Regional Infrastructure Fund to provide up-front capital for major infrastructure schemes
- private market funding related either to new development, Private Finance Initiatives, or other financial vehicles such as tolling or charging regimes.

Joint Working and Delivery Agencies

The alignment of investment decisions across a range of sectors is essential to achieving timely delivery of infrastructure in relation to development. It requires good communication and co-ordination between planning and delivery bodies at national, regional and local levels. Better alignment of planning and programme cycles will be an outcome for transport under the new approach set out in Delivering a Sustainable Transport System, and other bodies should seek to influence and align with the national programme cycles that emerge. Local authorities should also align their revenue expenditure to support capital programmes. A single Regional Implementation Plan, produced and updated by the RPB, will act as a means of improving the alignment of funding for the full range of infrastructure critical to the delivery of the RSS.

Implementation, Monitoring and Review

The successful implementation of sub-regional strategies requires strong leadership, and is most effective where powers are coherent. For the major growth areas, there is evidence of local delivery vehicles, involving one or more local authorities and partner bodies, looking sufficiently robust to manage the funding and delivery of both development and infrastructure. Planning authorities in other sub-regional areas and in strategic development areas should consider whether a similar approach, or one including a development partnership, would facilitate more effective and timely implementation.

Coordination with Adjoining Regions

The South East region is large and diverse, but it cannot be viewed in isolation. There are strong links with London and the East of England which are likely to evolve and grow in significance over the period of the Plan. It will become increasingly important to work jointly with neighbouring regions to ensure consistency of policies and their implementation across the greater South East. It will therefore be necessary to:

- undertake background work where there are potential inconsistencies and/or omissions between RSSs, or to improve the evidence base for subsequent reviews, including on housing, labour market issues and waste
- where possible seek to synchronise the process of future RSS reviews to assist a genuinely joined up approach to planning of the greater South East, taking account of the existing and emerging Government policy framework including the Planning Act 2008, the Housing Green Paper and the White Paper emerging from 'Delivering a Sustainable Transport System'.

The Implementation Plan

A non-statutory Implementation Plan should be produced by the RPB which should set out for each policy and priority proposal the implementation mechanism, the organisations responsible for delivery, the current status of proposals and the timescale for key actions. The sub-regional dimension of implementation, including specific delivery mechanisms and agencies relevant to the delivery of the sub-regional strategies will also form a part of the Implementation Plan. The RPB and other key stakeholders who are responsible for the Implementation Plan are encouraged to take note of the recommendations of the Examination-in-Public Panel in revising the current version of the Implementation Plan.

The Implementation Plan should contain a section that is regularly updated, preferably as part of the annual monitoring process to keep track of delivery of this strategy and funding for major investments. It should be kept under review as an evolving non-statutory, region-wide document giving a comprehensive picture of strategic infrastructure requirements and their delivery. It should aim to be an exemplar of proactive, co-ordinated realism.

Monitoring

POLICY IMR1: MONITORING THE RSS

The regional planning body will annually assess and report on the progress towards achieving the objectives of the Plan's policies and the sub-regional strategies, and indicate how the results of monitoring will influence actions at both regional and sub-regional levels.

Annual monitoring will cover both regional and sub-regional levels and will particularly focus on assessing the following:

i. **the delivery of housing and its effectiveness in the context of best available evidence on housing need and demand**
ii. **economic growth including any important changes in regionally significant business sectors and the changes in employment levels**
iii. **the management of the region's natural resources, in particular with regard to any changes in resource consumption and indicators of behavioural change**

Implementation, Monitoring and Review

> iv. **the delivery of regionally and sub-regionally significant social, physical and environmental infrastructure**
>
> v. **action that will be taken to maintain and, in particular, to enhance the effectiveness of delivery in the above areas.**

As a part of annual monitoring, the RPB will work with planning authorities and other regional partners to monitor key assumptions underpinning the RSS and to assess their robustness and continued relevance. The monitoring should be used to inform action to manage and where necessary to review the Plan. The results of monitoring will be reported annually through the regional annual monitoring report (AMR).

Working collaboratively with key partners, a separate non-statutory regional monitoring framework (RMF) will be produced by the RPB which should include:

- an indication of the likely structure of the regional AMR
- the proposed system for monitoring the delivery of sub-regional strategies
- the arrangements for the supply and interpretation of data for monitoring purposes
- proposals for co-ordinating, facilitating and/or taking forward any actions that may stem from annual monitoring.

The RPB will ensure that the monitoring framework includes SMART (Specific, Measurable, Agreed, Realistic, Timed) targets and where possible indicators relevant to monitoring behavioural change, assessing progress on smart growth, and assessing the impact of new housing and other development on the integrity of internationally designated nature conservation sites.

A significant additional source of information will be the National Indicator Set (NIS), This is a local performance management framework, and overall monitoring through the NIS will provide a useful context for monitoring for the RPB, local strategic partnerships, and for local planning authorities in relation to the local social, economic and environmental conditions.

The RPB and SEEDA will work together to lead the work to develop and keep up-to date an agreed regional evidence base. On matters that are likely to have a significant inter-regional/cross-regional boundary dimension, the RPB will actively engage in joint and/or co-ordinated evidence gathering and analysis with neighbouring RPBs, with a view to taking a consistent approach to actions needed.

The 'Plan, Monitor, Manage Approach'

The RPB has a key role in the 'plan, monitor, manage' approach to housing provision. A strong 'plan' function to provide clear long-term guidance is a central theme to this RSS, and the proposed monitoring framework will provide a sound basis for securing an effective 'monitor' element. While individual local authorities will take primary responsibility for managing the delivery of growth in their areas, the RPB will have a key coordinating role in the 'manage' process. A challenging and central aspect of this role will include:

- an advisory role to local authorities, particularly in the early stages of implementing the proactive mechanisms required by PPS3: *Housing*
- assistance in helping to remove blockages to housing delivery on major sites, such as acting as a bridge to central government departments and liaising with the Highways Agency and other providers
- interpreting the results from individual local authority trajectories for the overall delivery of housing at the regional and sub-regional scales for inclusion in the AMR
- setting out the actions to be undertaken at regional level where actual performance does not reflect the regional housing (and previously developed land) trajectories
- using the findings as input to the RSS review process.

Further actions that could be taken by the RPB to overcome obstacles to delivery or to influence the quality of delivery could include:

- seeking to augment mechanisms to increase affordable housing provision, including working more closely with the Regional Housing Board and the Housing and Communities Agency, and seeking to influence national funding regimes
- targeting economic interventions and regeneration funding on a common set of priorities
- developing the proposed Regional Infrastructure Fund to forward fund site infrastructure to remove blockages and kick-start other initiatives such as the provision of SANGS in the Thames Basin Heaths SPA
- working with health, education, water and transport providers to align priorities
- taking action seeking to overcome obstacles to delivery or seeking to influence the quality of delivery, e.g. through producing good practice guidance.

Review of the RSS

This RSS sets a long term strategy and a sustainable approach to managing the development of the region. However, there are a number of significant gaps in the strategy. Reviews on Gypsies and travellers' accommodation and on the primary aggregates apportionment are underway at present and these will help address some of these gaps. The need for a review on employment land provision based on updated job estimates/targets has also been recognised.

The limitation of readily available bottom-up evidence on housing means the RSS policies to address the need and demand for long term housing also need to be revisited through a future review. This will ensure that the region plans for additional and longer term housing growth to maximise its contribution to the national house building target set out in the Housing Green Paper. Any additional housing growth will need to be planned and accommodated in a sustainable way.

The NHPAU has recently advised the Government on a range of housing targets for each region (*Meeting the Housing Requirements of an Aspiring and Growing Nation*, June 2008). In considering NHPAU's advice, the Government has sought the views of regional partners in the light of current housing market conditions. Given that current and emerging RSSs provide a stretching framework for housing delivery over the next few years, the Government has agreed not to require an immediate review, but is working closely with regional partners in the South East to develop a work programme and review timetable which takes account of the outstanding issues, the NHPAU's advice, proposals for eco-towns and new Growth Points, and the need to manage the transition to new single integratedRegional Strategies which the Government is introducing through the Local Democracy, Economic Development and Construction Bill, and which forms part of the reforms announced by the Review of Sub-National Economic Development and Regeneration. However, those discussions should not in any way delay the need for rapid progress on delivery of the RSS and the strategy and direction of growth as currently set out. Local authorities and others should therefore ensure that the South East Plan is reflected in and implemented via their LDFs, LTPs, Local Area Agreements and other relevant policies and programmes without delay.

Appendix 1 - Saved Policies

27 Appendix 1 - Saved Policies

27.1 The publication of this final version of the South East Plan means that all the saved policies which had been extended by the Secretary of State in the following structure plans are no longer in force:

- Berkshire Structure Plan 2001-2016
- Buckinghamshire County Structure Plan 1991-2011
- East Sussex and Brighton & Hove Structure Plan 1991-2011
- Surrey Structure Plan 2004
- Hampshire County Structure Plan 1996-2011 (Review)
- West Sussex Structure Plan 2001-2016

27.2 The saved policies in the Oxfordshire Structure Plan 2016 were extended by the Secretary of State in September 2008 after the publication of her Proposed Changes to the draft South East Plan. It was not possible, therefore, to set out at that stage which of those policies would be expressly replaced by policies in the South East Plan. These are set out in the table below.

27.3 In relation to the Kent & Medway Structure Plan 2006, the Secretary of State has decided that none of its policies should be extended so these will cease to have development plan status when their three-year saved period expires on 6 July 2009.

Oxfordshire Structure Plan 2016 - adopted October 2005

Policy	Policy Title and Purpose	Replacement RSS Policy
G1	General Strategy	SP2, SP3, TC1, TC2, CC7, CO1
G2	Quality and design of development	CC6, H5, BE1, BE2
G3	Infrastructure and service provision	CC7
G4	Green Belt	SP5, CO4
G5	Development outside settlements	RE3, C3
G6	Energy and resource conservation	NRM11, NRM12, NRM15, NRM16, W2, W5, W6
T1	Sustainable travel	T1, T5, CO5
T2	Car parking	T4
T3	Public transport	T1, T2, CO5
T4	Freight	T11, T12
T5	Networks for pedestrians and cyclists	T5, CO5
T6	Networks for motorised travel	T1, T3, T14, CO5
T8	Development proposals	T1
EN1	Landscape character	C3, C4, CO1,
EN2	Biodiversity	NRM5
EN4	Historic and cultural heritage	BE6
EN5	Oxford's architectural and historic heritage	BE6, CO1
EN6	Archaeology	BE6
EN7	Geology	NRM5

Appendix 1 - Saved Policies

EN10	Water resources and waste water infrastructure	NRM1
EN11	Proposals for new reservoirs	NRM3
E1	Provision for employment development	RE1, RE2, RE3, CO2
E2	Oxford City	CO2
E3	Employment land provision in towns	RE2, RE3, CO3
E4	Small firms and local employment diversity	RE3, CO1
E5	Tourism and culture	TSR2, TSR4, TSR7, S5
E6	Employment and housing	CC7, CO1, RE5, H1, H2
H1	The amount and distribution of housing	H1, CO3, AOSR1
H3	Design, quality and density of housing development	H5
H4	Affordable housing	H3
TC1	Principal locations for development	TC1, TC2
TC2	Maintaining and enhancing centres	TC2
R1	Countryside recreation	TSR2
R2	Access to the countryside and rights of way network	C6
R3	The River Thames	C7
R4	Other waterways	TSR2
EG1	Proposals for renewable energy development	NRM15
EG2	Combined heat and power	NRM12
EG3	New generating plant	NRM11
M1	Mineral working	M3, W14
M4	Old mineral workings	W14
WM3	Landfill	W13

The following saved policies have been extended but have not been replaced by this RSS:

T7: Service areas

H2: Upper Heyford

M2: Sand and gravel

28 Glossary

List of Abbreviations

AMR	Annual Monitoring Report
AONB	Area of Outstanding Natural Beauty
AQMAs	Air Quality Management Areas
AQS	Air Quality Strategy
ATWP	Air Transport White Paper
BATNEEC	Best Available Technology Not Entailing Excessive Cost
DBERR	Department for Business, Enterprise and Regulatory Reform
BIDs	Business Improvement Districts
BRE	Building Research Establishment
C&D	Construction and Demolition Waste
C&I	Commercial and Industrial Waste
CAP	Common Agricultural Policy
CHP	Combined Heat and Power
CO_2	Carbon Dioxide
CTRL	Channel Tunnel Rail Link
DaSTS	Delivering a Sustainable Transport System
DCLG	Department for Communities and Local Government
Defra	Department for Environment, Food and Rural Affairs
DfT	Department for Transport
DPD	Development Plan Document
DWP	Department for Work and Pensions
EiP	Examination in Public
ESPACE	European Spatial Planning: Adapting to Climate Events
FGD	Flue Gas Desulphurisation
GDP	Gross Domestic Product
GHS	Global Hectares
GOSE	Government Office for the South East
GVA	Gross Value Added
HA	Highways Agency
HEFCE	Higher Education Funding Council for England
HRA	Habitats Regulations Assessment
ICT	Information and Communications Technology
ICZM	Integrated Coastal Zone Management
LAAs	Local Area Agreements
LDD	Local Development Document
LDF	Local Development Framework
LDS	Local Development Scheme
LDV	Local Delivery Vehicle
LSC	Learning and Skills Council
LSPAs	Local Skills for Productivity Alliances
LSPs	Local Strategic Partnerships
LTP	Local Transport Plan
MBT	Mechanical and Biological Treatment
MKAV	Milton Keynes Aylesbury Vale
MKSM	Milton Keynes South Midlands
MPA	Minerals Planning Authority
MPG	Minerals Planning Guidance Note
MPS	Minerals Planning Statement
MRFs	Materials Recovery Facilities
MSW	Municipal Solid Waste
MW	Mega Watts
NHPAU	National Housing and Planning Advice Unit
NHS	National Health Service
NO_2	Nitrogen Dioxide
NSCA	National Society for Clean Air
ODPM	Office of the Deputy Prime Minister (now DCLG)

Glossary

Ofwat	The Water Services Regulation Authority
PDL	Previously Developed Land
PM10	Particulate Matter
PPG	Planning Policy Guidance Note
PPS	Planning Policy Statement
RDF	Refuse Derived Fuel
RDPE	Rural Development Programme for England
RES	Regional Economic Strategy
RMF	Regional Monitoring Framework
RPB	Regional Planning Body
RPG9	Regional Planning Guidance for the South East
RPG9a	Thames Gateway Planning Framework
RPG9b	Strategic Guidance for the River Thames
RSF	Regional Sustainability Framework
RSPA	Regional Skills for Productivity Alliance
RSS	Regional Spatial Strategy
RTS	Regional Transport Strategy
SA	Sustainability Appraisal
SAC	Special Area of Conservation
SANG	Suitable Accessible Natural Greenspace
SDA	Strategic Development Area
SEA	Strategic Environmental Assessment
SEEBF	The South East England Biodiversity Forum
SEEDA	South East England Development Agency
SEERA	South East England Regional Assembly
SEERAWP	South East England Regional Aggregates Working Party
SERTAB	South East Regional Technical Advisory Body for Waste
SFRA	Strategic Flood Risk Assessment
SMEs	Small and Medium Enterprises
SPA	Special Protection Area
SPD	Supplementary Planning Document
SRA	Strategic Rail Authority
SSSI	Site of Special Scientific Interest
SUDS	Sustainable Urban Drainage Systems
STW	Sewage Treatment Works
WDD	Waste Development Document
WDF	Waste Development Framework
WEEE	Waste Electrical and Electronic Equipment
WPA	Waste Planning Authority
WRAP	Waste Resources Action Programme